Parsley, Peppers, Potatoes & Peas

Other titles of similar interest from Gramercy books:

Big Kitchen Instruction Book

Granny's Recipes, Remedies, and Helpful Hints

Recipes from Granny's Kitchen

Parsley, Peppers, Potatoes & Peas

A Cook's Companion For Handling, Using & Storing A Garden's Bounty

Pat Katz

Gramercy Books

New York

This 2002 edition is published by Gramercy Books™, an imprint of
Random House Value Publishing, Inc., a division of Random House, Inc.,
280 Park Avenue, New York, New York 10017, by arrangement with
Harley & Marks, Inc. Point Roberts, Washington.

Gramercy Books™ and design are trademarks of
Random House Value Publishing, Inc.

Printed in the United States of America

Interior design by The Typeworks

Random House
New York • Toronto • London • Sydney • Auckland
http://www.randomhouse.com/

Library of Congress Cataloging-in-Publication Data

Katz, Pat, 1934-
    Parsley, peppers, potatoes & peas : a cook's companion for handling, using & storing a
garden's bounty / [Pat Katz]
        p. cm.
    Originally published: Point Roberts, WA : Hartley & Marks Publishing, c1997.
    Includes index.
    ISBN 0-517-22005-9
      1. Cookery (Vegetables) 2. Cookery (Fruit) 3. Vegetables. 4. Fruit. I. Title.

TX801 .K377 2002
641.6'5—dc21
                                                            2001053201

9 8 7 6 5 4 3 2 1

Contents

Apples	1	Garlic	121
Apricots	7	Gooseberries	124
Artichokes	9	Grapes	126
Asparagus	11	Herbs	131
Beans, dry	12	Herb Roots	140
Beans, fresh	17	Herb Seeds	143
Beets	19	Jam and Jelly	146
Blackberries	22	Jerusalem Artichokes	150
Blueberries	23	Kale	153
Broccoli	25	Kohlrabi	153
Brussels Sprouts	26	Leeks	154
Cabbage	27	Lettuce	156
Canning	31	Melons	157
Carrots	45	Mulberries	159
Cauliflower	46	Mushrooms	160
Celeriac	48	Mustard (Greens and Seeds)	162
Celery	49	Nuts	164
Cherries	50	Okra	171
Chestnuts	52	Onions	172
Chicory	56	Parsley	176
Chinese Cabbage	58	Parsnips	177
Cold Storage	59	Peaches	178
Collards	64	Peanuts	180
Comfrey	65	Pears	183
Corn, dry	66	Peas	185
Corn, sweet	74	Pectin	187
Cranberries	78	Peppers, hot	190
Cucumbers	80	Peppers, sweet	193
Currants	82	Persimmons	196
Dandelions	84	Pickling	197
Drying	87	Plums	203
Eggplant	99	Potatoes	205
Elderberries	101	Quinces	210
Figs	103	Radishes	211
Freezing	104	Raspberries	213
Fruits	112	Rhubarb	214

Roses	216	Strawberries	260
Rutabagas	219	Sunflowers	261
Salsify	220	Sweet Potatoes	264
Sauerkraut	222	Swiss Chard	266
Seaweed	226	Tomatoes	267
Seeds	229	Tomatoes, green	274
Soybeans	233	Turnips	277
Spinach	240	Vegetables	278
Sprouts	242	Vinegar	280
Squash, summer	248	Watercress	286
Squash, winter and pumpkin	250	Watermelons	287
Steam Cooking	254	Index of Recipes and Food Ideas	291
Stir-Frying	257	Subject Index	294

Apples ✿

It is hard to imagine a food more versatile than the apple. It is everyone's favorite for eating raw, for making sauce and juice, and for drying. Apples are as delicious in salads or in cooked meat and vegetable dishes as they are when made into desserts. A winter's supply of apples stored in several ways—some in a root cellar or other cool place, some canned, and some dried—guarantees a diet that is healthy as well as varied and pleasant. The doctor who stays away when an apple is eaten every day might easily be increased to three who stay away every day, one for eating a raw apple, one for a glass of apple juice or a dish of applesauce, and one for a handful of dried apple rings.

There are apple varieties numbering in the thousands, among them early and late varieties, and special varieties for particular regions and climatic conditions with additional variations in size, color, flavor, and texture of the fruit. Those who plant their own apple trees can choose heirloom varieties, or apples known for their special flavors and textures, rather than the standard commercial varieties. Also many wild or untended apple trees are worthwhile for the excellent juice and sauce that can be made from their fruit.

HANDLING APPLES

Apples should not be picked until they are at the peak of ripeness. It is also important to pick them carefully without bruising them or damaging the fruiting spur, the small branch from which the apple grows. Bruised apples and windfalls should be used without delay, since they spoil quickly. Methods of storage and preparation depend to a large extent on the apple's variety. Early varieties do not keep well in cold storage and are usually canned or dried. Late varieties will keep for months in cold storage and are also good for canning and drying. The ways of cooking and canning apples will depend on their various textures and flavors. Some varieties break down when cooked, making them very good for applesauce, but unsuitable where a chunky texture is wanted. Very tart apples are outstanding for cooking, but mouth-puckering eaten raw. Very sweet or bland apples taste best in mixtures with tart fruits. (Refer to COMBINING SWEET AND TART FRUITS, in the FRUITS section.)

APPLE STORAGE

Canning

Chunks or Slices (For varieties that hold shape when cooked.) Drop several cups into boiling juice, syrup, or water. Cook 5 min., lift out with strainer, fill jars. Repeat with more apples. (Optional: Put whole spices in jars.) Add boiling cooking liquid, ½ in. headroom. Process boiling water bath. Pints: 15 min. Quarts: 20 min.

Baked

Core, put 1 teaspoon honey, dash cinnamon in each apple. Bake at 375°F for 40 to 60 min. until half done. Pack in jars, add boiling juice or syrup, ½ in. headroom. Process boiling water bath. Pints or quarts: 20 min. Refer to the CANNING section, below, and to PICKLING CRABAPPLES, in the PICKLING section.

Cold Storage

See APPLES IN COLD STORAGE, below.

Apples are very often sprayed with chemicals to prevent damage from insects and disease, and in some areas it is difficult to grow useable apples without sprays. This makes unsprayed, homegrown apples and wild apples especially precious, but all apples—even sprayed ones—are worth using. (Refer to INSECTICIDES IN FRUIT, in the FRUITS section.)

Crabapples

Any apple variety with very small fruits might be called a crabapple, but the name is generally associated with flowering ornamentals, or wild varieties with small, sour, sometimes astringent fruits. Though sour crabapples can be used in all the same ways as sour apples, it is easiest to make juice from them, because they can then be cooked without peeling, coring, or removing stems. Some ornamental crabapple fruits are so bland as to be almost tasteless. These are good pickled whole, or when cooked with strongly-flavored fruits; by themselves they are not very useful.

APPLES IN COLD STORAGE

Only fall-maturing varieties of apples keep well in cold storage. Early apples can be refrigerated from one to several weeks, but no longer. Different varieties of fall and winter apples keep for different lengths of time. Some must be used by January while others will keep until May.

Long-storage apples must be perfect, without blemishes or bruises, and with their stems left on. The ideal conditions for storing apples are 32°F, with high humidity. In a root cellar or in similar conditions, apples keep well in open containers. If to be kept in a cool, dry place, they should be individually wrapped in newspaper, or packed in a closed container to retain moisture. The traditional container is an old-style milk can, but a box lined with a plastic bag with a few holes cut in it can be used just as well. Some other materials that work as packing are dry leaves, straw, and shredded paper.

Loose apples should not be stored in the same area as cabbage, cabbage family vegetables, turnips, or potatoes. The apples may absorb vegetable odors, and their moisture and gases may cause potatoes to sprout. It is nice to have a quite separate storage area for fruits, but if that is not possible, apples should always be packed in a dry material, as described.

Drying

(Superb flavor!) Peel, core, slice. Spread on trays or thread on string and hang. Dry until leathery, so no moisture shows when broken and squeezed. For making fruit leather from sauce, refer to the DRYING section.

Freezing

(Least practical method. Texture poor when thawed, but acceptable if cooked.) *Chunks or Slices* Sprinkle with ½ teaspoon ascorbic acid powder diluted in 3 tablespoons water, or pack in liquid. Refer to LIQUIDS IN WHICH TO FREEZE FRUIT, in the FREEZING section.

3 medium apples = about 1 pound = about 1½ cups applesauce; 1 bushel apples = 16–20 quarts applesauce or 2–3 gallons cider

APPLE IDEAS

Apple Muffins, Pancakes, Baked Goodies

Raw apples chopped, sliced, or grated

When time for careful packing is limited, or a special storage space not available, most fall-maturing apples will keep 2 months or so in any cool place, such as an unheated bedroom. It is important that the temperature remain above freezing. Those apples not quickly used can be preserved in other ways when time permits.

Stored apples should be checked periodically for spoilage. If the proverbial bad apple is not removed, it very definitely will spoil the whole barrel or bagful. When first stored, they do not have to be checked very often, but toward the end of their storage life they should be checked every week or two. (Refer to COLD STORAGE OF FRUITS, in the COLD STORAGE section.)

APPLESAUCE

There is almost no limit to the amount of applesauce a family can use in a year. It is very good plain, and goes with everything from pancakes and pork chops to yogurt. It can be used in baking, in desserts such as fruit gelatines and ice creams, and dried to make fruit leather. It is the perfect way to use imperfect apples and windfalls, or wild apples that need trimming to remove wormy or damaged places.

Any variety of apple can be made into sauce. Some make delicious sauce with nothing added at all, while others taste best if perked up with lemon juice, or sweetened with honey or another sweetener. Traditional spices, such as cinnamon and cloves, herb seeds such as fennel and caraway, lemon or orange peel, and other flavorings can be added to taste. Delicious sauces can also be made by combining apples with other fruits.

Applesauce can be prepared with a variety of textures as well as flavors. It can have a smooth, purée-like texture, a coarse texture, or a chunky texture. Smooth applesauce is easiest to make, since the apples do not have to be peeled or cored, but many people prefer a chunky or coarse applesauce.

Smooth Applesauce

Wash apples and cut them in quarters or eighths, trimming away bad spots. Do not peel or core. Put the pieces in a pot with enough water to almost but not quite cover them. Bring to a boil, stirring occasionally to cook them evenly. When very soft, purée and remove skins and seeds with a food mill or strainer. If the sauce is too thin it can be simmered uncovered

are as versatile for baking as raisins. For a dozen apple muffins, add 1 cup of chopped raw apple to the dry ingredients and put a round slice of apple on top of the batter for each muffin. Just before baking a drizzle of honey and dash of spice can be added as a finishing touch. With pancake batter either dip in sliced apple rings and fry, or add chopped or grated apple to the batter. Try chopped or grated apple in any baked goods that go well with a fruit flavor, such as oatmeal cookies.

Apple Desserts with Herb Seeds
Instead of the traditional spices used to flavor apple desserts, try crushed or powdered herb seeds. Anise, fennel, caraway, coriander, and dill are all very good. Refer to the HERB SEEDS section.

Apple Slump
For this old-fashioned dessert, heat sweetened applesauce in a wide pot with a tight lid. Add one of the above herb seeds for flavor if desired.

in a heavy pot over low heat to concentrate it. Stir often to prevent sticking and burning. It can be canned as soon as it is thick enough to suit family tastes.

Chunky Applesauce

Prepare apples by peeling, coring, and cutting in quarters or eighths. (Peeling is optional, but the texture of the peels in the sauce can be bothersome. An apple peeler and corer makes that job quick and easy.) (See USING PEELS AND CORES, below.) To prevent darkening, the apple pieces can be sprinkled with lemon juice as they are prepared, but this is not necessary if they are to be cooked at once.

Put the apples in a pot, and cover about ¾ of them with water. (More water can be added later, if necessary. Apples become dry in storage and therefore they need more cooking water than freshly picked apples.) Cook until they are very soft. Textures differ according to variety; some break down completely and some remain in large pieces. Either way tastes good. The sauce can be canned as soon as the apples are cooked through.

Canning Applesauce

Stir boiling hot applesauce for an even thickness and ladle into canning jars, allowing ½ inch headroom. Process in a boiling water bath, for 10 minutes for both pints and quarts. (Refer to the CANNING section.)

Apple Butter

Applesauce is easily made into apple butter by cooking it with sweetening and spices until very thick. (Refer to MAKING JAMS AND FRUIT BUTTERS, in the JAM AND JELLY section.) To make it without sweetening see *Apple Cider Butter,* below.

APPLE CIDER

Apple cider is the juice of raw apples made by grinding or crushing apples to break down their cell walls and then pressing to extract juice. It is called sweet cider when fresh, and hard cider after it begins to ferment. Apple "juice" is strained from cooked apples or it is cider that has been strained to clarify it and heated to keep it sweet. (Refer to the FRUITS section.)

Making apple cider is a traditional fall activity for many households. It is an excellent way to use windfalls and bruised or imperfect apples, but the cider must be made soon after the

---

Prepare dumplings according to any favorite recipe and cook them in the applesauce. Sweeten only the sauce, not the dumplings.

Baked Applesauce

For a particularly delicious applesauce, bake whole apples without peeling or coring them. When they are soft, scrape the sauce away from the peels and cores.

Apple Tea and Apple Beer

Dry some apple peels and store them in a jar. To make tea, pour 1 or 2 cups boiling water over a handful of peels and let steep for a few minutes, as for herb tea. Other flavorings, such as mint leaves or rosehips, can be included. For apple beer, begin as for making tea, but let sit at room temperature for about 2 days, then strain and drink. The flavor is fruity and sometimes a little fizzy.

apples are gathered. Even one spoiled or moldy apple can ruin the flavor of a whole batch of cider. Wash apples before making cider, especially if they have been recently sprayed, but there is no need to remove stems, peels, or cores. A blend of sweet and sour apples makes especially good cider.

It is possible to make small amounts of cider by cutting up apples, grinding them in a meat grinder, then pressing them in a fruit press. It is even possible to crush apples with a mallet, tie the mash in a cloth bag, and squeeze or press to extract juice. Extractors for making carrot juice will extract small amounts of cider, but heavier equipment is needed if cider is to be made by the gallon. Homestead-sized cider presses are widely available, and advertised in magazines and catalogs featuring country items. They have two parts: one that grinds the apples and one that presses them. It is important that the grinder does a good job at reducing the apples to pulp. If coarse apple pieces are left, not all of the cider can be squeezed. Pulp from a bushel of apples should yield 3 gallons of cider compared to about 2 gallons when coarsely ground. After pressing, cider is usually strained through a sieve.

Fresh cider stays sweet for only a day or two at room temperature. If refrigerated immediately, it will stay sweet for a week or more. Many people like cider best when it is just beginning to ferment and has a light fizziness. When completely fermented it becomes cider vinegar. (Refer to the VINEGAR section.)

The pulp left from pressing cider is called pomace, and can be used to make pectin. (Refer to USING APPLE PEELS AND CORES, below. Also see the PECTIN section.)

Canning or Freezing Cider

Cider can be heated to a boil and canned like any fruit juice, but the flavor stays fresher if it is canned like grape juice (p. 129). Though freezing also preserves the fresh flavor, finding freezer space can be a problem. A frozen concentrate can be made (refer to CONCENTRATED JUICE, in the FREEZING section), but this is time consuming and impractical for large quantities.

Cider Syrup

For an intensely sweet syrup, boil cider in an open kettle until reduced to about ¼ its original volume. This can be canned by the open kettle method. (Refer to the CANNING section.)

Cider syrup can be used to sweeten and flavor baked goods, fruit desserts, and in other foods where a fruit flavor is welcome. It is also good served with pancakes or waffles. For "ciderade," mix a few tablespoons of syrup with ice water.

USING APPLE PEELS AND CORES

Most of the vitamins and minerals in apples are in or right under the skin, while both skins and cores are rich in pectin and flavor. There is, therefore, ample reason to save and use them. As the pomace, or pulp, left from pressing apples for cider is composed largely of peels and cores, it is also valuable.

There are many warnings against eating apple seeds because of their cyanide content. They *can* be dangerous if eaten in large quantities, but swallowing an occasional seed or using peels and cores in the ways described here is absolutely harmless. The leftover seeds and other solids are always strained off and eventually discarded.

The most basic way to use peels and cores is for making juice. Cover them with water, bring to a boil, and cook until the apple parts are soft. Strain through a cloth. This juice can be used as a drink or made into jelly or pectin. The juice from pomace is blander than the juice from unpressed peels and cores. This makes it ideal for pectin, but not so good for beverages or jellies unless other flavors are added. (Refer to the JAM AND JELLY and PECTIN sections.) To make vinegar from fresh peels and cores refer to the VINEGAR FROM MASHED FRUIT, TRIMMINGS, OR CULLS, in the VINEGAR section.

Apple peels and cores can be dried and stored for later use. They are spread out on trays and dried in a food dryer, or any warm, airy place. They can then be reconstituted with water and used in any of the above ways, or for APPLE TEA AND APPLE BEER (see APPLE IDEAS, above).

APPLE RECIPES

Apple Cider Butter

(MAKES 3–4 PINTS)

1 gallon cider	3 quarts apples, cored, peeled, and
cinnamon, optional	cut in small pieces

Put the cider in a large kettle and boil down to about 2 quarts. Skim off foam as it forms. Add the apple pieces and continue cooking, stirring frequently until thickened. This may take up to an hour. Add cinnamon, if desired. Pour into containers and seal as for open kettle canning. (Refer to the CANNING section.)

APRICOT STORAGE

Canning

Leave whole or pit. Blanching and peeling optional.

Hot Pack

(Preferred, except for varieties that fall apart easily.) Simmer 2–3 min. in boiling syrup, juice, or water. Drain, pack. (Optional: 1–2 pits per jar for flavor.) Add boiling cooking liquid, ½ in. headroom. Process boiling water bath. Pints: 20 min. Quarts: 25 min.

Raw Pack

Fill jars, add boiling syrup, juice, or water, ½ in. headroom. Process boiling water bath. Pints: 25 min. Quarts: 30 min. Refer to the CANNING section. Also see CANNING FRUIT JUICE AND SAUCE, in the FRUITS section, and *Apricot Chutney*, below. Caution: If overripe, add 2 teaspoons lemon juice per pint, 4 teaspoons per quart.

Drying

Arrange halves cut side up. Dry until leathery. To use like raisins, dry chopped pieces. Excellent for fruit leather. Refer to the DRYING section.

Freezing

Blanch 30 seconds in boiling water to prevent tough skins. Remove pits.

Large quantities of this butter can be made in one batch. The only limitation is the size of the kettle. In the past it was sometimes made outdoors in a copper kettle using as much as 25 gallons of cider at a time.

Cider Butter Leather

Fruit leather made by drying this butter comes out rich and sweet, almost like candy. (Refer to DRYING FRUIT, in the DRYING section.)

Apricots

Sweet, fresh tree-ripened apricots are treats unknown to many people. The ripe fruit does not keep long or ship well, so to enjoy them at their peak, one has to live where apricots grow, or raise one's own. The best apricot-growing areas are in the western half of the United States and Canada. Elsewhere it is best to buy dried apricots. They rank with raisins and prunes as superior snack foods, and are good in all kinds of cooked mixtures as well. The apricot's flavor is quite intense and gives a special zing to foods even when added in small amounts. In pastry or cookie fillings, poultry stuffings, and sauces for meat, apricots provide the touch that makes a dish memorable.

As apricots are high in vitamin A, and contain respectable amounts of other vitamins and minerals, they are a valuable fruit from every point of view.

HANDLING APRICOTS

After apricots are picked sugar no longer forms, so they must be left on the tree until fully ripe. Though they change color if picked green, they will never lose their astringency. When very ripe they become soft, tending to fall apart with cooking, but their fine flavor remains intact. For canning it is best to pick them just before they get soft. For juice or purée, soft apricots are excellent. If they become overripe, however, they may lose acidity, and it is then necessary to add lemon juice or vinegar when canning them.

Apricots for drying are sometimes picked while firm be-

Optional: Sprinkle with ascorbic acid solution or lemon juice. Pack in liquid. Refer to the FREEZING section.

2–2½ pounds fresh apricots = 1 quart canned or 1–1½ quarts frozen; 5 pounds fresh = about 1 pound dried; 1 bushel = 20 to 24 quarts canned

APRICOT IDEAS

Apricot Nectar Treats

Apricot nectar is a purée that is thin enough to drink. If a good supply is canned, many special treats are ensured. It can be made into frozen apricot desserts or apricot gelatin.

Apricot Nectar Milkshake

Mix 1 cup nectar, 1 cup milk, and 2 scoops preferred ice cream. Or make a blender concoction with apricot nectar, yogurt, an ice cube, and maybe a banana to sweeten and thicken it.

Baked Apricots

Preheat the oven to 300°F. Arrange pitted apricots in a shallow, buttered baking dish. They can be 2 or 3 layers deep. Drizzle with honey or vanilla sugar (sugar that has had a vanilla bean enclosed with it). Bake until the apricots are soft, 30 to 40 minutes. For a delightful breakfast version of

cause the dried fruit has a better shape, but they are sweeter if left on the tree until soft and ready to drop. If there is grass under the tree they can be gathered after they drop. Soft apricots will flatten into thin pieces when dried.

Apricots from wild or volunteer trees may have wiry fibers around the pits. The best way to remove them is to cook the fruits, and put them through a food mill or strainer to make a smooth purée or juice. It is necessary to add pectin to apricots when making most kinds of preserves. (Refer to the PECTIN section.)

this dish, set the apricots on buttered slices of bread on an oiled baking sheet, sweeten, and bake.

Plums and peaches are also good baked in these ways. Plums bake a little faster and peaches a little slower than apricots.

Sautéed Apricots

Slice an onion and a green pepper and sauté them for 5 minutes or so in a little butter or oil. Add fresh apricot halves, and sauté slowly until they are soft. Can be used as a side dish with meats.

Apricot Nut Sauce

Mix dried apricots with whole or chopped nuts of any kind, cover with water, and soak for about 2 days. This makes a delicious, rich sauce. For a favorite Middle Eastern combination, soak dried apricots with a few prunes and raisins, halved almonds, and either pistachio nuts or pine nuts. Rose water (refer to the ROSE section) is usually added for more flavor.

A quick version can be made by pouring boiling water over the dried apricot and nut mixture, and soaking for a few hours. However, the long soaking gives the richest flavor. Sherry or another liquor may be used instead of water for a festive touch.

Apricot Pits and Kernels

The kernels inside apricot pits have a strong almond smell and taste, and have been used in small amounts to flavor other foods. Since these kernels also contain a cyanide compound, eating them in large numbers is dangerous. There is no harm in putting 1 or 2 pits in a jar when canning apricots, nor in canning whole, unpitted apricots, since the pits are eventually discarded. However, recipes are questionable if they call for shelling these pits for chopping into jams or other mixtures.

It is possible to remove the cyanide from shelled apricot kernels by soaking them in many changes of warm (about 140°F) water over a period of 24 hours. They should taste free of any bitterness and will then be safe to use like almonds. Apricots, plums, cherries, peaches, and almonds are closely related botanically and all have almond-flavored kernels, but apricot kernels are used most often because the pits are easier to shell and have bigger kernels. Commercial macaroon paste has also been made from apricot kernels, and oil is extracted from the kernels of all of these fruits for various uses.

APRICOT RECIPES

Apricot Chutney

(MAKES 3–4 PINTS)

3 pounds apricots, pitted and quartered
1½ cups (about) vinegar
1 cup (about) honey or 1½ cups sugar

1 cup raisins or other dried fruit, chopped if pieces are large
1–2 cloves garlic, minced, optional

1 ½ cups onions, chopped
1 sweet pepper, chopped, optional
1–2 teaspoons mixed spices (such
  as cinnamon, cloves, allspice)

small piece ginger root, minced,
  optional
1 teaspoon cayenne or other hot
  pepper, or to taste

Mix all ingredients in a kettle and bring to a simmer, stirring several times. Taste and adjust amounts of vinegar and sweetener. Simmer uncovered until the apricots are soft and the chutney has thickened, usually about 30 minutes.

Ladle into canning jars, and process 10 minutes in a boiling water bath. (Refer to the CANNING section.)

The flavor of the chutney improves after it sits for a month or two. It goes well with curries and wherever chutneys are enjoyed.

Fruit Chutney

Most fresh fruits in season can be used instead of apricots. Plums or peaches are good. Seasonings can be adjusted to taste. Mixtures of fruits can also be used.

Artichokes

Globe artichokes, also called burr artichokes, are the unopened flower buds of a plant in the thistle family. They are interesting vegetables to cook and fun to eat, but are difficult to grow in most places. They are perennials, ordinarily requiring a long growing season, with a mild winter and a cool summer. The California coast suits them perfectly. However, they should become more common in other areas in the future, thanks to a newly developed annual variety that can be grown in home gardens where the growing season is fairly long.

Cardoon and Wild Thistles

Cardoon is closely related to artichokes. It has been raised since early Roman times for its stalk and the midribs of its leaves, which are peeled, then cooked as a vegetable. Wild thistle stalks and leaf midribs, when big enough, are eaten in the same way.

ARTICHOKE STORAGE
Canning

Trim off outer leaves, tips, then trim to fit wide mouth jars. (Optional: Tie leaves together with string.) Boil 5 min. in 1 gallon water with ¾ cup white vinegar, 1 tablespoon salt added. Lift out, pack, add boiling cooking liquid, ½ in. headroom. Optional: Add 1 teaspoon lemon juice per quart for flavor. Process 240°F, 11 pounds pressure. Pints: 25 min. Quarts: 30 min. Refer to the CANNING section.

Drying

Slice hearts uniformly. Steam until cooked through. Dry until hard. Refer to the DRYING section.

Freezing

Trim off outer leaves, tips, or remove, leaving hearts. Blanch 7 min. in boiling water. Optional: Add lemon juice to water or dip hearts in lemon juice. Refer to the FREEZING section.

ARTICHOKE IDEAS
Artichoke in Salads

Add cooked and sliced or chopped artichoke to salads of all kinds. It adds a special touch to tossed green salads, and goes well with egg, potato, shell-

The roots and very young leaves of both plants can also be eaten, and it is possible to extract a rennet for making cheese from the flowers of some species.

Wild thistles of one kind or another grow almost everywhere, and are a good survival food because they are easily recognized at any time of the year. Cardoon seeds for garden plantings are listed among the herb seeds in many seed catalogs. (The Jerusalem artichoke is an entirely different plant, not related to artichokes or thistles.)

HANDLING ARTICHOKES

Artichokes should be cut with 1 to 1½ inches of stem, while the buds are still compact, with tightly closed leaves or bracts. An artichoke's size does not necessarily reflect its age or maturity. The top bud on a plant is usually the largest, and the side buds become smaller the lower down they grow on the plant. Only the fleshy bases of the leaves, the hearts, and the stems can be eaten when fully formed buds are cut from a mature plant. However, the buds can be cut early, before the choke develops, and then all parts are edible, except perhaps the sharp tips of the outer leaves.

The cut surfaces of artichokes, cardoon, or wild thistle discolor quickly when exposed to air, so prepare them just before cooking, or else sprinkle them with lemon juice or another acidic liquid. Whole artichokes can take anywhere from 20 to 60 minutes to cook depending on their size and maturity. Poke with a fork to test for doneness.

If just the hearts are wanted for a recipe, the leaves can be steamed separately until tender, and the fleshy parts at their base used in salads or other mixtures. To clean artichokes, hold them by the stems and swish them up and down in cold water.

ARTICHOKE RECIPES
Pickled Artichoke Hearts, Middle Eastern Style

(MAKES 1½–2 QUARTS)

½ cup lemon juice (from 3–4 lemons)	12 artichokes
lemon peels	½ cup corn oil or other salad oil
salt, optional	

Artichokes

10

fish, or chicken salads. In a salad is a good way to use leaves when preparing artichoke hearts alone for another recipe. (To prepare the leaves, steam them and scrape or cut off the tender part at the base of each.)

Creamed Artichoke, Wild Thistle, or Cardoon Stalks

Slice or chop the cooked vegetable. Mix into a cream sauce, and serve with mashed potatoes, rice, or on toast.

Fried Artichokes

Slice tender, young artichokes, roll in seasoned flour or dip in batter, and sauté in oil or fat until browned on both sides. If the artichokes are not very tender, pre-cook them first. Baby artichoke buds, 1 to 1½ inches, can be fried whole in deep fat. When drained, sprinkle with pepper (salt optional), and arrange on a platter for an unusual hors d'oeuvre.

ASPARAGUS STORAGE
Canning

Whole Spears Trim to jar length. (Optional: Cook trimmings in the water used for blanching and filling jars to add flavor.) Blanch 3 min. in boiling water. Pack upright in jars, add boiling blanch-

Put lemon juice (and salt, if desired) in a bowl. Trim stems, leaves, and chokes from the artichokes, leaving the hearts. If these are large, cut them in half. Take each heart and rub it with a squeezed-out lemon rind, then place it in the lemon juice. When all the hearts are ready, take them out of the juice and arrange them in a lidded glass jar. Add the oil to the lemon juice and beat with a fork until well combined. Pour over the hearts in the jar, adding more oil if not completely covered. Seal with a tight lid for at least a month before eating. They will keep indefinitely in a cool place.

Asparagus

There is no other vegetable like asparagus. It has its own special look and taste, and its own special season. When the first spears push their way up in the garden, it is proof that spring has truly begun. These first spears are a delight to eat, and are also known as a spring tonic, good for the kidneys and bladder.

Asparagus is the first vegetable of spring because, in temperate climates, it is the only perennial vegetable maintained in home gardens. An established asparagus bed is an asset yielding dividends for many years. Starting one is like planting a tree; the hope and promise of good things to come are planted with it.

Asparagus grows wild in many places, and in spite of more than 2,000 years of cultivation, there is little difference between the wild and domesticated plants. Knowing where wild asparagus grows is almost as good as having a patch in the back yard. One folk name for asparagus is sparrowgrass.

HANDLING ASPARAGUS

Asparagus should be harvested before tops begin to open, or "feather out." Flavor is still good, though, even when they are slightly open. The spears should be cut or broken off at ground level, or just below. Breaking is preferred because there is less risk of damaging nearby underground spears. Morning is the best time for harvesting, as the stalks tend to dry out and toughen later in the day. It is important to refrig-

ing water, ½ in. headroom. Process 240°F, 11 pounds pressure. Pints: 25 min. Quarts: 30 min. *Cut Pieces* Blanch 2–3 min., pack, add boiling blanching water, ½ in. headroom. Process as for spears. Refer to the CANNING section.

Drying
Chop or slice thin. Dry until hard. Excellent for soup. Refer to the DRYING section.

Freezing
Use whole spears or cut in pieces. Blanch 2 min. if slender, 3–4 min. if medium or thick. If using rigid containers, alternate spear and stem ends for better fit. Quality retained 8–12 months. Refer to the FREEZING section.

3–4 pounds = 1 quart canned or 1½–2 quarts frozen

ASPARAGUS IDEAS
Asparagus Salads
Sliced raw asparagus, including the peeled white bottoms of the stalks, is very flavorful in all kinds of salads. The raw spears are good to munch just like carrot or celery sticks. (For some delicious dips, refer to the following recipes: *Indonesian Peanut Sauce*, p. 182; *Spanish Parsley Sauce*, p. 177.)

Cooked, chilled asparagus spears

erate asparagus soon after it is harvested, because sitting at room temperature will also dry and toughen it.

The outside of the bottom of an asparagus stalk is too tough and stringy to eat. If the stalks are to be eaten by hand, the tough part can be used as a handle. Otherwise, the outer layer of the bottom of the stalk should be peeled off, leaving only the tender white inner part. Another alternative is to cut off the bottoms to be cooked for soup stock or the liquid for canning asparagus. The bottoms can also be peeled, chopped, and added raw to salads, or cooked in soups. If asparagus was grown in sandy soil there may be sand under the scales on the stalks. The easiest way to get rid of it is to scrape off the scales.

Steaming is the best cooking method for asparagus. The spears can be set upright in a tall pot with 1 or 2 inches of boiling water (which cooks the tougher bottoms longer than the tender tips), or they can be laid on a rack and steamed. For steaming upright they can be tied in a bundle to hold them in position. If a tall pot is not available, a coffee pot might be used, or a double boiler with the top section turned upside down over the bottom section for a lid. Or a domed lid can be shaped with aluminum foil to fit on a regular pot. Whenever practical, sort asparagus so as to cook spears of the same diameter together. Their cooking time will vary from 8 to 15 minutes, depending on thickness. When done, the spears should still be bright in color, and somewhat firm in texture.

Beans, dry

"Beans for dinner!"—not a fanciful pronouncement, but certainly a comfortable one. A pot of beans always means a satisfying meal, and is the epitome of solid dependability in food.

Dried beans of various kinds are eaten with appreciation everywhere in the world. Beans have always been important for winter diets because they are easy to grow and harvest, and they keep so well. Gardeners can easily raise a year's supply

also make a nice salad arranged on lettuce leaves.

Asparagus Steamed with New Potatoes

When steaming asparagus upright in a tall pot, cook small new potatoes in the pot around the bottoms of the stalks. The asparagus and new potatoes go very well together with a little butter.

Baked Asparagus

Steam asparagus until just barely tender, then spread in a shallow, oiled or buttered baking dish. Sprinkle with melted butter or olive oil, grated cheese, and pepper, and season with lemon juice and nutmeg if desired. Bake only a few minutes to heat through and brown lightly.

Asparagus Instead of Bamboo Shoots, Stir-fried

Slice asparagus spears about ¼-inch thick diagonally, and use them for stir-frying instead of bamboo shoots. They cook in the same amount of time, and go well with Chinese seasonings.

DRIED BEANS STORAGE

Canning

(For precooked convenience.) Soak. Use *Basic Beans, Traditional Method,*

without special skills, equipment, or storage facilities. Beans are also a worthwhile source of protein. If eaten with grains or dairy products, they equal meat in protein value.

There are many varieties of beans, including some native to America and some with origins in other parts of the world. They are distinguished by different colors, sizes, and shapes, by their cooking characteristics, and by the areas in which they grow well. With the exception of soybeans, they are all similar in composition and nutritional value. Because soybeans are higher in protein and fat, and lower in carbohydrates, they must be handled differently. (Refer to the SOYBEANS section.)

DRIED BEAN VARIETIES

Adsuki Beans

These small, reddish black beans are grown primarily in Asian countries, and require a fairly long growing season. More easily digested than many other kinds of beans, they also have a unique flavor. They are often cooked in combination with rice.

Black-eyed Peas or Cowpeas

Despite their names these are beans, not peas. There are several other local names for them in the southern United States where they are popular. Good both when freshly shelled or when dried, they are especially enjoyable in mixtures with other vegetables.

Broad, Fava, Horse, or Windsor Beans

These names all refer to one kind of bean, commonly grown in Europe. They like cool weather, and so are cultivated like peas. They are eaten either freshly shelled or dried. The large seeded types originated in the Mediterranean area, while the small seeded ones are from the Middle East.

Garbanzo Beans, or Chick Peas

The round, rather bumpy shape of these beans is distinctive, as is their nutty flavor and somewhat firm texture. They are very well-suited for use as snacks and as additions to salads. There

---

under RECIPES, below, and boil 30 min., or soak with *Quick Method* and bring to boil. Drain, pack, add the boiling cooking water, 1 in. headroom. Process 240°F, 11 pounds pressure. Pints: 1 hour, 15 min. Quarts: 1 hour, 30 min. Refer to the CANNING section.

Storage
Will keep indefinitely at any temperature, but high quality retained longer if stored below 50°F.

Drying
See HANDLING DRIED BEANS, below.
   1 pound dry = 1½–2½ cups dry = 6 or more cups cooked

DRY BEAN IDEAS
Cooking Beans Ahead
Precooked beans are useful for numerous recipes and for adding to soups, salads, casseroles, and mixed vegetable dishes. So it is an excellent idea, when cooking beans for one dish, to prepare an extra amount. This can

are many delicious, special recipes for these beans, such as *Hummus*. (Refer to the SEEDS section.)

Kidney, French, and other Common Garden Beans

There are many bean varieties of this general type. They originated in Central and South America, and are the beans now most commonly grown in North America. Among them are the fresh green or snap home garden beans, and also many of the dried beans.

Lentils

Though these small, flattened beans grow in tiny pods with only 1 or 2 seeds per pod, one plant may produce 100 to 150 pods. They are grown extensively in Europe, Asia, and northern Africa, but are not common in American gardens, probably because they require more space than other beans. They are a cool-season crop, cultivated like peas. Lentils are quick cooking, and much appreciated for soups and stews.

Lima Beans

There are many kinds of lima beans, with a variety of sizes and colors. Some are called "butterbeans" because of their smooth, soft, buttery texture. All limas are good when used either freshly shelled, or dried.

Mung Beans

These small, round, greenish beans are most familiar when used for sprouting. (Refer to the SPROUTS section.) However, they are also good when cooked like lentils in soups or stews. They grow best in warm climates.

Scarlet or White Runner Beans

These large, coarse-podded beans are native to the tropical parts of Central and South America. Scarlet runners are often grown as ornamentals because of their showy red flowers. Both kinds of runner beans can be used dried, freshly shelled, and as green beans, if the pods are picked very young. The cooked, dried beans make a fine soup, and add interest to salads and mixed dishes because of their large size.

---

then be refrigerated for a week or more to be used as needed.

Hot Beans with Raw Vegetables

Heat plain cooked beans and, just before serving, mix with fresh chopped tomatoes and other raw, chopped or grated garden vegetables. Grated carrot, summer squash, and chopped leafy greens all go well with the tomato and beans. Minced parsley and other fresh herbs, such as chives, basil, or summer savory, can be sprinkled on top. Black-eyed peas are especially good prepared in this way.

Beans with Noodles or Grains

Mix hot cooked beans with hot cooked, drained noodles or grain of any kind. Use an equal amount of each. Season to taste. Some good seasonings are butter, pepper, grated Parmesan cheese, or minced parsley and garlic.

Green noodles look and taste outstanding when mixed with white beans. In the South black-eyed peas are mixed

HANDLING DRIED BEANS

Drying and Shelling

During dry weather, some varieties of beans can be left on the plant until the pods are completely dry and brittle. Some varieties split open and "spill the beans" when completely dry, and so must be picked in time. Mature beans left out too long in damp weather may sprout or mold while still in the pods.

Beans can be harvested as soon as the pods become thin, limp, and start to lose color. At this stage the whole plant can be pulled, and hung upside down in a dry, airy place, like an attic, until the pods are completely dry. Or the pods can be picked and spread out in a single layer to finish drying. Though one can shell the beans immediately and then finish drying them, this is usually more work than shelling the brittle pods.

Small quantities of dry beans are easily shelled by hand. A family bean-shelling and story-telling evening makes the chore a pleasant one. Larger quantities can be shelled by threshing and winnowing after the pods are dry and brittle. To do so, put the pods, or the entire plant, in a sack or large cloth bag, and tramp on it, or hit it with a mallet or baseball bat until all the beans have been knocked out of the pods. Pull out any large stalks, then winnow by pouring beans from one container to another in a brisk wind to blow away pieces of pod. Another alternative is to shake the beans on hardware cloth, or a screening with the right size mesh to let only the beans fall through.

Storing Dried Beans

To exclude rodents and insects beans should be stored in a tightly closed sturdy container. Problems with weevils can be prevented by pasteurizing the beans before storage to kill insect eggs. Spread the beans on trays and put them in a 175°F oven for 10 to 15 minutes. Cool, then store. Beans cannot be sprouted after pasteurization. A dried hot pepper can be placed in each container to repel insects.

Dried beans should be sorted before use to remove any small rocks or clumps of dirt mixed with them. Beans that float will not germinate and may have insect damage. There is no harm in eating the floaters, but the damaged ones may be unattractive. Though dried beans keep indefinitely, it is best to use

with rice, and seasoned with bacon fat, to make a dish called "Hopping John."

Bean Porridge

Heat cooked beans with enough soup stock or vegetable cooking water to cover them generously. For 1½ to 2 quarts of this mixture, moisten ½ cup cornmeal with water (which prevents lumping) and stir it in. Leftover cooked beef, pork, game, or other meat, chopped in small pieces can be added as well. Cook about 30 minutes, stirring often.

This makes a thick, hearty porridge that was once popular in New England. It was made in large quantities in winter to be set out in pots to freeze. Then a pot could be taken along when working in the woods and heated over a camp fire for a quick, hot meal.

Bean Patties and Loaves

Mashed cooked beans, and most thick bean mixtures can be seasoned, and shaped into patties or loaves for frying or baking. A beaten egg, bread crumbs, tomato sauce, or catsup, minced pars-

them within a year. As they get older they need a longer soaking and cooking time, and beans stored for several years may never get soft, no matter how long they are cooked.

Preventing Gas

When eating beans, some people are made very uncomfortable by the formation of gas in the digestive tract. For those who are bothered, there are several different ways to minimize the problem:

- Cook beans together with seaweed. The seaweed's flavor goes well with beans, and it is especially effective in reducing problems with gas. For convenience, kelp powder can be used to season bean recipes. (Refer to the SEAWEED section for a special recipe.)

- Eat beans together with generous amounts of raw or cooked green vegetables. Other folk remedies are seasoning with ginger, or serving with vinegar, or olive oil.

- Discard beans' soaking water, and cook them in fresh water. Some water soluble nutrients will be lost, but this method works well enough to make the loss acceptable.

- Try eating BEANO, a nutritional supplement that will counteract gas.

DRIED BEAN RECIPES

Basic Beans

1 part dry beans

3–4 parts pure, soft water (Hard or mineralized water, or "off" tastes, such as chlorine or sulphur, give beans a poor flavor.)

OPTIONAL ADDITIONAL INGREDIENTS:

ham bone, or piece of salt pork

vegetable seasonings (may include any or all of these: onion, carrot, celery, green, black or red pepper, garlic)

herbs, chopped (such as parsley, bay leaf, savory, or others)

tomatoes, fresh or canned

oil, butter, or other fat

salt

---

ley and onion, or a variety of other seasonings can be added. Loaves can be baked with strips of bacon on top, if desired. Usually it takes 45 to 60 minutes in a moderate, 350°F oven, to bake a loaf with beans in it.

FRESH BEAN STORAGE

Canning

Green, Snap, or Wax Trim, cut to uniform size.

Hot Pack

Boil 5 min. Pack. Add boiling cooking water, ½ in. headroom. Process 240°F, 11 pounds pressure. Pints: 20 min. Quarts: 25 min.

Raw Pack

Pack tightly, add boiling water, ½ in. headroom. Process as for hot pack.

Fresh Shelled Limas, Butter Beans, or Others

Hot Pack

Boil 3 min. Pack loosely, add boiling cooking water, 1 in. headroom. Process 240°F, 11 pounds pressure. Pints:

Two methods for soaking and cooking beans follow. (A third alternative, pressure cooking, can be used if manufacturer's directions are carefully followed to avoid a clogged vent. However, the texture of some varieties will be poor, especially if skins are tough.) For the very best flavor and texture the traditional method is recommended.

Traditional Method

Soak the beans in water overnight or until their size is at least doubled. (Optional: Drain and add fresh water to cover.) Bring to a boil, then reduce heat and simmer very slowly until the beans are tender. This may take 2 hours, or it may take all day! Both soaking and cooking times will depend on the bean's variety, its growing conditions, and its time in storage.

Quick Method

Bring the beans to a boil in water, and simmer 2 minutes. Remove from heat, cover, and let stand 1 hour or until beans have doubled in size. (Optional: Drain and add fresh water to cover.) Simmer until the beans are tender.

If using a ham bone or salt pork, add it when the beans begin to cook. Vegetable seasonings and herbs can go in near the beginning of the cooking time if a blend of flavors is desired, or near the end of the cooking time if distinctive flavors and textures are preferred. If neither ham nor salt pork is used, chopped vegetables can be sautéed in oil or fat before they are added. Tomatoes should be added towards the end of the cooking time, as their acids may keep beans from getting soft. If salt is used it should also be added towards the end because it toughens the skins of some kinds of beans.

Beans, fresh

Green, snap, and wax beans used to be called "string beans" because of strings along their seams that had to be removed, but most modern varieties are stringless so the name has fallen into disuse. Tender young bean pods, by any name, remain a favorite

40 min. Quarts: 50 min. Add 10 min. for very large beans.

Raw Pack
Pack loosely, do not press or shake, add boiling water, 1 in. headroom. Process as for hot pack. Refer to the CANNING section.

Drying
(Canning or freezing is preferred.) *Green, Snap, or Wax* Optional: Steam cook 15–20 min. Spread on trays. Or raw, string on a thread and hang. Dry in shade until leathery. (These, called "Leather Britches," need long soaking and cooking to tenderize.) *Fresh Shelled* Pre-cook, dry until hard. Refer to the DRYING section.

Freezing
Green, Snap, or Wax Trim, cut to uniform size. Blanch in boiling water 3 min. *Fresh Shelled* Blanch in boiling water, 1–2 min. if small, 3 min. if medium, 4 min. if large. Refer to the FREEZING section.
1½–2 pounds green, snap, or wax =

Beans, Fresh

🐚

18

vegetable, the kind nobody talks about yet everyone likes. Garden favorites because they grow well everywhere, they taste especially good when cooked immediately after they are picked.

The tender young bean pods are the first good tasting stage. Later on, the pods can be picked and shelled for the fresh, tender beans inside. These are generally known as fresh or green shelled beans, to differentiate them from mature, dried beans. Though it is possible to eat most varieties of beans in all stages of development, they are usually bred for a particular use, for which they are most productive and best tasting. For descriptions of some distinctive varieties refer to the BEANS, DRIED section.

HANDLING FRESH BEANS
Tender Young Bean Pods

Besides green and wax or yellow there is also a purple podded bean, and all are good treated in the same ways, regardless of the pod's color or shape. Pods should be picked when they are almost full size, but before the shapes of the beans inside show clearly. They should snap crisply when broken. If the tips at the stem end are tough, they can be broken off. Any strings along the seams of the pods will come off with the tips.

Beans can be cooked whole, sliced, or broken into bite-sized pieces. Breaking is preferred because it prevents the tiny, developing beans in the pods from falling out. While whole beans or pieces can be prepared by steaming them their flavor is often better if they are boiled briefly in plenty of water. This is because most steamers do not cook the beans quickly enough. A special way to slice raw beans is lengthwise in the French style. This helps to tenderize pods that are a little tough. Different styles of bean slicers or "frenchers" are sold in many stores and mail order catalogs. Stir-fried frenched beans are particularly good.

Fresh Shelled Beans

For shelling when fresh, pods should be picked after the shape of the bean shows clearly, but before they become limp or dry. It is good to test shell a few beans to see if they are ready, before picking a large batch. Small manual or electric bean and pea shellers are available that make quick work of shelling

---

1 quart cooked; 4–5 pounds unshelled = 1 quart shelled and cooked

FRESH BEAN IDEAS
Snap Beans as Dried Beans

If snap beans become tough before they can be picked, leave them to mature completely, and harvest them as dried beans. (Refer to the BEANS, DRIED section.) They can also be used as fresh shelled beans, but snap bean varieties tend to make better dried beans than fresh shelled beans.

Green and Wax Beans in Salads

Tender green beans, or wax beans, add a nice flavor when chopped raw into salads. They are also very good simply eaten whole as a raw snack, or served with dips. For an attractive display, arrange fresh green beans with wax beans and purple podded beans.

Fresh Beans with Nuts

Sauté chopped nuts such as cashews, raw peanuts, or cooked chestnuts, in butter until lightly browned, then toss them with hot, cooked snap or shelled beans. If desired, season with pepper, and a sprinkling of minced, fresh herbs, such as savory, basil, chives, or parsley.

fresh (but not dried) beans or peas. These shellers are carried by many seed and garden supply catalogs.

Some excellent varieties of beans for shelling fresh are black-eyed peas, broad beans, lima beans, and soybeans. (Refer to HARVESTING AND SHELL-ING GREEN SOYBEANS, in the SOYBEANS section.)

FRESH BEAN RECIPES

Succotash

(MAKES ABOUT 4 CUPS)

Many bean and corn mixtures are called "succotash." It is an Amerindian dish whose name comes from the Narragansett word "misiskquatash" (made with kidney beans, corn, and bear fat). Most modern versions are made with fresh shelled beans.

2 cups fresh or canned shelled beans	pepper, to taste
2 cups whole kernel corn	¼ cup cream
1 tablespoon butter	salt, if desired

Put the beans in a saucepan, cover with water, and cook until tender. Time will vary with the type of beans. Add the corn, butter, and pepper, and cook until the corn is tender. If there is extra liquid, drain it off. (It can be saved for soup or other cooking.) Add the cream and remove from heat. Season with salt, if desired.

Tomato Succotash

When adding corn, also add a chopped fresh tomato or 1 cup stewed tomatoes. Omit the cream. Other vegetables such as chopped onion, green pepper, okra, or celery can also be included.

Beets 🌿

Beets are, in a sense, subject to discrimination because of their color—the redness is so penetrating that everything they touch turns "red as a beet." The first consideration, when combining beets with other foods, is apt to be how the mixture will look,

Barbecued Bean Bundles

Cook whole snap beans until just barely tender. When cool enough to handle, group them in bundles of 5 or 6 beans. Then wrap a slice of bacon around each, and pin together with a toothpick. Broil, turning several times until the bacon is cooked. Sprinkle with pepper, or serve with barbecue sauce if desired. These look as good as they taste.

BEET STORAGE

Canning

Sort for size. Cook (see instructions below) until skins slip. Trim, peel. Pack whole, sliced, or diced. Add fresh boiling water, ½ in. headroom. Process 240°F, 11 pounds pressure. Pints: 30 min. Quarts: 35 min. Refer to the CANNING section. *Beet Greens* Refer to CANNING SPINACH, in the SPINACH section.

Cold Storage

Root cellar ideal. Do not wash or trim roots, leave 1–2 in. of tops. Pack in damp sand or other damp material. Late varieties keep all winter. Refer to the COLD STORAGE section.

Beets

✤

20

rather than how it will taste. If beets only kept their color to themselves, they would be as versatile as carrots or potatoes! Their pleasant, sweet taste and firm texture would be welcome wherever vegetables mix. However, facts are facts and beets dye red. If one or two are added to a dish, its name may be changed to suit its new color. Thus "Hash" with added beets becomes "Red Flannel Hash," and beets are valued some of the time just because they color other foods.

Beet greens as well as roots are valuable. Beet plants were grown as greens for many centuries before the fleshy rooted varieties were developed. The greens taste very much like their close relative, Swiss chard, and can be used in the same ways. (Refer to the SWISS CHARD section.)

HANDLING BEETS

Beets can be pulled at any age. Baby beets, ranging from large marble to golf ball size, are tender and sweet, delicious raw as well as cooked. Medium sized beets can be used whole or sliced. Fully-grown, fall-maturing beets will keep for months in a root cellar retaining their sweet, delicate flavor. Though they sometimes develop woody cores, these are easily pulled out after the beets are cooked. Cut cooked beets in half to see if their center rings are fibrous or tough. If so, remove them.

Cooking Raw Beets

When beets are cooked by themselves, it is important not to cut into them until after they are done. If cut, flavor and color leach out into the cooking or steaming water. If the beets are to be made into soup or a mixed stew the leaching will not matter. To prepare beets for cooking, cut the tops off an inch or two above the crown. Do not cut the tap root or rootlets. Rinse well without scraping or damaging the beet's skin. Then steam or boil until tender. This can take from 30 minutes to more than an hour depending on the size of the beets.

Beet cooking water is very often thrown away, but it should not be. It has nutritional value, and according to some, it is a blood builder. (Why not, considering its color?!) When possible, use beet cooking water in beet recipes, or include it in soup, or in vegetable drinks.

Drying

(Excellent) Optional: Pre-cook until tender. Slice thin, or grate coarsely. Dry to very tough or brittle. Refer to the DRYING section. Also see DRIED VEGETABLE PICKLES, in the PICKLING section, and cooking directions, below. *Beet Greens* Refer to DRYING SPINACH, in the SPINACH section.

Freezing

(Large beets' flavor is better with other storage methods.) Pre-cook until tender. Trim, peel, and slice or dice, if desired. Refer to the FREEZING section. *Beet Greens* Refer to FREEZING SPINACH, in the SPINACH section.

2½–3 pounds, tops removed = 1 quart cooked

BEET IDEAS
Baked Beets

Whole beets, untrimmed except for tops, are very good oven baked like potatoes, and served with butter. Large beets may take as long as 3 hours to bake, so put them in early. Trimmed and peeled beets can be baked in the pan with roasting meat, but will change the color of the meat

Cooking Dried Beets

Put dried beets in a saucepan and cover with water. Let soak 15 minutes, or a little longer if pieces are large. Heat to a simmer and cook until tender, usually 15 to 30 minutes. These can be used in any of the recipes in this section. (Also refer to DRIED VEGETABLE PICKLES, in the PICKLING section.)

BEET RECIPES
Old-Time Hot Borscht

(MAKES 8–12 BOWLS)

6–8 medium beets
¼ cup vinegar (red wine vinegar is best)
3 tablespoons (about) bacon fat or butter
1 cup onion, minced
1 clove garlic, minced
1½ cups cabbage, shredded
1 cup carrots, coarsely grated or cut julienne style
sour cream or yogurt, optional

½ cup celery, thinly sliced, optional
1½ quarts beef or pork stock
2 cups fresh or canned tomatoes, chopped
1 bay leaf
½ teaspoon thyme
pepper and salt, optional
1 or more cups leftover cooked meat, chopped, optional

The day before the soup is wanted, cook the beets in water to cover. Drain, saving the cooking water. (Or the beets can be cooked in the pot when the soup stock is made, and removed when done.) Grate the beets or cut them julienne style. Mix about ½ cup beets with the vinegar, and soak overnight.

The next day, heat the fat or butter in a soup pot, and gently sauté the onion, garlic, cabbage, carrots, and celery in it until they are limp. Add the soup stock, tomatoes, bay leaf, thyme, pepper, and salt. Add the beets and any beet cooking water, but continue to reserve the beet and vinegar mixture. Heat to a boil, and simmer about 30 minutes. Add the leftover meat.

Just before serving add the beet and vinegar mixture, and adjust seasonings, if necessary. Sour cream or yogurt can be added to each bowl of soup.

and other vegetables if allowed to touch them.

Beet and Horseradish Relish
Mix 1 part grated cooked beet and 1 part grated raw horseradish, or other preferred proportions. Add as much vinegar as the mixture will absorb. Some people like to add a little honey also. This keeps refrigerated for about a month.

Raw Beets in Salads
Small amounts of grated or very thinly sliced raw beet are delicious in many kinds of salads. They can also be used as a colorful garnish on cottage cheese or potato salads.

Stuffed Beet Salad
Cook medium or large beets and scoop out their centers with a spoon to make a hollow for stuffing. Cut a slice off the bottoms so that they sit firmly. Chop up the beet centers with onion, celery, and cooked leftover vegetables such as peas or green beans. Moisten with mayonnaise, and stuff the beets. They look very nice arranged on lettuce leaves. Plain sliced beets are also good with these dressings.

Polish Style Beets for Roast Meats

3 cups grated, cooked beets	1 cup meat broth or pan drippings
1 medium onion, minced	1–2 cloves crushed garlic
3 tablespoons butter	4–6 tablespoons lemon juice or
2 tablespoons flour	wine vinegar

Grate about 3 cups of cooked beets, and make a sauce for them as follows: Sauté a minced, medium sized onion in butter or other fat until limp. Stir in flour, and continue stirring until the flour browns lightly. Add either meat broth or defatted pan drippings mixed with water. When thickened to a sauce, add the beets and crushed garlic. Simmer a few minutes more. Just before serving, flavor with lemon juice or wine vinegar.

Very good served with roast or pot roasted meat, especially dark flavorful meats like mutton, venison, and other game.

Blackberries

Blackberries are prolific when they grow in a place that suits them. A vigorous patch of wild blackberries can easily yield as much as a family can eat fresh, with plenty left for making juice and other good things for the winter. If there are wild blackberries nearby there is usually no need to cultivate them, though the price from picking them may be a few scratches.

As there are thousands of overlapping varieties of blackberries, both wild and cultivated, it would be confusing to try to pinpoint a particular one. They may differ in size, flavor, seediness, and thorniness, but most varieties taste good and can be used in the same ways. A local, wild berry affectionately called "sow tits" may be as big, juicy, and flavorful as the properly named varieties, like loganberries and boysenberries.

HANDLING BLACKBERRIES

Pick blackberries when the dew has evaporated on a dry day. Avoid picking after heavy rains because the berries are more watery then and less sweet. Long sleeves, long pants, and a hat

---

BLACKBERRY STORAGE

Canning

(Seeds of some varieties may become too prominent when cooked.) Mix 2 tablespoons warm honey with each quart berries. Let stand 2 hours or until juice collects. Heat to a boil, fill jars, ½ in. headroom. Process boiling water bath. Pints: 10 min. Quarts: 15 min. (Or may pack raw as for RASPBERRIES.) Refer to the CANNING section. Also see CANNING FRUIT JUICE AND SAUCE, in the FRUITS section.

Note: Overly ripe berries may lack acid. Add 2 teaspoons lemon juice per pint, 4 teaspoons per quart.

Drying

(Poor flavor when dried whole.) Leather excellent. Refer to the DRYING section.

Freezing

Pack gently. Leave plain or cover with liquid (see LIQUIDS IN WHICH TO FREEZE FRUIT, in the FREEZING section). Best eaten partly thawed. May freeze fresh seedless purée (see SEEDINESS IN BLACKBERRIES, below). Refer to the FREEZING section.

5–8 cups fresh = 1 quart canned or frozen; 1 quart fresh = 1–2 cups juice

are a help when picking in a tangled thorny patch. Berries too high to reach can be brought closer by gently lowering the stem with a curved walking stick.

Fully ripe blackberries come off the plant readily, and can be picked more quickly than most other kinds of berries. Tightly attached berries should be left to ripen another day or two. As blackberries bruise easily they should be handled gently, and put in shallow containers so that the weight of the top berries will not crush the ones on the bottom. After they are picked they should not sit out in the sun, or they will lose color and sweetness. If the berries are gathered cleanly, washing them may not be necessary. If they must be washed, do it quickly, just before they are used. Blackberries will keep only a day or two in the refrigerator.

Seediness in Blackberries

The seeds in fresh blackberries are not troublesome, but in most wild blackberries and some cultivated varieties they become more prominent after cooking or freezing and may be disliked. They can easily be removed by pushing the fresh berries through the fine screen of a food mill or other strainer. The seedless purée can be made into jam, ice cream, or fruit desserts. If some contrast in texture is preferred a mixture of purée and whole berries can be used.

Blueberries

Until the twentieth century there were no cultivated blueberries. Wild blueberries were, and still are, an important fruit in these regions of North America with the necessary moist acid soil. American Indians and early settlers picked huge quantities and dried them for winter. Today wild blueberries are more apt to be canned or frozen, but are as popular as ever. Wild berries generally have more flavor than cultivated ones, and their small, firm shape makes them better for baking.

There are several related species that are called blueberries or huckleberries, or, in some places, bilberries, wortleberries,

BLACKBERRY IDEAS
Blackberry Apple Combinations
Blackberries and apples go well together in dozens of ways. They can be mixed to make juice, sauce, jam, pie, or fruit leather. Apples can be stewed in blackberry juice. Blackberries can be crushed, sweetened, and used as the filling in baked apples. The possibilities are restricted only by the limits of one's imagination.

BLUEBERRY STORAGE
Canning
This method is best for whole berries to use in baking: Put 2–3 quarts in a square of cheesecloth, hold corners, dip in boiling water until spots of juice show, about 30 seconds. Dip in cold water, drain, pack, ½ in. headroom. Do not add water or sweetener. Process boiling water bath. Pints: 15 min. Quarts: 20 min. Refer to the CANNING section. Also see CANNING FRUIT JUICE AND SAUCE, in the FRUITS section, and *Blueberry Marmalade,* below.
    Note: Overly ripe berries may lack acid. Add 2 teaspoons lemon juice per pint, 4 teaspoons per quart.

Cold Storage
Small, dry wild berries keep 3–4 weeks refrigerated in tightly closed contain-

or cowberries. The names are used differently in different locations. A species called blueberry in one place might be called huckleberry in another, but the confusion is not important, since all are edible and can be used in the same ways. Whatever the name they use, for eating fresh, most people like the softer, dusty-blue berries better than the black, shiny kinds with the hard seeds.

Garden Huckleberries

Seeds for garden huckleberries are sold in some catalogs. They are an annual, unrelated to blueberries, producing fruit in one season. The raw berries do not have a very good flavor, but they are acceptable cooked. Their flavor is best after light frosts.

HANDLING BLUEBERRIES

The full flavor and sweetness of blueberries develops several days to a week after they turn blue. They are ripe if they fall off the bush when touched. Commercially sold blueberries are often picked too soon, which accounts for some of their lack of flavor. If gathered carefully from a clean spot, blueberries should not need washing. They can immediately be put into containers, and refrigerated or frozen, or spread on trays for drying. At times it may be easier to gather berries by shaking them onto a cloth or plastic sheet, and remove the debris afterwards.

BLUEBERRY RECIPES

Blueberry Marmalade

(MAKES ABOUT 3 HALF-PINT JARS)

4–6 tablespoons orange or lemon peel, coarsely grated or thinly sliced	½ cup homemade pectin, optional (refer to the PECTIN section)
1¾ cups honey or maple syrup	5 cups blueberries
	½ teaspoon nutmeg

If the orange or lemon peel is too strong or bitter in flavor, boil it for 10 minutes in plenty of water and drain.

Heat the sweetening, orange or lemon peel, and pectin to a

---

ers. If soft, cultivated berries keep 1–2 weeks.

Drying

Optional: Blanch briefly to crack skins and speed drying. Spread on trays, dry until hard. Refer to the DRYING section.

Freezing

Excellent packed plain. Small wild berries stay separated, so may be used in baking without thawing. Refer to the FREEZING section.

5–8 cups fresh = 1 quart canned or cooked

BLUEBERRY IDEAS
Dried Blueberries in Meat Stews

Stew beef or other red meat with onions, then add dried blueberries about 30 minutes before it is done. This is a favorite American Indian combination.

Blueberries with Breakfast Cereal

Blueberries are good with cold cereal and superb with hot cereal. Stir fresh, frozen, or canned blueberries into hot cereal just before it is served. Add milk and a sprinkle of nutmeg and enjoy.

BROCCOLI STORAGE
Canning

Not recommended. (It becomes strong tasting and discolored.)

boil in a deep pot. (Pectin is necessary for a firm set, but the flavor and texture are good without it.) Watch the pot if using honey because it may foam up suddenly. Add the blueberries and nutmeg, and cook uncovered, about 20 minutes or until the marmalade thickens somewhat. Pour into jars and seal. (Refer to the JAM AND JELLY section.)

Raspberry Marmalade

Use raspberries instead of blueberries. Instead of nutmeg try using cinnamon or a pinch of cloves.

Broccoli

Broccoli is a relatively new vegetable in the new world, and an old one in the old world. It has become popular in North America only in the last thirty to fifty years, but has been cultivated in Italy since the time of the ancient Romans. Large-headed broccolis are favored in North America, while sprouting varieties are preferred in Mediterranean and Asian countries. Sprouting broccoli is very leafy and tender with small buds. It is cooked like other leafy greens.

Broccoli and cauliflower are closely related members of the cabbage family. Though their heads, or buds, look alike except for color, their flavor and texture are quite different, and they taste best with different kinds of seasonings. The green vegetable taste of broccoli calls for the same seasonings that suit leafy greens, green beans, and other green vegetables, for example, onions, garlic, vinegar, tomato, olive oil, or crumbled crisp bacon. Cauliflower, with its milder flavor and crisper texture, goes better with the kinds of seasonings used with potatoes. Broccoli is far richer in vitamins and minerals, especially vitamin A, than cauliflower.

HANDLING BROCCOLI

Heads of broccoli should be cut after the buds are fully formed, but before they start to open. The stalk and small leaves should be used along with the head, since they are equally good to eat.

Cold Storage
Heads keep about 2 weeks if refrigerated. Whole plants pulled just before hard frost keep 4–5 weeks in a root cellar.

Drying
Slice uniformly thin. Steam 10 min. or until cooked through. Dry until brittle. Refer to the DRYING section.

Freezing
(Preferred storage method.) Prepare (see below). Slice stalks and florets no thicker than 1½ in., or chop coarsely, then blanch. Steam chunks: 5 min. Boil: 3 min. If chopped, steam 1–2 min. Refer to the FREEZING section.

2–3 pounds fresh = 1 quart frozen

BROCCOLI IDEAS
Broccoli in Salads
Raw broccoli is good added to most kinds of salads. The peeled stalks are especially fine because their flavor is a little milder than the tops. They can be cut into rectangles to eat like carrot sticks, or slices can be marinated in an oil and vinegar dressing for several hours to make a special broccoli stalk salad. Leftover cooked broccoli is very good in salads, especially vegetable salads and aspics.

If the plant is left growing after the central head is cut, it will produce many smaller side shoots for later harvest. These, too, should be cut or broken off before they begin to open.

The inner parts of thick broccoli stalks are very tender and delicious when they are peeled. They are good raw or cooked with the florets. To peel the tough stalks, cut away a strip at the base of the stalk and pull until it comes off. Peeled stalks should be cut in chunks the same size as the florets.

De-bugging Broccoli

Various little bugs and worms like to hide themselves in broccoli heads. The standard method for driving them out is soaking in salt water for ½ to 1 hour. This works, but it is too drastic a step to take against such small problems. More harm is done by the soaking, which removes water soluble nutrients and adds unwanted salt, than could possibly be caused by the eating of an occasional harmless bug. However, it is not necessary to resign oneself to eating bugs with one's broccoli. If the broccoli is swished vigorously in a pan of cold water after it is cut or broken into separate florets, most bugs and worms will be dislodged. A second rinsing will do the rest. With broccoli that is to be blanched in boiling water for freezing, any bugs and worms will sink or float off after they are killed.

Brussels Sprouts

Are Brussels sprouts a gentle, real-world version of an improbable science fiction creature? What else could have one neck with dozens of heads, grow in the garden, and taste delicious? This cabbage family plant, which originated somewhere in Europe—possibly in Belgium as the name suggests—needs cool weather and some frosts to do well. Where growing conditions are right they are a pleasure to have in the garden. They do not take too much space, are very productive over a long period of time, are easy to harvest, and usually continue into early winter after other vegetables have disappeared. Brussels sprouts are also a pleasure in the kitchen. They have the elegance and flavor

---

Broccoli with Herbs, Roman Style

Do as the ancient Romans did and embellish broccoli with any combination of their favorite herbs: savory, mint, lovage or celery leaves, coriander leaves, scallion or a small onion or leek, and cumin seeds. Steam the broccoli florets and peeled stalks until tender, then put them in a saucepan with a little olive oil and wine or wine vinegar. Add a generous amount of minced herbs (crush cumin seeds if using them) and heat for 2 or 3 minutes to blend flavors.

BRUSSELS SPROUTS STORAGE

Canning
Quality poor. Watery, soggy, and generally unpleasant, except when pickled.

Cold Storage
Dig plants before hard frost, holding damp soil around roots. Keep about 2 months in root cellar or similar conditions. Budded sprouts often mature in storage.

Drying
Slice ½ in. thick. Steam 10 min. or until tender. Dry until crisp. Refer to the DRYING section.

of a fancy gourmet vegetable, no matter how simply they are cooked or how often they are served.

HANDLING BRUSSELS SPROUTS

The lowest sprouts on the stalk are harvested first. They tend to be smaller and looser-leafed than sprouts that form later, but they are still very good. Picking them encourages more sprouts to form. Each sprout is simply twisted to break it off from the stalk. Brussels sprouts need very little preparation. The base of the sprout is trimmed, if necessary, and wilted leaves are pulled off. When sprouts are large, sometimes a cross is cut in the base to make them cook evenly throughout.

After all the sprouts have been harvested, the tops of the plants can be eaten. The inner rosettes of leaves at the top are very tender, with the typical Brussels sprouts flavor. They cook very quickly, and are good served like cabbage or other leafy greens. If wished, the stalks can be peeled like broccoli stalks, to cook or eat raw. The lower leaves of Brussels sprouts plants can be picked early in the season while they are tender and cooked as greens.

Cabbage

Cabbage is the "head" and most important vegetable of the cabbage family. Usually it is a green head, but it can also be a red head or a Savoy curly head. Its nearest relatives are kale and collards—the leafy greens, broccoli and cauliflower—the buds, kohlrabi—the bulbous stem, and Brussels sprouts—a lot of little heads. All of these vegetables have the same ancestor, the sea cabbage, a small wild plant that grows in some coastal areas of England and Europe. Head cabbage is grown in temperate zones throughout the world, and has always had special value as a winter vegetable because it stores so well. Sauerkraut is also a winter staple. (Refer to the SAUERKRAUT section.)

Since cabbage is eaten in so many places, there are many different approaches to preparing it. Gardeners who want to depend on cabbage as a major winter vegetable have a rich

Freezing
Blanch in steam or boiling water. Small: 3 min.; medium: 4 min.; large: 5 min. Refer to the FREEZING section.

Live Storage
Mulch well in garden. Will keep most of the winter where weather is not too severe.
    about 2 pounds fresh = 1 quart cooked

BRUSSELS SPROUTS IDEAS
Baked Sprouts
Cook Brussels sprouts until almost tender. They can be cooked in chicken stock or other soup stock if desired, or use leftover sprouts. Butter a shallow baking dish and put the sprouts in it. Add several spoons of soup stock, cooking water, or water. Sprinkle with grated cheese or bread crumbs, and dots of butter. Bake about 15 minutes in a hot oven.

CABBAGE STORAGE
Canning
(Possible but not recommended because of strong taste and mushy texture, unless pickled.) Refer to CANNING SAUERKRAUT, in the SAUERKRAUT section. Also see *Spiced Pickled Cabbage for Canning*, below.

heritage of recipes and ideas to draw upon, and can look forward to eating it often without getting tired of it.

HANDLING CABBAGE

Cabbage is best if it has matured in cool weather. When spring cabbage is harvested early, it is tender and delicate in flavor and excellent for salads, but if it is left in the garden after hot weather arrives it is apt to taste bitter or strong. Fall cabbages can be harvested whenever they are big and firm enough to be useful. Cabbage for storage is best left in the garden until just before the first hard freeze. Light frosts will not hurt it and even seem to improve the flavor.

When the cabbage is pulled or cut, remove only the toughest outer leaves. Keep as many green leaves as possible, as they contain more vitamins and minerals than the white inner leaves. If necessary, wash the cabbage before preparing it, but do not soak it. Soaking removes water soluble nutrients. Usually, the tight inner part of the head does not need washing.

Cold Storage

See STORING WINTER CABBAGE, below. Also see KEEPING SAUER-KRAUT IN COLD STORAGE, in the SAUERKRAUT section.

Drying

Shred coarsely, or slice thinly. Steam blanch 8–10 min. (optional). Dry until ribs are tough, leafy parts crumble. Refer to the DRYING section.

Freezing

Shred, chop, or cut in wedges. Blanch in boiling water. Shredded or chopped: 1½ min. Wedges: 3 min. Refer to the FREEZING section.

  1 pound = 1 quart shredded raw

CABBAGE IDEAS
Cabbage Seasonings

Cabbage is particularly good with herb seeds. Anise, dill, and caraway seeds, and juniper berries are especially complementary. Tart flavors such as tomato, sour apple, or a splash of vinegar also go well. Cured meats like ham, bacon, sausage, or corned beef are other favorites with cabbage.

Storing Winter Cabbage

Any kind of cabbage will keep several weeks in a cool place like the refrigerator. Fall and winter varieties will keep 2 or 3 months under the right conditions. After long storage they do lose some of their color, flavor, and nutritional value, but they are still one of the best, most useful green vegetables to keep in cold storage.

Cabbage keeps very well in root cellars and in most outdoor storage arrangements such as mounds, pits, and insulated areas in outbuildings. Ideal conditions are 32°F with a fairly high humidity, but some variation is tolerated. Cabbages should be protected from temperatures below 30°F. Though they will keep in storage areas such as basements and unheated rooms, they give off a strong odor that can penetrate throughout a house, so most people prefer outdoor storage. The odor can be minimized if cabbages are wrapped in newspaper or packed in sand, leaves, or peat moss.

There are two ways to harvest cabbages for storage. One is to pull up the whole plant, leaving the stalk for a handle; the other is to cut off the head at its base. In either case, pull off loose outer leaves so that the head is fairly compact. Cut heads are then wrapped in several layers of newspaper or packed in damp sand, dry leaves, damp peat moss, or a similar material. They are then ready for the cold storage area.

Cabbages with stalks are either hung upside down in root cellars, or packed upside down in hay, straw, or dry leaves, and put in outdoor storage pits, mounds, or other protected areas. Sometimes cabbages for hanging in root cellars are hung first at room temperature for a few days to "paper over," where the outer leaves dry to a paper-like texture and protect the inside of the head.

Though it is possible to keep cabbage with less time and attention than required by these methods, some spoilage is likely. One traditional method was to simply pull cabbages and pile them in a windrow in the field without any trimming or careful stacking. A layer of hay 2 or 3 feet thick was thrown on top. In the winter when they were dug out they would often be frozen, but if used immediately they would still be good.

If stored cabbage should start to go bad because of a warm spell or any other reason, it can be saved by making sauerkraut, or by freezing or drying.

Moisture Content

The moisture content of cabbage varies considerably with the growing season and the way it was stored. A high moisture content means no extra liquid will be needed when making sauerkraut. It also means the cabbage will not fry or sauté well, because it will stew in its own juices. Before frying cabbage, recipes sometimes recommend sprinkling chopped or shredded cabbage with salt, letting it sit for a while, and then squeezing it to remove moisture. This step is unnecessary when cabbage is already somewhat dry. Since stored winter cabbage tends to get drier with time, it is excellent for frying or sautéeing. If recipes requiring this step are prepared only in winter, the use of salt can be avoided entirely. (In stir-frying the moisture content does not matter, as the quick, high heat seals moisture in.)

Preventing Strong Odors or Digestive Upsets

Cabbage is sometimes avoided because of its reputation for giving off strong smells while cooking, or for causing gas and stomach upsets. These problems are due more to the cooking method

Cabbage Instead of Lettuce

Young tender raw cabbage is as versatile as lettuce in salads. It is good in every combination from tossed green salads to aspics. Small, rounded cabbage leaves are very nice for holding a serving of a hearty potato or egg salad. Wedges of cabbage are good with any kind of dressing. Mature winter cabbage is best in salads if it is chopped small or shredded before it is added.

Cabbage and Fish Salad

Flake leftover cooked fish and mix with shredded or finely chopped raw cabbage. Add other shredded or chopped salad vegetables to taste, and moisten with mayonnaise. Sprinkle with paprika if desired.

Stir-fried Cabbage

Shredded or thinly sliced cabbage is very good in many stir-fried mixtures. To stir-fry alone, heat lard, chicken fat, or oil very hot. If wished, stir in minced garlic. Add the cabbage and stir-fry 1 minute or until it brightens in color. Add several tablespoons of soup stock or water, cover, and cook 3 to 5 minutes or until the cabbage is just

than the cabbage itself. When cabbage is overcooked in a lot of water at high temperatures its sulfur compounds break down, causing odors and digestive upsets. But if it is steamed, or stewed in a minimum of water at moderate temperatures for 10 to 15 minutes, or only until it is tender, these problems will not develop. Cabbage cooked by baking, sautéeing, or stir-frying is problem free. Preparations containing liquids, like soups and stews, can be troublesome, especially when reheated, and cabbage is not a good choice for use in soup stock. However, it is good when added to soups or stews just a few minutes before serving.

CABBAGE RECIPES
Spiced Pickled Cabbage for Canning
(MAKES 4–6 QUARTS)

2 small cabbages, or 6 to 8 quarts finely shredded (red cabbage is best)
⅛ cup plain or pickling salt (refer to the PICKLING section)
¼ cup mustard seed
2 quarts vinegar (wine vinegar is very nice)
½ cup honey or 1 cup brown sugar
¼ cup pickling spices (or a mixture of whole cloves, mace, allspice, peppercorns, celery seed, and cinnamon stick)

In a large bowl, sprinkle layers of cabbage with salt. Mix well and let sit 24 hours in a cool place. Drain and set out in the sun on a rack for 2 or 3 hours, or put in a cloth bag and hang over the sink for about 6 hours. The cabbage should become quite dry in this time. Mix the mustard seed with the cabbage, and pack in clean canning jars, leaving ½ inch headroom.

Meanwhile, heat the vinegar, sweetening, and spices to a boil and cook 5 minutes. Let cool, then strain to remove the spices. (If preferred, a spice bag can be used.) Pour the vinegar mixture over the cabbage in the jars, dividing it evenly between them. Run a knife around the perimeter of the jar to remove bubbles. If necessary add plain vinegar to fill the jars, leaving ¼ inch headroom. Adjust the lids and process in a boiling water bath, 15 minutes for pints, 20 minutes for quarts. Since the jars start out cool, place them in warm, not boiling, water. Start to time when water boils. (Refer to the CANNING section for further directions.)

---

tender. Pepper, salt, or other seasonings are optional. Refer to the STIR-FRYING section.

Baked Cabbage
Grease a baking dish and put precooked, chopped or shredded cabbage in it. Leftover cabbage or frozen and thawed cabbage can be used, if desired. Add a little light cream, soup stock, or water. Sprinkle the top with bread crumbs, grated cheese, and dots of butter. Bake in a hot oven until browned on top, about 20 minutes.

Creamed Cabbage
Cook shredded or chopped cabbage until just tender, and drain if necessary. Make a cream sauce. Just before serving mix the hot cabbage with the hot cream sauce. This mixture can be baked in the same way as BAKED CABBAGE, above. Seasonings such as dill leaves or seeds, celery leaves or seeds, and onion or garlic are good.

This pickle can also be packed in tightly closed containers and stored in a cool place without cooking or canning. It will keep 1–2 months.

Canning

The canning process was invented when the French government offered a prize to the inventor of a practical method for food preservation. Nicolas Appert won the prize in 1810 when he devised a way of sealing food in glass containers and cooking them in boiling water. That process is essentially the same as modern boiling water bath canning. The heat of the cooking destroys enzymes and microorganisms that would cause food spoilage, and the airtight vacuum seal prevents recontamination from exposure to air.

Since then, years of research and experience have established exact requirements for home canning most foods. When modern canning instructions are followed carefully, safe, high quality canned foods are assured.

REQUIREMENTS FOR CANNING HIGH- AND LOW-ACID FOODS

The most important fact to know about canning is that high- and low-acid foods have different canning requirements. Acidic foods, those with a pH of 4.6 or below, including most fruits, tomatoes, and pickles, are safe to can at 212°F (100°C), or at boiling temperature. Low-acid foods, those with a pH above 4.6, including vegetables, meat, and fish, must be canned in a pressure canner so as to maintain a temperature of 240°F (121°C). The reason for the difference is that the toxins that cause botulism poisoning cannot develop in acidic foods, but can develop in low-acid foods unless very high temperatures are used when processing them. (See BOTULISM POISONING, below.)

Most foods fall clearly into either the high-acid or low-acid group, but there are some borderline cases. All home canning guides clearly state which foods are acidic enough for boiling water bath canning, and which require pressure canning. Where there is doubt about a food, such as low-acid tomatoes, lemon juice or citric acid can be added to increase acidity. (Refer to the STORAGE directions for each food section for the necessary quantities and precautions.)

Many people find it practical to can only acidic foods, such as fruit, tomatoes, sauerkraut, relish, and pickles. Often, vegetables and meat are frozen, or perhaps dried, or salt cured. This eliminates the need for a pressure canner and the more painstaking processing it requires.

Botulism Poisoning

The bacteria that cause botulism poisoning are confusing because they are quite harmless in some circumstances, and highly dangerous in others. *Botulinum spores* are widely distributed in the environment, are not toxic themselves, and ordinarily do not cause any trouble. However, under certain circumstances the spores germinate and multiply to produce a highly poisonous toxin. In stored foods, these spores must either be prevented from germinating and producing the toxin, or they must be destroyed.

Botulinum spores are difficult to destroy, and it takes a combination of high temperature (240°F in home canning, usually) and time to kill them. There are, however, many substances and conditions that prevent their germination and growth. Most stored foods are safe because the spores cannot grow in them for one reason or another. They cannot grow when sufficient acid is present, with a pH of 4.6 or lower. Nor can they grow in concentrations of salt above 10%, and of sugar above 50%. Such physical conditions as temperatures below freezing, and dehydration or lack of moisture also prevent growth. The spores will grow in a vacuum, or partial vacuum, where it is moist and warm. Conditions inside a sealed can or jar of a low-acid food are perfect for the germination and growth of the botulinum spores and the production of poison. For this reason the spores must be killed when low-acid foods are canned. This requires heating every bit of the food to a temperature of 240°F, including the inside of food chunks, for an adequate time. The time given for processing each low-acid food in a pressure canner is carefully tested to make absolutely sure this happens.

Poisons produced by the botulinum spores are easier to destroy than the spores themselves, since boiling at 212°F will destroy the poison. This is why canning instructions say to boil home canned, low-acid foods for 15 to 20 minutes before eating them as an extra safety precaution. Remember that the boiling will not affect the spores, and they will still produce toxins if conditions are right—for example, if the food is recanned improperly.

Another dangerous aspect of botulism poisoning is that there may be no obvious signs of spoilage. Sometimes bubbling and foam, a swelled can, a spurt of liquid when the can or jar is opened, or a strange look or smell before or during cooking will indicate trouble, but these signs are not always present. If there are any suspicions that botulism toxins are present, destroy the food so that no person or animal can eat it. *DO NOT* touch or taste it. Burn the food or bury it in a deep hole, or boil it, jar, lids, and all, and then throw it out.

Acidic foods should also be carefully destroyed should they mold, because certain molds raise the pH enough for botulism poisons to develop.

A generation ago in some areas people regularly canned low-acid foods at boiling temperature apparently without botulism problems. Perhaps there were very few botulism bacteria present in those regions, or perhaps those people were just lucky. It is neither safe nor sensible to rely on previous successful use of this method. There is now so much movement of people, food, and soil that the botulinum spores are sure to be present everywhere, whether they once were or not—and considering what is known about botulism, who wants to depend on luck?

However, worries about botulism poisoning should not discourage people from home canning. Actual cases of poisoning are very rare, and huge quantities of food are canned at home every year without any hint of a problem. As long as the danger is understood, and each food is properly processed, canning is an excellent and safe way to preserve low-acid, as well as high-acid, foods.

CANNING AT HIGH ALTITUDES

The altitude at which food is canned will affect the processing requirements. Because air pressure decreases with higher altitudes, water boils at temperatures below 212°F. At altitudes above 1,000 feet boiling water bath canning is done at a lower temperature, and to compensate, processing times must be increased. Decreased air pressure also affects pressure canner processing, but a temperature of 240°F must still be reached inside the canner. To do so, the canner's pressure is set higher at altitudes over 2,000 feet. Processing times remain the same. The following chart gives adjustments at various altitudes.

ALTITUDE ADJUSTMENTS FOR BOILING WATER BATH CANNING

Feet above sea level	If processing time required is 21 minutes or less, add:	If processing time required is 22 minutes or longer, add:
1–2,000	2 minutes	4 minutes
2,001–4,000	4 minutes	8 minutes
4,001–6,000	6 minutes	12 minutes
6,001–8,000	8 minutes	16 minutes

Feet above sea level	*When 11 pounds pressure is required at sea level use:*
2,000–4,000	12 pounds
4,001–6,000	13 pounds
6,001–8,000	14 pounds

CANNING CONTAINERS

Glass jars are the most popular containers for home canning. It is possible to use tin cans, but there are more complications. For information about them, see the references at the end of this section.

Jars made especially for canning are often called "mason" jars, after their inventor, John L. Mason. The commonly used sizes are pints and quarts, but half-pint jars are handy for foods to be used in small amounts. Although half-gallon mason jars are sold, their use is not advised for boiling water bath or pressure canning. They are too big for safe processing, and most canning instructions do not give processing times for them. Pint and quart jars come in standard and wide mouth sizes. The wide mouth jars are best for packing large pieces of food.

One of the nicest things about canning jars is that they are reusable year after year if well cared for. However, they cannot be handled too roughly, and the old ones must be protected from drastic temperature changes. Another requirement when canning in glass jars is a dark storage place, as exposure to light will gradually reduce the food's quality.

Canning Lids

Modern canning lids are usually two-piece, screw band metal lids. The actual lid is a round, flat disc with a rubber-like sealing compound around the edge. This lid can be used only once. The other part is the band, or ring, which screws onto the jar and holds the lid in place during processing and sealing. These rings are reusable as long as they remain free of rust or corrosion, and screw on easily. One or the other of the two lid sizes, regular and wide mouth, will fit most styles and sizes of modern canning jars, regardless of brand.

There may be small variations among the canning lid brands, but they basically all work in the same ways. They must be boiled in water for about 5 minutes to soften their sealing compound before they are set on the filled jar. Follow the directions that come with the jar lids. The rings are then screwed down firmly, but not fully tightened. The lids then have enough give so that air escapes during processing, but they still hold the lid in place so that a vacuum seal forms as the jars cool. One person's idea of firmly tightened may be different from another's, so some leeway in the tightness of the canning lids can be allowed. Very tight lids could cause breakage during processing, or the lids could buckle and not seal, though this is unusual. When the jars have cooled completely the rings should be removed and reused.

Some old-style lids, such as zinc ones with porcelain liners, and glass lids on jars with wire bales, are still in use. Both require new rubber rings every time they are used. These lids are only partially sealed before processing, and the final seal is made when the jars are removed from the canner. Directions for using such lids usually come with the rubber rings.

Recycling Canning Containers

Using old jars or bottles that originally contained commercially processed foods is condemned in most canning guides. However, many people have successfully made limited use of some of these containers, and the practice is not going to disappear. Instead of dismissing the whole idea, why not explore the circumstances where this has worked and those where it has not?

Only jars that originally contained food should be considered for recycling. But because commercial food jars are not always made as strongly and carefully as regulation canning jars, their use is limited. They should never be used for pressure canning as the stresses are simply too great.

There are two kinds of jars with reuse value. First, there are those jars, especially mayonnaise jars, that fit standard canning lids. These have been used quite successfully for boiling water bath canning. They must be pint or quart sizes so that the processing time will be standard. There is the possibility that a jar will crack during canning, or that a lid will not seal properly, but the same thing can happen with regulation canning jars, and must always be watched for. Any jar that fails to seal after one or two tries should be thrown out.

To check a jar for flaws, run a finger around the rim, feeling for irregularities or nicks. Then set the jar upside down on a flat surface, and see if it touches all the way around the rim. Test the canning lid and ring together on the jar to make sure they screw down firmly. Sometimes a ring will fit well by itself, but when screwed down with the lid it will not work. If a jar passes all these tests it can be tried for boiling water bath canning. One experienced user of recycled jars says they are more dependable than the old-tinted mason jars that some people still use.

The second kind of commercial jars with some limited reuse value are those whose screw-on lids have a plasticized sealing compound around the rim for making a vacuum seal. These jars can only be used for open kettle canning of very acidic foods, or very sweet foods, such as jams, jellies, pickles, concentrated fruit juices, or maple syrup. They are not safe for boiling water bath canning, because the lids will not necessarily form as effective a seal as regulation canning lids. Also, the shapes and sizes of these jars are too irregular for accurate timing.

Before using these jars for open kettle canning, check the lids and jars carefully. They must both be in perfect shape. The lids should have no scratches, rust, or dents, and the sealing compound around the inside of the rim should be unmarred. Lids that have been pried off the jar cannot be reused.

Always boil the jars and lids before using them. Then follow the directions under OPEN KETTLE CANNING, below. Check the seal after the jars have cooled. Usually the lids will look or feel slightly concave. If the contents are liquid, turn the jar upside down and watch for a stream of bubbles from around the inside jar rim, indicating a faulty seal. Random bubbles are not significant. Do not try the lids, since that would break the seal. Later on, if any signs of mold or other spoilage should appear, throw out the jar and its contents. It is best to reuse this kind of commercial lid only once, although some of them will reseal several times.

CANNING METHODS

It is very important to use the correct canning method for each kind of food. As described above, all low-acid foods are canned in a pressure canner, while most acidic foods are canned in a boiling water bath canner. Two other canning methods, steam bath canning (not to be confused with pressure canning), and open kettle canning, are also described below. These are used only for canning acidic foods. Another food storage method used for a few very acidic fruits is cold water canning, but it is not really canning in spite of the name. (Refer to COLD WATER CANNING, in the COLD STORAGE section.) The outmoded method called oven canning described in some old cookbooks is never safe to use.

Boiling Water Bath Canning

This canning method works by submerging jars of food, ready for processing, in boiling water, and cooking them at a full boil for the required time. It is the preferred method for canning fruit, tomatoes, and pickles.

A deep canning kettle or a large, deep pot with a rack and a lid is necessary. The pot must be deep enough to hold the jars on the rack, 1 or 2 inches of water above them, and about 2 inches of air space to prevent boiling over. A pot for quarts should be 11 to 12 inches deep, and 9 to 10 inches deep for pints. Some commercial canning kettles are not deep enough, so measure before buying. A kettle that is too shallow will probably not seal jars properly. The racks that come with canners are usually basket shaped, with high or folding handles for lifting all the jars at once. A rack can be improvised by placing several old canning lid rings in the pot and setting a round, cake cooling rack on them. A more permanent rack can be cut from hardware cloth (small mesh wire fencing) to fit the pot, then stapled to strips of wood for support. With an improvised rack, a pair of tongs is essential for lifting jars out of the boiling water. Special canning tongs can be purchased, but some other kinds of tongs may work. Try them ahead of time to make sure. It is also helpful, but not essential, to have a wide mouth funnel for filling jars without getting food on the rims. Other equipment that may be needed will already be in most kitchens.

To begin canning, fill the kettle about half full of water. If the food to be canned is hot packed (see CANNING, STEP BY STEP, below), bring the water to a boil and have extra water boiling as well. If the food is raw packed, have warm water in the kettle. When the jars have been filled and the lids adjusted according to directions, set them in the water on the rack. The jars should not touch each other, or the sides of the kettle. Add enough water of the correct temperature to cover the jar tops by 1 to 2 inches, pouring the water around the jars, not directly onto the lids. Cover and bring to a boil. Begin timing after the water has reached a full boil, and keep the water boiling for the entire processing time. (Adjust the processing time for high altitudes as described in the chart above.) When processing is complete, remove the jars from the kettle and set them in a draft-free place where they will not be disturbed for 12 hours. (See CANNING, STEP BY STEP, below, for details of preparing, packing, and storing.)

Steam Bath Canning

This method worked in the same way as boiling water bath canning, except that it used the heat of steam from the boiling water. It is labeled unsafe in modern canning guides because regulation processing times have not been developed. As well, in a home canning situation it is impossible to make sure that the steam reaches and remains at the temperature of boiling water.

Open Kettle Canning

Open kettle canning is accomplished by pouring boiling hot food into hot, sterile jars, and sealing them immediately with sterile lids. The method is successful only with very acidic fruit juices, syrup, jam, and jelly. It is not a substitute for most boiling water bath canning, and is discouraged in modern canning guides. There is a possibility of contamination when the food is exposed to the air before sealing, and the lids do not seal well if the food cools too much when the jars are filled. At high altitudes the boiling temperature is lower, making it more difficult to have everything hot enough to seal properly. If jars do not seal, spoilage, such as mold or rotting, may occur, and the food must be discarded.

The advantages of open kettle canning are that it saves time and fuel, and makes it feasible to can one or two jars of fruit juice, syrup, or preserves without setting up a full-scale canning operation. Very acidic fruit juices, maple syrup, and other syrups, and jams and jellies may be canned by the open kettle method or by the more secure boiling water bath method, except for some jellies, whose texture will be damaged by the extra processing.

Steps for Open Kettle Canning

1. Boil jars and lids at least 5 minutes to soften the sealing compound on the lids. Keep jars and lids at a simmer until they are to be used.
2. Have the liquid to be canned at a boil. Remove only 1 or 2 jars from their boiling water. Fill them immediately almost to the brim with the boiling liquid. If necessary, wipe jar rims with a paper or cloth towel dampened by dipping in boiling water. Remove lids from their boiling water with tongs and seal immediately. Screw lids down firmly.
3. Turn the jars upside down for about 30 seconds, letting the hot liquid reheat the inside of the lid. Let the jars cool, and test for a seal as for any canning procedure.
4. Success depends upon having everything ready, and then working quickly. It is important to fill and seal only 1 or 2 jars at a time so that nothing can cool before it is sealed. Tongs, pot holders, and other equipment should be laid out before beginning.

Pressure Canning

The only safe way to can low-acid foods is in a steam pressure canner. Only a pressure canner can reach and maintain the required temperature of 240°F. (See REQUIREMENTS FOR CANNING HIGH- AND LOW-ACID FOODS, above.)

Pressure cookers that are not designed for canning are not recommended. They are usually too small, and do not heat up and cool off at the same rate as the canners. If one must be used, add 20 minutes at 11 pounds pressure to the required processing time. Large steam pressure canners are expensive, but will last for many years if properly cared for.

Many brands and styles of pressure canners are available. They operate differently, so their enclosed instructions must be followed. Note especially the directions for cleaning the safety valve and petcock openings. A piece of string is normally pulled through them after every use. If the canner has a dial gauge, it *must* be checked every year to ensure its accuracy. The canner's manufacturer, or, in the U.S., a local Agricultural Extension Office, should be able to check it.

Many people prefer to freeze low-acid foods rather than can them. The advantages of canning are that canned foods are stored without electricity and without the fear of power failure or unplugged freezers, and they can be used immediately without thawing.

The basic procedure for pressure canning is as follows. Put several inches of water in the canner. Heat it to a boil if the jars are filled with very hot food; otherwise, just warm the water. Set the filled jars, with their lids adjusted, on the rack in the canner. Follow the directions that came with the canner for all procedures, including closing the lid, venting air, raising pressure to the necessary level, and maintaining it, cooling naturally, opening the vent, and finally removing the cover and the jars.

Most canning at sea level is done at 11 pounds of pressure. If the altitude is above 2,000 feet, adjust the pounds of pressure used according to the high-altitude chart, above, to maintain a temperature of 240°F.

CANNING, STEP BY STEP

1   PREPARE CANNING LIDS AND JARS

Check each jar to make sure there are no nicks or cracks. Run a finger around the rim to feel for flaws. Inspect lids to make sure they are perfect. Wash and rinse the jars. If necessary for the canning method used, bring them to a boil in a pot of water and leave them in it to stay hot. Follow the package directions for the lids, or wash and boil them for 5 minutes. The lids and jars can be boiled in the same pot and left there until needed.

2   PREPARE FOOD AND FILL JARS

(Information for canning a specific food is given under the Storage heading in each food section. Also included is the feasibility of canning.)

Prepare food just before it is processed, one kettle or canner load at a time.

There are two methods for packing food in jars—raw pack and hot pack. Delicate foods that break or crush easily, such as fresh fruits, are usually raw packed. Dense foods that take a long time to heat through are usually hot packed, and foods that must be cooked in preparation are also hot packed. Some foods can be packed either way.

RAW PACK   This method is sometimes called cold pack. Prepare the raw food by washing, trimming, peeling, coring, or cutting as necessary. Pack the pieces of food close together in clean jars. Leave as little space as possible between pieces without crushing or damaging the food. Add hot liquid to fill the jar, unless the food's own juices will fill it. Boiling water, stock, syrup, or a pickling liquid may be used. Leave the required headroom both when packing the food and adding liquid.

HOT PACK   Prepare the food as necessary, and cook or partially cook it according to the directions for that food. For foods with a processing time of less than 10 minutes, pack or pour the hot food into jars that have been kept hot after being boiled for 10 minutes. (The water bath canner may be used to do this and the water saved for use in processing.) Pack pieces of food close together without crushing. Add boiling hot cooking liquid or water to fill the jars, if necessary, leaving the required headroom both when packing the food and adding the liquid. It may be easier to ladle foods such as soup and fruit sauces into jars. A wide mouth funnel will facilitate ladling or pouring, and will keep the jar rims clean.

3   REMOVE BUBBLES, CLEAN RIMS, ADJUST LIDS

Run a plastic knife or similar tool, such as a spatula's plastic handle, around the inside of the jar between the food and the glass to dislodge bubbles. A shake or light tap on the table will also help settle the food and loosen bubbles. Check the headroom and add more liquid if necessary. Wipe the jar rim with a damp cloth or paper towel, making sure no food or juice is stuck to the rim. Set the lids in place and tighten according to their package directions. If two-piece screw lids are used, set the flat lid piece on the jar with the sealing compound against the rim. Screw on the ring firmly but do not use full strength to tighten it.

4   PROCESS THE FILLED JARS

Using the method appropriate for the food, process the jars for the required time. (See CANNING METHODS, and chart for altitude adjustments, above.)

5   COOL JARS, CHECK LIDS

Carefully remove the hot jars from the canner, and set them in a draft-free place where they will not be disturbed. After 12 to 24 hours remove the rings from two-piece lids. Check the seal on each jar. Most metal lids will be slightly concave, or sunken in, if they are sealed. If the jars are sticky or have food on the outsides, wash them in warm water, then rinse and dry.

6   STORE IN A COOL, DARK, DRY PLACE

The ideal storage place for canned goods is dark, dry, and above freezing but below 50°F. High temperatures and exposure to light destroy some of the vitamins in canned food. Light can also bleach out color. Dampness can cause metal lids to rust and lose their seals. If a dark storage area is unavailable, keep the jars in boxes, or wrap or otherwise cover them. If they cannot be kept cool enough, use canned goods before hot summer weather sets in. In winter, store them away from heat sources, but also prevent freezing, as this may cause the seal to break.

Properly canned and stored foods will keep indefinitely, but they gradually lose quality, so it is best to eat them within a year.

7   USING CANNED FOODS

Check canned foods for signs of spoilage before using. Is the seal loose or broken? Is there mold, gas, slime, or a spurt of liquid when the seal is broken? Does the food smell bad, or look discolored? (This does not apply to fruit that darkens at the top of the jar. See below.) If any of these signs are present, destroy the food as described below.

As a precaution, boil all home-canned, low-acid foods for 15 to 20 minutes before eating them. This is a final insurance against botulism poisoning, since boiling destroys any toxins. Leafy greens, corn, meat, poultry, and seafoods need a full 20 minutes of boiling because of their density, but it can usually be incorporated into the normal food preparation. *The food should not be tasted before it has been boiled.* If there is a spurt of liquid when a jar is opened, or an odd smell, or a lot of foaming, when the food is boiled, it should be destroyed. These are also signs of botulism toxin production.

It is important to use the liquid surrounding canned foods, as many of the vitamins and minerals are in it. Liquid from canned vegetables and meats can be used for making soup or in mixed dishes, if it is not otherwise needed.

8   DESTROY SPOILED OR SUSPECT CANNED FOOD

Destroy such food without touching or tasting. This is most important with low-acid canned foods. It should not be given to animals. Spoiled food should be burned, buried deep, or boiled for 20 minutes and discarded.

CANNING FRUIT

(Also refer to individual fruits, and CANNING FRUIT JUICE AND SAUCE, in the FRUITS section.)

Most fruit is acidic enough for boiling water bath canning. Some tomatoes and fruits may vary in acidity, so it is recommended that 2 tablespoons of lemon juice or ½ teaspoon of citric acid be added to each quart. If such a precaution could be necessary, it is noted in the canning instructions for the individual fruit.

Sweetening Canned Fruit

Fruit is commonly canned in a sweetened syrup, but this is not essential. Plain water or unsweetened fruit juice can be used instead. The addition of a sweetener helps to retain the fruit's color and, to some extent, its flavor and texture, but the amounts needed are much less than are usually recommended. Very, very light syrups can be used to good effect.

LIQUID SYRUP FOR CANNING FRUIT

Fruit Juice

Any fruit juice with a compatible flavor can be used. Sweet juices go well with tart fruits, and tart juices go well with bland or sweet fruits. (Refer to COMBINING SWEET AND TART FRUITS, in the FRUITS section.)

Pectin

Thin, homemade pectin can be used as the canning liquid for any fruit, but it is especially good with tart fruits. (Refer to the PECTIN section.)

Very Light Syrup

Use 2 to 3 tablespoons honey or sugar per quart of water. Include any juice collected while preparing the fruit. Use the cooking water if the fruit is hot packed.

Light Syrup

Use ¼ cup honey or ½ cup sugar per quart of water. Include any juice collected while preparing the fruit. Use the cooking water if the fruit is hot packed.
• Have ready about 1 cup of liquid per pint, or 2 cups per quart of fruit to be canned.

Darkening and Other Difficulties with Canned Fruit

The best way to prevent darkening of fruit is to prepare it in small batches, and pack and process it without delay. However, lemon juice or an ascorbic acid solution (1 teaspoon crystalline ascorbic acid in a cup of water) can be used as a dip for fruit pieces, or to sprinkle over peeled or cut sections. Avoid soaking fruit in water because of the loss of water soluble nutrients.

Darkening of the top fruit in a jar is caused by too much headroom. The fruit will be good to eat if the jar's seal is tight and there are no signs of spoilage. If fruit floats in its jar, it may have been packed too loosely, or in a very heavy syrup, or the fruit may have been very ripe. Floating does not affect the fruit's eating quality, only its appearance. Often fruit that was hot packed looks better in the jar than raw packed fruit.

CANNING PICKLES

(Also refer to individual pickle recipes.) Most pickles and relishes are canned in a boiling water bath. They are acidic because vinegar has been used, or acid has been produced during fermentation. (Refer to the PICKLING section.) There is a variation for a few kinds of pickles, however, which should perhaps not be called canning. For this, pack vegetables raw with seasonings, and pour a boiling hot vinegar solution over them. Use at least 1 part vinegar to 1 part water. Then seal the jars, with no further processing, and store in a cool place. The flavor and texture of the raw vegetables are retained. The vegetables should be packed loosely enough to allow room for more liquid than usual. If using regular canning lids, leave the rings on the jars to ensure a tight seal.

CANNING VEGETABLES

(Also refer to individual vegetables.) All vegetables, except tomatoes, must be pressure canned at 240°F. The hot pack method is usually recommended over the raw pack, because air is driven out of the food before processing, resulting in a better product. To save nutrients, the water used to prepare the vegetable should be used as the canning liquid. It is not necessary to add salt when canning vegetables.

Vegetable mixtures should be processed and timed according to the vegetable that requires the most time. Even when tomatoes are included, the mixture must be pressure processed as for the slowest-cooking vegetable.

Canning Leafy Greens

All leafy greens can be canned as for spinach. (Refer to the SPINACH section.) Greens that hold up well after long cooking are the best for canning, but it is generally better to freeze greens if possible. Dandelion greens and many wild greens can be canned, as well as Swiss chard, turnip tops, beet tops, and mustard greens.

CANNING CAUTIONS

- Can fresh, high quality foods only. Mature or fully grown foods are better to can than young or immature foods because they stand up better during processing.
- Prepare foods cleanly, using clean cutting boards and utensils. Chill foods before preparing them if possible, to slow down spoilage organisms.
- Pay close attention to headroom requirements for canning jars. If there is too little headroom, food can be forced between the lid and jar rim, preventing a seal. If there is too much headroom, space is wasted. A large air space can also prevent a seal.
- Handle hot foods, hot liquids, and hot jars carefully, to prevent accidents. Keep children away from the canning area. Tip canner lids away from people when opening, to prevent steam burns. Hold hot jars away from the body when moving them.
- Protect glass jars from drastic temperature changes. Do not pour very hot foods into cold jars. Do not set jars of hot food on a cold metal surface. Set them on padding or a wooden board. Avoid cold drafts against hot jars.

REFERENCES

Ball Blue Book, published by the Ball Corporation, Muncie, Indiana, 47302.

Hertsberg, Ruth, *Putting Food By,* The Stephen Greene Press, 1982.

"Is It Safe to Can In Mayonnaise Jars?", *Organic Gardening,* August, 1983. (A short, but helpful article showing how mayonnaise jars can be safely used.)

USDA Home and Garden Bulletin No. 8, Home Canning of Fruits and Vegetables, published by U.S. Dept. of Agriculture.

CARROT STORAGE

Canning

Leave whole if small. Slice, dice, or cut to matchstick size if large.

Hot Pack

Cover with boiling water, bring to boil, drain. Pack, add boiling cooking water, ½ in. headroom. Process 240°F, 11 pounds pressure. Pints: 25 min. Quarts: 30 min.

Raw Pack

Pack tightly, 1 in. headroom. Add boiling water, ½ in. headroom. Process as for HOT PACK. Refer to the CANNING section.

Cold Storage

Root cellar is ideal. In dry storage place, pack in damp sand or other damp material for cool but dry storage area. Winter varieties keep 6 months. Overwinter in mulched garden row in moderate climate. Refer to the COLD STORAGE section.

Carrots

Carrots can appear in every dish on the menu from soups, salads, and main dishes, to desserts. Their sweet flavor and aroma, and their bright orange color make them a welcome food, worldwide. They make a basic seasoning for stews, sauces, and soups everywhere in Europe. They are stir-fried and stewed in China and most other Asian countries, and are a standard item in most North American refrigerators.

White, purple, yellow, and red carrots exist, but orange is the color for which they are known. The orange is caused by their high carotene content. Since carotene becomes vitamin A when it is digested, orange carrots are especially nutritious. However, to break down their cells and to make the carotene available to the body, carrots must be either cooked, very finely grated, or juiced.

Homegrown fresh carrots taste infinitely better than most store carrots. Carrots keep so well that unfortunately most commercial suppliers let them sit for a long time, losing flavor, before selling them. Even the last carrots to come out of the home root cellar in early spring are better than most store carrots. The home gardener who can grow enough carrots to store for a year-round supply is lucky, indeed.

HANDLING CARROTS

Carrots can be harvested whenever they are big enough to use. Many people like the delicate flavor of baby carrots pulled as thinnings. Others prefer the full flavor of larger carrots. It is best to cut off the green tops when the carrots are pulled, as the greens drain vitality and flavor from the roots if left on. Some people use sprigs of carrot greens in salads or cook a few like spinach. There have, however, been occasional reports of stomach upsets as a result.

Harvest carrots for cold storage before heavy frost. Leave ½- to 1-inch of the stem on, but do not otherwise trim or wash them. For immediate use cut off the crown and trim off root hairs. Wash the carrots and scrub with a vegetable brush, if necessary. Do not scrape them unless the skins are in very bad shape, as there are many vitamins in the outside layer. It is pos-

Drying
Steam whole, and cook through, 20–30 min., optional. Slice or shred. Dry until leathery or brittle. Refer to the DRYING section.

Freezing
Leave whole if small. Slice, dice, or cut to matchsticks if large. Blanch in boiling water. Whole or large pieces: 5 min.; small pieces: 2–3 min. Refer to the FREEZING section.

2½–3 pounds without tops = 1 quart cooked; 1 bushel, 50 pounds, without tops = 16–20 quarts canned or frozen

CARROT IDEAS
Carrot Drinks
Raw carrot juice is a well-known tonic, but a special juice extractor is needed for making it. However, many carrot drinks can be made in a blender, with raw chopped carrots or cooked carrot purée. For a sharper taste, add lemon juice. A good cocktail can be made by blending carrot and such vegetables as cucumber, green pepper, onion,

sible to blanch carrots in boiling water and easily peel off a very thin skin, but except for looks, there is little reason to do it.

The texture and appearance of carrots can be varied greatly by the way they are cut. Long slim carrot sticks are nice for snacks and with vegetable dips. In salads, carrots are good grated, sliced thinly crosswise, cut to julienne or matchstick size, and shaved lengthwise into curls. Various kinds of vegetable slicers make most of these slicing jobs quick and easy. For cooking, carrots can be left whole, cut in chunks, or cut as for salads. Mashing or puréeing them after cooking is another possibility. Steaming is the most nutritious way to cook whole carrots or large pieces. (Refer to the STEAM COOKING section.)

and celery with tomato juice. Lemon juice or vinegar, a dash of Tabasco sauce, and such herbs as parsley and basil also go well.

Mashed Carrots

Cook and mash carrots with potatoes or other vegetables. They can also be cooked alone, mashed, and then seasoned as a vegetable side dish. Mashed or puréed carrots can also be substituted for puréed pumpkin in many recipes, including pies, puddings, and ice cream. Refer to the recipes in the SQUASH, WINTER AND PUMPKIN section.

CAULIFLOWER STORAGE
Canning

Not recommended! It becomes discolored and strongly flavored.

Cold Storage

Keeps in root cellar 1–2 months, refrigerated about 1 month. Refer to the COLD STORAGE section.

Drying

Separate into florets and cut into ½-inch-thick slices. Steam 6–8 min. or until cooked through. Dry until tough or brittle. Refer to the DRYING section.

Cauliflower

How to win new friends and please old ones? Give them cauliflower freshly cut from the garden. The cool greenness of the tight inner leaves contrasting with the whiteness of the compact head of curds is pleasing to the eye, while the crisp texture and mild flavor will please the palate. Who could resist a vegetable that is delightful to eat raw, delectable cooked alone or in mixtures, and good looking as well?

A cauliflower is a large, compact head of flower buds. The buds are sometimes called curds (because of their white, cheese-like appearance). This member of the cabbage family is not as nutritious as its greener relatives, though it does have a respectable amount of calcium. But it has a mild flavor and crisp texture and is delicious raw or cooked. Cauliflower leaves are also quite good if prepared in the same ways as cabbage.

Cauliflower, which means "flowered cabbage," grows very much like broccoli, though its flavor is quite different. For a comparison, refer to the BROCCOLI section.

HANDLING CAULIFLOWER

Cut cauliflower heads after they have grown to their full size, but before they start to open or "rice." Leave as many tight leaves clinging to the head as possible. Not only do the leaves have a good flavor but they also contain more nutrients than the white curds. When cauliflower is harvested for fall storage it should be cut together with many of the protective leaves, or else it should be pulled roots and all. Whole plants can be kept by planting the roots in damp sand in the root cellar. According to some reports immature heads stored in this way will grow and fill out during storage.

Avoid soaking cauliflower in salt water, an unhealthy practice often recommended to remove bugs. Instead, rinse thoroughly in a pan of cold water which should remove all of the bugs from the florets. If one escapes notice when a whole trimmed head is rinsed it will come out in the water used for steaming or boiling. (Refer to DE-BUGGING BROCCOLI, in the BROCCOLI section.)

Many recipes call for precooked or partially cooked cauliflower, and steaming is the best way to do this. Florets take from 8 to 15 minutes, and whole heads from 20 to 30 minutes, depending on size. To steam whole heads, set them stem side down in the steamer. To boil whole heads, put them stem side down in about an inch of water. This allows the tougher stem to cook more than the tender curds.

Enjoy cauliflower raw in salads, and with dips, as well as cooked. If only the tops of the florets are used raw, the stalks can be pickled. (See the recipe below.)

CAULIFLOWER RECIPES
Pickled Cauliflower Stalks

(MAKES 1−1½ QUARTS)
(See also MAKING FERMENTED PICKLES, in the PICKLING section.)

1 pound cauliflower stalks	½ teaspoon cayenne or
2½ tablespoons plain or pickling	other hot pepper,
salt	to taste
1 tablespoon mustard seeds,	3 cups water, boiled
crushed, or ½ teaspoon mustard	and cooled
powder, or to taste	

Cut the cauliflower stalks into 2- to 3-inch-long, finger sized sticks, blanch them in boiling water for 30 seconds, then drain. Pack the sticks into a 1½- to 2-quart jar. Add salt, mustard, cayenne, and water. The water should cover the stalks completely. Put a clean cloth over the jar mouth, tie it in place or use a rub-

Freezing
Break or cut florets into 1-inch-thick pieces. Blanch in boiling water 3 min. Refer to the FREEZING section.

3 pounds = 1 quart prepared;
12 pounds = 4–6 quarts frozen

CAULIFLOWER IDEAS
Leftover Cauliflower, Baked
Arrange cooked cauliflower in a buttered baking dish. Cover with white sauce or cheese sauce or sprinkle with bread crumbs, grated cheese, or both. Bake until it is heated through and the top is browned, about 20 minutes. Add a garnish of parsley when it is served.

Cauliflower Greens
Cook tender cauliflower leaves in the same ways as cabbage. Their flavor is surprisingly pleasant.

Cauliflower Salads
Raw cauliflower florets or cooked florets that are still somewhat crisp are very good in salads. They can be added to tossed salads or arranged on a bed of lettuce with other ingredients and served with a dressing. Some ingredients that combine well with cauliflower are sliced cooked beets, green peppers or pimiento, chopped scallions, parsley sprigs, olives, cooked

ber band. Keep in a warm place for 2 days. Stir once each day. Then keep in a cool, dry place for about a week, after which the pickles should be fermented and ready to eat. Refrigerated, they will keep for about a month.

Pickled Kohlrabi Sticks

Cut kohlrabi into sticks and pickle in the same way.

shrimp, or other seafoods, and crisp, fried bacon crumbs. Mayonnaise makes a good dressing.

Cauliflower Fried in Batter

Pre-cook cauliflower, or use leftovers that are tender but not soft. Florets or cauliflower sliced into thin wedges can be used. Dip in pancake batter or another favorite batter, or in lightly beaten egg and then in bread crumbs or flour. Fry in a generous amount of oil or other fat in a frying pan, or deep fry. Refer to the *Tempura* recipe, in the FRUITS section.

CELERIAC STORAGE

Cold Storage

Keeps all winter in root cellar or similar conditions. Can be packed in damp sand or other damp material. Refer to the COLD STORAGE section.

Drying

Thinly slice or grate roots. Precooking optional. Dry until hard or brittle. Excellent in soups and stews. Spread leaves and minced stalks on trays. Dry until leaves crumble and stalk bits are hard, for use as an herbal seasoning. Refer to the DRYING section.

Celeriac

Celeriac is a type of celery grown for its large root. Also called knob celery, celery root, or turnip rooted celery, it is a flavorful and practical root vegetable that is generally overlooked. Home gardeners can grow it and store it as easily as carrots, beets, and other root vegetables. It is easier to grow than regular celery and will flourish in a much greater range of soils and climatic conditions.

Celeriac has a pleasant, celery-like flavor that tastes delicious cooked by itself, or mixed with other vegetables and meat. In France and other European countries, it is often served with game meats. Celeriac tops look and taste like celery, but do not form thick stalks. They make an excellent herbal seasoning, and can be used wherever a celery flavoring would be welcome.

HANDLING CELERIAC

Celeriac reaches about 4 inches in diameter but can be pulled as soon as it is large enough to use. (If it will be stored in the root cellar, it should be pulled in late fall just before the heavy freezes.) After pulling, cut off tops about an inch above the root and shake out as much dirt as possible. Wait to trim it further until just before use. (For using the tops refer to CELERY section.)

Celeriac requires a lot of trimming because the tops and rootlets grow out of a large part of its surface in twisted tangles. The soil works into the creases and cannot be washed out. Parts of the root may have to be peeled, to get it clean.

Celeriac discolors easily, but this does not affect its flavor.

Chilling before preparation will slow down discoloration. Or it can be sprinkled with lemon juice, vinegar, or ascorbic acid solution.

Celeriac cooks like any other root vegetable, adding an exceptional flavor to soups and stews. Grated raw celeriac is good in salads.

Celery

Large, fleshy celery stalks were first developed in the 18th century. Before that, celery looked like an herb and was used as one. A clump of thin-stemmed, leafy green celery might be grown next to parsley, so that a few sprigs of each could be conveniently picked for flavoring soups, stews, and salads. The leaves of the modern celery plant are often used as a flavoring in cooking, like their early herbal counterpart, while the crisp stalks are a favorite raw vegetable snack and salad ingredient.

The home gardener who can grow thick, crisp celery stalks is fortunate, because it does not grow well everywhere. However, most gardeners can take a hint from the past and grow celery as an herb. Ordinary celery seeds will produce leaves and stems for seasoning, even if thick stalks never form. The tops of celeriac plants, and the leaves of the herb lovage, also provide a celery flavor. Celery seeds are another source of celery flavor. (Refer to the HERBS section.)

HANDLING CELERY

Harvest celery for immediate use by cutting the root just below the soil surface. (Some root is needed to hold the stalks together.) Do not wash the celery until it is to be used, as it keeps best dry. When celery is harvested for fall storage, pull the plant roots and all, so it can be "replanted" in the storage area.

A few leaves for seasoning can be taken from celery plants as needed. When the main crop is harvested, a supply of leaves can be dried or frozen. Powdered or crumbled dried leaves can be used instead of celery salt when it is called for in recipes, avoiding the salt.

Celery is a good mixer. Raw, it goes with every kind of

Freezing

Tops only. Refer to FREEZING HERBS, in the HERBS section.

CELERIAC IDEAS
Celeriac in Soup Stock

Include whole, trimmed celeriacs in the pot when cooking soup stock. Let simmer 45 minutes to an hour, or until tender. Remove celeriac, drain, and use in any cooked celeriac recipe. The soup stock will be much improved by the celeriac's flavor.

CELERY STORAGE
Canning

Cut 1 in. pieces, cover with boiling water, boil 3 min. Drain, pack in jars, add boiling cooking water, 1 in. headroom. Process 240°F, 11 pounds pressure. Pints: 30 min. Quarts: 35 min. *Celery and Tomato* Boil equal parts celery and fresh chopped tomato 5 min. Pack 1 in. headroom. Process as for celery alone. Refer to the CANNING section.

Cold Storage

Pull with roots in late fall. Replant in damp sand or soil. Will keep most of winter in root cellar or protected outdoor storage area. Refer to the COLD STORAGE section.

salad, vegetable dip, and stuffing. Cooked, it blends with all kinds of meats and vegetables. In fact, it is so busy mixing and joining, that it is not often featured alone. The following recipes are unusual because celery is the main ingredient.

CELERY RECIPES

Celery and Carrots in Cider

(MAKES ABOUT 6 SIDE SERVINGS)

outside stalks from a head
  of celery
1 pound (about) carrots
2½ cups apple cider or apple juice
pepper, salt, optional
parsley, chopped, for
  garnish

Cut both the celery and carrots into 2-inch sections, then slice each section into several sticks. Heat the cider to a boil and add carrots. Simmer for 15 minutes. Add the celery and season lightly with pepper and salt, if desired. The seasoning will get stronger as the cider becomes concentrated. Cook until both the celery and carrots are tender, about 20 more minutes. Remove the vegetables from the pot, and keep them warm in a serving dish. Boil the cider over high heat until it is reduced to about ¼ cup. Pour over the vegetables and serve sprinkled with parsley. Excellent as a side dish with roast meats.

Cherries

The season for fresh cherries is short and sweet, so the provident person who is lucky enough to have surplus cherries will want to capture some of the sweetness and flavor for other seasons of the year. Canned cherries, dried cherries, cherry juice, cherry preserves, and all the delicacies that can be made from cherries are sure to cheer the dreariest winter day. One only hopes that the dreary days come to an end before the cherries.

Though cherries are usually classed as either sweet or sour, some varieties are in between. Sweet cherries are most often

---

Drying

Stalks Slice ¼ in. thick. Optional: Steam 4 min. Dry until brittle. *Leaves* Refer to DRYING HERBS, in the HERBS section. Stalks and leaves can be powdered to use as seasoning. Refer to the DRYING section.

Freezing

(Useful in cooked dishes only.) *Stalks* Slice 1 in. pieces or smaller. Blanch 3 min. in boiling water, 4 min. in steam. *Leaves* Refer to FREEZING HERBS, in the HERBS section, and to the FREEZING section.

  1 pound trimmed = 3–4 cups chopped

CELERY IDEAS

Celery Bread Crumb Stuffing

Combine 2 parts chopped celery with 3 parts bread crumbs. Season with such herbs as sage, thyme, marjoram, and savory, and onion, pepper, and salt, to taste. Moisten with meat juice or soup stock. Other ingredients like grated carrot or cooked, chopped chestnuts can be included. Use to stuff poultry or vegetables.

CHERRY STORAGE

Canning

Pit (see below), or prick unpitted with

enjoyed plain. Even when canned, dried, or frozen, they are delicious plain. It is sour cherries that are best for cooking and making juice. Wild cherries, almost always sour and flavorful, make a fine juice, and are good in mixtures with blander fruits. When they can be picked in large enough amounts, wild cherries are well worth the effort.

HANDLING CHERRIES

Cherries keep best if picked with stems left on, but people with their own cherry trees may prefer to pick them without stems so as to avoid damage to the trees' fruiting twigs, or to have them ready for use without the extra step of removing stems. Cherries picked stemless should be eaten or processed very soon or they will spoil at the spot where the stem was removed.

Sour cherries become sweeter if left on the tree for an extra week or two after they first ripen, but will require protection from birds.

Cherry juice is an excellent, but often overlooked, way to use cherries. The best juice comes from sour cherries. Sweet cherry juice tastes bland and is best mixed with sour cherry juice or another tart juice. (Refer to the FRUITS section.) Cherries are sometimes candied, but dried, sweet cherries are healthier, and can be used in the same ways. Maraschino cherries are heavily processed, not worth the trouble of making at home, and not really even worth eating. Their processing involves a long soak in lime and sulphur dioxide followed by cooking and draining. This makes them white and flavorless, so then they are sweetened, artificially flavored, and dyed red. Instead, use cherry preserves or dried sweet cherries.

Pitting Cherries

For many uses cherries must be pitted, and doing large numbers by hand is tedious at best. Some use the looped end of a clean hair pin or paper clip, pushing it in at the stem end to hook the pit and pull it out. Others find it easiest to slit the cherry with a small knife and pick out the pit. Always work over a bowl to catch the dripping juice. Less juice will drip out if the cherries are chilled before pitting.

large needle to prevent bursting. Unpitted hold shape best.

Raw Pack
Shake down in jars, add boiling syrup or other liquid, ½ in. headroom. Process boiling water bath. Pints: 20 min. Quarts: 25 min.

Hot Pack
Heat slowly in pot, add water to prevent sticking if unpitted. Sweetening optional. When they boil, pack in jars, add boiling water if necessary, ½ in. headroom. Process boiling water bath. Pints: 10 min. Quarts: 15 min. Refer to the CANNING section. Also see CANNING FRUIT JUICE AND SAUCE, in the FRUITS section.

Drying
Pitted (see below) preferred. If not, crack skins in boiling water to speed drying. Dry sweet cherries until leathery, sticky; sour cherries until hard. Or make fruit leather. Refer to the DRYING section.

Freezing
Pitted (see below) preferred. (Pits may add almond flavor.) Pack plain, or sweetened, or covered with liquid. (A pectin pack is excellent. Refer to the

Anyone who pits cherries regularly will find it worthwhile to buy a cherry pitter. There are several kinds. The simplest is a small hand-held tool that pits one cherry at a time. There is also a fairly inexpensive pitter that clamps onto the table and is turned by hand. It does the job quickly and can also be used to pit canned, black olives.

Uses for Cherry Pits

A dilute juice for a fruit drink can be made from cherry pits and the bits of fruit left on them. Cover with water, heat to a boil, then strain off the juice. Chill, sweeten if needed, and use like lemonade.

The kernels inside cherry pits can be used in several ways. In the Middle East the kernels of black cherries, called "mahleb," are crushed and used as a food flavoring. An American Indian use was to stew black wild cherry kernels together with the fruit, some maple syrup, and some apple cider to be used as sauce for cornmeal or puddings. The kernels of cherries and other stone fruits are sometimes pressed commercially for the oil in them. The leftover press-cake has been used as a stock feed.

Cracking cherry pits for the kernels is like shelling very small nuts. If the pits are crushed with just enough pressure to crack the shells, the kernels can be picked out.

Chestnuts

The loss of the American chestnut to the blight was a great loss of valuable food for the people where it grew. Chestnuts are an excellent carbohydrate food. People can and have lived on them. A family with a supply of dried chestnuts in the attic can enjoy chestnut dishes all winter, ranging from salads and vegetable mixtures to soups, stuffings, sandwiches, snacks, and desserts.

Chestnuts are a common food in Korea and some other Asian countries, and in Italy and the Mediterranean area. In some places, they are used as livestock feed. There is hope that the chestnut will again become common in North America. Some blight-resistant varieties of Asian and European chestnut

---

PECTIN section.) Sweet cherries hold color best in liquid or sprinkled with lemon juice. Refer to the FREEZING section.

2–2½ pounds = 1 quart unpitted; 1 bushel (56 pounds) = 22–23 quarts unpitted

CHERRY IDEAS
Cherries with Maple Syrup or Maple Sugar

Sour cherries are especially good sweetened with maple syrup or sugar. They can be stewed in a little maple syrup, or in their own juice with maple sugar. The American Indians often used this combination. The *Maple Fruit Preserves* (in the JAM AND JELLY section) are excellent made with sour cherries.

CHESTNUT STORAGE
Cold Storage

Chestnuts mold quickly in damp root cellars, but need high humidity to prevent drying. If refrigerated in plastic bags with a little dry peat moss, they keep 2–3 months.

Drying

See DRYING CHESTNUTS, below.

trees are being planted in home orchards, particularly the Chinese chestnut, which has about the same range as the peach tree. Researchers are also working to protect the American chestnut from the blight, and some progress has been made towards that goal.

HANDLING CHESTNUTS

Chestnuts should be gathered about every other day during the fall ripening season. If they lie on the ground long they become moldy or wormy. Shaking the tree may knock more chestnuts down. If the burrs fall to the ground unopened, store them in a cool place until they open, usually within a week. Fresh chestnuts are somewhat astringent, but improve if held at room temperature for a few days. They should then be refrigerated or dried or frozen.

Peeling Chestnuts

Chestnuts have an outer shell and an inner skin or pellicle. It is possible to peel raw chestnuts by cutting through the shell with a knife, but it is slow work. The inner skin sticks to the nut and is hard to remove. Peeling is much easier when the nuts are hot, so they are usually cooked by boiling or roasting and peeled before they cool. Cook about 10 minutes in boiling water or roast for 15 to 20 minutes in a moderate oven. The shells should be slit with a knife or pricked with a fork before roasting to prevent bursting. This is not essential when boiling, but many people prefer to do it anyway, as the opening makes a handy place to start peeling.

Remove the chestnuts from the heat a few at a time so they do not cool too much, and cut or pull off the shells as soon as they can be handled. The pellicle or inner skin will come off with the shell, as long as the chestnuts are still very warm.

If whole nutmeats are not important a quick method is to cut the chestnuts in half with a heavy knife. Drop the halves in boiling water and cook until the nutmeats fall from the shells.

Drying Chestnuts

Chestnuts will dry in the shell if kept in a dry airy place, such as an attic. If there are mice or other rodents, put the chestnuts in large metal cans that have many small ventilation holes punched

Freezing

May be frozen in the shell, but space is saved if precooked and peeled (see below). Package in plastic bags or other containers. Quality retained 1 year. Thaw at room temperature, or drop in boiling water and cook approx. 5 min. Also freeze as CHESTNUT PURÉE (see below). Refer to the FREEZING section.

1 pound = about 1½ cups shelled

CHESTNUT IDEAS
Stewed Chestnuts with Vegetables or Fruit

Peeled chestnuts make an excellent side dish when cooked until tender in water or soup stock. They are especially tasty mixed with most cooked green vegetables or with stewed prunes, apples, or other fruits.

Sautéed Chestnuts

Heat oil or butter in a frying pan. Toss cooked chestnuts in it for a minute or two just before serving. They take the place of potatoes or rice in a meal, and are delicious mixed with hot, cooked green vegetables. Refer to FRESH BEANS WITH NUTS, in the BEANS, FRESH section.

in them. After a month or so the meats will shrink to hard lumps inside their shells. They will keep a year or more. The dried nuts can be reconstituted and used like fresh chestnuts, or shelled and ground into flour.

To shell dried chestnuts, cut the shell with a sturdy knife. The inner skin will usually come off when the shell is removed. If it does not, drop the nut in boiling water for a minute to loosen the skin. Shelled dried chestnuts can be reconstituted by soaking several hours or overnight in water, then cooking in the same water until soft. Dried chestnuts can also be soaked and cooked until soft before they are shelled. They are then shelled as for fresh chestnuts.

Another way to dry chestnuts is to cook and peel them fresh (see above), then spread them on racks or trays and dry in a food dryer or other warm, dry place. This works well for small quantities but would probably be too time consuming for a big fall harvest. These dried cooked chestnuts require less soaking and cooking time for reconstitution than the dried raw nuts. They can also be ground for flour.

Chestnut Stuffing

Mix cooked, chopped chestnuts into bread crumb stuffing for poultry or meat. This is a traditional stuffing for the holiday turkey. Chestnuts are also good in rice stuffings, and in stuffings with dried fruits such as prunes. One Italian poultry stuffing combines ½ pound cooked macaroni, 2 diced apples, 1 cup pitted, quartered prunes, 1½ cups cooked, chopped chestnuts, and 1 egg, seasoned with butter, salt, pepper, and oregano.

Creamed Chestnuts

Cook chestnuts until very tender and add them to your standard cream sauce. They also add flavor to most creamed vegetable dishes.

Boiled Chestnut Snacks

Instead of roasting chestnuts, boil them in their shells in salted water for a few minutes. Let people peel their own

Chestnut Flour

Dry, hard chestnuts grind easily in a grain mill. For some mills it may be necessary to first break the chestnuts into small pieces with a hammer or nutcracker. Some meat grinders, blenders, and food processors will also grind chestnuts.

Chestnut flour can be substituted for some of the wheat flour in recipes for baked goods. To make a purée for recipes that require it, slowly add boiling water to the flour, stirring constantly until the desired thickness is reached. If flour from precooked dried chestnuts is used, the purée can be sweetened for an instant chestnut pudding.

Roast Chestnuts

Roast chestnuts are a popular snack all over the world. They are seasonal, since only fresh chestnuts can be roasted. In China, chestnuts are roasted in hot sand. To try this, heat a pan of sand in the oven or on top of the wood stove until it is too hot to touch. Embed some chestnuts in the sand. Do not cut slits in the shells because sand will get in. They can be pricked with a needle, but they do not seem to explode as easily as those roasted on coals. Stir the sand and chestnuts a few times for even cooking. They will be done in about a half hour.

To roast chestnuts on an open fire cut a slit or an X in them, or prick with a fork. Cook in the coals at the edge of a fireplace or on charcoal, turning them often so they do not burn. After a few minutes taste one to see if they are done. Everyone peels their own chestnuts, as hot as they can stand handling them. Chestnuts can also be shaken over a fire in a perforated container like an old-fashioned corn popper, or set on the surface of a wood-burning stove and turned frequently. They will also roast in a pan in the oven in about 20 to 30 minutes.

Chestnut Purée

Peel chestnuts (see above), and simmer them in water or soup stock, or in a mixture of half water or soup stock and half milk. Cook over low heat for an hour, or until quite soft. Purée in a food mill or blender. Purée can also be made from flour. (See CHESTNUT FLOUR, above.)

Chestnut purée is a classic accompaniment to game meats. It is usually seasoned with butter or a little of the meat juice, and served like mashed potatoes. The purée can be reheated in a double boiler or over very low heat. If overheated it will become thick and heavy.

Chestnut purée thinned with soup stock or meat juices makes delicious gravy. If it is very thin, and vegetables are added, it makes a tasty soup.

Desserts can also be made from chestnut purée. Cook the chestnuts in water, or water and milk. The purée sweetened with honey is already a pudding.

CHESTNUT RECIPES

Most recipes call for precooked chestnuts. Dried chestnuts that have been reconstituted, or thawed frozen chestnuts are just as good as freshly cooked, peeled chestnuts.

Jim's Mother's Chestnut Butter

(When chestnuts could be gathered by the barrelful in the fall, chestnut butter sandwiches were an everyday school lunch for many children.)

Peel raw chestnuts and grind in a meat grinder. After the first grinding, salt them lightly, if desired, and put them through the grinder several more times, until the mixture is fairly smooth. Use as a spread for bread. Make small batches at a time, because the butter sours easily. (Cooked chestnuts can also be used, and

chestnuts as soon as they are cool enough to handle. Chestnuts dried in the shell (see DRYING CHESTNUTS, above) can be boiled for a snack in this way, but it takes a long time. If they are soaked in water for several hours, then simmered on a stove for several more hours, they will be very good.

Chestnuts and Corn

The American Indians made a mixture of chestnuts and corn that was wrapped in green corn shucks and boiled for 2 hours or so. Various mixtures are suggested in different references to native Indian cooking. Whole kernel corn and peeled chestnuts can be ground together, and wrapped and cooked like tamales. Boiling water can be poured over a mixture of cornmeal and chestnut flour to make a dough that can be wrapped. Cotton cloth or aluminum foil can be substituted for corn shucks if they are not available.

some may prefer their flavor over that of the raw nuts.)

When fresh chestnuts are no longer available, peel and grind dried chestnuts. Mix the resulting flour with enough butter to make it spreadable. This chestnut butter improves after a day or two as the chestnut flavor becomes stronger.

Korean Chestnut Balls

Grind cooked, peeled chestnuts as for chestnut butter. Omit salt. Flavor with a little honey or cinnamon and shape into small balls. They are traditionally rolled in chopped pine nuts, but any chopped nuts can be used.

Chicory 🌿

Chicory, with all of its diversity, should not be overlooked by the home gardener. Many seed catalogs offer five or six varieties: some for salad greens such as endive, escarole, and radicchio, a red-leafed variety from Italy; and some with large roots for winter forcing, such as witloof chicory, also known as Belgian endive. The greens are much more versatile than lettuce, since most varieties will grow during hot summer weather as well as cool fall and mild winter weather, and they are also good cooked as a pot herb like dandelion greens. For a superb winter salad delicacy, chicory roots can be forced. Witloof chicory produces a tightly packed head of blanched leaves shaped like an oversized cigar, while another forcing variety, *Barbe de Capucin,* has loose pink and white leaves. Another way to use chicory roots is to dry and roast them for a coffee-like beverage.

Wild chicory, which grows abundantly in some regions, can be used in the same ways as cultivated chicory. Both the leaves and roots, however, have a more bitter flavor. The leaves should be gathered and used in early spring along with dandelion leaves, which they greatly resemble when young. (Refer to the DANDELIONS section.) Wild roots can be forced and are good for drying and roasting, but they must be dug before they produce a flower and seed stalk.

CHICORY STORAGE

Canning

Leafy tops Handle as for spinach. Refer to SPINACH and CANNING LEAFY GREENS, in the CANNING section.

Cold Storage

(Preferred method for leafy heads and roots.) *Leafy heads, Endive, Escarole* Pull with roots, tie heads to blanch, replant in sand or soil. Store in root cellar or similar conditions. Keeps 2–3 months. *Roots* Store in root cellar to keep all winter. Refer to the COLD STORAGE section. Also see WINTER FORCING OF CHICORY ROOTS, below.

Drying

Leafy tops Refer to DRYING LEAFY GREENS, in the DRYING section. *Roots* Cut uniform sticks or slices. Dry until hard or brittle.

Freezing

Refer to FREEZING LEAFY GREENS, in the FREEZING section.

HANDLING CHICORY

With planning, chicory leaves for salads and cooking can be harvested all year. In spring, there are thinnings, and perhaps shoots from broken root tips remaining in the soil. Varieties such as endive and escarole are usually harvested in summer and fall since they withstand both heat and frosts well. Open-headed varieties are tied closed about 3 weeks before harvest to blanch them, making them crisper, tender, and less bitter. Often the outer green leaves are cooked and the inner leaves used for salads. Endive and escarole can be stored longer than most salad greens and enjoyed well into winter. Forced roots also provide chicory leaves in winter.

Winter Forcing of Chicory Roots

Forcing simply means providing conditions to start a plant's spring growth early. Most varieties of chicory root will produce a leafy head when forced, as long as they have not yet produced a blossom and seed stock. However, the varieties developed especially for forcing are the most dependable. Generally, only straight, undamaged roots should be forced. Less than perfect roots are best for drying and roasting, or even cooked as a vegetable. Dandelion roots can be forced or roasted in the same way as chicory.

Dig the roots late in the fall, just before hard freezes. Trim the tops to about 1 inch above the crown. The roots can be trimmed to 9 or 10 inches if they are inconveniently long. A practical forcing method for a small planting is to "re-plant" the roots close together in containers of soil or sand as soon as they are dug and trimmed. Store the containers in a cold place where they will not freeze, such as a root cellar. When wanted for forcing, move them to a warm, dark place. A 60°F room is fine. If the room is lighted, cover the containers with large cardboard boxes, or another covering that will keep out light and allow growing space. Forced chicory grown in light becomes too bitter to enjoy. The soil or sand should be kept barely damp and the containers should have drainage holes, because the roots will rot if they are too wet.

Within 2 to 3 weeks, blanched heads of chicory will grow large enough to use and can be cut. A second growth usually appears after the first cutting. It is not as delicate, but can still be used for salads. The spent roots can then be added to the compost pile. If containers of chicory roots are brought in from cold storage and forced at regular intervals, this delicacy can be enjoyed all winter.

Forced chicory is so crisp and flavorful raw that it is easy to find ways to use it. It is also tasty cooked, but in winter, when homegrown, raw vegetables are at a premium, it seems a shame to cook it. Recipes for cooking Belgian endive appear in most French and Italian cookbooks.

A simple way to enjoy witloof chicory, or Belgian endive, is to serve one head to each person as a first course. The leaves can be pulled off and eaten one by one. As the center is approached, the leaves become increasingly crisp and delicious, with the most delicate heart leaves to be enjoyed last. A dip or salad dressing can be provided. Belgian endive leaves are also excellent when stuffed like celery.

Bitterness in Cooked Chicory

The greatest problem when cooking chicory is its varying degrees of bitterness. In cultivated varieties, especially those with blanched leaves, the bitterness is diminished to a pleasantly sharp flavor. The mildest chicory is usually one harvested in cool weather. Exceedingly bitter greens or roots can be cooked in one or more changes of water, as for some wild foods, but of course vitamins and minerals will be lost. Moderate bitterness in cooked greens can be balanced by serving them with lemon juice or vinegar, or by using them in recipes with milk. Recipes for dandelion greens can be used since their greens are very similar. (Refer to the DANDELIONS section.)

Large, cultivated chicory roots are a tender and quick-cooking vegetable, but they also have a characteristic sharp flavor. They are good added to stews and soups in small amounts, but opinions will vary about their flavor when served alone.

Chinese Cabbage

The possibilities for using Chinese cabbage are just beginning to be understood in western countries. This vegetable is certain to increase in popularity, as it is very productive, grows well in cool weather, and keeps well. Best of all, it lends itself to western cuisine as readily as to Chinese and other East Asian cooking methods. It can be the main ingredient in a tossed salad French or Italian style one day, and appear stir-fried Chinese style the next.

There are scores of varieties of Chinese cabbage. The vari-

CHINESE CABBAGE STORAGE

Canning

Possible, but poor texture. Refer to CANNING LEAFY GREENS, in the CANNING section.

Cold Storage

(Best storage method.) Keeps refrigerated approx. 1 month. For root cellar or similar storage, pull plant with roots, replant in sand or soil. Or cut varieties with tight heads, pack in straw. Some varieties keep 3–4 months. Refer to the COLD STORAGE section. Also see KEEPING SAUERKRAUT IN COLD STORAGE, in the SAUERKRAUT section.

Drying

(Common in China.) Separate leaves, dry whole, sliced lengthwise down stalk or shredded. Steam blanch 3–5 min. or until wilted, optional. Spread with minimum overlapping. Dry until leafy parts papery, stalks brittle. Pour

ous names and characteristics can be confusing, due to different translations, and the constant introduction of new varieties. There are, however, several notable types. Best known are the "heading" types, which include michili and wong bok. These form large, oval or cylindrical heads with wide, white stalks and blanched centers. The celery cabbage sold in groceries is of this type, with an especially tall, celery shaped head. The loose leaf types are another group. Many look like Swiss chard, with thick, white stalks and dark green, rounded leaves, but loose feathery leaves and other variations also occur. This group is sometimes called mustard cabbage, and is often listed under "greens" in seed catalogs. Bok choi and pak choi are among this type.

Despite distinctive differences in looks and some difference in taste and texture, all Chinese cabbages can be used in similar ways, and are interchangeable in recipes.

HANDLING CHINESE CABBAGE

Most varieties of Chinese cabbage have better flavor and texture when harvested in cool weather, in either spring or fall. If harvested in fall before heavy frosts, long-keeping varieties can be stored all winter. (Refer to the COLD STORAGE section.) Some varieties also do well in insulated cold frames and cool greenhouses.

Raw Chinese cabbage is delicious in salads. The thick, crisp stalks can be sliced like celery. The leafy parts are like lettuce, with a peppery flavor. Stir-frying is an ideal way to cook Chinese cabbage, or it can be cooked like spinach or mustard greens, if the heavy stalks are allowed extra cooking time. The best method is to place the stalks in the pot or steamer first, with the leafy parts on top.

Chinese cabbage seeds can be used for seasoning in the same way as mustard seeds. They can also be ground for prepared mustard. (Refer to the MUSTARD (GREENS AND SEEDS) section.)

Cold Storage

When mechanical refrigeration was developed, and refrigerators became standard home equipment, most old methods for keeping food cold became obsolete. However, one old method

boiling water over to reconstitute, or add to soup or stew. Refer to the DRYING section.

Freezing
(Possible, but poor texture.) Refer to FREEZING LEAFY GREENS, in the FREEZING section.

CHINESE CABBAGE IDEAS
Chinese Cabbage in Soup
For a crisp, fresh addition to soup, put a small mound of shredded or sliced Chinese cabbage in each soup bowl. Ladle very hot soup over it. The Chinese cabbage will cook slightly, but retain its freshness, and the soup will be cooled to just the right temperature for eating. Chinese cabbage can also be added to the soup pot just before serving, but if it sits very long, or is reheated, it will become an ordinary vegetable soup without distinctive texture or flavor.

is as practical as ever—using the earth's coolness for storing vegetables, fruits, and other foods. A well-designed root cellar is the most sophisticated arrangement, but other possibilities are underground pits, insulated mounds, and simply leaving root vegetables in the ground under a heavy mulch for digging during winter thaws. Use can be made of unheated space, such as an attic, spare room, pantry, or basement. If available, a well-insulated outbuilding or spare refrigerator are also good storage spaces. The modern gardener with an interest in storing homegrown food all year will want to use every method available, whether old or new.

Requirements for cold storage are so variable, depending on climate, the foods to be stored, and individual circumstances, that everyone has to work out the best methods for themselves. Information on designing and building root cellars and other cold storage structures is available from many sources, including U.S. Department of Agriculture bulletins and state agricultural department publications. (See the REFERENCES at the end of this section.)

FACTORS AFFECTING COLD STORAGE OF FOODS

Temperatures above freezing and below 40°F are best for storing most foods, but anything below room temperature will help to delay spoilage. When temperatures drop low enough to freeze foods, special storage techniques are required. (Refer to the FREEZING section.)

The temperature at which various foods will freeze and be damaged also varies. Most root vegetables, onions, and apples will survive a few degrees below freezing without damage, while potatoes are damaged by even slight frost. If stored foods should be exposed to below-freezing temperatures, check them often for the next week or two. They may appear to be all right at first, and then show signs of spoilage later.

Besides temperature, other factors affecting cold storage are humidity, air circulation, and light. Root cellars and similar storage areas provide an even, cold temperature between 32 and 40°F, a high humidity, and darkness. A well-designed root cellar has ventilation providing adequate air circulation, but a closed underground pit has very little. Attics and unheated rooms are likely to fluctuate in temperature, but are still useful if the temperature stays above freezing and below room temperature. Humidity is usually lower in unheated rooms than in a root cellar, which is better for some foods. Attics are the driest storage areas available in most houses. Some foods will need protection from light in storage areas with windows. Refrigerators provide an even, cold temperature and darkness, but have no air circulation and low humidity. Humidity is usually lower in frost free refrigerators than in models that need defrosting.

COLD STORAGE OF
ROOT VEGETABLES AND TUBERS

Also refer to specific root vegetables and tubers.

Root vegetables and tubers are among the most practical fresh or raw foods for cold storage. Root cellars are ideal, but these foods also keep well in other cool areas if protected from drying out and freezing. They do best at temperatures between 32 and 40°F with a humidity of 90 to 95%, in darkness and with some air circulation. They will keep all winter under the right conditions.

The best varieties of root vegetables and tubers for storage are those bred for long keeping. Planting must be timed so they mature in fall and can be harvested just before heavy frosts. Dig and handle the roots carefully to avoid injury or bruising. If undue spoilage has been a problem, freshly dug roots can be left in the sun for a few hours to kill bacteria that could cause spoilage. Shake dirt from vegetables but do not wash them before storage. Water is more likely to cause spoilage than dirt. The only trimming needed is to cut off the tops of root vegetables to ½- to 1-inch above the crowns. Be careful not to cut into the root itself, and do not trim rootlets or root hairs. Whole roots and tubers keep best, and large, unblemished roots keep the longest. Sort out small and imperfect roots and store separately for early use.

Some packing material or covering is necessary for root vegetables stored in less than ideal conditions. In a good root cellar they keep well simply laid in bins, but packing material may increase storage life there as well. Packing or covering keeps roots moist, provides darkness, and offers some protection from fluctuating temperatures. Damp sand, peat moss, or dry leaves make good packing materials. Other possibilities are wrapping each root in newspaper, or putting small bunches in plastic bags with a few air holes. Rutabagas can be coated with paraffin or wax. Damp sand is excellent if the vegetables will be stored in low humidity. The sand can be lightly sprinkled if necessary. Buckets, bins, plastic pans, and sturdy boxes are good storage containers. They should have drainage holes so moisture cannot collect. Leave the top uncovered, or use a top with holes in it.

Towards the end of their storage life, root vegetables often show signs of growth. Leaves sprout or tiny root hairs may grow. If tops grow on beets or turnips they can be used for greens. Roots lose flavor and food value quickly once they start to grow, and should be used immediately. Extras can be dried or fed to livestock.

Carrots, Celeriac, Chicory Roots, Horseradish, Jerusalem Artichokes, Parsnips, Salsify

Where winter is not too severe, these vegetables can be left in the garden over the winter. They will stay in excellent condition until spring growth starts, as long as they do not freeze severely, or suffer rodent damage. They should be heavily mulched and their rows or beds well-marked, for digging during winter thaws and in early spring. It may be practical to harvest part of a crop in fall for indoor cold storage, and leave part in the garden for early spring use.

Jerusalem artichokes do not keep well after they are dug. They are best left in the ground until needed. Freezing in the ground does not damage them.

COLD STORAGE OF ABOVE-GROUND VEGETABLES

Also refer to specific vegetables.

Many above-ground vegetables that mature in fall can be stored in a root cellar or similar storage conditions. They may keep only 1 or 2 months or all winter, depending on the vegetable and storage techniques. Cabbage keeps all winter stored in several ways. Cucumbers, cauliflower, kohlrabi, tomatoes, and eggplant keep up to 2 months. A few vegetables require less humidity than in a root cellar. Onions keep best in a cold, dry place, while winter squash and pumpkins prefer a moderately cool, dry place.

Cauliflower, Celery, Chinese Cabbage, Endive, Escarole, Kale, Kohlrabi, Leeks

An excellent and simple way to store these vegetables is to pull the whole plant, roots and all, and "replant" them in moist sand or soil. Pull the plants in dry weather, and do not wash them. Check for slugs or other pests and pick off as many as possible by hand. Store in a root cellar or in similar storage. Endive and escarole tops are best tied to make compact heads for close packing, and the tops of leeks cut to a uniform length.

Where winters are mild, all these vegetables can be heavily mulched in the garden and pulled as needed through the winter.

COLD STORAGE OF FRUITS

Also refer to specific fruits.

The winter-keeping or late varieties of many fruits can be stored in a root cellar or similar conditions. Apples and pears will keep all winter, while citrus fruits, grapes, quinces, and firm, small berries will keep from one to several months. It is necessary, however, to store most fruits separately from vegetables, particularly potatoes, turnips, and cabbage family vegetables. The fruits can absorb odors, or give off odors or moisture that harm the vegetables. The root cellar can be divided into separate areas, or the fruits can be kept in closed containers.

Fruit must be checked often for spoilage. It is quite true that one bad apple (or orange or grape) will spoil the whole barrel (or box or bag). If spoiled fruit is found, wipe any mold or wetness off adjacent fruits before repacking.

Cold Water Canning: Cranberries, Green Gooseberries, Lemons, Limes, Rhubarb, Wild Plums

These firm and very acidic fruits can be kept raw in cold storage by a process called cold water canning. It is not actually canning, however, since there is no vacuum seal. The cold water is really just a packing material that prevents contact with the air, thereby extending storage life. Fruit must be fresh, raw, and unblemished. Wash in cold water if washing is necessary.

Sterilize jars with lids that seal tightly. They can be any size and can be, but do not have to be, canning jars. Fill the jars with fresh, whole fruit without crushing it. Rhubarb can be cut in any convenient length. Wash a deep pail and scald it with boiling water. Put a jar of fruit in the pail and run cold drinking water into the jar until it overflows and the water is well above the jar top. Put the jar lid on under water and seal tightly. Remove the jar, empty the pail, and repeat with the next jar. This procedure drives out air bubbles and seals in the fruit without any air space.

Store the jars in a cool, dark place. The fruit will keep for months if the storage place is cold enough. Just above freezing is ideal. The water will become flavored and can be used with the fruit.

SUGGESTIONS FOR VEGETABLES AND FRUITS IN COLD STORAGE

- Check stored foods often, especially towards the end of the storage season. Remove spoiled foods and any spoiled material on nearby foods.
- Keep track of the amounts of remaining foods. If there is too much of something, consider preserving it another way while it is still in prime condition. Most of the vegetables and fruits kept in cold storage are also good dried, particularly root vegetables, potatoes, onions, and apples. Canning, pickling, and freezing are other alternatives.

• If stored foods dry out or lose flavor so they are unacceptable for people, feed them to livestock or pets. Some animals will prefer them cooked. There is no need to trim or wash these foods. Simply cook them in a big pot of water.

COLD STORAGE OF FOODS IN CROCKS

Many foods can be packed in crocks or similar non-corrosive containers, covered with pickling liquid, brine, fat, or oil to exclude air, and stored in a cold place for the winter. They should normally be used before warm spring weather arrives. In spite of differences in foods their storage needs are similar. They keep best between freezing and 40°F. Containers should be covered to keep out dust and pests. The food must be well-covered by the pickling liquid, brine, fat, or oil because it will spoil if exposed to air. If food tends to float, a weight must be used. (For some examples of food stored in crocks, refer to the PICKLING and SAUERKRAUT sections.)

REFERENCES

Agriculture Canada, Publication 1478/E, "Home storage room for fruits and vegetables," 1978.

Hertzberg, Ruth, *Putting Food By,* The Stephen Greene Press, 1982.

USDA Home & Garden Bulletin No. 119, "Storing Vegetables and Fruits in Basements, Cellars, Outbuildings, and Pits."

Collards 🌿

Collards or collard greens have the same botanical name as kale, which suggests that the two of them should be as alike as twins. If so, each twin has gone its separate way. Collards are favorite greens in the southeastern United States because they tolerate the summer heat and winter coolness equally well. In mild, somewhat humid climates they are a year-round vegetable. Kale is a northern green, especially beloved in Scotland. (Refer to the KALE section.) These two vegetables can often be interchanged in recipes, but prepared in traditional ways they are markedly different.

Some of the best ways to cook collards come from southern Black cooking traditions, but they can be enjoyed as a summer,

---

COLLARD STORAGE

Canning

Possible, but flavor and texture are poor.

Drying

Cut off stalks. Steam 8–10 min. (optional). Spread in thin layer. Dry until crumbly. Refer to the DRYING section.

Freezing

Blanch leaves 3 min. in boiling water. Refer to the FREEZING section.

COLLARD IDEAS

Creamed Collards

Chop collards coarsely and cook as you would spinach (refer to the SPINACH section), without seasoning. In a separate pot gently sauté a minced onion in about 2 tablespoons butter or other fat. When the onion is golden, stir in 1 tablespoon flour. Blend well and add 1 cup milk. Stir constantly over low heat or in a double boiler until it thickens to a smooth sauce. Season with pepper and salt, if

fall, and early winter vegetable almost everywhere. They have a mild cabbage flavor, and can be cooked like cabbage or any leafy green. They are rich in vitamins A and C and in minerals.

HANDLING COLLARDS

Collards taste best when picked young from fast growing plants. The leaves should be almost full-sized for cooking, but quite small and young for salads. The lowest leaves can be harvested progressively as the plant grows, leaving a tall stalk with a rosette of leaves on top. Eventually, the whole rosette can be harvested.

Since collards in the South can be harvested fresh most of the year, long-term storage is seldom necessary. In the North they can be frozen or dried for winter and spring use, and will keep up to a month in the refrigerator or root cellar.

Collard greens are cooked like spinach, except that they require a longer cooking time, 10 to 20 minutes depending on age and toughness. (Refer to COOKING SPINACH, in the SPINACH section.)

Comfrey

Comfrey is highly regarded as a medicinal herb with well-documented success in speeding the healing of many kinds of sores, bruises, and boils. Early spring comfrey greens are appetizing cooked like spinach, but later in the season their leaves are too fuzzy and their taste too bland and mucilaginous to be appealing. The late greens are improved if chopped small and cooked with other more flavorful ingredients. Comfrey's extraordinary nutritional value makes it worth eating often. It is unusually high in protein and vitamin B12, and is rich in many other vitamins and minerals. The protein and B12 are especially important to vegetarians.

HANDLING COMFREY

The first spring comfrey leaves make the best greens for cooking or salads. For salads, chop them small to minimize fuzziness and use in small amounts. Cook the leaves like spinach, using

desired, add the hot, cooked collards, and serve.

COMFREY STORAGE
Canning
Refer to CANNING LEAFY GREENS, in the CANNING section.

Drying
Leaves Trim stalks, spread with minimum overlap. Dry until crumbly. *Roots* Slice to uniform size. Dry until hard or brittle, or grind to powder. Refer to the DRYING section.

Freezing
Leaves Blanch in boiling water 2–3 min. Refer to the FREEZING section.

COMFREY IDEAS
Comfrey as a Nutritional Supplement
Mince fresh comfrey leaves or crumble dried leaves, and add to soups, stews, salads, and casseroles, or anywhere parsley would be added. Their bland flavor is not especially noticed, but the dish's nutritional value is increased.

the water that clings to them after washing plus a few extra tablespoons. Comfrey greens are good cooked with other, stronger-flavored greens.

Comfrey leaves that grow after the first harvesting are not as tasty as the first leaves, even if they are young and tender. Cooking these later leaves is mostly a matter of disguising their flavor. They are best cut fairly small and mixed with stronger-flavored ingredients.

It is possible to eat comfrey roots as a vegetable, but they are more enjoyable steeped in milk for a soothing beverage, or dried, roasted, and ground for a coffee-like drink. An effective compress for human or animal bruises, abscesses, and boils can be made from the root. Wrap a clean slice of root loosely in gauze or cheesecloth. Mash with a mallet or the flat side of a heavy knife to flatten the compress and free the root juices. Dip the compress in boiling water to sterilize it and apply it to the sore. Leave on overnight if possible, using tape or a cloth binding.

Most herb books list other ways to take advantage of the healing properties of comfrey.

Blenderized Comfrey

Put comfrey leaves in a blender or food processor and liquify with milk, soup stock, vegetable juice, or water. Use as the liquid in sauces, gravy, or soup, or as a fresh vegetable drink.

DRY CORN STORAGE
Canning

See CANNING HOMINY, below.

Drying

See HANDLING CORN and DRYING HOMINY, below.

$1/3$ cup dry corn = about 1 cup cornmeal; 1 cup corn for popping = about 5 cups popped

DRY CORN IDEAS

(The Cornmeal Mush recipe is required in most of the following ideas.)

Corn, Dry

Corn is native to the American continents, and was vital to the survival of most North, Central, and South American Indians. Soon after their arrival in the new world early settlers learned from the Indians how to grow corn, and it helped them survive and prosper just as it had the Indians. The settlers found corn to be more versatile than other grains, because it could be eaten fresh as a vegetable or left to dry and stored for later use. It was also easy to harvest by hand, without special tools. Today, modern homesteaders appreciate corn and grow it for many of the same reasons.

There are literally hundreds of races and varieties of corn with an amazing range of characteristics. A corn plant can be as small as two feet, or as tall as twenty. It can mature in two months or in eleven. An ear can be the size of a man's thumb or two feet long. The kernels can be yellow, white, blue, black, brown, and varying shades in between. And less spectacular, but most important, there are varieties suited to a wide range of climates and soils.

The commonly grown modern varieties are distinctly divided between those used dry for cornmeal, hominy, and animal feed, and sweet corn for eating fresh. Most corn intended for dry use is too starchy and tough to be enjoyable fresh, while mature, dry sweet corn is not as flavorful or practical as specialized dry varieties. However, if sweet corn should pass its prime for eating fresh, it can be used as dry corn. A few old varieties of corn, such as the blue or black corn from the southwestern United States and Mexico, are good both fresh and dried.

Fresh corn is discussed in the CORN, SWEET section, which follows this section.

Dry or field corn varieties are grouped according to the kernels' texture. When the starch is very hard it is called flint corn. Popcorn is an extremely hard kind of flint corn. Dent corn kernels combine both hard and soft starch, and the unequal drying causes a dent to form in the top of each kernel. Another variety, sometimes called flour corn, has very soft, mealy kernels that are easily ground or chewed. It is commonly used by South American Indians. Some seed catalogs carry the different dry corn varieties in small quantities which is nice for the adventurous home gardener.

CORN'S NUTRITIONAL VALUE

Corn has a rather poor reputation regarding its nutritional value. But though it is not exceptionally high in nutrients, it is a valuable carbohydrate food with some protein, vitamins, and minerals, and should not be crossed off anyone's food list. The open-pollinated varieties have higher protein levels than most hybrids. Since corn is low in lysine, which is one of the essential amino acids in protein food, high-lysine corn has been developed. Another way to increase protein value is to eat corn with foods that are high in lysine, such as beans. For example, several tablespoons of soy flour added to cornmeal in recipes considerably increases the protein value. The American Indians combined corn with a great variety of vegetables, nuts, and seeds, often by drying and grinding the other food and mixing it with cornmeal. This no doubt enhanced the nutritional value of the corn, as well as producing many interesting flavors.

Yellow corn is preferable to white as it contains more vita-

Cornmeal Mush
1 part cornmeal, or grits (allow about ¼ cup per serving)
3–4 parts liquid (water, or half water and half milk)
salt, optional

Mix the cornmeal with enough of the cold liquid to moisten it. Heat the liquid to a boil and stir in the wet cornmeal gradually to prevent lumps. Bring the pot of cereal to a boil, then set on low heat, or put in a double boiler. Stir occasionally until done. If necessary, more water can be added during cooking.

The proportions of liquid to cornmeal and the cooking time depend on the type of cornmeal, and on personal tastes. Long cooking in more liquid makes a soft, creamy gruel, or congee. Cooking times can vary from 15 minutes to an hour or more.

Salt should be added towards the end of the cooking time.

Hot cornmeal mush is excellent with yogurt or buttermilk. Other favored additions are butter, honey, or maple syrup.

min A. It is also worth noting that corn, like any other plant, contains more nutrients when grown on good soil and in good growing conditions.

HANDLING CORN

Harvesting

Large plantings of dry corn for human consumption are harvested with the same machinery as dry feed corn for animals. Where good dry feed corn is available, some can simply be appropriated for household use, though it may need sorting to remove pieces of cob, or winnowing to blow off bits of chaff.

When growing a small stand of dry corn, pick the ears when they are fully mature, and dry them in an airy place safe from rodents. One way to dry them is to pull back the husks from each ear, then tie a bunch of ears together by the husks, and drape them over a wire in a protected, airy place. If a tin can lid is strung on each end of the wire, mice will not be able to get at the corn.

Shelling Kernels

Corn should be shelled only after it is completely dry. Either the whole cob can be stored and then shelled a few ears at a time, as needed, or the whole crop can be shelled at once. Of course, the shelled kernels take up less space than ears. They are stored like other grains, in a cool, dry, and well-protected place.

To hand shell small amounts of corn, grasp the ear firmly with both hands and twist in opposite directions to dislodge the kernels. Small hand-held shellers can be purchased to make the job easier, or, for larger amounts of corn, there are hand-cranked shellers that do about 10 bushels an hour.

Cornmeal

Any dry corn can be ground to make cornmeal, including field corn, popcorn, Indian corn, and dry sweet corn. Taste and texture will vary with the kind of corn used. Corn with softer starch makes a very floury meal. Dent corn makes a somewhat floury meal, while flint corn or popcorn make a grainy meal.

Home ground cornmeal is whole grain and therefore more nutritious than degerminated commercial cornmeal. Whole grain cornmeal works better in recipes than the degerminated kind. This is especially true for recipes that require cooking the

---

Cornmeal to Replace Potatoes

Make cornmeal mush to serve in a mound with a dab of butter in the center instead of mashed potatoes. This goes well with eggs for breakfast, or with meat and vegetables for dinner. Cornmeal mush with yogurt, sour cream, or cheese is a common dish in Romania, called mamaliga. Hominy grits are good eaten in the same ways.

Polenta

Cooked yellow cornmeal mush is called polenta in Italy, and eaten with tomato sauce and grated cheese instead of pasta. The polenta can be cooked plain, or seasoned with butter and grated cheese. For the latter, stir 2 to 3 tablespoons butter and ½ to 1 cup grated Parmesan type cheese into several cups of hot mash that have almost finished cooking.

cornmeal in water and then using it in other mixtures such as bread dough. When recipes call for water ground or stone ground cornmeal it is whole grain meal that is wanted, so any home ground meal will work no matter what type of mill is used. The difference for cooking seems to lie in the greater thickening power or more cohesive quality of the whole grain cornmeal.

Corn Starch

Corn starch is pure starch refined from corn, and cannot be made at home. Potato starch, however, can easily be made. It is essentially the same and can be substituted for corn starch in recipes. (Refer to MAKING POTATO STARCH, in the POTATOES section.)

Occasionally in recipes there is confusion between corn flour and corn starch. If small amounts are called for to thicken liquids it is corn starch that is wanted; if larger amounts to serve as a basic flour are required, use a finely ground or floury cornmeal.

Parched (Browned) Corn

Two quite different corn preparations are called parched corn. One is dry corn that has been browned in the oven or a heavy dry frying pan. The other is cooked sweet corn that has been dried. (Refer to the CORN, SWEET section.)

Both dry kernels and cornmeal can be parched. Spread the corn in a thin layer in a shallow pan, and roast in a low, 250–300°F oven until browned, but not black. Stir often. Whole kernels will take much longer to parch than meal. To parch corn on top of the stove, put a thin layer of kernels or meal in a heavy, dry frying pan over very low heat, stirring often, until it is browned. Whole kernels will take up to 2 hours; meal will take about half an hour. A wood-fueled heating stove can often be used for this kind of parching.

Parched corn brings a pleasant flavor to bread and baked goods. Lightly parched, it makes a flavorful cooked cereal. It is also a common ingredient in coffee-like beverages.

Popcorn

Popcorn is a very hard variety of flint corn. It pops when moisture trapped in the kernel expands and explodes the kernel as it is heated. Too dry popcorn will not pop properly. Instead it only

Fried Cornmeal Slices

Hot cornmeal mush can be poured in a dish, cooled, sliced, and fried. It is especially good when cooked with other ingredients to flavor it. The polenta mixture described above is very good fried. To make another good mixture, sauté a little minced garlic, onion, and green pepper, with about ¼ pound ground meat in the cookpot. Add about 2 cups of water or soup stock, ½ cup cornmeal, and any desired seasonings. Cook as for ordinary cornmeal mush. The cooked cornmeal slices can be dusted with flour before frying if they are sticky.

Cornmeal Layers for Casseroles

Pour hot cornmeal mush in an oiled, round casserole. When cool and firm, turn it out, and slice across it to make 2 or 3 round layers. Put the bottom layer back in the casserole, add sauce or filling layered with the cornmeal.

partly splits with a muffled pop, or scorches without popping at all. When too moist, it makes an especially loud sound, yet the popped kernels are small and tough.

When drying popcorn, test pop some every so often. Then, when it pops perfectly, store it where it will not get any dryer. It can be shelled, and put in airtight containers in a cool place, or the ears can be kept at about 32°F, with a humidity of 85%.

If popcorn becomes too dry it can be moistened by putting it in a jar with a tablespoon of water for every 3 or 4 cups of corn. Close the jar tightly, and shake well twice a day for several days. If it still does not pop well, add a little more water and leave for another few days.

HOMINY, OR HULLED CORN

The only practical use for dry corn, other than making cornmeal, is making it into hominy. Kernels of dry corn cooked in plain water will have an unpleasantly tough, skin-like hull that interferes with eating them. Hominy is prepared by cooking in a solution of hardwood ashes, lye, or lime to remove the hulls. This treatment also gives the corn the characteristic flavor and texture that many enjoy. The dough for tortillas and tamales is made by grinding hulled corn or hominy. Hominy grits are made by drying and grinding hominy.

Traditional hominy is made from white corn with big kernels. White flint, or the blue or black varieties of corn are preferred for tortilla dough. However, yellow field corn can be treated to remove hulls, and then used for hominy or tortilla dough. It will have the same flavor.

Hominy or hulled corn loses vitamins during processing, but retains its protein and carbohydrate value. These have been enough to make it a basic life-sustaining food for large groups of people in the southern United States and Mexico. The many hominy dishes, especially tortillas, are popular everywhere.

MAKING HOMINY

The basic proportions for making hominy are 1 quart dry corn to 1 gallon of any of the following:

Corn with Nuts or Seeds

The American Indians often mixed corn with either chopped or ground nuts and seeds. Cornmeal mush is quite good cooked with chopped nuts or sunflower seeds.

Hominy and Beans Stew

Cook hominy and any kind of dry beans separately. Mix them together with some of their cooking water, chopped onion, green pepper, parsley, or other vegetable and herb seasonings. Cook about 30 minutes to blend flavors. This is stew if it is thick and soup if extra water or soup stock is added.

Hasty Pudding

As the name suggests this is a quick and easy old-fashioned dessert. It is simply hot cornmeal mush with a dab of butter, some molasses, maple syrup or honey, some milk or cream, and a sprinkle of cinnamon and nutmeg.

Hardwood Ashes

Put about 1½ quarts clean hardwood ashes in a big enameled or stainless steel pot. *Do not use aluminum.* Add 5 quarts of water. Boil 15 minutes, then let sit away from the fire until the ashes settle. Pour off the clear water to use—about a gallon. It will feel slippery to the fingers because it is a lye solution.

Slaked (Hydrated) Lime

(Do not use quicklime, calcium oxide, which is dangerous to handle, or agricultural lime, which does not work.) Mexican grocery stores sell slaked lime for making tortillas, and some other grocery stores sell hydrated or pickling lime as a pickling aid. Use about 4 tablespoons slaked lime mixed in 1 gallon of water.

Cooking the Corn

Heat the corn in the solution and boil until swelled with the skins ready to slip. To test if it is done, remove and rinse a few kernels, rubbing them to see if the hulls loosen. To prevent changes in flavor or texture, it is best not to leave the hominy in the solution any longer than necessary. The time will vary according to the type of corn and the solution used, but it is usually between 1 and 2 hours.

When the hulls are loosened, drain and rinse the corn in hot water several times. Then rub the kernels between the hands until the hulls come loose. The dark specks at the base of the kernel are usually also rubbed loose. When the hominy is rinsed the hulls will float off. They can plug a sink drain so it's best to catch them in a strainer. The hominy must be well rinsed to remove all taste of the hulling solution. Soaking for several hours in 3 or 4 changes of water is sometimes recommended.

Cook the rinsed hominy in fresh water until it is tender and ready to eat. Time will vary for different kinds of corn. Some will just need heating to a boil, and some may need to cook for an hour.

Canning Hominy

Pressure can only! Pack hot cooked hominy in jars and add boiling hot water, leaving ½ inch headroom. Optional, add ¼ teaspoon salt to pints, ½ teaspoon to quarts. Pressure process at 240°F, 11 pounds pressure. Pints: 60 minutes; quarts: 70 minutes. (Refer to the CANNING section.)

Drying Hominy

Spread cooked hominy on trays or screens. Dry until brittle in a food dryer or very low oven. Soak to reconstitute before cooking. Use like regular hominy.

Making Grits

Coarsely grind dried hominy to make grits. Use as a cereal. Grits are good served with butter, like mashed potatoes.

Hominy grits are usually made from white corn, but yellow corn tastes just as good. Grits tasting a lot like hominy can be made by coarsely grinding very hard flint corn or popcorn, or by coarsely grinding barley. Hard corn or barley grits are easier to prepare and more nutritious than hominy grits, since they do not need treating to remove hulls. They can be substituted for hominy grits in recipes.

TORTILLAS

Tortillas have been Mexico's basic bread since ancient Aztec times, and they are still made in the same ways today. Marian Hengerford, who stayed with an Indian family in Chiapas, Mexico for a while, describes how they made tortillas in a letter to *Countryside* magazine, April, 1976.

"First of all they started with dried-on-the-stalk field corn. The corn was stored in the husk until the day before use, when it was husked and shelled. The corn kernels were put in an earthenware pot over a fire with water barely covering the kernels. The lime was obtained by gathering snails in the rivers and creeks and burning the shells to a powder. This concentrated lime was added, about a handful to a pot of kernels, and boiled until the corn was kind of soft. It did seem similar to making hominy. The Indians said the snail shells made the kernels pop open easier.

The softish kernels were rinsed in woven baskets in running water until the water ran clear. A slight draining occurred as the kernels were carried back to the kitchen in the basket. Only then was the grinding done. The kernels were forced through a grinder once and then the resulting mash was ground again. This gives the basic tortilla dough. The liquid came only from the water that stuck on the kernels after washing. If it was too dry to pat into shape a little water might be added, but not often and not in large quantities."

Tortilla Dough

Make hominy ("nixtamal" in Mexico) in any of the ways described above. Grind it twice in a meat grinder to make a workable dough ("masa"). If it is too dry to hold together, work in a little water, but do not let it become sticky. In Mexico, balls of dough are patted out by hand to make thin, round tortillas. Newcomers to the art of tortilla making will find it much easier to flatten the dough between damp cloths. Put an egg-sized ball of dough on a damp cloth. Cover with another damp cloth and press with a small board to make a tortilla 4 to 5 inches across and ⅛ inch thick. It takes practice to make perfect tortillas, but they taste good even if oddly shaped. (A tortilla press can also be bought to shape the tortillas more quickly.)

Cook the tortillas on a hot dry griddle or frying pan, for about 2 minutes on each side. They should remain flexible. To keep them warm and a little moist, wrap them in a damp towel, adding tortillas to the stack in the towel as they are cooked.

Tortillas will keep about a week in the refrigerator. Before refrigerating, put waxed paper between each one, wrap a damp cloth around them all, and put them in a plastic bag. Freeze them for long storage. For the freezer put waxed paper or freezer wrap between them and seal them in plastic bags.

Masa

In some areas, stores sell masa harina, a special flour for making tortilla dough. A similar flour can be made at home by grinding dried hominy as finely as possible. (Regular dried corn does not work.) To use this flour, work in warm water until the right consistency is reached; 2 cups masa harina and 1⅓ cups warm water are the usual proportions.

Tortilla Chips

Tortilla dough can also be made into flavorful crackers. Work seasonings to taste into the dough. Chili powder, salt, and a bit of cayenne pepper make a good flavor, but any seasonings, from onion juice to curry powder can be used. Flatten the dough as for tortillas and cut it into squares or triangles. Bake the chips on an oiled cookie sheet, or fry them in a lightly oiled pan until they are crisp.

DRY CORN RECIPES

The following recipe originated with American Indians or Mexican Indians— the first experts in corn cookery.

North Woods Doughboys

(MAKES ABOUT 6 SIDE SERVINGS)

This particular name comes from an 1875 cookbook, but the recipe represents a very old and basic way to cook cornmeal. The same sort of mixture was called "hoecake" when baked on a hoe over an open fire, and "ashcake" when it was buried to cook in hot ashes at the edge of the fireplace. The ashes were rinsed off just before the cake was eaten. One old recipe suggests putting the ashcake between two cabbage leaves while baking to keep it clean. Other early versions were called "Johnnycake," "corn pone," or just "pone," from "apone," an Indian name for them.

1 cup cornmeal
2 tablespoons soy or peanut flour, optional (not part of early recipes)
¼ teaspoon salt, optional

1 tablespoon lard or other fat, optional
2–2½ cups boiling water
fat or oil, for frying

Mix the cornmeal, soy or peanut flour, salt, and lard in a heat proof bowl. Pour in boiling water, a little at a time, stirring constantly. Keep adding water until a soft dough is formed. As the water is added the cornmeal thickens and requires more water.

Heat fat or oil in a frying pan, then put in spoonfuls of the dough, flattening them to about ½-inch thick with the spoon. Fry until nicely browned on both sides. (The dough can also be fried as one large, flat cake.)

SWEET CORN STORAGE
Canning
Cut from cob (see below).

Whole Kernel Hot Pack
Use 2 cups water per 4 cups kernels. Heat to boil, stirring often. Drain, pack in jars, add boiling cooking water, 1 in. headroom. Process 240°F, 11 pounds pressure. Pints: 55 min. Quarts: 1 hr. 25 min.

Whole Kernel Raw Pack
Fill jars loosely, 1 in. headroom. Add boiling water, ½ in. headroom. Process as for HOT PACK, above.

Cream Style Hot Pack
(Pints only, too dense for quarts.) Add 2 cups boiling water per 4 cups cream style corn. Heat to boil, stirring to prevent scorching. Fill pints, 1 in. headroom. Process 240°F, 11 pounds pressure, 1 hr. 25 min.

Corn, Sweet

A hundred years ago when corn was eaten fresh it was called green corn, meaning immature corn. Since then a series of newer, sweeter varieties have been developed for eating fresh which quite reasonably are called sweet corn. In fact, the latest varieties are so sweet that some people find them cloying to the taste.

Whatever variety is preferred, sweet corn is a favorite food that everyone can enjoy with one qualification. Although considered a vegetable, it should not replace green vegetables, as it does not contain the same important vitamins and minerals. It is actually a grain and should be considered a carbohydrate in meal planning. So eat it instead of potatoes or bread, and serve green vegetables or salad with it. (Refer to CORN'S NUTRITIONAL VALUE, in the CORN, DRY section.)

The prime time for picking sweet corn is rather short lived. If picked too early the kernels are small and lacking in flavor; if picked too late the corn is doughy, or starchy and somewhat tough. Some people can judge ripeness by feeling the ears of corn. When they feel full and give a little when pressed they are ready. Other indications are silk that is turning brown and dry, tips that are rounded and full, and kernels that yield "milk" when dented with a fingernail. Sweet corn will stay at its best for only a week or two, so eat, can, dry, or freeze it without delay. If it is only a little past its prime it can be used for making the *Corn Relish* or BAKED CORN-OFF-THE-COB recipes, below. It can also be left to mature and dry and be used as dry corn.

Standard varieties of sweet corn become less sweet as soon as they are picked, and their sugar begins changing to starch. If the corn cannot be rushed to the kitchen and cooked immediately, it should be refrigerated, or kept in a cold place to slow down this process. It can be husked before refrigeration. New extra sweet varieties hold their sweetness better than older varieties, and their immediate processing is not so important.

Whether sweet corn is canned, dried, or frozen is largely a matter of convenience, since quality is excellent with all three. Though today canned and frozen corn are most common, in the past huge quantities of sweet corn (sometimes called parched corn) were dried for winter use. When prime quality sweet corn is cooked immediately, and then dried, it tastes just as good as canned or frozen corn. (See RECIPES, below.)

Blanching or Boiling Corn-on-the-Cob

Ears of corn can be steamed, but unless the steamer holds the heat very well, boiling cooks the corn faster. For best results, bring a large pot of water to a rapid boil. Add only enough ears of corn so they will not be crowded in the pot, and the water quickly returns to a boil. When one batch is done, take it out with tongs, and repeat. The corn will cook in 3 to 10 minutes, depending on the size of the ears.

Cutting Whole Kernel or Cream Style Corn

The two ways to cut corn from the cob are whole kernel and cream style. Either style can be frozen or canned, but for drying

---

Cream Style Raw Pack
Fill pints only, 1½ in. headroom. Add boiling water, ½ in. headroom. Process 240°F, 11 pounds pressure, 1 hr. 35 min. Refer to the CANNING section. Also see *Corn Relishes,* below.

Drying
(Excellent quality!) Cook on cob, cut whole kernels (see below). Spread, dry until brittle. To use, soak several hours or overnight and cook approx. 30 min. Refer to the DRYING section.

Freezing
Whole Kernel or Cream Style Blanch ears 4 min. in boiling water, then cut (see below). *On-the-Cob* (Slim cobs best.) Blanch in boiling water 6–10 min. according to size. Thaw completely before cooking. Refer to the FREEZING section.

the corn is cut whole kernel. For canning and some recipes corn is cut raw; for freezing and drying it is precooked.

To cut whole kernels, hold the ear against a cutting board, stalk end down, and slice off the kernels top to bottom with a sharp knife. Cut close to the cob but not into it. For cream style corn slice off only the tips or top halves of the kernels. Next, scrape the cobs with the back of the knife to force out the milky juice and the hearts of the kernels. Then combine the cut tips and the scrapings. Cream style corn can also be made by grating the corn off the cob with a hand grater.

The special hand-held tools that adjust for cutting whole kernel or cream style corn probably save more time when cutting cream style than whole kernel. A knife is quite as efficient for cutting whole kernel corn.

A device for holding the corn can be made by cutting a clean wooden board to fit in a cake pan. Drive a 3- or 4-inch nail completely through the board, then put it in the pan with the nail sticking up. Impale one end of the ear of corn on the nail, hold the other end steady with one hand, and cut off the kernels. The pan catches the cut kernels.

Using Corn Husks

Husks from sweet corn or fresh field corn are traditional food wrappings, and too tough to be edible. Though best known as wrappings for tamales, they can also be wrapped around other mixtures.

To remove the husks as whole leaves, cut off the ears of corn at their base just where the kernels begin. The husks can then be unwrapped leaf by leaf. They are sometimes blanched in boiling water before use, or tough or dry husks can be soaked in water to make them pliable.

If fresh husks and silk are not wanted, many animals like eating them. An old-time use for dry husks was as a stuffing for pillows and mattresses.

Using Leftover Corn Cobs

A lot of flavor is left in the cobs after the corn is removed. Cook them in water to cover for half an hour, then drain off the liquid. Sweet corn cob cooking water is good as a soup base or used instead of water in any corn recipe. Years ago, cooking wa-

---

1 bushel with husks = 6–10 quarts prepared; 3–5 pounds with husks = 6–12 ears = 1 quart prepared

SWEET CORN IDEAS
Corn Omelets

Cooked sweet corn is delicious in any style omelet. For a fluffy omelet add the corn to well-beaten egg yolks and seasonings. Fold in stiffly beaten whites. Cook in a buttered frying pan until the bottom has browned. Fold the omelet and turn out on a heated plate. For a western style omelet, sauté the corn in butter, if desired with sweet peppers and tomato. Then add the lightly beaten eggs. Turn when almost set, or finish like scrambled eggs. Garnish with minced chives or scallions.

ter from the red cobs of dry field corn was used with pectin and sugar to make corn cob jelly. Dry corn cobs are also used for smoking meat, as kindling for starting fires, and even for making pipes. Fresh corn cobs are used to feed livestock.

SWEET CORN RECIPES

Corn Fritters

(MAKES ABOUT 6 SIDE SERVINGS)

2 cups cream style corn, fresh, frozen, or canned

2 eggs, separated

pepper, salt, optional

¼ cup flour

Mix the corn with the egg yolks, pepper, and salt. Stir with a fork to blend in the yolks completely, then mix in the flour. Beat the egg whites until stiff and fold them into the batter. Heat a well-oiled griddle or frying pan and drop oyster-sized tablespoons of batter on it. Brown on both sides and serve hot. These are good both for breakfast with syrup, or for supper with meat and vegetables.

Canned Corn Relish, Shaker Style

(MAKES 5–6 PINTS)

2 cups corn, cut raw from the cob

2 cups onions, chopped small

2 cups ripe tomatoes, chopped small

1½ teaspoons celery seed

2 cups cucumbers, chopped small

2 cups vinegar

2 cups cabbage, chopped small

¾ cup honey or 1 cup sugar

1 teaspoon turmeric

1 teaspoon salt, optional

Combine the corn, onions, tomatoes, cucumbers, and cabbage in a large pot. Mix the honey or sugar, celery seed, turmeric, and salt, if desired, with the vinegar, and add to the vegetables. Heat to a boil and simmer, uncovered, about 20 minutes, stirring often. Pour boiling hot into hot canning jars, adjust lids, and process 10 minutes in a boiling water bath. (Refer to the CANNING section.)

Baked Corn-off-the-Cob

Sweet corn that has just passed its prime is best for this. Cut the corn from the cob and scrape off the rest. Mix with melted butter, and pepper. Put in a deep layer in a buttered baking dish. Bake in a moderate, 350°F oven until set and crusty brown on top. With salad, this makes a nice lunch, or serve as a side dish with dinner.

Super Sweet Corn in Desserts

New super sweet corn varieties can be used to sweeten desserts. Try adding ½ cup corn to recipes for cookies, puddings, custard, or fruit bread. Whole kernel corn will impart a chewy texture while cream style corn blends in more completely. For a smooth mixture the corn can be puréed.

Canned Corn Relish, Yankee Style

(MAKES ABOUT 5 PINTS)

5 cups cooked corn, cut from cob
½ cup green pepper, chopped small
½ cup sweet red pepper, chopped small
1 cup onion, chopped small
1 tablespoon mustard seed
2 teaspoons celery seed
½ teaspoon turmeric
½ cup honey or ¾ cup sugar
2 cups vinegar
1 teaspoon salt, optional
½ cup celery, chopped small

Mix all ingredients and simmer slowly for 30 minutes, stirring often. Pack boiling hot in hot canning jars, adjust lids, and process 10 minutes in a boiling water bath. (Refer to the CAN-NING section.)

This relish was often eaten as a sandwich spread in the past and is quite good that way.

Cranberries

Everyone is familiar with cranberry sauce for the holiday turkey, and with the store-bought bottles of clear red juice that list water and sugar ahead of cranberries in the contents. Not many are familiar with cranberry cultivation, as their growing requirements make them impractical for the family garden. Only those who live near cranberry bogs or places where they grow wild can harvest them. Northeastern American Indians and early settlers gathered them in huge quantities. As they keep better than most fruits they were carried on ships to prevent scurvy, and exported to Europe packed in barrels of water.

A few wild berries are enough like cranberries to be used in the same ways. Cranberry bush (or high bush cranberry) is well-known and sometimes cultivated for fruit in far northern regions. A wild berry known variously as cowberry, foxberry, lingonberry, and rock cranberry is often gathered in northern Europe and used like cranberries.

CRANBERRY STORAGE
Canning
(Sweeten before canning for best color and flavor.)

Whole Sauce
Prepare *Extra Special Cranberry Sauce* (add oranges after opening), or use any sauce recipe. Pour boiling hot in jars, ½ in. headroom. Process in boiling water bath. Pints and quarts: 10 min.

Jellied Sauce
Cook 2 pounds berries in 1 quart water until popped. Put through strainer or food mill. Sweeten to taste, heat to boiling. Process as for WHOLE SAUCE. Refer to the CANNING section. Also see CANNING FRUIT JUICE AND SAUCE, in the FRUITS section.

Cold Storage
(Very practical.) Raw berries keep for weeks refrigerated. To store for several months, wash well in cold water, let dry, or pat dry with clean towel. Pack in sterilized jars, seal with sterilized lids. Refrigerate or keep in other cold place. Refer to the COLD STORAGE section. Also see COLD WATER CANNING, in the same section.

HANDLING CRANBERRIES

Cranberries are gathered in the fall, and can be kept in cold storage all winter. Where protected by snow they will sometimes stay in good condition on the plants through the winter. Extra cranberries are easy to can, dry, or freeze for year-round use. Home canned cranberry juice is excellent. Cranberries are high in pectin and jell readily when cooked with sweetening. (Refer to the PECTIN section.) Since cranberries are so tart they are good combined with sweet fruits. They blend especially well with sweet apples, sweet oranges, and raisins. (Refer to COMBINING SWEET AND TART FRUITS, in the FRUITS section.)

If cranberries are abundant, use them in recipes for other tart fruits. They will give their own special flavor to recipes for rhubarb, sour or crabapples, sour cherries, or currants and gooseberries.

CRANBERRY RECIPES

Extra Special Cranberry Sauce

(MAKES ABOUT 1 QUART)

¾ cup honey or maple syrup
½ cup water
4 cups cranberries

1–2 oranges, peeled and chopped, medium

Bring the honey or syrup and water to a boil. Add the cranberries and cook until they have popped, from 5 to 10 minutes. Cool completely, then mix in the chopped oranges. Let sit an hour or more before serving. This sauce can be made a day ahead.

Cranberry Gravy

½ cup cranberry sauce (jellied or whole)
2 cups chicken or turkey gravy

Mix cranberry sauce with chicken or turkey gravy. Jellied sauce will keep the texture of the gravy smooth, but whole cranberry sauce also tastes good. This is a festive way to serve up the leftovers of a roast chicken or turkey dinner.

Drying

Crack skins by dunking in boiling water 15–30 sec. Spread in single layer on trays and dry until hard. Or make fruit leather. Refer to the DRYING section.

Freezing

Pack dry, clean raw berries in rigid containers to prevent crushed fruit. Seal and freeze. Prepared relish or sauce can also be frozen. Refer to the FREEZING section.

1 pound = 4 cups

CRANBERRY IDEAS

Raw Cranberry Relish

Grind cranberries in a meat grinder or food chopper with such raw fruits as apples, oranges, and pineapple. Add ground or grated orange peel, raisins or other dried fruits, and honey to taste. For a mixture to go with beef or game meats, grind a small piece of horseradish root with the cranberries. When oranges are not used, a little lemon juice will be good.

Cranberries in Baking

Cut raw cranberries in half, or chop them very coarsely, and add to muffins, pancakes, or fruit breads. They can take the place of blueberries in muffins and pancakes.

Cucumbers 🌿

Cucumbers are one of the oldest known garden vegetables. They have been cultivated for over 3,000 years in parts of Asia and Africa, and there are seemingly over 3,000 uses for them. These include numerous ways to prepare them raw, to pickle them, and, less well-known, to cook them.

All cucumbers do not look alike. The green, cylindrical varieties are the most common, but there are many others, ranging from the Apple or Lemon cucumbers (which are shaped like the fruits), to the Sikkim variety grown in the Himalayas, which reach up to 15 inches long and 6 inches around. Also notable are the large, smooth skinned European and English cucumbers grown mostly in greenhouses, and the long, slender Chinese and Japanese varieties which are quite ridged and warty. The latter are easy to grow, and their mild flavor is excellent in salads, pickled, and cooked.

HANDLING CUCUMBERS

Any cucumber over an inch long can be harvested, but they are usually allowed to grow to at least 3 or 4 inches. Often cucumbers are harvested small and immature for pickling, while medium sized ones are picked for salads. When full-sized cucumbers are about to turn yellow they are excellent both cooked as a vegetable or pickled like fruit. (Refer to the *Spiced Pickled Fruit* recipe, in the PICKLING section.) Where garden space is limited, a single variety can be grown and picked at different stages for different purposes.

It is best to cut cucumbers leaving a short stem on each. Pulling may both injure the vine, and break the skin at the stem end where spoilage can start. Careful cutting is most important with whole pickling cucumbers and those to be kept in cold storage for some time. Homegrown cucumbers should not be peeled unless skins are tough, but waxed or sprayed store cucumbers must be peeled. Eating the skins is said to prevent gas and, of course, saves valuable nutrients.

Under imperfect growing conditions the cucumber's stem section sometimes becomes bitter. If several slices are discarded from this end, the rest of the cucumber is usually good.

CUCUMBER STORAGE
Canning
(Practical for pickles only.) Refer to the PICKLING section.

Cold Storage
Pack large, firm, unblemished cucumber with stem left on in damp sand or other protective material, and store in root cellar or similar condition. Storage life up to 2 months. Refer to the COLD STORAGE section.

Drying
Slice thinly or chop small. Dry until brittle. Use in soup or stew, or use crisp slices as chips with dips. Refer to the DRYING section.

Freezing
(Not acceptable raw except in a vinegar solution.) See VINEGARED CUCUMBERS, below. Juice and cooked dishes may be frozen.

1 bushel raw cucumbers = 40–45 pounds = 14–24 quarts, pickled

CUCUMBER IDEAS
Cucumbers and Herbs
Cucumbers are delicious with most fresh-from-the-garden herbs. Minced chives, scallions, dill leaves, fennel,

A slight bitterness can be counteracted by vinegar dressings.

As cucumbers contain a lot of moisture they are sometimes sliced and pressed between two plates or small boards, with a weight on top to remove juice. A sprinkling of salt before pressing is often recommended to draw out liquid, but the salt can be avoided if slices are very thin. Another way to remove juice is to grate cucumbers or chop them small, and then squeeze them in a cloth. Pressed or squeezed cucumbers, being somewhat limp and dry, will absorb salad dressings instead of diluting them as do fresh slices. Cucumber juice is flavorful added to vegetable juice mixtures, aspics, and soups.

Cooked Cucumbers

Mature cucumbers are surprisingly delicious cooked. They are prepared much like summer squash or zucchini and can be used in the same recipes. However, their texture will be firmer and their flavor somewhat different. Even overripe, yellow cucumbers can be cooked if they are first peeled and seeded.

Cucumber Pickles

The best pickling cucumbers are immature, firm, small, and freshly harvested. If kept for even a day at room temperature they may later become hollow or shriveled after pickling. It is best to pick cucumbers on a dry day, as they will be waterlogged and less flavorful right after a heavy rain. For whole pickles, use unblemished cucumbers, cut to leave a small bit of stem, and remove any remnants of blossom. Less perfect cucumbers, if firm and fresh, are good for pickled slices, chunks, or relish, but must still be firm and fresh.

There are numerous cucumber pickle recipes, but only a few general types. Most often vinegar is the pickling agent, but a few depend on lactic acid (formed by natural fermentation) to preserve and flavor the cucumbers. In these salt is used to draw out the sugars and juice, providing the right conditions for fermentation. The process is like making sauerkraut. (Refer to MAKING FERMENTED PICKLES, in the PICKLING section.)

Pickles made with vinegar may be sweet or sour. The most nutritious are those made with a minimum of salt and sugar. (Refer to THE NUTRITIONAL VALUE OF PICKLES, in the PICKLING section.)

basil, parsley, or summer savory are good individually or in combinations sprinkled over cucumber slices. They make a good salad without other seasoning, but a salad dressing or yogurt can be added.

Vinegared Cucumbers

For a cool, refreshing, summer side dish, marinate sliced or chopped cucumbers in vinegar for 15 minutes or longer. A mild homemade cider vinegar or wine vinegar is ideal. If harsher, stronger tasting vinegar must be used, dilute it half-and-half with water. Serve the cucumbers in the vinegar, or drain and sprinkle them with minced herbs, as described above.

Cucumbers can also be frozen in a half vinegar, half water mixture. When thawed and drained they can be added to salads.

Cucumber Soup

Chopped cucumber is very good added to most vegetable and meat soups for the last 10 or 15 minutes of cooking. For an all cucumber soup, cook several chopped cucumbers in chicken, rabbit, or veal stock. Purée the mixture and enrich with milk and a little cream. Season with pepper, herbs, and salt, if desired. If a thick-

CUCUMBER RECIPES
Squeezed Cucumber Relish

(MAKES 4 PINTS)

12 (about) medium to large cucumbers (enough to make 2 quarts after squeezing)	¼ cup honey or ½ cup sugar (increase for a sweeter relish)
5–6 onions, grated or chopped small	1 teaspoon turmeric
	cayenne or other hot pepper, to taste
2 cups vinegar	1 teaspoon salt, optional

Grate the cucumbers, or chop them finely. Put them in a cloth-lined colander over a bowl, and gather the ends of the cloth to make a bag. Tighten, twist, squeeze, and press the bag to remove as much juice as possible. (Reserve the juice for soups or juice mixtures.) In a large pot combine onions, vinegar, honey or sugar, turmeric, pepper, and salt, if desired, with the cucumber. Heat to a boil, uncovered, stirring frequently, and boil 5 minutes. Pour into clean hot jars, adjust lids, and seal. Process in a boiling water bath for 10 minutes. (Refer to the CANNING section.)

---

ened soup is preferred, melt 2 tablespoons butter in the soup pot, stir in 2 tablespoons flour, then add the other ingredients.

CURRANT STORAGE
Canning

Remove stems (see HANDLING CURRANTS, below). To process, refer to the GOOSEBERRIES section. Also see CANNING FRUIT JUICE AND SAUCE, in the FRUITS section.

Drying

(Not the same fruit as commercially dried currants, but very good.) Optional: Crack skins by blanching 15–30 seconds in boiling water. (Unnecessary if picked by stripping.) Dry until hard. Refer to the DRYING section.

Freezing

Package plain whole, or sweeten either whole or crushed with honey, sugar, or syrup. Refer to the FREEZING section.

1½–2 quarts fresh = 1 quart crushed or cooked, or 2–3 cups juice

---

Currants

Currants have a compelling, tart flavor that makes them extraordinary in jelly and preserves. Sauces made with red currant jelly or preserves are a popular accompaniment for ham and roast meat in England and France. One fancy red currant preserve is Bar-le-Duc, named after the French town where it originated. Each currant in it is pricked with a pin to absorb the syrup in which it is cooked so that it becomes plumply beautiful.

In the United States before the 1920s currants were a fairly common fruit. In the Twenties most currants and gooseberries were uprooted, because they were found to be an alternate host for white pine blister rust, and white pine timber far overrode currants or gooseberries in importance. However, currants can still be grown or gathered wild in many places, and they remain both delicious and useful.

There are red, black, and white currant varieties. Because they are closely related to gooseberries they can be used in the same ways. Currants are a good source of vitamin C. Black currants, which have the most vitamin C, are also the most susceptible to white pine blister rust.

There is some confusion about dried currants. Those sold in stores are not actually currants, but a special kind of dried grapes. In recipes, "currants" often means the dried grapes rather than the true fresh currants. True currants are good dried, but as they dry hard they usually need soaking to reconstitute them.

HANDLING CURRANTS

Currants will stay on the bush for 4 to 6 weeks after they change color or begin to ripen. As they hang, they become sweeter, and some varieties will become sweet enough to eat fresh. The black varieties are sweeter than the red. Pectin content is highest when currants are underripe or when they first ripen, so pick them early for jam or preserves. The red varieties contain the most pectin.

Pick currants on a dry day after the dew has evaporated. They can be picked one by one, removing the stem from each, or whole clusters can be broken off at once, or they can be stripped from the plant by holding a container under them and running a hand down each cluster. Though stripping damages the currants, it will not matter if the fruit is to be used immediately. Currants that are to be stored even for a few days should be picked more carefully, however.

Stemming Currants

If currants are to be cooked for juice or jelly their stems need not be removed. They can be strained out after cooking as they do not affect flavor. When it is necessary to remove stems, mix the currants with enough flour to coat them, then roll them gently between the palms of the hands until the stems come off. Then rinse away flour and stems together. The currants' little tails will rub off with the stems, but they are not noticeable if left on, even when eaten fresh or cooked whole. Even stems can be left on and eaten like the tails if the slight chewiness is not minded.

Currant Juice

Do not overlook this delicious specialty. Fresh, uncooked juice is very good in punch, and for sherbet; the canned juice is good

---

CURRANT IDEAS

Currants in Fruit Mixtures

Combining currants with other fruits is an old and excellent idea. They go especially well with raspberries, but are also good with cherries, early apples, and other fruits that ripen around the same time. Such combinations make delicious juice and punch, jams and jellies, sherbet, ice cream, and pie or tart fillings. Currant-raspberry pie is exceptional.

Fresh Currants in Baked Goods

Use currants instead of blueberries in pancakes, muffins, and fruit breads, and add a little grated citrus fruit peel.

Fresh Currants Over Ice

Pick currants after they have become somewhat sweet. Spread them over a clear cube of ice in individual bowls. According to one very old recipe book, "Of a sultry morning nothing is more refreshing."

used like any tart juice. Currant wine used to be popular. (Refer to MAKING FRUIT JUICE AND SAUCE, in the FRUITS section.)

Dandelions 🌿

Dandelions can be a dandy vegetable, but their name actually comes from the French *dent-de-lion,* or tooth of a lion, describing the sharply indented leaf margins.

Dandelions are collected wild more often than cultivated, but some seed catalogs do carry seeds for big-leafed varieties that do not get as bitter, or blossom as quickly, as the wild plants. The best wild dandelions for eating grow undisturbed in fields and open places. Though it may not seem so to those who strive for perfect lawns, mowed dandelions are somewhat stunted. The rage that some people feel towards dandelions in their lawns would be dissipated if they could discover the joys of eating them. They might even decide to stop mowing their lawns so the dandelions could reach their full potential!

HANDLING DANDELIONS

Wild dandelion greens are harvested from early spring, when the first little leaves appear, until mid-spring when they begin to blossom. When the greens become too tough and bitter to enjoy, the blossoms can be harvested and used instead. The roots can be dug all year, depending on the way they are to be used. Starting with the crowns in spring, dandelions are practically a year-round vegetable. However, do not gather dandelions close to busy roads, because of contamination from car exhausts and winter treatments to remove ice.

Dandelion Crowns

In very early spring, when the first leaf tips begin to show, dig the plants and cut off the rosettes of beginning leaves and buds, or cut the plants an inch or two below the soil's surface with a sharp knife. They will be pale yellow or white with a crisp tex-

---

DANDELION STORAGE

Canning

Cook young greens in minimum water until wilted. Cook older greens in large pot of boiling water 10 min., drain to remove bitterness. Pack, add boiling water, 1 in. headroom. Process 240°F, 11 pounds pressure. Pints: 1 hr. 10 min. Quarts: 1 hr. 30 min. Refer to the CANNING section.

Cold Storage

Roots Refer to WINTER FORCING OF CHICORY ROOTS, in the CHICORY section.

Drying

To dry greens refer to the SPINACH section. For tea refer to DRYING HERBS, in the HERBS section.

Freezing

Blanch tender leaves 1½–2 min. in steam or boiling water. Blanch tough leaves 5 min. in boiling water. Refer to the FREEZING section.

   2–3 pounds raw greens = 1 quart cooked

ture and mild flavor. They are delicious in salads. They can also be cooked quickly in a minimum of water, seasoned with butter and pepper, and served as a hot vegetable. Some like to cook the little, partially formed flower buds separately for a special treat.

Delicate, blanched leaves can be encouraged by piling soil over the plants, so that more leaves are blanched as they grow, or buckets can be turned upside-down over the plants to keep them in darkness. Roots forced in winter will also produce crisp, blanched leaves.

Dandelion Greens

The greens are the most prolific, useful part of the dandelion. Large amounts can be gathered, and canned or frozen for winter. Years ago they were salted down (salt cured) and stored, but that is the least nutritious way to handle them. Early spring greens are tender enough to use raw for salads, or cook in the water left on them from washing. Later in the season they become gradually more tough and bitter. Then they are best cooked in a large pot of boiling water for about 10 minutes and drained. This takes away some of the bitterness. Bitterness can also be handled as with their close relative, chicory greens. (Refer to the CHICORY section.)

Sand and dirt particles tend to collect in dandelion greens, and it is best to immerse them in several changes of cold water. Light bits of debris will float off, and the leaves can then be lifted out of the water, leaving sand and dirt behind. Picked greens wilt quickly, so refrigerate or prepare them without delay.

Dandelion Blossoms

Dandelion blossoms are good prepared like squash blossoms or elderberry flowers (refer to the SQUASH, SUMMER section), though they are best known for making dandelion wine. Gather the blossoms on a dry day and, most important, remove the stems and calyx (the outer ring of leaves around the blossoms). The inner green ring that holds the blossoms together can be left in place, though it does not matter if they fall apart. The blossoms can be pinched off the plant with the fingers, leaving stem and calyx behind, or picked and held by the stem while the blossoms are pinched or snipped off with scissors. If carefully picked from a clean place they will not need washing.

DANDELION IDEAS

Dandelion and other Greens

Use dandelion greens in recipes for mustard greens, spinach, chicory, and other greens. They are delicious seasoned with minced ham, crisp crumbled bacon, vinegar, lemon juice, and sliced or chopped, hard-boiled eggs. Try mixing them with other spring greens, especially those with a bland flavor, such as comfrey.

Dandelion Beet Salad

Mix fresh, young dandelion greens or blanched crowns with cooked, sliced beets and pour a French or Italian dressing over them. Minced chives or scallions, and other salad greens or vegetables can be included.

Dandelion and Pasta

Mix hot, cooked dandelion greens with hot, cooked spaghetti or noodles. Toss with olive oil or butter, and Parmesan or another grated cheese. Serve immediately.

Dandelion Roots

If dug in early spring, when the crowns are harvested, dandelion roots make a pleasant cooked vegetable. They should be peeled since the skin is very bitter. Slice the roots, and bring to a boil in plenty of water. Drain to remove any remaining bitterness, then cook and season like carrots, or other root vegetables.

Dandelion roots can also be roasted for a beverage, and forced in winter for their blanched leaves, as for chicory roots. (Refer to the CHICORY section.)

DANDELION RECIPES

Spicy Stir-fried Dandelion Greens

(MAKES 6 SMALL SIDE SERVINGS, OR APPETIZERS FOR 6 TO 10)

1 tablespoon honey or sugar	¼ teaspoon cayenne pepper
2 tablespoons vinegar	2 tablespoons oil
1 tablespoon soy sauce	1 pound dandelion greens

Combine the sweetening, vinegar, soy sauce, cayenne pepper, and 1 tablespoon of the oil. Mix in the greens and marinate about 30 minutes. (The greens do not need chopping as they cook down enough to be handled with a fork or chop sticks.)

Drain the greens, saving the marinade. Heat a wok or heavy frying pan, and add the remaining tablespoon of oil. Stir-fry the greens 2 to 3 minutes. Add the marinade and heat quickly, stirring to combine thoroughly. This lively stir-fry is equally enticing served cold as an appetizer, or hot, with rice.

Dandelion Blossom Punch

(MAKES ABOUT 8 CUPS. DOUBLE AMOUNTS FOR A PARTY.)

1 quart dandelion blossoms, stems and calyx removed	½ cup honey or 1 cup sugar
2 quarts boiling water	1 orange
	½ lemon

Pour the boiling water over the dandelion blossoms and let stand overnight. Strain out and discard the blossoms. Add the sweetening and bring to a boil. Thinly slice the orange and lemon with their peels. Pour the boiling blossom water over them, then let stand at room temperature for 3 days. Strain, pour over ice cubes or chill in the refrigerator, and enjoy. The flavor evokes a pleasantly herbal soft drink.

Drying 🌿

In a dry climate it is direct, simple, and natural to dry food for storage. Even in humid climates the drying of certain foods, such as grains, mature beans, and herbs is taken for granted, and many other foods can be dried with some special attention. Primitive man learned very early that dry nuts, seeds, and fruits would keep all winter, and mankind has depended on dried foods ever since. Even with modern, mechanical refrigeration and freezing, and sophisticated canning techniques, there is a place for dried foods. Everyone depends on stored dry grains and flour, and dried fruits are widely used. In some parts of the world drying is an important means of storing vegetables, meat, and fish, as well. In China, huge quantities of vegetables and seafoods are dried, both commercially and in the home. These dried foods play an important and delicious part in Chinese cooking.

Anyone interested in food self-sufficiency is bound to consider drying as a method for storing at least some foods. It costs little or nothing and requires very little equipment, although specialized equipment is available. Dried foods are light, compact, and easy to store. Most can tolerate storage temperatures ranging from room temperature to way below freezing, so they can be stored anywhere if kept in protective containers or packages. Their quality is excellent for 6 months to a year or more, and they keep almost indefinitely without spoiling.

Still other advantages of dried foods are their flavor, nutritional excellence, and convenience. In dried fruits, for instance, natural sugars and nutrients, particularly minerals, are concentrated, making them an especially healthy, ready to eat sweet treat. The concentrated flavor of dried vegetables makes them outstanding when used as a seasoning. Dried vegetable shreds, flakes, or powder, kept handy on a kitchen shelf, can be added to soups, stews, or sauces in the same way as herbs. If desired, instant seasoning or soup mixtures can be prepared ahead. Dried mixtures which include meat are popular as hiking and camping foods, since they are easily carried and prepared.

Another virtue is that drying offers a different way to process familiar, plentiful foods. There is less monotony when foods, such as apples, are preserved in a variety of ways. If some are stored in the root cellar, some canned, and some dried, they will be three times as enjoyable.

Home drying is experiencing a renaissance as a modern food storage method. Many new and old ideas for drying foods

---

DRYING

Yield: Most dried foods are reduced to one fourth or less of their original volume and weight.

are surfacing, with many approaches, opinions, and sometimes disagreements to consider. Anyone who likes trying new things should enjoy experimenting with drying, using a variety of foods. There are probably plenty of interesting possibilities that have not been thought of yet.

FOOD DRYING FACTORS

Food dries when warm, dry air circulates around it, so temperature, humidity, and ventilation or air movement must be considered, along with the type and preparation of the food to be dried.

Food can be dried at temperatures ranging from about 90 to 150°F. However, caution is necessary when temperatures are either very low or very high in this range. At 90°F, humidity must be low, and air circulation must be good, or the food will spoil before it can dry. Food will not dry outdoors in humid 90°F weather, but it will dry very well on a breezy 90°F day in the desert. To dry foods successfully in spite of high humidity, extra heat and good ventilation must be provided.

When drying at high temperatures, in the 130 to 150°F range, care must be taken that food does not cook, or form a crust that seals in moisture and prevents complete drying. Foods are most apt to cook or form a crust at the beginning of the drying process, when they are full of moisture. Directions for using electric food dryers usually advise beginning with temperatures around 120°F and increasing as drying progresses.

Different drying temperatures and techniques can affect the texture and flavor of the food dried. For instance, slices of zucchini, cucumber, or banana dried quickly at a high temperature become crisp chips. Dried more slowly at a lower temperature, the zucchini or cucumber is papery rather than crisp and the banana is leathery and sweeter.

The ways in which dried foods will be used depends a great deal on their texture. If leathery but chewable, or crisp, they will probably be good eaten as is. If tough, or hard, or brittle, the food will need moistening or soaking, and probably cooking, before it is eaten. If hard foods can be ground to flakes or powders they may be very useful and versatile as seasoning ingredients.

METHODS AND EQUIPMENT FOR DRYING FOOD

Food can be air dried, solar dried, or dried with an artificial heat source. All home drying methods do essentially the same job, reducing the food's moisture to about 10 to 20% of the original content. Commercially, there are highly specialized dehydration methods that remove almost all the moisture, but these are not possible for use at home. Powdered milk, for instance, cannot be made at home.

The most practical home drying method changes with different circumstances, but one item of equipment is always useful. This is a movable drying tray or rack, or better yet, a set of them.

Drying Trays

Conveniently sized trays or racks that will fit both outdoor and indoor drying situations are ideal. The same trays may then be used as shelves in dryers, or hung over a wood stove, or propped up in the sun on the south side of the house. The best trays have bottoms that allow air circulation. Wooden frames or old window screens with fiberglass or plastic screening are excellent. Do not use metal screens or hardware cloth as the metal may contaminate the food. Some drying trays have wooden slats or dowels placed ¼- to ½-inch apart, to hold the food. This wood should be a variety that will not flavor or stain the food. Cheesecloth or other cotton cloth can be laid on these trays if food is likely to drop through. Trays must always be positioned so that air can move under them.

Outdoor Drying

Nothing sounds easier than putting food outdoors and waiting for it to dry, and nothing is easier—if Mother Nature cooperates, the air is clean and dust free, the bugs and birds and rodents keep their distance, and the food itself is suitable for drying.

For outdoor air drying, warm, sunny, low-humidity weather is necessary. In some places, the entire summer is good for drying. In others, the requirements are a good weather forecast, luck, and a back-up system to finish drying food indoors. Anyone who has made hay in a humid climate knows the problems.

Food can be dried in either sun or shade, but generally fruit is sun dried and vegetables are protected from direct sunlight (see below). There are many ways to arrange food outdoors so that warm, dry air can reach it. It may be hung on clotheslines, threaded on strings and hung from eaves or under porch roofs, or it may be spread on racks or trays in the sun, or in an airy, shady place. The intense heat on a flat or gently sloping roof, or the reflected heat from a south facing wall, can sometimes be used to advantage. Screened enclosures are often used for protection from animals, and a light cloth cover will protect food from dust. Often it must be covered at night, or taken indoors away from night dampness and dew. When drying outdoors the best method must be worked out according to individual circumstances and the food to be dried.

In humid or cool climates a solar dryer can make the difference between the success and failure of outdoor drying.

Solar Dryers

Any enclosure that traps the sun's heat and allows good air circulation can be used as a solar dryer. Generally, achieving air circulation is a greater challenge than collecting heat. Enclosures heat quickly in the sun, as anyone knows who has climbed into a closed car on a sunny day.

Home built solar dryers range from finished cabinets with removable trays to temporary glass- or plastic-covered structures with sides open for air to circulate. Cold frames can be converted for summer use as solar dryers. They must be propped up so that air enters under the food and exits at the top, above the food. Old cars can be used if openings for air circulation can be made and covered with screen or cloth. Heat can be increased by painting a solar dryer flat back, and arranging a plastic or glass panel so it faces the sun. A thermometer that measures up to 200°F, like an oven or dairy thermometer, is an important aid.

Plans for building solar dryers are available from many sources. Ready-made dryers can also be purchased. (See REFERENCES at the end of this section.)

Indoor Drying

Most homes have warm, dry areas suitable for drying food. Attics are usually good places for drying herbs, nuts, and small quantities of grain. For foods that need more attention, the dry heat that radiates from wood-burning stoves, furnaces, or appliances, such as refrigerators and hot water heaters, can be used. Do not, however, put food directly in the path of hot air from a furnace because of dust and possible contamination from fumes. In a pinch, food can be dried in a regular oven if the temperature can be set as low as 150°F and the oven door propped open for ventilation. Ovens are too expensive and inefficient to be used often for drying, but they may save a batch of food during rainy weather. Food can be dried in the heat left in the oven or warming oven of a wood-burning cookstove after the fire burns out, as long as it is moved when the fire is rebuilt.

The same trays used outdoors or in solar dryers can be hung or propped up over the indoor heat source. If the area is dusty, lay a light cotton cloth over the food.

The most carefree, though not the cheapest, way to dry food is with an electric dryer.

Electric Dryers

Home electric dryers are becoming more and more popular. Plans for making them are available from many sources, or they can be purchased ready to use. (See REFERENCES at the end of this section.) Units with built-in thermostats and controlled airflow take the guesswork out of food drying and ensure uniform results. They are, for many people, worth the expense.

BASIC FOOD DRYING STEPS

PREPARATION   Harvest food carefully, avoiding washing, if possible. If necessary, rinse quickly. Cut large pieces to a uniform size.

SPREADING OUT TO DRY   Spread pieces of food in a thin layer on drying trays or racks, or hang or otherwise arrange so that air circulates freely around it. Begin drying as soon as possible after preparation and avoid interruptions in the drying process.

REARRANGING WHILE DRYING   Stir, turn, or rearrange pieces of food to be sure they dry evenly. Change the position of drying trays if necessary. Check the temperature often, and adjust if required.

TESTING FOR DRYNESS   When food appears dry, cool a few pieces. Cut or break leathery foods and squeeze. If moisture appears, drying is incomplete. Break hard or brittle pieces to see if they are dry inside. Check the larger pieces particularly. The pieces that dry first can be removed. Do not leave thoroughly dry food in a dryer at higher temperatures. It may scorch.

OPTIONAL PASTEURIZATION   If contamination by insect eggs is a possibility, pasteurize the dried food by putting it, still spread out, in the oven at 175°F for 10 to 15 minutes according to the size of the food pieces. Another way to destroy insects and eggs is to freeze the dried food at 0°F for 3 to 4 days. Insect infestation is most likely on fruits dried outdoors.

STORAGE   Cool dried food to room temperature before sealing in airtight containers. See STORING DRIED FOOD, below.

PREPARATION FOR DRYING

Dried food of high quality results from properly prepared fresh food of high quality. Though preparation varies for different foods, generally small, uniform slices or pieces of food dry faster and better than large chunks. Mechanical slicers, choppers, and graters are helpful to achieve uniformity.

Different sources recommend different predrying treatments for various foods. Most of these treatments are optional, and some are unnecessary where small batches of food can be quickly prepared and set to dry. However, there are other treatments which are very helpful. These are described with their pros and cons in the following pages. For more extensive information see the REFERENCES at the end of this section.

DRYING FRUIT

(Also refer to the storage information in individual fruit sections elsewhere.)

Most fruits dry easily and well. Their acids and sugars help protect them from spoilage as they dry. Completely ripe or slightly overripe fruit makes the sweetest, most flavorful dried fruit.

Predrying treatments are seldom necessary if small batches of fruit are handled quickly. Anti-oxidant and sulphur treatments prevent darkening of the fruit and, in some cases, minimize vitamin loss. Darkening is more likely with sun drying, but it does not affect flavor, so there is no real need to prevent it. If desired, however, darkening can be minimized by dipping the fruit in lemon juice, pineapple juice, or ascorbic acid just before drying. Occasionally blanching or precooking is suggested for fruit, but it is of no particular benefit, except to crack the skins of firm berries. If necessary, however, cooked fruit can be dried successfully.

Sun drying is the traditional method for drying fruit, and the results make delicious snacks. The sun seems to bring out sweetness and flavor, but fruit dried indoors or in the shade is also excellent.

Home-dried fruit intended for long storage must be more leathery, or drier, than most commercially dried fruits. The latter are kept moist with preservatives and other controls that are neither available nor desirable for home use. (The extra moisture also means the fruit weighs more for sale by the pound.) Home-dried fruit should feel tough, and no moisture should show if a piece is cut and squeezed. Berries and a few other fruits will be hard when dried, rather than leathery.

If fruit is dried quickly and in large pieces, it may need conditioning before it is stored. Conditioning ensures that all the fruit is evenly dried. Put the dried fruit in open containers in a dry, airy place at about room temperature for 10 days to 2 weeks. Stir the fruit every day. It can be packaged and stored.

Fruit Leather or Roll-Ups

Drying puréed fruit to make a thin, pliable sheet of "leather" is a delicious way to preserve it for snacking. Leather is usually made from raw fruit, but cooked fruit, such as smooth applesauce, is also very good. Combinations of sweet and tart fruits, and variations that include ground or finely chopped nuts and seeds, are delicious. Honey or other sweetening may be added, as well as such spices as cinnamon or nutmeg. Thin purées, like those from juicy berries, are easier to dry if they are first thickened. One method is to process chopped raw apple in a blender with the purée. Chia seeds and ground flax seeds are also good thickeners. The very thick pulp left from making fruit juices, particularly apple, can also be used. There are many possible combinations.

Drying Fruit and Other Purées

Spread purées in a layer about ¼-inch thick on a non-stick surface. A lightly oiled baking sheet, freezer wrap, or heavy plastic make convenient drying surfaces. Spread the purée as evenly as possible with a table knife or the back of a spoon. If using a dryer with several stacked shelves or trays, cover the right half of one tray, the left half of the next and so on. This allows air to circulate easily around the food. Sun drying is an excellent method for fruit leather.

Dry fruit purées until the top surface becomes less sticky and the sheet of fruit holds together in one piece. Then turn it over to dry the other side. Dry until leathery and somewhat tough. The sheet should be pliable, but not soft. Some fruit leathers may remain a little sticky even when dried. Purées other than fruit may become too crumbly for turning. These can just be loosened or crumbled and left until they are uniformly dry.

Store fruit leather and other dried purées in airtight containers. (See STORING DRIED FOOD, below). Fruit leather may stick together when stored, so it is a good idea to put waxed paper between layers. If the leather is to be rolled, lay waxed paper on each sheet and roll them up together.

Drying Apples, Melons, Pears, Persimmons, Quinces

Core or remove seeds. Peeling is optional and depends on the toughness of the skins. They tend to become more tough or hard when dried. Slice the fruits about ¼-inch thick and lay on drying trays, preferably one layer deep. Turn slices once or twice during drying. Slices may also be threaded on strings and hung to dry. It may be necessary to use spacers, such as short sections of plastic straws, between slices to keep them from bunching. Another way to dry these fruits is to dice them for use like raisins. Dry until leathery and somewhat tough.

Drying Stone Fruits

Stone fruits are usually halved and pitted before drying, and large fruits like peaches must be pitted to dry properly. It is best not to peel stone fruits because skins are thin and tender, and they also hold in juices. Peaches can be rubbed to remove fuzz. Arrange pitted halves on drying trays, cut side up, so that juice collects in the hollows. Turn them when the cut side is dry enough not to stick to the drying tray. Stone fruits may also be cut in wedges or slices, or diced for drying. The smaller pieces dry fastest. Turn them several times during drying, and dry until leathery. Very sweet fruit may be sticky when dry, but it should not be soft inside or show moisture when squeezed.

Drying Small, Firm Fruits such as Blueberries, Grapes, Rosehips, Cherry Tomatoes

These fruits when whole have naturally waterproofed skins which slow the drying process. If the skins are cracked, the fruits dry much more quickly, but this is optional. Each berry or fruit can be nicked with a knife, but it is much quicker to blanch them in boiling water to break the skins. (This is sometimes called "checking," because of the fine, often checkered, pattern of the breakage.) Put them in a strainer or colander in small batches and immerse in rapidly boiling water for 15 to 30 seconds, then dunk them in cold water and drain. Spread in a single layer on drying trays. If the fruit might fall through the trays, spread cheesecloth or any thin cotton cloth on the tray first.

Some of these fruits will become hard and others leathery when dry, but there should be no moisture inside when a fruit is broken open.

Drying Soft Berries

Soft berries are slow to dry and do not retain their original flavor. They are probably best dried as fruit leather. If dried whole they become hard, and can be ground for the fruit meal described below, or used for tea. They are not especially good as snacks or cooked fruit.

If possible, avoid washing soft berries. Otherwise, rinse them very quickly. Spread in a single layer on drying trays. (Large strawberries should be cut in half.) Begin drying immediately and do not interrupt the drying process unless they are almost dry, as they spoil easily. Dry until hard, with no moisture showing when broken open.

USING DRIED FRUIT

Often the kinds of fruit dried at home are less sweet than familiar commercially dried fruits, such as raisins, dates, figs, and prunes. Most of the fruits with an extra high sugar content grow in warm climates. Dried sweet cherries are one of the sweetest dried fruits from a temperate climate. They also make delicious snacks, but some other dried fruits may be too tough or hard to enjoy as is. These fruits can be moisturized for snacking. They are also delightful additions to baked goods, or they can be soaked for a day or two to make "stewed fruit" without any stewing.

Moisturizing Dried Fruits

Dried fruit that is too tough or hard to chew can be softened in several ways. In a humid climate, it can simply be taken out of its container and exposed to the air for a few days. In a dry climate, a slice of raw apple can be added to the container. The dried fruit can also be covered with water, drained immediately, and kept in a closed container for a day.

Fruit Meal

Fruit that becomes hard when dry, such as rhubarb and most berries, can be ground in a mill or blender. This meal is excellent added to baked goods, sprinkled on cereal or other foods, or made into herb tea (refer to the HERBS section). A quick jam or sauce can be made by mixing the meal with a little hot water, letting it sit a few minutes, and then mixing in honey to taste.

If dried fruit should accidentally have a browned, faintly scorched flavor because of drying too long at a high temperature, it can often be used as fruit meal.

DRYING VEGETABLES

(Also refer to the storage information in individual vegetable sections elsewhere.)

The quality of most dried vegetables is best when dried away from direct sunlight, as the sun fades them and leaches out flavor. (If using an outdoor dryer designed to expose foods to sunlight shining through glass or plastic, cover the glass or plastic in a way that leaves ventilation holes open. Cloth or wood can be used.)

Small vegetables, or those that have been chopped, grated, or thinly sliced, dry more quickly with better quality than larger chunks. Small pieces are also more convenient because they need less soaking and cooking time. They can be easily added to soups, stews, and sauces. Flaked or powdered vegetables make an almost instant seasoning. The starchier, dried vegetables, such as potatoes, winter squash, and mature beans and peas, can be ground and used as flour.

Blanching or cooking is recommended for many vegetables before drying. Raw, unblanched vegetables cut into small pieces dry well, but many lose flavor and vitamins after 6 months or so of storage. Precooked vegetables should retain quality for a year or more. In addition, precooking softens tissues, so vegetables dry faster and need less soaking and cooking time afterward. Vegetables used only for seasoning, such as onions, do not need blanching. With other vegetables, blanching is probably best unless they will be used within a few months.

Although called blanching, the cooking of vegetables before drying is much more complete than the quick blanching required before freezing. Generally, vegetables should be cooked through. Cooked, leftover vegetables can be dried successfully as long as they have not been mixed with butter or oil. Steaming is the best precooking method, because it removes fewer nutrients and is less apt to add unwanted water.

Drying Root Vegetables, Tubers, Winter Squash

These solid, non-watery vegetables dry very well. They taste like the fresh vegetable after soaking and cooking. Soaking and cooking times vary according to the size and toughness of the pieces. Large, tough pieces may need to soak an hour or longer, and cook a half hour or longer. Use the same water for soaking and cooking. If grated, finely chopped, or very thinly sliced before drying, vegetables can be added to soups, stews, and sauces without soaking.

Precooking or blanching is optional, but flavor is retained longer in storage if it has been done.

It is often practical to store root vegetables and tubers in the root cellar until midwinter and then, when there is time, dry those that might not be used by spring. If dried root vegetables are left over when a new crop comes in, they can be roasted and ground for a beverage.

Drying Onions, Sweet and Hot Peppers, Mushrooms

These and other vegetables used primarily for seasoning do not need precooking or any other treatment before drying. Chop them small or slice very thinly, so they can be added directly to foods without soaking. If brittle when dried, they can be crushed to flakes as for hot peppers.

Drying Asparagus, Green Beans, Sweet Corn, Eggplant, Okra, Summer Squash

For these and most other vegetables, precooking or blanching is optional, but improves the quality; sweet corn must be precooked (refer to the CORN, SWEET section). Thin slicing or chopping of larger pieces will improve their quality.

Before using, these vegetables should be soaked in water to cover until they have swelled to their original size, then simmered until tender.

Drying Leafy Greens

(Also refer to DRYING HERBS, in the HERBS section.) Although some greens, especially cabbage and Chinese cabbage, are dried and used in large quantities, drying is not most people's choice for storing greens. Freezing generally preserves their fresh flavor best, but some do well in cold storage and some are good canned. If greens must be dried, their color and flavor are best preserved by first steam blanching. Where necessary, prepare greens by cutting out heavy midribs and stems. Cut large leaves in half. Some greens may be shredded. Put small batches loosely in a steaming basket and steam until wilted, about 5 minutes for tender greens, longer for coarse or thick leaves. Spread on drying trays, with a minimum of overlapping. Most greens will be crumbly when dried.

Reconstitute dried leafy greens by pouring boiling water over them in a saucepan and simmering until tender, usually about 10 minutes.

USING DRIED VEGETABLES FOR SOUP

Dried vegetables are ideal for making soup. They have been precut to a small size before drying, so no preparation is necessary, except perhaps a few minutes of soaking. Drying intensifies the flavor of most vegetables, improving the soup. A mixture of dried vegetables can be kept handy for quick soups of all kinds. If dried vegetables are ground to a powder, they make an almost instant vegetable broth.

Dried, Chopped Vegetable Soup Combinations

Vegetables must be dried separately and mixed after drying. A vegetable combination that is good fresh, such as onion, celery, carrot, and green pepper, is also good dried. Dried herbs, and vegetables such as mushrooms, okra, or tomato can be included to taste.

Dried vegetables in a soup mixture should be about the same size so they cook in the same amount of time. Vegetables which require a long soaking time, such as dried sweet corn, should not be included. They can be soaked separately and added to soup. A soup combination made of vegetables chopped small or grated requires a short cooking time. Add 1 to 2 tablespoons dried vegetables to each cup of cold water, soup stock, or other liquid. Heat and simmer about 10 minutes, and the soup is ready.

Some strongly-flavored vegetables, such as chopped, dried asparagus, make delicious soups, but are not good in combinations, except with a few vegetables, such as onion or potato.

Vegetable Soup Powder

Any dried vegetable soup mixture can be ground to a powder in a blender, grain mill, or other grinder, as long as the vegetables have been completely dried until brittle or crumbly. If they are at all pliable, they will gum up the grinder. A few vegetables, such as onions, may be brittle when dried but absorb enough moisture later to become pliable again. These can be dried briefly in a low oven or food dryer just before grinding. Store the powder in an airtight container and try to use within 6 months, as it loses flavor with time.

Mix vegetable soup powder with water or soup stock, heat to a boil, and it is ready. The powder can also be added to hot water or soup stock and simmered briefly.

STORING DRIED FOOD

The key to safe storage of dried food is first making sure the food is completely dried, then protecting it so it cannot reabsorb moisture. Foods dry enough for storage have a characteristic look and feel. Some will be hard or brittle, some crumbly or papery, and some leathery or tough. If in doubt about a food's dryness, continue drying until there is no doubt. If food is dried in large or thick pieces, break open a few to check the inside for moistness. Dried food should be cool when packaged, as it can sweat if enclosed while still warm. If moisture should collect inside storage jars of dried food, open them and spread out the food to dry a while longer. With experience it becomes easier to tell when a food is thoroughly dry.

Where the climate is humid, it is essential to keep dried foods in airtight, moisture-proof containers. Even in dry climates, sealed containers are best to keep out insects and rodents. Jars or cans with tight lids are best. Containers with loose lids can be used if waxed paper is laid over the container's mouth and pressed down with the lid to seal it.

Some dried foods fade and lose flavor when exposed to light, so opaque containers or a dark storage area are recommended. Cool, dry storage areas are best, but most dried foods can tolerate ordinary room temperatures, and good packaging can protect them from high humidity.

Damage is sometimes caused by insects or eggs that get on dried food before it is packaged. If this is a problem, they can be destroyed by pasteurizing the dried food. (See BASIC FOOD DRYING STEPS, earlier in this section.)

Moist or partially dried fruit can be stored in the freezer as a handy snack, but it is more economical to dry the fruit completely, store it in the regular way, and then moisten it for eating. (See MOISTURIZING DRIED FRUITS, earlier in this section.)

Dried foods retain their quality for 6 months to a year or even several years, depending on the food type and its preparation.

REFERENCES FOR DRYING

DeLong, Deanna, *How To Dry Foods,* 1979, H.P. Books. (A new edition is expected in 1988.)

Hertzberg, Ruth, *Putting Food By,* The Stephen Greene Press, 1982.

MacManiman, Gen, *Dry It, You'll Like It,* 1975, Living Foods Dehydrators, P.O. Box 546, Fall City, Washington, 98024. (This booklet includes plans for building an electric dryer.)

USDA Farmer's Bulletin, No. 984, *Farm and Home Drying of Fruits and Vegetables.*

Eggplant

There is a novelty variety of eggplant whose small creamy white fruits look like hen's eggs, but the most familiar varieties look more like purple-black ostrich eggs. In between are many shapes and colors including a long, thin, almost snake-like variety, and another with stripes. In the Mediterranean region, the most popular are small and elongated, like a small zucchini squash. In spite of such variations, all eggplants respond to cooking in much the same way.

Eggplant is a challenging vegetable. On its own it whets no one's appetite, but in the hands of a good cook it can be transformed into extraordinary dishes, some so renowned as to be legendary. Imam Bayildi is the eggplant dish that made the Imam faint—whether from shock at the cost of the olive oil it soaked up, or from delight at its flavor is not known. Moussaka is claimed by both the Greeks and the Turks, and is enjoyed throughout the Middle East. In France, Ratatouille is a classic vegetable stew, and Caponata and Eggplant Parmigiana are two of many superb eggplant dishes from Italy. Excellent but un-

---

EGGPLANT STORAGE

Canning
(Not attractive, so best in mixed dishes.) Slice, or cube. Salt lightly, cover with cold water. Soak 45 min., drain. Boil in fresh water 5 min. Drain, pack, add boiling cooking water, 1 in. headroom. Process 240°F, 11 pounds pressure. Pints: 30 min. Quarts: 40 min. Refer to the CANNING section.

Cold Storage
Harvest before frost. Keep in root cellar or refrigerator up to 2 months. Refer to the COLD STORAGE section.

Drying
(Quality is good.) Slice to ¼ in. thick. Cook until tender, 5–10 min. in boiling water with 6 tbsp. vinegar or 4 tbsp. lemon juice added per gallon. Dry until brittle. Refer to the DRYING section.

Freezing
(Tends to be soggy when thawed.) *Slices or Cubes* Blanch 4 min. in boiling water with ½ c. lemon juice or vinegar added per gallon. May separate slices to be used for frying (refer to FREEZING SLICES, in the FREEZING section). Refer to the FREEZING section generally.

1 pound = about 3 cups diced raw; 2 medium eggplants = about 1 quart cooked

Eggplant

heralded eggplant dishes come also from India and the Far East, and from the southern United States. Wherever eggplant is grown, there is a way to make it taste delicious.

Aubergine is the French and British name for eggplant, and some cookbooks use that term.

HANDLING EGGPLANT

Eggplant can be harvested as soon as its skin becomes glossy. Young eggplants of about ¼ to ½ their full grown size are especially tender and delicious. If left too long before picking, eggplants become seedy, often tough and bitter as well. Bitterness may also occur if picked before the skins become glossy, or when stunted from poor growing conditions.

Eggplant is not well-suited for long-term storage. Although it can be canned, dried, and frozen, it is not as useful after processing as most other vegetables. It loses its special texture and may change flavor slightly. The best ways to preserve it are dried plain, or frozen in such dishes as vegetable stews and casseroles that contain a minimum of oil or fat. It freezes well in tomato mixtures. Otherwise, it is best enjoyed as a summer vegetable, and as late into the fall as it will keep in the refrigerator or root cellar.

Eggplant is virtually always cooked before it is eaten. Cooking methods range from frying through stewing, stuffing, mashing, and charcoal broiling whole. If the eggplant is to be sliced or cut before cooking, delay cutting until the last minute to prevent darkening.

Removing Bitterness from Eggplant

The ideal approach to bitterness is to avoid it by using only young, freshly harvested eggplants. There are, however, several ways to remove bitterness should it occur. Halves, slices, or cubes of eggplant can be blanched for 3 or 4 minutes in boiling water with a little vinegar added, then patted dry with a towel. (This is similar to preparing it for freezing or drying. Refer to the food storage information above.) Another method is pressing or squeezing out the bitter juices. If very

---

EGGPLANT IDEAS
Small Eggplant, Roasted Whole

Select one small, unblemished eggplant per person. Roast the eggplants on a rack in a moderate oven until the stem end feels soft, about 45 minutes. Feel them rather than puncturing to test for doneness. They swell up while roasting, and it is more fun to let everyone do his own puncturing and seasoning. Have butter or olive oil and lemon wedges on the table when the eggplant is served. Minced parsley and garlic or onion can also be on hand.

Eggplant Cakes

Finely mince raw eggplant together with a little onion. Squeeze out as much moisture as possible by hand, or by twisting in clean cloth. The volume will be considerably decreased. Mix eggplant with 1 or 2 lightly beaten eggs and enough flour to hold the mixture together. Season with pepper, and such herbs as parsley or celery leaves. Cook as thin patties in a well-oiled frying pan, turning once to brown both sides.

Mashed Eggplant

Cook the eggplant whole by steaming, boiling, baking, or charcoal broiling until soft. Instead of broiling over

thinly sliced or chopped small, eggplant can be pressed under a plate or a small board weighed down with something heavy, such as a rock or container of nails. Moisture will collect on the pieces in about an hour, and can be removed by patting them dry with a towel. Grated or minced eggplant can be squeezed in a towel like grated cucumber to remove juice. (Refer to the CUCUMBERS section.)

For very bitter eggplant, the most effective treatment is sprinkling the cut pieces with salt and draining them for an hour. They can be weighted down for quicker draining. (Salting vegetables is usually an objectionable practice because it causes loss of vitamins and minerals, but as eggplant is poor in these, the loss is minimal.) After draining, rinse the pieces in cool water, squeeze gently, and pat dry with a towel.

These treatments also make eggplant more pliable and cause it to soak up less oil when cooked, often desirable even when no bitterness is present.

Elderberries

Most species of elderberries do not taste particularly good raw, but they improve greatly when cooked. They are truly delectable if dried and then cooked, and are also appreciated for their juice, which is delicious canned, or can be made into jelly and wine. (Refer to the JAM AND JELLY section.)

Elderberry flowers are also edible, and are sometimes called elder blow. Fresh elderflowers can be added to pancakes and muffins, or dipped in batter and fried as fritters. Dried flowers can be used like an herb for tea or for flavoring. Fresh or dried, they are known as a flavoring in vinegar and as an ingredient in homemade cosmetics. Wild elderberries are common in many places and can be harvested in large quantities. They are also easily cultivated. This easy availability plus their remarkably high vitamin C content makes elderberries a valuable fruit, well worth including in any family's food supply.

charcoal, the eggplant can be set directly on top of a moderately hot wood-burning stove, and turned often, until the skin on all sides is blackened and the inside is soft. Peel, pull, or rub off the skin. Mash the eggplant with a fork, or in a food mill or blender. Season and serve as a side dish, or mix with bread crumbs, egg, and seasonings and fry as patties.

Eggplant Dip
Mash cooked eggplant as above and beat in a little olive oil, lemon juice, crushed garlic, and salt, to taste. Yogurt can also be included. Serve the dip sprinkled with minced parsley. The flavor is especially good when the eggplant is charcoal broiled or cooked on the stovetop as described above.

This Middle Eastern favorite goes well with flat, Middle Eastern style bread. It is also delicious as a raw vegetable dip.

ELDERBERRY STORAGE
Canning
Caution! Add 2 tablespoons lemon juice or ½ teaspoon citric acid to every quart of juice, sauce, or whole berries before processing to increase acidity. For whole berries refer to the BLUEBERRIES section. Also see CANNING

ELDERBERRY RECIPES

Dried Elderberry Chutney

(MAKES ABOUT 4 PINTS)

2 cups cider vinegar
½ cup honey
3 cups dried elderberries
1 large onion, minced
    1 clove garlic, pressed
      or minced

½ lemon, finely sliced with peel
1 teaspoon ginger powder or minced
    fresh root
¼ teaspoon cayenne or other
    hot pepper
1 tablespoon mixed pickling
    spices

Heat the vinegar, honey, and 1 cup of water to make a syrup. Add the elderberries, onion, garlic, lemon, ginger, and cayenne. Tie the pickling spices in a small square of cheesecloth and add to the pot. Simmer, uncovered, stirring often to prevent sticking, until the mixture has cooked down and thickened. Remove the cheesecloth bag, and pour into hot canning jars. Process 10 minutes in a boiling water bath, as described in the CANNING section.

Fresh Elderberry Chutney

Omit the cup of water and use 2 pounds of fresh instead of dried berries. The elderberries can be mashed before they are added to the pot.

Elderflower Face Cream

(FROM "THE FARMERS WEEKLY," COUNTRYWISE BOOKS, 1966.)

"Melt 1 lb. pure lard in saucepan and add as many handfuls of elderflowers (stripped from stalks) as lard will cover. Simmer gently for about 1 hour. Strain through fine sieve or muslin. Before pouring into small screw-top jars, add a few drops of oil of lavender or other good scent. Use when cold. I make this face cream every year; my grandmother—and no doubt many other people's grandmothers—used it lavishly, for they found it unfailingly good." *Miss A. Williams, Cardiganshire*

Other versions say to add a few drops of turpentine instead of lavender, or to use vaseline or cocoa butter instead of lard.

FRUIT JUICE AND SAUCE, in the FRUITS section, and *Dried Elderberry Chutney*, above.

Drying

(Excellent. The flavor improves with drying.) Blanch briefly to crack skins (optional). Spread on trays and dry until hard. Refer to the DRYING section. For elderflowers refer to DRYING HERBS, in the HERBS section.

Freezing

Dry-pack plain raw elderberries in containers, or make sauce or juice. Refer to the FREEZING section.

ELDERBERRY IDEAS
Elderberry and Tart Fruit Combinations

Elderberries combine exceedingly well with tart, sour, or even astringent fruits. Those maturing around the same time as elderberries (crabapples, sour grapes, wild plums) are ideal, but rhubarb or cranberries that have been canned, frozen, or dried are also excellent. The proportions can be half and half, or to taste. Try making juice, jam and jelly, and pie. Refer to COMBINING SWEET AND TART FRUITS, in the FRUITS section.

Figs

Figs were one of the first cultivated tree fruits. They were grown in the Mediterranean area in ancient times, and were important in the lives and mythology of the early Greeks and Romans. In the story of the founding of Rome, a fig tree overshadowed the wolf's cave where the twins, Romulus and Remus, were raised. The tree symbolized the future prosperity of the race.

In North America, figs are grown commercially in California and Texas, and in home gardens in most of the southern United States. If given special care and protection, they will grow in regions with moderately cold winters. Fresh, tree-ripened figs are delicious, but as they do not keep well people who live outside their growing area can seldom enjoy them. Dried figs, however, are available and appreciated everywhere. Where figs are called for in recipes, dried figs are almost always what is meant.

Figs have a reputation as an herbal medicine. When fresh, they can be made into a poultice for boils and infections. They are also taken for insomnia, and as a laxative. The sap of unripe figs will curdle milk, so it is sometimes listed as a vegetable rennet for making cheese.

HANDLING FIGS

The time for harvesting figs depends on the variety and the intended use. Some varieties bear fruit twice a year. Figs grown in a marginally cool climate must be harvested before they are completely ripe because they sour if left on the tree. Figs for drying are often left to fall off the tree by themselves.

Figs can be canned or frozen, and are delicious pickled, or in jams and preserves, but drying is the primary preservation and storage method.

Drying Figs

Figs from the family tree in a marginal growing area should be picked when ripe, and dried like any other fruit. Small figs can be dried whole, but large ones should be cut in half and dried like peach halves. (Refer to the DRYING section.) Whole figs can be blanched in boiling water for 30 to 45 seconds before drying to crack the skin and make them dry faster.

FIG STORAGE
Canning

Select firm but ripe fruit. Do not peel or remove stems. Pour boiling water over, simmer 5 min. *Caution!* Lemon juice or citric acid must be added when processed in a boiling water bath. Drain, pack, add 1 tablespoon lemon juice per pint; 2 tablespoons per quart. If using citric acid, add ½ teaspoon per quart. Add boiling light syrup or cooking water, ½ in. headroom. Process in boiling water bath. Pints: 1 hr. 25 min. Quarts: 1 hr. 30 min.

Pressure process (omitting lemon juice), 240°F, 11 pounds pressure. Both pints and quarts: 10 min. Refer to the CANNING section.

Drying

(Preferred storage method for most varieties.) See DRYING FIGS, below.

Freezing

Cut off stem. Peel (optional). May dry pack plain or cover with any of the liquids listed in LIQUIDS IN WHICH TO FREEZE FRUIT, in the FREEZING section.

2–2½ pounds fresh = 1 quart canned or frozen

In warm, dry areas where figs are abundant, they are left on the tree until they are partially dry and fall to the ground. The ground is mowed or cleared ahead of time for easy gathering. They must be gathered every 2 or 3 days to prevent molding and insect infestation. Commercial figs are often sulfured or fumigated at this point, but such questionable treatments can be omitted by the home grower.

The partially dried figs are spread on racks or trays to finish drying. In some Mediterranean regions they are spread on a bed of rushes. Drying in the shade is recommended for some varieties, because the sun will toughen the skin. Figs are dried until firm and leathery, and no juice should show when they are squeezed. Keep dried figs in airtight packaging, like any other dried fruits.

In Lebanon, anise seed is used to ward off insects. After drying, each fig is individually dipped in a pan of boiling water containing a spoonful of anise seed. The figs are then spread out and redried before packaging.

FIG IDEAS
Dried Figs in Fruit Juice
Soak dried figs in orange, apple, or other fruit juice for several hours, or overnight. Serve like stewed fruit. A quicker method is to soak for a few minutes, then simmer over low heat until tender. For stuffed figs, drain the soaked figs, make a slit in each, and stuff with nutmeats. Roll in coconut or finely chopped nuts. Serve the rich soaking juice as a beverage.

Fig Parfait
For a fig parfait, chop or slice fresh figs and arrange in layers in a mold or dish, with sweetened whipped cream. Sherry, rum, or another liquor can be sprinkled over the figs or added to the whipped cream for flavoring. Freeze until solid and unmold for serving. Instead of whipped cream, softened vanilla ice cream can be used, then refrozen.

Freezing 🌿

Running a home freezer throughout the year is the most modern way to preserve food, but freezing foods for later use is as ancient as the presence of humankind in cold climates. Primitive peoples almost certainly kept food frozen in outdoor caches during the winter, and a few millennia later a nineteenth century cookbook gives directions for the proper thawing of food stored outdoors in below freezing weather. The advent of the home freezer has changed freezing from an occasionally useful practice to a highly effective year-round storage method.

There are drawbacks to the use of a home freezer, but they have little to do with the way it preserves food. Freezing is the best way to retain the freshness of many vegetables, and a wide assortment of other foods. It is, instead, the expense of operation, the possibility of mechanical failure, and the dependence on outside power that limits the home freezer's usefulness. In sharp contrast to canned and dried foods which keep without special attention once processing is complete, frozen foods are always vulnerable. Something as minor as an accidentally unplugged electrical cord can spoil a year's food supply, while such major problems as power outages are entirely beyond individual control. While these are not reasons to avoid using a freezer, they are reasons for limiting its use by storing part of the household's supply in a more self-reliant way. In deciding which method to use it makes sense to save the freezer for foods that lose quality or are difficult to process when stored in other ways. Green vegetables should, for instance, have priority over fruits that are just as good or better canned, dried, or root cellared.

FROZEN FOOD QUALITY

The quality of the food coming out of the freezer can only be as good as the quality of what goes into it. If fresh food at its peak in flavor and ripeness is prepared, packaged, frozen, and thawed according to directions its quality will be excellent. If directions are ignored and food is simply tossed into the freezer it will not necessarily spoil—it might even taste good for a month or so—but then drying, freezer burn, or enzyme action begin to take their toll.

Other vital requirements for quality in frozen food are a properly functioning freezer, and good protective packaging to exclude air and retain moisture. Within these bounds there is room for experimenting and trying new ideas.

Freezer Types and Temperatures

For highest quality and longest storage life, food should be frozen quickly, and stored at 0°F or below. Food remains edible as long as it stays frozen, but it loses flavor and texture faster as the temperature gets higher. A food that retains full quality for a year when stored at 0°F, might taste good for only a month or two stored at 30°F. It is prudent to keep a thermometer in the freezer.

The best freezers are those in which temperature does not vary. A chest type is better than an upright because less warm air will get in when it is opened. A freezer without an automatic defroster is better than one with a defroster, because the warming of the freezer walls during the defrosting cycle may gradually reduce food quality.

PACKAGING FOODS FOR THE FREEZER

Packaging for freezing must be airtight and moisture-proof, with as little air space as possible around the food inside the package. Pack rigid containers closely to exclude air. Wrappings should press tightly against the food, and all packaging must have airtight lids or seals. Double wrapping is one way to ensure a tight seal. Whole packages, including rigid containers, can be sealed inside plastic bags or another layer of wrapping. Watch packages in the freezer for punctures or lids that do not stay sealed. Any questionable ones should be re-wrapped.

Rigid Freezer Containers

For freezing soft and liquid foods use rigid containers. The best ones are the special freezer cartons sold in many stores, or glass jars with flared or straight sides. Containers with "shoulders" can break from the pressure of food expanding as it freezes. Glass jars with two-piece canning lids that will bulge to accommodate expanding food are excellent, but recycled food jars with good lids can also be used. Plastic containers should have lids that snap into place to make an airtight seal. If they do not seal tightly press a strip of freezer tape along the edge of the lid. Plastic containers that once held cottage cheese or ice cream can be recycled for freezer use if seals are checked. It is also possible to use rigid containers without lids by fitting plastic bags in them and filling and sealing the bags. Square or rectangular plastic containers take less freezer space than round containers.

Always leave an airspace in rigid containers to allow for food expansion while it is freezing. The space needed will depend on the liquidity of the food and the shape and size of the container.

Plastic Freezer Storage Bags

There is considerable concern among scientists about the safety of certain plastics made flexible with a chemical called phthalate or DEHP, as it is highly carcinogenic in animals. As a precaution, until more conclusive research results are publicized, the thinner more flexible plastic bags and food wrappings are not listed for food storage in this book. The heavy, freezer-strength plastic bags, however, are very convenient for packaging non-liquid foods. Their big advantage is that air can be more completely removed from them, giving better protection to odd-shaped pieces of food, so these are included here. It is important to remove air before sealing them.

Though plastic bags cannot usually be reused in the freezer, they can be tested for leaks by blowing them up like a balloon, pinching them closed, and watching for escaping air. If reusing the good ones, it is best to use two, one inside the other.

Freezer Wrap

Firm chunks of food can be wrapped in special freezer paper and sealed with freezer tape. Use only tough moisture-proof wrapping. (Neither waxed paper, nor thin plastic, nor aluminum foil give adequate protection.) The wrappings must press against the food and be neatly and tightly folded to exclude air. Use a "butcher wrap" or "drugstore fold," or any method that folds the seams over twice to make an airtight seal. Though freezer tape that sticks at below zero temperature is best for sealing, cheap masking tape will usually hold if the strips go completely around the package and overlap.

SPECIAL FREEZING TECHNIQUES

Freezing Slices

It is often helpful to be able to separate frozen food slices without thawing them. They will thaw more quickly, or where appropriate, they may be cooked without thawing. For a separator, put a piece of freezer paper or waxed paper between each slice before it is frozen.

Freezing Before Wrapping

Some foods freeze best spread on trays in a single layer with each piece separated. When frozen solid they are quickly packaged and returned to the freezer. As they do not stick together they can be taken out in any quantity, large or small, to use as needed. Some foods to handle this way are dollops of whipped cream, slices of tomato, and other vegetable and fruit pieces.

Freezing Food Cubes

Foods to be used in small amounts are very convenient frozen in ice cube trays or muffin tins. The solidly frozen cubes are then packaged and returned to the freezer. Later, one cube at a time can be removed for use. A muffin tin cup holds about twice as much as an ice cube tray section. If it is difficult to remove frozen cubes from a muffin tin run water on the bottom of the tin, loosening one or two cubes at a time, and catching them as they fall. Baby foods and minced herbs can be conveniently frozen in cubes. (Refer to the HERBS section.)

Concentrated Juice

It is possible to make concentrated juice or syrup by partially freezing fruit juice or maple sap, draining off the liquid, and discarding the almost clear ice that remains. Repeat the freez-

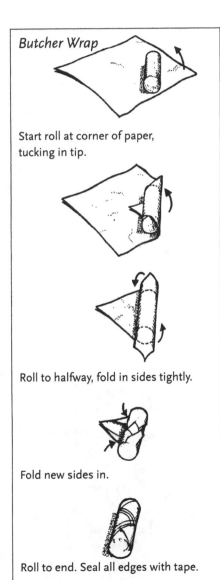

Butcher Wrap

Start roll at corner of paper, tucking in tip.

Roll to halfway, fold in sides tightly.

Fold new sides in.

Roll to end. Seal all edges with tape.

ing, draining, and discarding of ice several times or until the desired concentration is reached. It does take considerable time and attention to make a strong concentration with this method, but it has been used successfully both at home and commercially. Grape juice concentrated in this way retains the fruit's good, fresh flavor.

As the degree of freezing and draining time will vary under different conditions, those who want to try this approach must experiment for themselves. To avoid waste, only discard those ice crystals which are quite clear and tasteless.

FREEZING VEGETABLES

Freezing is the preferred way to preserve most green vegetables, as with this method they generally taste best and retain nutrients best. If stored at 0°F, they keep their high quality about 1 year. Most root vegetables and white or yellow vegetables are just as good or better canned or kept in a root cellar. Potatoes and cabbage do not freeze well in the home freezer, as ice crystals will form and break down their texture.

Wash and trim vegetables for freezing in the same way as for cooking. Cut large vegetables into uniform serving sized pieces. A quick precooking or blanching is recommended for vegetables before they are frozen.

Blanching Vegetables

Blanching is necessary to stop enzyme activity. Without it the vegetables gradually lose flavor and color and may also become tough. Anyone can discover that this is so by freezing a few test packages of raw vegetables, waiting six months, and then trying to eat them.

Blanching

Rapidly boiling water

Vegetables must be blanched quickly at a temperature as near boiling as possible, using boiling water, steam, or as an experiment, a microwave oven. (For the microwave, it is important to have even heating.) Steam blanching is often recommended because there is less leaching of nutrients into the blanching water, but it is harder to reach and maintain the necessary high temperature with steam. A good steamer with a tight lid is essential, and it is better to use boiling water than to make do with an inadequate steamer. (Refer to the STEAM COOKING section.)

Blanch vegetables in small batches of 1 to 2 pounds in plenty of boiling water or in a shallow layer in the steamer. An overload will slow down the blanching process and reduce quality. Generally blanching is complete when the vegetable changes color or turns a brighter green. Start timing only when the water has returned to a boil after the vegetables have been added. Steam blanching will take a minute or two longer than boiling water. (Blanching times are given in the storage information in each vegetable section.)

Once the vegetables are blanched, chill them quickly by dunking them in icy cold water for a minute or so to stop them cooking. This is most important for those green vegetables that overcook easily. Then drain, package, and freeze them at the coldest temperature possible. If ice water is not available, vegetables can also be cooled fairly well by spreading them out in a single layer on a clean cloth or other surface.

Frozen vegetables tend to taste best if cooked. Drop them, solidly frozen, into a small amount of boiling water in a saucepan, cover them, and cook just enough to heat them so they will not be over-cooked.

Freezing Leafy Greens

Greens which require from 10 to 15 minutes of cooking are better frozen than the very quick cooking greens, as they will withstand the rigors of both blanching for freezing and cooking again for serving. Such wild greens as dandelion and lamb's quarters are excellent for freezing, as well as kale, Swiss chard, and spinach, but Chinese cabbage, lettuce, and other delicate greens will lose texture and become mushy.

Blanch greens in boiling water, or cook them until wilted in just the water left on them from washing, rather than steaming them. (In a steamer the leaves tend to mat down into a solid layer, so that the steam cannot penetrate.) After cooking, spread the greens out to cool. If desired, chop them on a cutting board before freezing. Also freeze any liquid left from cooking greens, or use it in another way.

FREEZING GARDEN VEGETABLES
IN SOUP STOCK

Fresh garden vegetables frozen in stock make a very good base for all kinds of soups, bringing summer's flavors into winter meals.

Gather an assortment of vegetables, starting with such hearty ones as sweet corn, shelled green beans, and root vegetables. Add, perhaps, leafy greens, tomatoes, and onions, scallions, or chives. Include fresh herbs like basil or summer savory. Heat soup stock to a boil while cleaning, chopping, or otherwise preparing the vegetables. Use a minimum of stock for the quantity of vegetables. More liquid can be added once the soup mixture has been thawed. Put the slowest-cooking vegetables in the boiling stock first. When it returns to a boil add the quick-cooking vegetables and herbs, but do not add any other seasonings. Bring again to a boil, then chill quickly by setting the pot in a pan of cold water. When cool put the mixture in containers, label with the kind of stock and the primary vegetables used, and freeze. When thawed, other ingredients such as cooked chopped meat, cooked rice or noodles, and seasonings can be added. To save their garden fresh flavor, do not cook the vegetables any longer than necessary when making the soup.

(For precise freezing instructions also refer to the storage boxes in each specific vegetable section in the book.)

FREEZING FRUITS

Freezing is the best way to preserve the fresh taste of most kinds of berries, but other fruits are usually just as good canned, dried, or, in some cases, root cellared. Ice crystals form in many kinds of fruit when they are frozen, breaking them down and making them mushy when thawed. To avoid this, frozen fruits can be eaten only partly thawed.

Fruits may be packed plain for freezing, or covered with fruit juice or another liquid. Fruits that darken easily are usually covered with an acidic juice or with an ascorbic acid solution. Some fruits will be good made into fresh juice for freezing. (Refer to FRESH FRUIT JUICE, in the FRUITS section.) There is seldom any point in cooking and then freezing fruit. If fruit is to be cooked it is much more practical to can it for storage.

(For precise freezing instructions also refer to the storage boxes in each specific fruit section in the book.)

LIQUIDS IN WHICH TO FREEZE FRUIT

Fruit Juice

Use juice made from the fruit to be frozen or use any complementary fruit juice. If the fruit darkens easily use an acidic juice like orange, grapefruit, pineapple, or water flavored with lemon juice. (Refer to COMBINING SWEET AND TART FRUITS, in the FRUITS section.)

Pectin

Thin or diluted homemade pectin has a good flavor and a smooth pleasant texture. It will add healthy sweetness to the fruit and help prevent darkening as well. (Refer to the PECTIN section.)

Ascorbic Acid Solution

An ascorbic acid solution is often recommended to prevent darkening. Unlike other liquids it does not add flavor. Proportions for the solution vary from ¼ to ¾ teaspoon crystalline ascorbic acid dissolved in one quart of water. Use the larger amount for the fruits most subject to darkening.

Syrup

For a very light syrup heat 2 to 3 tablespoons honey, or maple syrup, or sugar in a quart of water. Bring to a boil, then cool completely. For a light syrup use ⅓ cup honey or maple syrup, or ½ cup sugar per quart of water.

Note: If the fruit floats in the liquid, crumple a piece of freezer wrap and put it on top of the fruit in the container to hold the fruit down. Otherwise the top pieces may darken.

FREEZING COOKED FOODS

Bread and other baked goods and many kinds of precooked mixed dishes are excellent frozen. Most people experiment to find out which dishes in what amounts are most practical for them.

For some it works well to make extra baked goods and cooked dishes to put in the freezer in the winter and early spring. The baked goods and cooked dishes can then be used during the busy late spring and summer months, making new space in the freezer for the season's harvests.

FREEZING CAUTIONS

- Remember that foods that have been frozen and thawed will spoil much more quickly than fresh raw food. Most spoilage organisms are not killed by freezing, but merely held in an inactive state. Once thawed, the organisms can quickly spoil food tissues already broken down by ice crystals during the freezing process.
- Keep a close eye on the freezer and be prepared to take action if it should stop for any reason. A generator might be used during a prolonged power outage, or use dry ice to keep the food frozen. Avoid opening the freezer when there are problems. Another alternative during freezing weather is moving the food outdoors in animal-proof containers. If the food does begin to thaw, can or dry as much as possible. Some of it can also be salted. The rest must be cooked and eaten, or perhaps cooked and returned to the freezer when it is again in operation. (If food is only partly thawed, with ice crystals still showing in it, it can safely be refrozen, but quality may be

noticeably lessened.) If foods are above refrigerator temperature, only the frozen fruits or other acid foods should be used or refrozen. Spoilage of fruit will show as fermentation or other quality loss.

- Keep the freezer as full as possible, as it takes less power to operate a full freezer. Empty and unplug a freezer with very little in it until it is needed again.

- Be aware that the flavors of some foods, especially seasonings, can change while they are stored in a freezer. Onions and salt lose strength over time. Others, such as pepper, cloves, garlic, celery, and sweet pepper may become strong or bitter tasting. Do not store highly seasoned foods for too long, and if possible plan to add seasonings when the food is cooked.

- Purées made in a blender or any device that whips air into them will lose quality faster in the freezer than sauces or purées made with a food mill or any method that mashes rather than whips. Cooking will drive the air out of blenderized foods, but then the fresh raw flavor will be lost.

Fruits

The ultimate in food enjoyment is surely the savoring of ripe, freshly picked fruit. No instruction book can improve the taste of a juicy, sun-warmed strawberry or a crisp apple picked on a cool fall day! Recipes and ideas for cooking, storing, and otherwise using fruit become helpful only after everyone has enjoyed as much as they want of the fresh fruit.

SEMI-TROPICAL FRUITS

These fruits grow only in limited areas of the southern United States, but as they ship well, they are seen in stores in many places.

Avocados

There are two main types of avocados that grow in North America—large avocados with rough or bumpy seeds from Florida, and smaller ones with smooth seeds from California and Hawaii. Avocados are not sweet, but are oil rich, containing unsaturated fatty acids and vitamins A and E. The fruits are not

---

FRUIT STORAGE

Canning

Refer to the CANNING section. Also see CANNING FRUIT JUICE AND SAUCE, below.

Cold Storage

Refer to the COLD STORAGE section.

Drying

Refer to the DRYING section.

Freezing

Refer to the FREEZING section. Also see FREEZING FRUIT JUICE AND SAUCE, below.

ripe until they feel soft when pressed. Firm fruits will ripen if kept at room temperature for several days to a week, or longer. When ripe, the stiff outer rinds peel off easily. Avocados are usually eaten raw and are delightful additions to salads with orange or grapefruit segments, or tomatoes. Mashed avocado is good in everything from soup to ice cream, but is best known as guacamole (avocado sauce), a versatile Mexican sauce. Mashed avocado can be frozen if 2 teaspoons of lemon juice are mixed with every cupful. To keep avocados after they have been cut open, leave the seed in the part to be stored, squeeze the cut part with lemon or lime juice, wrap it well, and refrigerate.

Citrus Fruits

Most people think of citrus fruits as oranges, grapefruits, lemons and limes, but there are many others. One is the kumquat, a distinctive fruit that looks like a miniature orange and is eaten in its entirety, rind and all. A large fruit called variously shaddock, pompelmous, or pummelo, is probably the parent of grapefruit. The most ancient of the citrus fruits is citron. Only its rind is edible, candied or pickled. (The citron melon whose rind is pickled is not related.)

Fresh, frozen, and canned citrus fruits and juice are shipped almost everywhere in North America, and are very familiar. Despite this, however, many have never tasted citrus fruits at their best—as fresh, tree-ripened fruit. Eating these, or drinking their freshly squeezed juice, is a heady experience, particularly the first time. If there is ever an opportunity to obtain them through special ordering, or during a trip to a citrus growing region, the experience is well worth the extra effort and expense.

Dried Citrus Peel

Most dried peels make a flavorful seasoning for a variety of foods. Though used in the same ways as fresh grated rind only one third as much is needed. Since most commercial citrus fruits have been heavily sprayed with chemicals, their peels cannot be recommended for eating. Whenever a source of unsprayed fruit becomes available, dry as much peel as possible for future use. When dwarf lemon, lime, or orange trees are grown as house plants, the peel of their fruits can be dried. Such peels generally taste good even if the fruit itself does not.

To prepare peels for drying, scrape or pull off any remaining fruit. Cut them in strips or any convenient size, and spread

---

FRUIT IDEAS
Mulled Fruit Juice

To mull means to heat and spice a beverage. Mulled cider is traditional, but most fruit juices are also excellent mulled. Heat the juice slowly with a cinnamon stick, a few whole cloves, and other whole spices, if desired. Thin slices of orange or lemon can be added. Strong juice can be diluted with water or blander juice. If it is tart, add honey. Heat slowly to blend flavors, then remove it from the stove before it boils.

For a festive occasion, homemade wine can be mulled. Mix it with juice for a mulled punch.

them out in a warm, airy place. A food dryer works well, but the peels will dry at room temperature also. Once they are hard or brittle, store them in an air-tight container. They can be ground in a blender or other grinder as needed, or they can be ground and then stored. However, if pre-ground they lose flavor faster. The different kinds of citrus peel can substitute for each other in recipes; though the flavor varies, the results are all good. As well, a teaspoon of dried citrus peel instead of a teaspoon of vanilla in baked goods, puddings, and other desserts is a surprisingly delicious substitution.

Kiwis

This well-travelled fruit originated in China, then moved to New Zealand where an unimaginative name, Chinese gooseberry, was changed to the catch-ier kiwi to make it more marketable, and now has taken the U.S. and Canada by storm. The fuzzy brown-skinned fruit, with its attractive lime-green flesh and soft edible black seeds, is familiar in grocery stores everywhere. The brown-skinned variety grows only in mild climates, but a new green-skinned, northern-hardy variety is now available from some plant nurseries. The plants are vines which grow much like grape vines.

Brown-skinned kiwis must be peeled before use. Press them to determine ripeness, as the skins always look the same. Their sweet-tart flavor is at its best when they are firm, yet not hard. If they soften too much they become bland and flavorless. Smooth, green-skinned kiwis do not need peeling, and are smaller and somewhat sweeter. Kiwi fruit is very high in vitamin C and potassium.

Kiwis are most often used sliced, to take advantage of the stunning color contrast between green fruit and black seeds, but they can also be eaten whole, halved, or chopped. They make a perfect addition to most fruit cups and salads, and can be cooked like any tart fruit. Slices are easily dried to make a delight-fully tart snack. No doubt they can also be frozen and canned successfully, but officially tested methods are not yet available.

Olives

Though olive trees will grow in many locations across the southern United States, they bear fruit only in certain areas of California and Arizona. To be pro-ductive they must have dry hot summers and cool winters. Olive oil is the most important olive product, and has often replaced butter and animal fat. Pressing olives for oil is similar to pressing apples for cider. Fully ripe olives are picked in winter when they contain the most oil, then ground, seeds and all, pressed, then reground, and pressed a few times more. The first pressing produces virgin olive oil, and later pressings a denser, greener oil with a stronger olive flavor. Many prefer the flavor of the later pressings.

The familiar, canned, green and black olives are picked when underripe, then processed in lye or salt to remove bitterness. The shriveled black olives, often called Greek olives, are picked after frosts, when they are no longer bitter. They are usually salt cured and stored in olive oil.

Pomegranates

The name means apple with many grains. They are also known as Chinese apples. Pomegranates are eaten fresh, or pressed for juice. To open, cut off the crown and slice through the rind from top to bottom in strips, without cutting into the red, juicy "seeds." The fruit can then be pulled apart along its natural divisions. It is refreshingly tart eaten as is. The seeds can also be added to salads, and sprinkled on foods for garnish. Fresh pomegranate juice is excellent. Separate the red seeds from the white pith before pressing, and do not press hard enough to crush the seed's kernel, which will give an off flavor. The seeds can also be cooked and strained to make juice. Grenadine, a sweet syrup used to flavor beverages, is usually made from pomegranates.

INSECTICIDES IN FRUIT

Most commercial fruits are treated with insecticides or other toxic chemicals at some time during growth and storage. Traces of them inevitably get inside the fruit where they cannot be washed or peeled off. It is well worthwhile, therefore, to raise or buy organically grown fruit, and to use wild fruit and fruit from neglected trees. If, however, the choice is between commercially raised fruit and no fruit at all, it seems best to eat and enjoy commercial fruit. However, processed fruit products that contain refined sugar or artificial sweeteners, preservatives, and artificial colorings and flavorings should certainly be avoided.

Insecticides on fruit skins are more successfully removed by washing in water containing a little vinegar or a few drops of detergent than by washing in plain water. Thorough rinsing is, of course, necessary. Peeling is another option, but this means the loss of vitamins, minerals, and flavor, which are often concentrated in or near the skin.

Fruit does not have to look perfect to taste delicious. Unsprayed or wild fruit may have superficial blemishes that can be trimmed off, or ignored. Seriously blemished or damaged fruit can often be trimmed and made into juice or sauce.

COMBINING SWEET AND TART FRUITS

The range among fruit flavors is very broad, but most fruits can, nevertheless, be categorized as either sweet or bland, or tart or sour. Flavor-enhancing combinations can then be suggested to make sweet or bland fruits more piquant, and tart or sour fruits more mellow and sweet. A common example is the lemon juice so often sprinkled on sweet fruits to enhance their flavor.

Mellowing combinations are particularly valuable for very sour fruits. Often, sour fruit is considered unusable except in heavily sweetened mixtures, such as jams, jellies, pies, and other desserts. Occasional treats of this kind are delicious, but there are less sugary ways to use sour fruit. Combining with sweet, bland fruits is ideal, since both flavors are improved and less additional sweetening is used. Fresh, dried, and canned fruits can be used, as well as juices and sauces. Very tart juices, from rhubarb, sour apple, or sour wild fruit, are useful when home canned in small jars for mixing with sweeter juices, and for adding to tea and other dishes instead of lemon juice.

SWEET-TART FRUIT COMBINATIONS

SWEET OR BLAND	TART OR SOUR
(The possibilities are infinite.)	
Sweet Apples	Sour Apples
Bananas	Sour Cherries
Domestic Blueberries	Most Citrus Fruits
Sweet Cherries	Crabapples
Elderberries	Cranberries
Melons	Currants
Mulberries	Gooseberries
Some Peaches	Kiwi
Pears	Pomegranates
Persimmons	Quinces
Rosehips	Rhubarb
Some Dried Fruits	Some Plums
(especially prunes, raisins,	Sour Grapes
figs, and dates)	Many Wild Fruits and Berries

MAKING FRUIT JUICE AND SAUCE

Juice can be extracted from most fruits, and sauce can be made from any pulpy fruit. Berry juice is delicious, and stone fruits like peaches, apricots, and plums make good juice or sauce. Juice is always popular, and it is amazing how much a family can drink when the supply is plentiful. Fruit juice can also be used in gelatins, and in many other mixtures.

There are two approaches to making both juice and sauce. One is to use raw fruit, and the other is to extract the juice or make sauce from cooked fruit. For fruits other than citrus, the second approach is easier, but fresh juice and sauce are delicious and worth some extra effort.

Fresh Fruit Juice

Juice is easily squeezed from oranges and other citrus fruits. Most soft, raw fruit can be pressed through a sieve or food mill, or whirled in a blender and squeezed in a cloth to extract juice. If the fruit is very juicy, the purée may be thin enough to drink without straining. Peeling fruit before juicing is usually unnecessary but large pits or seeds should be removed, and some chopping may be required. The small seeds in berries or grapes are removed when a food mill, squeezing strainer, or fine mesh sieve or cloth is used for straining. (Refer to SEEDINESS IN BLACKBERRIES, in the BLACKBERRIES section.)

Special equipment is needed to make juice from firm, raw fruits. They require chopping or grinding, then heavy pressure. Centrifugal juicers (best known for making carrot juice) will make juice in small quantities from most firm, raw fruits, but they are expensive and must be used almost every day to be worthwhile. Small quantities of juice can also be made by grinding firm fruit in a food chopper or processor and pressing it in a cloth bag under a heavy weight, or with an old-fashioned fruit and lard press. The equipment for making apple cider can be used for making juice from some other firm fruits. (Refer to the APPLES section.)

Juice from Cooked Fruit

When fruit is cooked until soft, the juice can easily be drained off or pressed out. The necessary equipment is a large cooking pot, and a big strainer or colander. If juice is made often, it would be worthwhile to purchase a steam juicer for extracting juice from fruit. Steam cooking can retain more of the fresh fruit flavor than boiling. A spigot or hose on the steamer drains off the juice when it is ready.

Peeling and seeding are generally unnecessary when cooking fruit for juice, since it will be strained later. Large fruits may be cut in pieces, and large pits may be taken out, if desired. A few peach or apricot pits can be left in for added flavor. Some water must usually be added, and the fruit must be stirred occasionally to help it cook evenly without sticking. Dry fruits may need to be covered with water. Fruits with tough skins, such as firm berries and grapes, should be mashed with a potato masher or similar tool to break the skins as they begin to cook. The flavor of some fruit juices is best if the cooking is kept at a simmer rather than a boil. (Refer to MAKING GRAPE JUICE, in the GRAPES section.)

To make clear juice strain through a cloth, allowing the juice to drip without squeezing the pulp. Juice strained through a sieve will be cloudy, but heartier in flavor. For a thick juice or nectar, some pulp should be pressed through the sieve with the liquid.

Homemade fruit juice is quite concentrated if made with a minimum of water and a long cooking time. Berries and wild fruits, in particular, make strong-flavored juices. These can be diluted for drinking, or used full strength to flavor gelatines, sherbets, and other dishes.

Pulp from Making Fruit Juice

There is a dryish pulp left when juice is extracted from raw or cooked fruit, which can be quite flavorful. A quick taste will determine whether it is worth saving. Spent pulp can be put in the compost pile. Pomace from making apple cider can be used for making pectin. (Refer to the PECTIN section.)

Most leftover pulp has enough flavor to make a second infusion of juice. Cover the pulp with water, heat to a boil, and strain. This juice can be mixed with the first batch, or used separately. Some very strong-flavored pulp can even be used for a third infusion. This diluted juice can be chilled, or poured over ice for a cool drink.

Other uses for fruit pulp are for making fruit sauce, butter, or leather, or fermenting it for vinegar. When a smooth-textured pulp is necessary, a strainer or food mill can be used to remove seeds, peels, and fibers. Thick, smooth pulp is ideal for making fruit butter (refer to the JAM AND JELLY section) and fruit leather (refer to the DRYING section).

Fruit Sauce

Most kinds of fruit make good sauces. Like juice, they can be made from either raw or cooked fruit. Soft, raw fruits can be mashed through a sieve, food mill, or food press. Other fruits can be peeled and cored or pitted as necessary, and puréed in a blender or food processor. Fresh fruit sauce should be eaten immediately since it darkens and loses flavor quickly.

Cooked fruit sauce can be made in several ways. Some fruits break down to a sauce when cooked, while others must be mashed or puréed. Most fruits can be "sauced" like apples. (Refer to the APPLES section.)

Canning Fruit Juice and Sauce

Acidic juices and sauces are among the easiest foods to can. (If a fruit's acidity is doubtful it is noted under CANNING in the box at the beginning of that section.) The juice or sauce should be heated to a boil, and poured into hot canning jars, leaving ¼ inch headroom for juice and ½ inch headroom for sauce. All modern canning guides require processing both pints and quarts for 10 minutes in a boiling water bath. (Refer to the CANNING section.) However, large quantities of acidic fruit juices are successfully home canned every year using the open kettle method. (Refer to OPEN KETTLE CANNING, in the CANNING section.) Thick sauces and purées should be processed in a boiling water bath, since it is hard to know if a thick sauce is heated to 212°F throughout, and hard to keep it very hot while pouring and sealing. All blenderized purées or sauces should be cooked uncovered for several minutes before canning to drive out the air bubbles whipped into them by the blender.

The quality of a few fruit juices, including grape juice and some berry juice, is best if it is never boiled. These juices should be heated to a simmer rather than a boil, or to about 190°F, before they are poured into jars. They must then be processed in a boiling water bath at 190°F for 30 minutes.

Freezing Fruit Juice and Sauce

Freezing is not as practical as canning for the majority of fruit juices and sauces. The quality of juice or sauce from cooked fruit is just as good or better canned, and no thawing is required before use. The flavor of some fresh, raw juices and sauces is quite special, and these may be frozen. It is also possible to make a concentrated fresh juice for freezing. (Refer to CONCENTRATED JUICE, in the FREEZING section.)

Sauces intended for freezing should be made by mashing the fruit, or pushing it through a sieve or food mill. Blender sauces and purées have had air whipped into them, and enzymes have been released that make them lose quality quickly. It is better to freeze fruit whole or in slices, then put it in the blender when it is removed from the freezer. Some fruits make delicious frozen desserts if puréed in a blender or food processor while frozen, and eaten immediately. (Refer to FROZEN PERSIMMON DESSERTS, in the PERSIMMONS section.)

FRUIT RECIPES

Fruit Tempura (Japanese Fruit Fritters)

(MAKES SNACKS FOR 6–8 PEOPLE)

BATTER:

1 teaspoon honey or sugar

1 egg, separated

1 cup (about) flour (half whole wheat and half unbleached is good)

Fruits (use one or several, or try other firm fruits):

apples, cored and sliced into ¼-inch-thick wedges

pears, cored and sliced into ¼-inch-thick wedges

bananas, sliced diagonally ½ to 1 inch thick

pineapple, canned or fresh, in chunks about 1 inch thick

oil for deep frying (one that does not burn easily)

1–2 tablespoons sesame oil, optional

To make the batter, mix the sweetening and egg yolk in a bowl, using a fork or wire whisk. Slowly add 1 cup of cold water, stirring constantly. Gradually add enough flour to make a batter of pancake consistency. Do not over-mix—the batter can be a bit lumpy. (This much can be done ahead of time and refrigerated for an hour or so.) Beat the egg white until stiff and fold into the batter.

Heat the oil or fat, including sesame oil if it is used, in a deep-fat fryer or wok to between 350° and 375°F. To test the temperature, drop in a bit of batter. It should sink, then rise immediately. Dip pieces of fruit in the batter one at a time and fry, turning once to brown evenly. They should cook in 3 to 5 minutes. Drain on a wire rack or paper and serve hot.

Vegetable Tempura

Cut vegetables into easily handled pieces, steam to precook, and chill completely. Deep-fry as for fruit, using the same batter.

Guatemalan Fruit Cup

(MAKES 6–8 CUPS)

4–6 large oranges, peaches, or other fresh fruit

3 tablespoons parsley, minced

2 tablespoons chives, scallions, or sweet onions, minced

2 tablespoons pimiento, cut in thin strips

1–2 avocadoes, cut in bite-sized pieces, optional

honey or other sweetening, optional

If using oranges, cut them in half and remove segments with a small spoon or knife, working over a bowl to catch the juice. Cut peaches or other fruit into bite-sized pieces, peeling if necessary. Combine the fruit and juice with the parsley, chives, scallions or onion, pimiento, and avocado, if desired. If tart, add sweetening, but do not let the mixture get too sweet. Serve in individual dishes, or scrape out orange peels and fill one for each serving. They make a delightful appetizer.

Garlic

Garlic is renowned as a seasoning and a medicinal herb. Since ancient times it has been credited with preventing or curing numerous disorders. Authorities on folk remedies and herbal or natural medicines praise it highly, and modern scientific investigators find it as remarkable as did their ancestors. However, it is garlic as a vegetable and a food seasoning that is most interesting to cooks and those for whom they cook.

There are, it seems, two kinds of people in the world: those who love and those who hate garlic. But no one should consider himself or herself among the haters without first tasting the best quality fresh garlic prepared in as many ways as possible. The unpleasantly harsh or bitter taste of very old or long-frozen garlic may be the cause of an initial dislike. (Another source of bitterness may be the use of chemical fertilizers during cultivation.) The best garlic is home grown and no more than a year old. Its peeled cloves are firm and almost white, neither limp nor turning yellow or brown, and its flavor is comparatively mild.

There are several plants besides regular garlic which have a mild garlic flavor. Elephant garlic, with its very large cloves, is mild and can be added to foods as liberally as onions. Garlic chives, or Chinese leeks, have a mild garlic flavor. Like regular chives, the tops are minced and used for garnishes, as in salads and cottage cheese. Wild garlic tops can be minced and similarly used when they first come up in the spring. The seed stalks that sometimes grow from garlic plants also have a mild garlic flavor. They can be cut and cooked as a vegetable. (See GARLIC IDEAS, below.)

Braiding Garlic

To begin braid, twist or tie three plants together.

Add new plants at even intervals during braiding.

Tie knot to finish braid.

HANDLING GARLIC

Pull or dig up garlic when the tops begin to wither and die. In moderate climates this happens in mid-summer. It should be harvested before the tops die back entirely when the bulbs are easy to locate. Garlic must cure, or dry, in an airy place. It can be left outdoors for a few days in the shade or in the field with the tops covering the bulbs, but should not be left in direct sunlight.

One way to store garlic is to trim the heads, leaving about 1 inch of the tops and a ½ inch of the roots, and keep them like onions in net bags or other porous containers. Another method is to tie the garlic tops in bunches, or to braid them for hanging. This must be done while the tops are still green enough to be flexible.

Hang the braids in a cool corner of the kitchen, in the attic, a spare room, or the pantry. A braid of garlic makes an irresistible gift from the garden. Such braids can even be saved and given as Christmas presents.

Peeling Garlic

Garlic's thin, papery peel generally has to be removed before use. When only one or two cloves are needed, it is easy enough to pull off the peels. Pressing each clove firmly with the side of a knife blade loosens the peels. To quickly peel a larger number, blanch the separated cloves by dropping them in boiling water for 2 minutes, then drain them. This loosens the peels so they will easily slip off. Small garlic peelers are also available from seed catalogs or wherever kitchen gadgets are sold.

Garlic can be added unpeeled to soups or sauces that are to be strained before serving. It is also possible to mash garlic unpeeled through a garlic press, but there will be more waste than with peeled cloves.

Crushing Garlic

When crushed or mashed, garlic releases a strong flavor that seasons food quickly. A garlic press is often used to force the garlic clove through little holes in the press, making a kind of purée. Other ways to crush garlic are to hit it with a mallet or knife handle, or to press it with the flat of a knife blade. Another method is to mince the garlic, then mash it with the back of a spoon in a small cup or bowl, or with a mortar and pestle. A little salt is sometimes mashed with it, helping to remove bitterness.

GARLIC STORAGE

Note: Most varieties of garlic keep easily from one year's harvest to the next in an airy place. (See HANDLING GARLIC, above.) No other storage method is needed, except for the sake of convenience.

Drying

Peel and slice cloves, then dry on trays until hard. Pulverize in a blender, or with mortar and pestle. Store in airtight containers. Replace once a year. Flavor gradually weakens while stored. Refer to the DRYING section.

Freezing

Not recommended. (With time the flavor becomes strong or bitter.)

Preserving in Vinegar or Oil

Peel cloves by blanching. Pack in jars, cover with vinegar or oil, seal tightly,

Garlic's Changing Flavor

Garlic's strength and flavor change dramatically with different methods of preparation. Garlic cloves used whole or sliced or minced are milder than crushed garlic. When cooked gently until well done, garlic is surprisingly mild and much different in flavor from either raw garlic or garlic sautéed quickly at high heat. Often, people do not even recognize the garlic taste when it has been simmered a while with other ingredients. Instead, they only notice an exceptionally good flavor. Roast garlic purée brings a subtle flavor to many dishes.

Even raw garlic does not have to be overwhelming. It can be mixed with fresh parsley to modify and complement its taste. These two are so compatible that the very best remedy for garlic breath is to eat a bunch of fresh parsley. In fact, whenever raw garlic is used fresh parsley is sure to taste good as well.

There is a distinctive flavor and aroma to sautéed, lightly browned garlic. Some expert cooks say never to brown garlic, but there are also delicious dishes that depend on the browned garlic flavor, so it is in the end a matter of personal choice. Many Chinese stir-fried dishes begin with browning a minced garlic clove.

Roast Garlic Purée

(MAKES ½–1 CUP)

5 heads of garlic (They should   salt, optional
    be firm, not sprouting. Home   1 tablespoon oil,
    grown are best.)   preferably olive

Wrap the garlic heads together in aluminum foil and bake in a hot, 400°F oven until soft, from 50 to 60 minutes. Test by poking through a clove with a thin-bladed knife. Unwrap and let the garlic cool until it can be handled. Pull off enough of the peels and root attachment to separate the cloves. Set a fine mesh sieve in a bowl and squeeze each clove over it so the soft center is forced out from the root end and into the sieve. Discard the skins and press the cloves through the sieve with the back of a spoon. Mix with a dash of salt, if desired, and the oil. This purée will keep for a month or more if packed in a small jar and refrigerated with a thin layer of oil poured over the surface.

Add the purée to soups, stews, mashed or puréed vegetables, and salad dressings. It can even be mixed with butter and

and refrigerate. Will keep for months. Use the vinegar or oil for seasoning as well as the garlic.

1 head garlic averages 10–12 cloves; ⅛ teaspoon powdered garlic = 1 small clove

GARLIC IDEAS
Stewed Garlic Seed Stalks

Cut seed stalks as soon as they appear in growing garlic plants. They are most tender then, and will also interfere with bulb formation if allowed to grow. Stew these stalks in a few tablespoons of water with a pat of butter or a little oil for about 10 minutes, and add a sprinkle of pepper, if desired. If there are too few stalks for a separate dish, they can be sliced and cooked with such vegetables as peas or green beans.

spread on bread for an hors d'oeuvre or snack. For those who like the purée, 20 or 25 heads can be puréed at once and stored in the refrigerator.

Gooseberries

Gooseberries are a passion for some people; their distinct and special flavor is like no other. They are closely related to currants, but this is apparent not so much in taste as in appearance, growth habits, and the berry bush's unfortunate hosting of white pine blister rust. (Refer to the CURRANTS section.)

The particular varieties of gooseberries cultivated in Great Britain and northern Europe do not generally grow well in North America because of climatic differences and their susceptibility to mildew. However, native varieties can be cultivated in most of the cooler regions of the continent. Though these do not grow as large or become as sweet as the European gooseberries, they are delicious nonetheless. Wild gooseberries are well worth picking when they can be found.

HANDLING GOOSEBERRIES

Gooseberries are picked at different stages of ripeness for their various uses. They are most useful for cooking and making preserves when they are full-sized, yet still green, firm, and very tart. At this stage they are high in pectin and as acidic as lemons or rhubarb, so they can be used in much the same ways. (Refer to COMBINING SWEET AND TART FRUITS, in the FRUITS section.) This is also the best time to store them by cold water canning. (Refer to the COLD STORAGE section.) As they ripen they become sweeter, a few varieties becoming sweet enough to eat raw. If left too long, however, they are apt to become mushy, or, in some locations, wormy. The sweetest varieties become reddish or purple when fully ripe, while other varieties turn yellow or a paler green. Sweet gooseberries are very good in fruit cups and salads. They can be soaked in muscatel or another sweet wine to make a festive dessert.

Some gooseberry bushes are so dense and thorny that the

GOOSEBERRY STORAGE

Canning

Trim tops, tails.

Hot Pack Unsweetened

Barely cover kettle bottom with cold water. Add berries. Bring to simmer, low heat. To prevent sticking, shake pot, do not stir. When hot through, fill jars, ½ in. headroom. Process 212°F, boiling water bath. Pints: 15 min. Quarts: 20 min.

Hot Pack Sweetened

Add ¼–½ cup honey or sugar per quart. Bring to simmer as above, omitting water. When cooked, let sit covered 2–3 hours to plump up berries. Fill jars; process as above, but start with warm instead of boiling water in canner.

Cold Pack

Put ½ cup hot syrup in each jar. (Refer to LIQUID SYRUP FOR CANNING FRUIT, in the CANNING section.) Fill with berries then syrup, ½ in. headroom. Process as above. Refer to the CANNING section. Also see CANNING FRUIT JUICE AND SAUCE, in the FRUITS section, and *Gooseberry Chutney*, below.

berries are difficult to pick. Such bushes are most easily harvested by wearing sturdy leather gloves and stripping the berries from the branches into a basket or other container set under them. The leaves, twigs, and other debris that comes off can also be partly removed by rolling the berries down a slightly tilted "ramp" into another container. As the leaves and twigs do not roll easily, most of them will be left behind. A final sorting can be done when the gooseberries are topped and tailed.

Removing Tops and Tails from Gooseberries

The tops or stems and tails or remnants of blossoms that cling to gooseberries do not always have to be removed by hand. If used in a juice or a strained sauce, they will be strained out during processing. Otherwise, each berry can be trimmed with scissors or by pulling off the tops and tails with the fingers. This is fairly easy to do when the gooseberries are large, but tedious if the berries are small. The tops and tails of small wild gooseberries are usually not very noticeable and can simply be ignored.

GOOSEBERRY RECIPES

Gooseberry Chutney

(MAKES 5–6 PINTS CANNED)

3 pounds tart gooseberries, topped and tailed
1 pound raisins
3–4 medium onions, chopped
2–3 garlic cloves, minced
1–2 cups honey or sugar

2 cups vinegar
¼ cup mustard seeds
½ teaspoon cayenne or other hot pepper
¼ teaspoon turmeric

Put all ingredients in a pot, bring to a boil, and simmer uncovered for about 2 hours. Stir often. Taste when almost done, and if necessary, adjust sweetening and vinegar. The mixture should be fairly thick.

Ladle boiling hot chutney into jars and process in a boiling water bath for 10 minutes. (Refer to the CANNING section.)

Rhubarb Chutney

Use chopped, fresh rhubarb instead of gooseberries. The turmeric can be omitted.

Cold Storage

See COLD WATER CANNING, in the COLD STORAGE section.

Drying

Trim tops, tails or winnow after dried. Dry until hard. Refer to the DRYING section.

Freezing

Trim tops, tails. Package dry and plain, or cover with syrup or other liquid. Refer to the FREEZING section.

about 2 pounds (5–8) cups fresh berries = 1 quart canned or frozen

GOOSEBERRY IDEAS

Elderflower or Mint Gooseberry Jelly

Use the juice of tart green gooseberries to make *Fruit Jelly with Honey* (recipe in the JAM AND JELLY section), or any other standard jelly. For the last 5 to 10 minutes of cooking add a sprig of mint or head of elderflowers. Remove the herb before bottling the jelly. The elderflowers can be enclosed in a cheesecloth to keep them from disintegrating.

As green gooseberries are rich in pectin they should jell readily.

Grapes 🌿

The earliest recorded cultivation of grapes was so long ago that it seems as if humankind has always grown them. The Bible says that Noah planted a vineyard, and there are mosaics of grape and wine production in Egypt dating back to 2400 B.C. Grapes were important in ancient Greece and Rome and continue to be important today in all temperate regions of the world. Through the centuries hundreds of different varieties of grapes have been developed to suit different climates and for different purposes. There are table grapes, raisin grapes, sweet juice grapes, and most specialized of all, wine grapes.

Home gardeners are restricted to varieties of grapes that suit their local climate, and there are likely to be limitations to the use of these varieties. The sweetest table grapes, for instance, do not make the best juice, and seedy grapes that are superb for juice will not make good raisins. Though wine grapes tend to make good juice and may also be good to eat fresh, growing them for vintage wines is beyond the scope of most gardeners.

There is no such thing as an all-purpose grape, nor is there ever likely to be one. However, new varieties are constantly being developed, and it is likely that gardeners in most areas will eventually have the choice of varieties suitable for most purposes.

The fruit is not the only edible part of the vine. The leaves are delicious stuffed or wrapped around meats while they cook, and a few can be laid on top of vegetables when they are pickled to make them crisp. In some cookbooks they are called vine leaves. (See USING GRAPE LEAVES, below.) Grape seeds are used as a coating for a special French cheese, and have been pressed commercially for their oil. Even the tartaric acid crystals that form in grape juice have a use: they are refined to make cream of tartar.

Some mention must also be made of wild grapes, as they can be picked in large quantities in some places. While some are sweet enough to eat raw, they are usually best made into juice and wild grape jelly.

HANDLING GRAPES

The Encyclopedia Britannica says truthfully that "a grape is ripe when it has reached the stage best suited for the use to which it is to be put." For eating raw and making sweet juice, grapes

---

GRAPE STORAGE

Canning

See CANNING GRAPE JUICE, below. For whole seedless or seeded grapes:

Hot Pack

Bring grapes to boil in water or syrup. Drain, pack in jars, cover with same boiling hot liquid, ½ in. headroom. Process 212°F, boiling water bath. Pints: 15 min. Quarts: 20 min.

Raw Pack

Fill jars without crushing. Add boiling water or syrup, ½ in. headroom. Process as above. Refer to the CANNING section.

Cold Storage

Catawbas, Tokays, Concords keep best. Pick when cool. Hold at 50°F until stems shrivel slightly. Arrange in shallow layers, or pack in straw. Will keep 1–2 months in root cellar. Best

should remain on the vine until fully ripe but still firm. If to be dried for raisins, they can be left on the vine until they begin to wither. For a tart juice or jelly they should be picked while still a little green, as they contain the most pectin then. Even grapes so green that their seeds are still soft can be used in an old-fashioned sour grape pie.

Seedy Grapes

Though grape seeds are perfectly safe to eat, they are a little hard to chew. It is easy enough to spit them out when eating grapes, but this is impossible with raisins. For drying, canning whole, or freezing, seedless grapes are almost a necessity. In juice-making, seeds are not a problem—in fact, the most flavorful juice grapes are seedy.

It is possible to cut open each grape and pick out the seeds, but this is a tedious process. One old cookbook suggests using a goose feather or a toothpick. Seeding a few grapes for a special salad or fruit cup in this way is not hard, but it is not practical for larger amounts. However, grapes with skins that slip off easily when squeezed can be seeded in the following way:

Separate the grape skins from the pulp and seeds by squeezing the grapes so that the pulp drops into a saucepan. They can be squeezed quickly, two at a time, one in each hand. Set the skins aside. Cook the juicy pulp until soft, then push through a sieve to remove the seeds. A food mill with a fine screen works very well. Mix this purée with the grape skins. If they are tough, the skins can be chopped. Do not discard them as most of the color and a lot of the flavor is in the grape's skin. This skin and pulp mixture will make many kinds of desserts, jams, and fruit leathers.

MAKING GRAPE JUICE

(Refer also to MAKING FRUIT JUICE AND SAUCE, in the FRUITS section.)

Grapes are among the best kinds of fruit for juice-making. Most families will drink as much grape juice over the winter as they can store. Because of their full, distinctive flavor, Concord type grapes are most popular for juice, but other somewhat tart varieties are also good. An overly sweet and bland juice can be combined with sour grape juice or another sour fruit juice for a pleasant combination. (Refer to COMBINING SWEET AND TART FRUITS, in the FRUITS section.)

separated from other foods. Refer to the COLD STORAGE section.

Drying
See MAKING RAISINS, below.

Freezing
(Seedless or seeded grapes only.) Remove stems. Dry pack or cover with juice or other liquid. Refer to the FREEZING section. Also see FREEZING FRUIT JUICE AND SAUCE, in the FRUITS section.

Note: Also see PRESERVING GRAPE LEAVES IN SALT, PICKLED GRAPES, and BRANDIED GRAPES, below.

4 pounds fresh grapes in clusters = 1 quart canned or frozen or ½ pound raisins

GRAPE IDEAS
Pickled Grapes
Firm, perfect grapes with stems removed will keep indefinitely if placed

Grape juice is best if prepared without boiling. Concord grape juice is acceptable after boiling, but loses its fresh flavor. The juice of other varieties will become completely flat and flavorless if boiled. Temperatures around 170°F are recommended. Cooking and canning temperatures should never exceed 200°F.

Fresh grapes are often crushed and pressed or squeezed to extract their juice. A squeezing strainer has a special spiral grape part that makes an excellent, somewhat thick or pulpy juice. Some small apple cider presses can be adapted for making grape juice. (Refer to MAKING APPLE CIDER, in the APPLES section.) When grapes are pressed like apples there is no need to remove the stems; they will not flavor the juice and may even help in the pressing.

Where pressing equipment is not available it is most practical to cook the grapes before extracting the juice. First, remove the stems, which add a harsh flavor when cooked, and put the grapes in a heavy kettle with just enough water to prevent sticking. Heat to a low simmer, being careful not to let the fruit boil, and stir often. To speed up the release of juice, as the grapes begin to simmer, mash them with a potato masher or kitchen mallet. When cooked through, about 30 minutes, or longer if amounts are large, strain off the juice. For a clear juice, allow to drip through a cloth without squeezing. Juice made in this way will be quite concentrated and can be diluted before it is used.

Other ways to make grape juice are with a steam juicer, like the one in the STEAM COOKING section, and by the quick canning method described below. These methods make a more diluted juice, requiring more storage space, but the juice's flavor is still quite good.

The pulp (or pomace) left from making grape juice can be used either for a second infusion of juice or in several other ways. (Refer to PULP FROM MAKING FRUIT JUICE, in the FRUITS section.)

A peculiarity of grape juice is that tartaric acid crystals and sediment form after it sits for a while. Though harmless, these spoil the look of the juice. To get rid of the sediment, let the juice sit for 24 hours in a cool place, then pour or siphon off the clear juice without disturbing the bottom. If grape juice has been canned without taking this step, the juice can still be poured off carefully when the jar is opened, leaving the sediment behind.

in jars and completely covered with vinegar. (Jars with ordinary lids are fine, and refrigeration is unnecessary.) Their flavor will be strong, and they are best used sparingly as a garnish for potato or meat salads, or with meats. For a milder pickle put a little sugar or honey in the jar with the grapes.

Grapes can also be spiced and pickled like other fruits. Refer to the *Spiced Pickled Fruit* recipe, in the PICKLING section.

Grapes in Salads

Seedless grapes or grapes that have been sliced and seeded bring a pleasant flavor to tossed salads. Try a mixture of sliced grapes, sliced cucumbers, and such minced fresh herbs as mint, parsley, and chives in an oil and vinegar dressing.

Generally, canning is the most practical way to store grape juice, but it is nice to also freeze some uncooked if there is enough freezer space. (Refer to FREEZING FRUIT JUICE AND SAUCE, in the FRUITS section.)

Canning Grape Juice

Because boiling spoils the flavor, grape juice is processed in a boiling water bath canner at a temperature of 190°F. (Refer to the CANNING section.) Use a dairy thermometer or other thermometer to check the temperature and make sure it never goes over 200°F.

Fill hot canning jars with the hot grape juice, leaving ¼ inch headroom. For both pints and quarts process at 190°F for 30 minutes.

Quick Canned Grape Juice

This method is best used with strongly-flavored, tart grapes such as Concord or wild grapes. More canning jars are needed since the juice is not concentrated, but the flavor will be good. Fill the jars about half full with clean, stemmed grapes. Optional: Add 1 or 2 tablespoons honey or sugar to each jar. Fill with boiling water, leaving ¼ inch headroom. Process both pints and quarts in a boiling water bath at 190°F for 30 minutes, or at 212°F for 15 minutes. (Refer to the CANNING section.) Wait at least a month before opening, giving the water time to soak up the grape flavor.

Some people use the grapes as well as the juice. To remove seeds put them through a food mill or strainer.

MAKING RAISINS

Raisins are exceedingly useful and popular dried fruits, and many who raise grapes are interested in making them. Most of North America's raisins come from parts of California where the climate is favorable for both growing and drying. However, grapes can be dried wherever they are grown, using the same methods used for drying other firm berries. (Refer to DRYING FRUIT, in the DRYING section.) What really curtails raisin making is the requirement of a sweet, seedless variety of grape; these do not grow everywhere. Seedy grapes can be dried, of course, but the seeds will become harder and more prominent, so that the raisins are not much fun to eat. They can, however, be soaked for their juice.

Frosted Grape Clusters

For a special dessert, cut a bunch of grapes into small clusters of several grapes each. Dip the grapes into warm syrup: half honey and half water warmed together can be used. Then sprinkle with some flavorful powdery or finely chopped mixture, such as finely chopped nuts, carob powder, crisply dried bananas pulverized in a blender, or any combination of these. Let the coated grapes dry on a rack for a few minutes to several hours before eating them. They can be refrigerated overnight, but will not keep much longer.

Brandied Grapes

Put perfect grapes, stems removed, in small jars. Cover with brandy or another liquor, seal, and store for 2 or 3 months. Both grapes and liquor improve in flavor. They can be used like brandied cherries.

There is not, as yet, any handy home device for seeding grapes. Instead there are new efforts directed towards developing sweet, seedless grape varieties adapted to most climates. In the meantime, some kinds of seedy grapes can be made into fruit leather. (See SEEDY GRAPES, above, and refer to *Fruit Leather,* in the DRYING section.)

Before they are picked for drying, grapes should ripen completely to fully develop their sugar content. Their sweetness will not increase after picking. In California grapes are usually sun-dried in clusters. They are rather slow to dry, taking an average of 3 weeks in the sun. When small quantities are dried they can be stemmed and blanched to check (crack) skins, which will speed up drying. (Refer to DRYING FRUIT, in the DRYING section.)

Sun-dried raisins are dark in color, while those dried in the shade are lighter. Their quality is excellent either way. The very light colored store-bought raisins have usually been lye dipped and sulfur treated to bleach them. The sultana variety of seedless grape is often bleached and dried. The dried "currants" sold in stores are actually a variety of small grape, specially raised for drying. Wine grapes are occasionally dried, then later soaked and the juice used for making wine. This juice has a brownish rather than a red or purplish hue.

USING GRAPE LEAVES

Grape leaves, also called vine leaves, add an unusual, slightly tart flavor to the foods with which they are cooked. They are widely used as cooked wrappings. Stuffed grape leaves (or "dolmas") are wonderful little cigar-shaped rolls made everywhere in the Middle East. A grape leaf is often put in a jar of pickles, not for flavor, but to keep the pickles crisp.

Grape leaves are best picked when they are about full-sized, yet still young enough to be tender, usually in June. (Though they can be used later in the season, they may be a little tough.) First, cut the stems off the grape leaves to be used as wrappings, then blanch them in boiling water for 2 or 3 minutes or until they are limp. If the leaves are to be salted to preserve them, they will only need rinsing before they are used.

Preserving Grape Leaves in Salt

The easiest way to preserve grape leaves is to pack them in salt in a jar or crock. Place the fresh, dry leaves one at a time in the container, sprinkling each leaf with plain or pickling salt. Cover and store, preferably in a cool place. Before use, rinse each leaf very thoroughly with cold water to remove the salt. The leaves will keep indefinitely.

Herbs   🌿

Herbs hold the same fascination for people today as they have through the ages. Old folk remedies for both physical and mental ills depended largely on medicinal herbs, and culinary herbs have been appreciated and explored as food seasoners over the centuries. These two herbal uses have, for the most part, remained quite distinct from each other, but there is now beginning to be a joining together of the two pathways. Though herbs are ostensibly regarded as food seasonings, we now ask more of them: they are to be an aid and a comfort in the constant battle waged by so many people against modern dietary excesses. Once it is understood that the affluent western world's diet is too rich in fats and sugar, too salty, and too full of artificial additives, a resolution is usually made to change to healthier fare. Then, eating habits of a lifetime must be broken, and in the process an empty, negative, and let-down feeling may arise. It is at this point that herbs come to the rescue. They can be more than a substitute for the flavors of sugar, salt, or anything else, and can fill flavor gaps in healthy and interesting ways. As well, herbs offer a delightfully positive way to be preoccupied about food. One can explore the diversity of flavors, aromas, medicinal benefits, and other delights of the world of herbs and, while doing so, leave behind the seemingly endless struggle against the urge to eat from the surrounding glut of unhealthy foods.

Tastes in herbs are personal. When specific directions are given for using herbs, they should be taken as suggestions, and when flat statements of their characteristics are made, they should be taken as opinions. There is no single right or wrong way to use an herb; instead there is the fun of trying many ways, learning perhaps, from others' suggestions and opinions, but in the end deciding for oneself. In any case, herb flavors will vary with their variety, the place they were grown, the season, and whether they are fresh or dried. The only way to understand a particular herb in a particular place at a particular time is to try it.

Gardeners are doubly blessed, as they have both the pleasure of growing herbs and the opportunity to explore their special qualities at a leisurely pace. Each can be tried while fresh at different stages of growth, as well as dried, and in combination with other herbs and seasonings.

HERB STORAGE

Drying
(Preferred method for most leafy herbs.) See DRYING HERBS, below.

Freezing
(Best for herbs that lose flavor if dried.) See FREEZING HERBS, below.

Live Storage
Maintain in garden, and as potted plants for a constant fresh supply.

Note: Also see PRESERVING HERBS IN VINEGAR OR OIL, below.

1 teaspoon dried herbs = 2–3 teaspoons minced fresh herbs

HERB IDEAS

Fresh Herbs with Meals
In some Middle and Far Eastern countries a bowl of nicely arranged fresh herbs sits on the table at meal time. Anyone can then nibble a refreshing

HANDLING HERBS

Herbs freshly gathered when needed are the nicest. Herbs growing near the kitchen door, and pots of herbs on the window sill, will provide some fresh herbs throughout the year, but some will still need to be dried or perhaps frozen. Though drying is the best way to preserve most leafy herbs, there are a few that will lose or change flavor, notably chives, tarragon, basil, dill, and parsley. These can be frozen quite successfully for use in cooking, but as they become limp after thawing their usefulness in salads or as garnishes is limited.

Drying Herbs

Gather leafy green herbs when they are most flavorful, just before they bloom. The best time is in the morning of a dry day after the dew has evaporated. If they are cut or picked neatly they should not need washing. But if they are dusty, rinse them quickly in cool water and then shake or pat them dry with a towel. Then put them in an airy, shady place to dry. Sunlight fades them and destroys flavor so shaded drying is essential. Herbs can be tied in bunches by the stems, or put loosely in net bags and hung in an airy attic, shed, or porch for drying. Take them down and store them as soon as they are dry, as they tend to lose flavor and collect dust if left hanging. If using a food dryer, never let temperatures go above 100°F, as higher temperatures destroy flavor.

Storing Dried Herbs

To store, rub or crumble the leaves off the twigs or stems and close them in airtight containers. As a precaution, especially in damp climates, check inside the containers after a few days to see if any moisture has collected. If so, spread the herbs out to dry a few more days. If using clear glass containers, store them in a dark place to retain full color and flavor. (Refer to the DRYING section for details.)

As the flavor of dried herbs gradually diminishes during storage, it is best to renew the supply once a year. Leaf pieces or crumbled leaves retain flavor longer than powder. Powder small amounts as needed, using a blender or mortar and pestle. Do not discard the herbs' dry stems and twigs as they create a nice pleasant scent when burned. Use them to put on the coals when food is charcoal broiling or put them in the fireplace.

---

herb as they eat. Try sprigs or leaves of parsley, chervil, mint, chives or scallions, watercress, dill, thyme, and coriander. Wild herbs and greens like chickweed, purslane, and sorrel can be included in the herb bowl, and some may like to add a fresh hot pepper as well.

Herbed Scrambled Eggs

Mince about a tablespoon of fresh herbs for each egg used, or substitute ½ to 1 teaspoon dried herbs, but fresh are best. Mix herbs and eggs and scramble as usual. Tarragon, savory, or thyme, with a little chives or scallions are very good. (Though other seasonings can be added, they are not necessary.) Sampling an unfamiliar herb with scrambled eggs is a good way to get to know it.

Herbs in Salads

Most salads are improved with herbs.

Freezing Herbs

Though sometimes herbs are blanched like vegetables before freezing, it is easier and just as good to make packets of a few sprigs each in amounts to be used at one time, and then freeze them. Use small freezer bags for these small portions, and put them in one large container when frozen. However, the best way to preserve the flavor of herbs in the freezer is to freeze them in cubes of ice. Chop or mince the herb and pack ice cube tray sections with it. Then add water to fill the tray, and freeze. When solid remove the cubes and store them in freezer bags. A cube will be just right for adding to soups and stews, and the flavor will be as good as fresh. Such cubes can also be thawed in a strainer, letting the water drain off, so that the herbs can be used in salads or cottage cheese. Favorite herb combinations can be minced together and frozen for a very convenient seasoning. For instance mixed celery leaf, parsley, and scallion cubes are very nice for adding to all sorts of dishes. See BOUQUET GARNI and FINES HERBES, under HERB IDEAS, below, for examples of some herb combinations, and refer to the FREEZING section for freezing details.

Preserving Herbs in Vinegar or Oil

Herb leaves covered with either of these will keep for months. Herbs like basil and tarragon which do not respond well to drying can be preserved in this way. Pack herb leaves loosely in jars, cover them with vinegar or oil, and store in a cool place. The basil flavor is best preserved if the vinegar is heated to a boil before it is added. Do not use cold pressed oils from health food stores because they become rancid too easily. As the herb will flavor the vinegar or oil, they too will be valuable for flavoring foods. Use the vinegar like any herb vinegar. (For suggestions, refer to the VINEGAR section.)

Cooking With Herbs

Herbs are surprisingly interchangeable in foods, considering their distinctly different flavors. Substitutions may not be appreciated when a particular herb is closely associated with a food, like oregano on pizzas and sage in breakfast sausages, but otherwise the possibilities are almost unlimited. Many different herbs and herb combinations will give zest and interest when cooked with foods as diverse as appetizers, main courses,

In spring, when herbs are mild and tender, toss in whole leaves or sprigs. During the summer and fall when herbs are stronger in flavor and coarser in texture, mince them so they can be distributed throughout the salad. Even very strong herbs like sage and oregano can be used in very small amounts if finely minced. In winter, use dried herbs to flavor salad dressings.

Bouquet Garni, an Herb Bouquet

A bunch of several herbs to be cooked in a stew, soup, or sauce for seasoning is a bouquet garni. With fresh herbs use string to tie the sprigs together by the stems like a bouquet for easy removal when their work is done. Tie dried herbs inside a small piece of cloth. Often included in a bouquet garni are parsley, bay leaf, thyme, basil, savory, rosemary, and celery or lov-

vegetables, and even desserts. There is great fun in growing an unfamiliar garden herb to try in ordinary and unexpected ways. Get to know it first by adding it to simple dishes, such as scrambled eggs or a plain broth, then combine it with other herbs and seasonings in various sauces, stews, casseroles, breads, and whatever else imagination dictates.

Herbs blend in best and will yield the most flavor if added for about the last 20 minutes of a food's cooking time. (Except for a few strong herbs, like bay leaf and sage, which can be cooked for several hours and still add flavor.) To introduce distinct and separate flavors rather than blending them into foods, add them in the last 5 minutes of cooking, or just before serving.

HERBS FROM THE GARDEN

(Also see the HERB ROOTS and HERB SEEDS sections.)

The following herbs and blossoms for seasoning are easily grown in most gardens, and are included in recipes throughout this book.

age leaves. Parsley, bay leaf, and thyme are often used together, but any herbs can be used in any combination.

Fines Herbes or Herb Seasoning for the Table

Throw out the salt shaker, and instead have ready an herb mixture for seasoning food just before it is eaten. Fines herbes can be a mixture of finely minced fresh herbs or a mixture of crushed or powdered dried herbs. Though these can be sprinkled on foods in the last few seconds of cooking, there is something special about adding them at the table. A classic French mixture is parsley, chervil, chives, and tarragon. Other herbs that are good in such mixtures are basil, thyme, rosemary, oregano, marjoram, sage, and fennel. Combine them in roughly equal amounts, or adjust proportions to taste.

Basil

Basil tastes best fresh. It has much less flavor after drying, but can be frozen or preserved in oil or vinegar. Its flavor in vinegar is retained best if it is heated enough to wilt the leaves. Fresh basil is delicious in salads, especially in tomato salads, and used fresh or preserved as a seasoning for cooked tomato mixtures. Put a leaf or small sprig in each jar when canning tomatoes. Minced basil leaves with butter are very good on peas, green beans, and other green vegetables. They are also an excellent seasoning to add to soups, to dried bean dishes, and sprinkled on most fish fillets and steaks just before serving.

Bay and Bayberry Leaves

Bay leaves come from the bay tree, a variety of laurel, native to the Mediterranean region. It must be distinguished from the American laurel which is poisonous. Though bay trees are not winter hardy in most of North America, they can be grown in tubs and brought indoors during cold weather.

Bayberry bush leaves, which grow wild along many North American coasts, can be used as a seasoning instead of bay leaves. Their flavor is different, but they complement many of the same foods. Both bay and bayberry leaves are easy to dry and store. Bayberry adds an especially nice aroma and flavor to shellfish dishes.

Borage

Tiny, newly formed borage leaves, minced and added to salads, give a delicate cucumber flavor. Add larger leaves to sauces for fish for the same effect. The young leaves can also be cooked and served like spinach or used in greens mixtures. Float the brilliant blue borage flowers on cool summer drinks or sprinkle them on salads for a startling touch of color.

Camomile

The yellow center of the camomile blossom is the prized part of the plant. Gather the flowers when they are in full bloom and dry them for making a soothing and flavorful tea. (See *Herb Teas,* below.) Should there be too much camomile to drink, take a nice soothing bath in it, as recommended by early herbalists.

Celery Leaves, Celeriac Leaves, Lovage

All of these have a strong, fresh celery flavor excellent for seasoning all kinds of soup, stews, and salads, especially potato salad. Lovage is also known as smallage or milage. The leaves and thin stalks of all of these plants dry very well. (Refer to the CELERY and CELERIAC sections, and for seeds, to the HERB SEEDS section.)

Chervil

Chervil can be used in about the same ways as parsley. Its flavor is mild and pleasant, so add generous amounts to foods. It is best fresh. It does not dry well, but can be frozen. When cooking, add it at the last minute because its flavor quickly disappears. It enhances the flavor of other herbs, which makes it important in *Fines Herbes* and other herb mixtures. Chervil roots are good cooked like carrots.

Chives, Scallions, Other Onion Greens

Though these related plants all differ in flavor their light onion taste makes them welcome in the same kinds of foods. They are

Pickled Nasturtium Buds and Seed Pods

Nasturtium buds and pods can be pickled by simply pouring vinegar over them, and keeping them in a cool place for a few weeks. For a more flavorful pickle, pick seed pods on a dry day and dry them in the sun, or in very low heat in a food dryer until they are firm to the touch. It may take one to several days. For the pickling liquid, heat 2 cups of vinegar with 2 bay leaves and 6 peppercorns. Bring to a boil, then remove from heat and let cool completely. Pack the seed pods in a jar, cover with the vinegar, seal, and store in a cool place for 3 or 4 weeks before using. The leftover liquid can be saved until more seed pods are collected and ready to pickle.

best fresh, but they can also be frozen. Chives can be grown in pots on the window sill for winter use. Scallions or onion tops can also be grown indoors. (Refer to the ONIONS section.) Freshly chopped chives or scallions are a perfect garnish for potatoes, eggs, fresh cheeses, soups, and salads. For garlic chives or Chinese leeks and wild garlic, refer to the GARLIC section.

Comfrey

Refer to the COMFREY section.

Coriander (Chinese Parsley, Cilantro)

Coriander leaves are used like parsley in many parts of the world. In Mexico and the Caribbean this herb is called cilantro. It is also popular in the Middle East, India, China (hence Chinese parsley), and other Far Eastern countries. The flavor of the fresh leaves is distinctive and strong, so try them cautiously at first. Float a leaf in soup, or mince a leaf or two and use as a garnish on stir-fried meat or chicken dishes. Then try the leaves in the FRESH TOMATO SAUCE, in the TOMATOES section. Coriander does not dry well, but can be frozen. The seeds are milder than the leaves. (Refer to the HERB SEEDS section.)

Dill

Fresh, feathery young dill leaves, sometimes called dill weed, are delicious in salads, and with potatoes, eggs, or fish. As the plant matures the leaves become tougher and less flavorful, but by then the flower umbels are forming so use them instead. An umbel or dill head is the classic flavoring for pickled cucumbers or other pickled vegetables. Use them before they reach full maturity and begin to dry out. For a constant supply of dill leaves and umbels through summer and fall resow the seeds several times. In winter use the seeds for flavorings. (Refer to DILL SEEDS, in the HERB SEEDS section.)

Elderflowers

Refer to the ELDERBERRIES section.

Fennel

Fresh fennel leaves have a light, licorice flavor well-known as a seasoning for fish, but they are also good used in the same ways as dill. Florence fennel, called finnochio in Italy, has thick bulbous stalks, and is a delicious vegetable either fresh or cooked. Fennel leaves can be frozen or dried. The seeds can be used like anise seeds. (Refer to ANISE SEEDS, in the HERB SEEDS section.)

Marjoram and Oregano

These two herbs are closely related. Oregano is sometimes called wild marjoram, and it has the stronger flavor. It is often used alone, while marjoram works well-blended with other herbs, especially thyme. Both are most familiar dried, but they are also very good when used fresh. They are excellent in the popular Italian style tomato sauces, and very good with all meats and fish, and they also enhance bean dishes, soups, and salads of all kinds. They are often suggested seasonings throughout this book. An example is *Herbed Tomato Juice Cocktail,* in the TOMATOES section.

Mint

There are many different kinds of mint, but peppermint and spearmint are the ones most often grown in the garden. Wild mint is widespread and varies greatly in flavor. Try samples from different locations to see which tastes best. The flavor of mint is strongest before it blooms, so cut it back occasionally to make new growth. In spring the tender new leaves are delicious in salads and fruit cups. Later the leaves become rougher and should be minced for eating fresh, or used in mixtures made in the blender. Dried mint is most often used for teas, but can be substituted for fresh mint in most recipes. Mint is good in herb combinations, and with meats and vegetables, as well as in drinks and desserts.

Nasturtium

The nasturtium is more than a pretty flower. It is an excellent herb with a brisk, peppery flavor. The leaves, buds, blossoms, and seed pods are all edible. Use fresh leaves chopped into salads, or minced to add to cottage cheese or cream cheese. Add them just before serving, since they can develop a bitter taste. The dried leaves can also be used as a peppery seasoning.

The blossoms provide a lovely splash of color floated in soups, or garnishing salads, appetizers, and desserts. Both buds and seed pods can be pickled to use like capers, but the pods have a firmer texture than the buds. The dry seeds can be made into a sort of mustard. (Refer to the MUSTARD (GREENS AND SEEDS) section.)

Parsley

Refer to the PARSLEY section.

Rose Petals

Refer to the ROSES section.

Rosemary

Rosemary is an interesting and versatile herb, equally good fresh or dried. It can be grown in the garden in summer, then kept in a pot in a cool place indoors during freezing weather. Used in the same ways as sage and thyme, it is outstanding with light meats like rabbit, chicken, veal, lamb, or pork. A few twigs or leaves sprinkled on the coals when charcoal broiling one of these will add an exceedingly pleasant aroma and flavor.

Sage

As sage is strong flavored it should be used with restraint. Mix parsley with it to tone down and complement its flavor. When dried its flavor is quite familiar, as the expected seasoning for poultry stuffings and breakfast sausage. Fresh sage has a somewhat different, milder yet delicious flavor. Mince tiny bits of it to add to eggs, cottage cheese, green beans, and eggplant and tomato dishes.

Savory

The two savories, summer and winter, differ somewhat in flavor, but can be used interchangeably. Winter savory has the strongest flavor. Both can be used fresh or dried. Summer savory is known for its affinity with green beans, but it goes well with many vegetables. Cabbage, Brussels sprouts, summer squash, and most vegetable mixtures taste very good seasoned with either savory. This herb also goes well with most meats and can be used instead of thyme.

Tarragon

While Russian tarragon is easier to grow, French tarragon is the most flavorful variety. In some recipes, tarragon is called by its French name, estragon. Use it fresh or frozen since drying changes its flavor. It is very good with cucumber pickles instead of dill, and is a common flavoring in vinegar. Try it with chicken, seafood, vegetables, and in salads. Some recipes featuring it are *Herb Vinegar,* in the VINE-GAR section, and SEASONED SAUERKRAUT, in the SAUERKRAUT section.

Thyme

The strong yet pleasant flavor of thyme is good both fresh and dried. It enhances so many foods, and complements so many herb and spice mixtures, that enumeration is difficult. For a start, however, try it in meat and vegetable stuffings, stews, and casseroles, and put some fresh sprigs on the table for nibbling with meals. (See FRESH HERBS WITH MEALS, under HERB IDEAS, above.) When adventuring with herbs, thyme is a must.

MAKING HERB TEA

There are several satisfactory ways to brew herb teas. Which to use will depend on personal preference and the characteristics of the ingredients used. Pure, good-tasting water is essential.

For delicately flavored teas, warm the teapot and put the herbs in it. Bring water to a boil and pour it over them. Let steep from 5 to 10 minutes, or according to taste.

For stronger herb teas, heat water in a non-aluminum pot or saucepan, and when it boils take it off the heat, add the herbs, cover, and steep. If a very strong flavor is wanted or the ingredients are in large pieces the pot can be kept on very low heat while it steeps for as long as 20 to 30 minutes. If necessary, use an insulating ring under the pot to prevent boiling. If one of the ingredients for tartness is used, it can be put in the saucepan with the cold water and brought to a boil before adding the herb leaves. Pour the tea into cups through a strainer, or simply let ingredients settle to the bottom before drinking.

Common Herb Tea Ingredients

Alfalfa leaves, dried

Camomile, dried

Celery leaves, dried

Citrus peel, dried (especially orange)

Comfrey leaves, fresh or dried

Clover blossoms, fresh or dried

Elderflowers, dried

Mint, fresh or dried

Parsley leaves, fresh or dried

Raspberry or strawberry leaves, dried

Rose petals, fresh or dried

Sage, fresh or dried

(To begin with use equal parts of each ingredient, then adjust to taste. For further experimentation, whole spices, such as a piece of cinnamon bark or a clove, can be included.)

Ingredients to add Tartness

Berries, dried

Rhubarb stalks, chopped, fresh or dried

Rosehip, fresh or dried and crushed

Sour apple slices, dried

Some Suggested Herb Tea Combinations

Mint with rosehip, rhubarb, or sour apple.

Celery, parsley, and comfrey.

Raspberry or strawberry leaves, with orange peel.

Sage with alfalfa, or clover.

Rose petals with parsley.

Camomile, alfalfa leaves, and comfrey.

Elderflowers with mint.

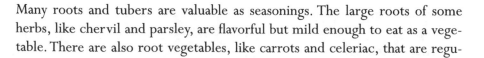
Proportions:

½–1 teaspoon dried herbs or about 2 teaspoons fresh herbs to 1 cup boiling water.

Iced Herb Tea

A strong infusion of any herb tea can be cooled and iced, or herb tea can be used instead of water when making lemonade. Iced mint tea is very refreshing.

Green Drink

(MAKES 4–6 VERY SMALL GLASSES)

fresh herb leaves (try mildly-flavored herbs such as comfrey or parsley with stronger flavors like mint, sage, scallion, or chives)

vegetable cooking water or juice, fruit juice, or water

vinegar, lemon juice, or small amount of a tart fruit

honey, or a sweet fruit

Remove any tough stems or stalks from the herbs and chop large leaves into small pieces. Put enough leaves loosely in a blender to almost fill it. Add vegetable cooking water or other liquid to about half fill the blender. Add vinegar or other tart flavor, and honey or other sweet flavor to taste. Blend until smooth. Taste and adjust seasonings, if desired. Serve immediately.

Change the ingredients in this drink with the seasons. In spring include wild greens, such as chickweed, wild onion, or wild mustard. It is as healthy and invigorating as a beverage can be.

REFERENCES FOR GROWING AND COOKING WITH HERBS

Boxer, A., and Back, P., *The Herb Book,* Octopus Books Ltd., London, 1987. (A complete reference on herbs for the kitchen.)

Edwards, John, *Roman Cookery,* Hartley & Marks, Point Roberts, WA, 1986. (Historical herbal recipes adapted for today.)

Stuart, M., *The Encyclopedia of Herbs and Herbalism,* Crescent Books, New York, 1979.

Herb Roots

Many roots and tubers are valuable as seasonings. The large roots of some herbs, like chervil and parsley, are flavorful but mild enough to eat as a vegetable. There are also root vegetables, like carrots and celeriac, that are regularly included in mixed dishes as seasonings, and there are ginger and horserad-ish, whose seasoning powers are well-known. When the root or tuber of any plant is used for its distinctive flavor it is, at least on these pages, an herb root.

Burdock Roots

These delectable roots are also known by their Japanese name, gobo, and are considered extraordinarily healthy in Japan. Their flavor is unique, but not over-powering, and they blend deliciously into meat, fish, and vegetable dishes. They are also good cooked alone. Burdock is biennial, and it is important, when gath-ering wild roots, to choose only the first-year plants, which are without seed stalks. The roots of second-year plants are tough and woody. Cultivated burdock has very long, tender roots. They are easily grown, but hard to dig up, because they break so easily. One solution is to grow them in high beds with wooden sides that can be removed for harvesting. Seeds are available from many seed catalogs.

Flavor any meat, fish, or vegetable stew with burdock root slices. Japanese style all-gobo dishes are made by cutting the roots into slices or slivers, then stewing them in stock or water with soy sauce for seasoning. To cut these sli-vers hold a root by the top end and pare off thin strips from the other end, turning the root while cutting as if sharpening a large pencil. To prevent dark-ening, the roots are slivered into a pot of water and left to soak until they are drained just before cooking. However, as nutrients are lost with the water, and the burdock will darken anyway if soy sauce is added, the soaking can be omitted. Gobo cooks in 10 to 30 minutes, depending on the size of the pieces.

Ginger Root

Powdered ginger can be made from dried ginger roots, but the fresh roots are more versatile and flavorful. Fresh ginger root is important in Chinese and other Asian cuisines. It can also be grated or finely minced to use in gingerbread, cookies, and cooked with fruits or fruit preserves. It is especially good with pears.

Ginger roots are actually tubers that are grown like pota-toes, but they require a very long growing season. It is possible to plant the tuber in a large pot, keeping it outdoors in summer and bringing it in when the weather gets cold, but it needs space, sunlight, and careful tending in order to produce new tubers. Fresh ginger roots are now sold in many grocery stores.

HERB ROOT STORAGE
Cold Storage
Most keep well in root cellars, or in similar conditions. (Optional: Pack in damp sand or other damp material.) Refer to the COLD STORAGE section.

Drying
Slice or shred, then dry until hard. Some are best powdered for use. Refer to DRYING VEGETABLES, in the DRY-ING section.

Freezing
Cook if practical, or package raw. Quality varies for different roots. Refer to the FREEZING section.

They will keep for months in damp sand in a cool place, but they spoil quickly if left in a plastic bag and refrigerated. They are better off uncovered at room temperature, and can be used even after they are quite shriveled. They can also be frozen and grated as needed without thawing.

Horseradish

Horseradish roots do not gain their distinctively hot taste and pungent smell until after they are grated. Their hotness is caused by a reaction between two separate chemicals which must be freed by grating. Freshly grated horseradish is hottest and best, so leave the roots in the ground and dig as needed or store them in a root cellar where they will keep all winter. (Refer to the COLD STORAGE section.) Horseradish can be preserved by drying and powdering, by grating and freezing, or by grating and covering it with vinegar and then refrigerating it. Though it will gradually lose hotness stored in any of these ways, it retains some flavor for 2 to 3 months. The young leaves are good cooked like spinach, while the cooked root has a bland flavor.

While it is being grated, horseradish is a tear-jerker, with fumes that are much stronger than those from chopping onions. Among the many suggestions for avoiding the tears are to grate the roots outdoors, letting a breeze blow away the fumes; to grate them near a hot stove so the heat carries the fumes upwards out of the way; or to let several people take turns grating, and when one succumbs let another take over. If using a blender or food processor do not lift the lid and inhale at the same time. A blender will cut the horseradish into separate little flakes that are good for freezing and can be taken out a spoonful at a time without thawing. By adding vinegar to the horseradish in the blender a quick relish is made.

Grated horseradish is very good in many sauces, dips, and salad dressings. Mixed half and half with catsup it makes a popular seafood sauce. Mixed sparingly with softened butter it becomes a sandwich spread, and mixed with applesauce or other fruit sauces or preserves it becomes a relish for meats.

Frozen Horseradish Cream

Grate a small to medium horseradish root and 2 to 3 medium apples, by hand or in a blender. Mix in 2 tablespoons honey and 2 cups yogurt. Freeze until mushy, stir with a fork, and freeze until solid. Just before use, let it soften enough to scoop out in balls. Serve with cold meats, fish, or fruit. For a salad, or an attractive side dish, put scoops of horseradish cream on peach halves or sliced persimmons, or decorate a platter of cold, sliced turkey or other meat with them.

Herb Seeds

Most herb seeds dry as they mature, and need no special processing for storage. Many retain their flavor in a closed container for several years.

The complete spice cabinet always includes an array of flavorful seeds for seasoning foods. Most of these can be home raised or gathered wild, and can to a surprising extent replace imported spices like cinnamon and cloves. Though the various seeds will not duplicate the specific flavors of imported spices, they offer a range of sharp, spicy, aromatic flavors which are intriguing to use in all kinds of dishes. The delight of desserts spiced with coriander, caraway, or anise seeds; the vim of vegetables seasoned with dill, or fennel seeds, or with juniper berries; the zest of sauces made with celery or mustard seeds—who can resist?!

HARVESTING HERB SEEDS

The first concern when harvesting small herb seeds is choosing the best time, which is after they are fully formed but before the seed pods are so dry that they shatter and scatter the seeds. Cut or pick the stalks or seed heads while they are still slightly green, and finish drying them on racks or trays in an airy place, preferably indoors, away from birds and rodents. If the seeds are very small, spread a cloth under them to catch any that fall. Another way to dry herb seeds is to tie a paper bag over the tops of a bunch of stalks, and hang them upside down so that the seeds will fall into the bag. It also sometimes works to tie a paper bag or cloth over the seed heads right on the plants in the garden, which will, at the same time, protect them from birds. If the plant is one whose seeds mature gradually, this way also catches the early seeds while waiting for the later ones. Some dry seed pods must be rubbed or crushed to loosen the seeds, and then winnowed to remove chaff and debris. (Refer to THRESHING AND WINNOWING, in the SEEDS section.)

If herb seeds are to be crushed to release more flavor, it is best to do so just before using them, otherwise the flavors dissipate. Seeds can be crushed with the back of a spoon against the side of a rounded cup, but a mortar and pestle is more effective. Seeds can be powdered in a blender, producing a texture which makes them especially good to use as spices in baked goods.

One to two cups of most kinds of herb seeds is enough for a year's supply of seasoning. If more seeds are gathered they make a gift that friends will appreciate.

Anise

The lightly licorice flavor of anise seeds is delicious in cooked apple desserts, sauerkraut, and other fruit and vegetable dishes, and with fish and meats, as well. Add a pinch to cooked carrots or cabbage, to stews or soups with vegetables, and to meat or fish dishes. The crushed or powdered seeds make a good spice in cookies and fruit breads. A pleasant tea can be made by boiling them for 5 minutes in water. A sort of anisette can be made by steeping anise seeds in brandy for 6 weeks. Anise leaves are also flavorful. Try a few minced in fruit salads or green salads.

Star-anise, which is associated mostly with Chinese cooking, comes from an entirely different plant, and has a considerably stronger flavor. Small amounts are good used like anise seeds.

Caraway

Rye bread with caraway seeds is a classic, but it is only one of many ways to use these versatile seeds. They are good whole in various kinds of cheese, soup, vegetable, and meat dishes. Try a few crushed in a potato salad. When crushed and used in baked desserts they have a delightful spicy flavor that is hard to identify. Mix some crushed caraway seeds with a little milk and honey and brush on loaves of raisin bread about 15 minutes before they come out of the oven, and everyone will be both delighted and mystified by the flavor. See SEASONED SAUERKRAUT, in the SAUERKRAUT section.

Celery, Celeriac, and Lovage

Commercially sold celery seeds for seasoning come from a wild, particularly strong tasting celery, but the seeds of cultivated celery, celeriac, and lovage are all worth collecting for their considerable celery flavor. The seeds are as versatile as the leaves, blending well with many other herbs and seasonings in all kinds of foods. They are very good in meat stews and sauces, crushed in salad dressings, and added to some breads and baked goods. Try adding a few to biscuit dough.

Coriander

In contrast to the overwhelming flavor of the leaves, the seeds are pleasantly spicy, and growing coriander is very worthwhile for the seeds alone. Ground or powdered coriander seeds are excellent in gingerbread and pumpkin pie and can replace cinnamon or cloves in most recipes. They are often used ground in sausages.

Dill

As the pleasantly haunting dill flavor tends to dominate in mixtures, these seeds become the primary seasoning. The flavor and texture are excellent in most hearty salads, including egg, potato, beet, seafood, and bean, and in most cooked fish, egg, and cabbage or sauerkraut dishes. They can often be used instead of celery or caraway seeds in recipes. Crush them just before use, for a richer flavor.

Fenugreek

Fenugreek is a legume resembling sweet clover. The seeds are slightly bitter, with a distinct curry aroma. (They are an ingredient in most curry powders.) They blend well with oregano, thyme, and other herbal seasonings for meat and vegetable stews, and soups. Crushing before use releases their flavor, and is important when brewing fenugreek tea. (Brew like the anise tea, above.) Fenugreek sprouts are unique and delicious, with an interesting taste eaten alone, or in salads and sandwiches. (Refer to the SPROUTS section.)

Juniper Berries

These are fruits, but because they have so little flesh they are used as seeds. If at all soft when gathered, dry them in an airy place before storing them. Juniper trees and shrubs are found almost everywhere. All their berries are edible, but as some have a stronger flavor than others taste them to judge the amount to use. The berries are good for seasoning meat and fish stews and cooked cabbage. They are often included in marinades for meat. They are also used for flavoring gin. Bruise the berries and the smell of gin is recognizable.

Mustard

Refer to the MUSTARD (GREENS AND SEEDS) section.

Poppy

Refer to the SEEDS section.

Sesame

Refer to the SEEDS section.

Jam and Jelly

Traditional fruit jams, jellies, and other preserves were almost always highly sweetened. There are now also many low-sugar fruit spreads, which were developed in response to current awareness of the harm caused by eating too much sugar. Some of the most delicious of these depend entirely on the natural fruit for sweetness, but they tend to resemble sauces and gelatines rather than old-fashioned jams and jellies. Other new spreads rely on artificial sweeteners, and sometimes preservatives as well, and cannot be recommended.

A great deal can be said in praise of both natural spreads made from sweet fruits, and the traditional jams and jellies which are often made from fruit so sour it is mouth-puckering. Well-made sour fruit jams and jellies have a wonderful, sweet-sour intensity that can only be described as mouth-watering, and since a scant teaspoon is enough to transform an ordinary slice of toast into a feast for the gods, even the most calorie conscious will find little to worry about.

MAKING JAM, JELLY, AND OTHER FRUIT SPREADS

Making a perfect, old-fashioned jelly takes careful attention to detail, while jams, fruit butters, preserves, conserves, and marmalades can be handled more casually, though they also have painstaking variations. Fruit, and sugar or another sweetener are the basic ingredients. Mild-flavored honey is excellent instead of sugar in some kinds of jelly, and in most of the other fruit spreads. Maple syrup is delicious in some preserves.

Pectin, which occurs naturally in some fruits, is essential for jelling jelly, and a help for setting or thickening other fruit spreads. For directions for making pectin, refer to the PECTIN section. The methods and recipes included here depend on fruit's natural pectin, or on the addition of homemade pectin. The pectin sold in stores requires different procedures and comes with its own instructions. Jams and jellies made with it will have a higher sugar content, unless labeled otherwise and there is a higher yield from a given amount of fruit. The flavor is less full and not as intense as that of old-style jam and jelly. A special low-methoxyl pectin, sold in some health food stores,

---

JAM AND JELLY STORAGE

Note: If sugar content is high, may be sealed with a thin layer of melted paraffin.

Canning

Pour, boiling hot, into hot jars and seal as for OPEN KETTLE CANNING. Refer to the CANNING section. Optional: Process jam and similar preserves (not jelly) in boiling water bath. Half pints, pints, or quarts: 10 min. Refer to the CANNING section.

Freezing

(The only storage option if made from raw fruit.) Fill containers, leaving ½ in. headroom. Cool, or let jell, before freezing. Quality retained 1 year. Refer to the FREEZING section.

JAM AND JELLY IDEAS
Freezing Fruit for Jam and Jelly

If there is freezer space, it is often convenient to freeze berries or other fresh

jells without added sweeteners. It cannot be homemade, and, in sour fruit preparations at least, little is gained as sweetening is often necessary for palatability.

Making Jelly

Tart, strongly-flavored fruits, such as wild berries and grapes, are best for traditional jelly. For a clear, sparkling jelly, the fruit juice must be strained from cooked fruit through cloth with no squeezing or pressing. The cloth can be tied or sewn into a bag and hung to drip overnight. (Refer to JUICE FROM COOKED FRUIT, in the FRUITS section.)

Before it will jell, fruit juice must contain acid, pectin, and sugar. Lemon juice, or another acidic juice, and homemade pectin can be added where needed. Another alternative is to combine fruits low in acid or pectin with fruits high in these. Apples are good in combinations because they are high in pectin and not too pronounced in flavor.

When ready, the juice is boiled with a measured amount of sugar until it reaches the jelly stage. The proportions necessary for jelling are from 1 to 1¼ cup of sugar per cup of juice. To jell properly, jelly must be made in small amounts. A good batch size is 4 cups of juice or less.

If using a jelly or candy thermometer to test for jelling the temperature should be about 220°F near sea level, and 8°F above the boiling point for water at higher altitudes. The jelly stage is usually reached after 10 to 20 minutes of boiling.

The classic test is made by spooning up a little of the boiling jelly, holding it well above the pot for a moment to cool, then pouring it off. If the last drops fall in two slow, separate drips, it is almost done. If the last drops slide off in one sheet, the jelly is done and should be poured immediately into jars or glasses. Another way to test it is to put a little jelly on a cool saucer and set it in the freezer for a minute to see if it jells.

If it has not jelled after 30 minutes of boiling, the mixture probably lacks pectin, acid, or sugar. The flavor can be damaged by too much boiling, so it is best to take the pot off the stove after half an hour and enjoy fruit syrup instead of jelly.

Jelly can be sealed in canning jars by the open kettle canning method (refer to the CANNING section), or it can be poured in glasses, cooled until it sets, and covered with a thin layer of

fruit in the summer, for making jam or jelly in the winter. The fruit should be packaged in the amounts needed for making one batch of jam or jelly. There will be more time for cooking it in the winter, and the heat from the stove will be welcome, rather than stifling.

Last Minute Jam

Make a quick jam in the blender using fresh, canned, or frozen fruit. Add raw apple pieces, or banana for thickening. Sweeten if desired. Enjoy right away on toast or waffles, or make really special peanut butter and jam sandwiches.

Jelly Melt Cereal

For a change from the usual, put a spoonful of jelly on a bowl of hot cereal and let it melt before "digging in." Yogurt instead of milk goes very well.

melted paraffin. It should NOT be processed in a boiling water bath, as continued cooking in a closed container will prevent a proper jell.

Making Jams and Fruit Butters

These are made by simply cooking fruit with a sweetener until thickened. Jam is made from chopped or mashed fruit, and butter is made from a smooth sauce or purée. The pulp left from making fruit juice can also sometimes be used. (Refer to PULP FROM MAKING FRUIT JUICE, in the FRUITS section.) The amount of added sweetening can be judged by taste. Some fruits need very little. The *Apple Cider Butter* recipe in the APPLES section can be made without any sugar at all. Fruits that are juicy and not likely to thicken in a reasonable time can be mixed with chopped apple or applesauce, homemade pectin, or powdered gelatine to make them set. Dry fruits may need the addition of water or fruit juice when cooked.

Jam and fruit butter must be stirred almost constantly while cooking to keep them from sticking and burning. Using a pot with a heavy bottom, moderate heat, and perhaps an insulating ring to diffuse heat will also help prevent burning.

Jams and fruit butters that are sweetened to taste may contain too little sugar to keep if sealed with paraffin, and should be canned by processing in a boiling water bath for 10 minutes, or else frozen.

Making Preserves, Conserves, and Marmalades

These are made of fruit cooked in syrup until the fruit is translucent and the syrup has reached the jelly stage. Preserves are usually made of large pieces of one kind of fruit. Conserves are a mixture of fruits, often with raisins and nuts added. Marmalade has shreds of citrus fruit peel cooked into it.

There are several ways to make these spreads. Fruits and sweetening can be mixed and cooked like jam, forming their own syrup. Fruit and sugar can be layered in a pot and left several hours or overnight, until juice is drawn out to form a syrup, and then it can be cooked. Syrup can also be made separately, with the fruit added to it and cooked. Citrus fruit peel for marmalade is usually cooked in water until tender, then both peel and cooking water are used. The peel can be grated or ground before cooking, or the orange, lemon, or other citrus fruit can be cooked whole and thinly sliced.

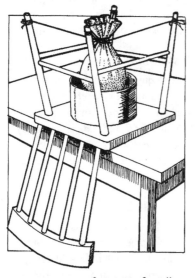

One way to strain fruit juice for jelly

Considerable sweetening is necessary to give the fruit in preserves, conserves, and marmalade their traditional appearance and flavor. The standard ratio is ¼ to ½ cup of honey or ½ to ¾ cup of sugar per cup of fruit. With this in mind, however, new versions can be adapted to taste.

If the syrup should thicken before the fruit is cooked, a little fruit juice or water can be added. If the fruit is done and the syrup remains too runny, the syrup can be drained and boiled separately as for jelly, and mixed with the fruit when it is almost done. These spreads should be canned rather than sealed with paraffin, unless they have been cooked to the jelly stage.

Uncooked Jam and Jelly

Fresh, raw fruit can be mashed or puréed, sweetened, and set with gelatine. A squeezing strainer will remove seeds and peels from many fruits while puréeing. Fresh fruit juice (refer to the FRUITS section) can also be jelled with gelatine. Sweetening is optional. Uncooked jams and jellies can also be made with commercial pectin according to the package directions, but large amounts of sugar or artificial sweeteners are required, whereas gelatine works without either. Natural or homemade pectin must be cooked with fruit before it can set.

Uncooked jams and jellies made with about equal parts fruit and sweetening will keep about 3 weeks in the refrigerator. Without sugar, they will keep about a week. For long storage they must be frozen.

RECIPES FOR JAMS AND JELLIES

These recipes feature sweeteners other than refined sugar, and are best made with fruit too sour to enjoy unsweetened. Their flavor intensity makes them satisfying eaten in very small amounts.

Fruit Jelly with Honey

(MAKES 4—5 HALF-PINTS)

3 cups tart, pectin-rich fruit juice, or 2 cups juice and 1 cup homemade
    pectin (refer to the PECTIN SECTION)   2 cups mild honey

Boil the juice and honey in a deep pot, as they may boil over in a shallow pot. Skim off froth as it appears. When the jelly stage is reached, pour into glasses or jars and seal. (See MAKING JELLY, above.)

Strongly-flavored fruits, especially wild fruits, are best for honey jelly. The jelly will not be as clear and bright as when made with sugar, but the flavor will be superb.

Maple Fruit Preserves

(MAKES 3–4 HALF PINTS)

1 cup maple syrup
3–4 cups berries, pitted cherries, sliced peaches, plums, or other fruit

1 apple, chopped, optional

Heat the maple syrup to a boil, then add the fruit. Simmer, uncovered, until the fruit has cooked through and appears translucent, 20–30 minutes. If the syrup is still very thin, strain it off and boil it separately for a few minutes, then add the fruit and boil again. Pour into jars and process in a boiling water bath for 10 minutes. (Refer to the CANNING section.) If the fruit is low in pectin, the apple will help thicken it.

Fruit and Nut Conserves

(MAKES 4–5 PINTS)

2 quarts tart berries or other
  fruit, seeded and chopped as
  necessary
2 cups honey, or add sweetening
  to taste

½ cup raisins, or chopped figs
  or prunes
½ cup nuts, chopped, or ¼ cup
  sunflower seeds
spices, grated lemon peel, or other
  flavorings, to taste, optional

Combine all ingredients in a large pot, and heat slowly, stirring constantly to prevent sticking. When juice has collected, increase the heat and stir occasionally. Maintain at a slow boil until the fruit is well-cooked and the mixture has thickened, about 20–30 minutes. Pour into jars and process in a boiling water bath for 10 minutes. (Refer to the CANNING section.)

Jerusalem Artichokes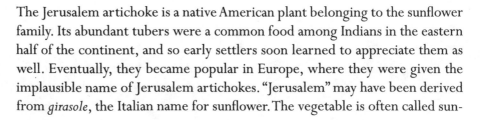

The Jerusalem artichoke is a native American plant belonging to the sunflower family. Its abundant tubers were a common food among Indians in the eastern half of the continent, and so early settlers soon learned to appreciate them as well. Eventually, they became popular in Europe, where they were given the implausible name of Jerusalem artichokes. "Jerusalem" may have been derived from *girasole*, the Italian name for sunflower. The vegetable is often called sunchoke, and is listed under artichokes in some older gardening books and cookbooks. If there is any confusion with globe artichokes, the description, or directions for preparation will clarify which is meant.

Jerusalem artichokes are easily grown where the climate is not too dry, and are found wild in many places. The tubers somewhat resemble small, knobby potatoes, and can be mistaken for fresh ginger roots. This versatile vegetable is crisp with a mild, earthy flavor when eaten raw, and tender, with an unobtrusive root vegetable taste when cooked. To go with their improbable name, Jerusalem artichokes are improbably delicious prepared in the same ways as cucumbers, both raw and cooked. A more descriptive name would have been cucumber-rooted sunflower.

HANDLING JERUSALEM ARTICHOKES

The Jerusalem artichoke tuber is a cold weather vegetable that is not ready to eat until after autumn frosts. It does not keep well after digging, which limits its commercial value, but makes it practical for the home gardener who can dig tubers as needed in the fall, during winter thaws, and in the spring before growth starts. Though very good when dried, frozen, or pickled for storage, they are most appreciated in winter and early spring when few other fresh homegrown vegetables are available. Dried slices, after being reconstituted by soaking, can be used in most recipes that require cooking. Both dried and fresh Jerusalem artichokes are especially good in stir-fried dishes.

People who feel compelled to peel Jerusalem artichokes are bound to dislike them because the job is so tedious. There is no reason the peels cannot be eaten. The tubers can be broken apart, scrubbed with a brush if necessary, then used. An alternative is to blanch them in boiling water, drain them, and rub the peels off. The tubers from newer hybrids are smoother and easier to clean than those from old strains or wild plants.

Steaming or boiling for 10 to 20 minutes is the basic cooking method for Jerusalem artichokes, but they can also be baked or sautéed. They have one peculiarity. If they are cooked much longer than is required to soften them, they will toughen or become hard again.

JERUSALEM ARTICHOKE STORAGE

Canning
Pickled only. See *Jerusalem Artichoke Pickles,* below.

Cold Storage
Will keep refrigerated 1–2 weeks only. Packed in damp material in root cellar will keep about 1 month. Refer to the COLD STORAGE section.

Drying
Slice to uniform size. Optional: Steam until tender, 5–10 min. Dry until hard. Refer to the DRYING section.

Freezing
Cut to uniform size. Blanch in boiling water with 1 or 2 teaspoons vinegar. Large chunks: 3 min.; sliced or diced: 1 min. Refer to the FREEZING section.

Live Storage
Leave in ground. Dig up in fall, winter, and early spring.

Jerusalem

Artichokes

152

Jerusalem Artichoke Salad

(MAKES ABOUT 6 SIDE SERVINGS)

1 pound Jerusalem artichokes, diced
2 tablespoons onion, minced, or
    2 scallions, chopped
¼ cup vegetable oil
¼ cup vinegar
1 teaspoon honey

1 tablespoon fresh herbs, minced,
    or 1 teaspoon dried herbs (mint is
    especially good, but parsley, thyme,
    and rosemary are also excellent)
lettuce, or other salad greens

Mix the Jerusalem artichokes, onion or scallion, oil, vinegar, honey, and herbs in a bowl. Let marinate at room temperature for an hour. Add greens and toss.

Jerusalem Artichoke Pickles

(MAKES 4 QUARTS, OR 8 PINTS, CANNED)

5 cups vinegar (refer to
    PICKLING VINEGAR, in the
    PICKLING section)
5 cups water
½ cup honey
1 teaspoon salt, optional
1 tablespoon turmeric,
    optional (it gives a golden
    color)

3 tablespoons pickling spices,
    tied in a cloth (refer to
    the PICKLING section)
4 quarts Jerusalem
    artichokes, cut in chunks
    or sliced
4 cloves garlic, optional

Heat the vinegar, water, honey, salt, turmeric, and pickling spices to a boil and simmer 15 minutes. Take out the pickling spices.

Meanwhile, pack the Jerusalem artichokes in clean, hot canning jars, leaving ½ inch headroom. If using garlic, put a whole clove in each quart jar, or a half clove in pints. Pour the boiling hot vinegar mixture into each jar, leaving ½ inch headroom. Adjust lids and process in a boiling water bath for 15 minutes. (Refer to the CANNING section.)

JERUSALEM ARTICHOKE IDEAS

Jerusalem Artichokes Simmered in Stock

Cover chunks or thick slices of Jerusalem artichoke with chicken stock or another soup stock, and simmer until tender, with most of the stock absorbed, 20 to 30 minutes. Do not overcook, or they will toughen. Serve with a lump of butter, a sprinkle of lemon juice or vinegar, and parsley for garnish.

Grated Jerusalem Artichoke in Soup or Salad

Grated Jerusalem artichoke is a good addition to most meat or vegetable soups, about 5 minutes before they are done. For salads, sprinkle grated Jerusalem artichoke with lemon juice or vinegar immediately after grating to keep it from discoloring.

Tomato Sauced Jerusalem Artichokes

Cut Jerusalem artichokes in chunks or slices and cook about 20 minutes in any well-seasoned tomato sauce. Serve with noodles or other pasta.

Kale

The handsome, dark green leaves of kale are likely to be the last green crop in the garden. As the cold deepens, their flavor sweetens, and kale comes into its own as the most delectable of winter vegetables.

Kale belongs to the cabbage family and is very closely related to collards (refer to the COLLARDS section), but it is individual in taste. Sea kale, considered to be a gourmet's vegetable, is another plant entirely. It grows wild along British and European Atlantic coasts.

HANDLING KALE

The kale season begins after autumn frosts, so never judge this vegetable by its flavor in warmer weather. If well-mulched, kale can be harvested in very cold weather, and may even last until spring. The early leaves that grow on overwintered plants are tender and delicious in salads. Otherwise, kale is best cooked. When preparing it, discard the tough stalks of large leaves. Leafy parts can be chopped, or torn with the fingers. Kale needs a longer cooking time than most greens, and should be steamed or boiled for about 20 minutes. If cooked with meat or potatoes, or a grain, such as oats or barley, simmer it from 30 to 40 minutes to mingle flavors.

Crispy Fried Kale

Heat several tablespoons of oil in a large frying pan or wok, and add crushed garlic and shredded or chopped kale. Fry, stirring often, over fairly high heat. Serve when crisp, in about 10 minutes.

Kohlrabi

The kohlrabi plant has its own special way of being a vegetable. Its stem enlarges just above the ground to form a round, firm bulb with a tuft of small leaves growing out of the top, and larger leaves here and there around the sides. The bulb tastes similar to the in-

---

Jerusalem Artichokes in Cucumber Recipes

Jerusalem artichokes do not taste anything like cucumbers, but they appreciate the same seasonings and can be prepared in the same ways. For instance, slice them raw and marinate in a vinegar mixture. Refer to *Vinegared Cucumbers*, in the CUCUMBERS section.

KALE STORAGE

Canning

Pressure can only!

Hot Pack

Cut out tough stalks. Steam until limp, about 10 min., tied in cheesecloth bag, or spread loosely on rack in large pot. Pack in jars, add boiling water, 1 in. headroom. Process 240°F, 11 lbs. pressure. Pints: 1 hr. 10 min. Quarts: 1 hr. 30 min. Refer to the CANNING section.

Cold Storage

Pull whole plants with roots. Replant in root cellar or protected outdoor frame, will keep 1 month or more. Refer to the COLD STORAGE section.

Drying

Refer to DRYING LEAFY GREENS, in the DRYING section.

ner stalks of its close relatives, cauliflower and broccoli, but is crisper and sweeter. Kohlrabi is delicious raw ("I eat 'em like apples," says one enthusiastic admirer), and it is delicious cooked. Even the leaves are tasty cooked like cabbage.

It is surprising that kohlrabies are not better known, since they are easy to grow and store, as well as being easy to enjoy in many different ways. Their name is German, taken from the Italian *caroli rape,* cabbage turnip.

HANDLING KOHLRABI

Harvest kohlrabies when small, between 2 and 4 inches in diameter. If they grow much larger, they become woody and strongly flavored. In close plantings they should be cut, since pulling disturbs the roots of adjacent plants. Plant kohlrabies intended for winter storage in summer, so that they are not overly large when harvested. Light frosts will not hurt them, but they must be pulled before heavy frosts.

Very small, tender kohlrabies do not need peeling. Peel medium sized bulbs, and save the leaves of all for greens. Raw kohlrabi is delicious sliced, chopped, or shredded in salads, or cut into sticks and eaten like carrot sticks. Small kohlrabies can be steamed or boiled whole, while larger ones are most often sliced or diced before cooking. Try them in the *Pickled Cauliflower Stalks* recipe in the CAULIFLOWER section.

Sautéed Kohlrabi

Slice kohlrabies thickly and steam until tender, or use cooked leftovers, or precooked, frozen and thawed slices. Sauté in butter or olive oil until golden brown. A half clove of garlic can be sautéed with them and removed, or add minced onion and curry powder to the butter or oil before the kohlrabi slices. Intense seasoning flavors blend well with this vegetable without overwhelming it.

Leeks ❧

Leeks are closely related to onions, with an onion-like smell and taste. However, they are not merely another kind of onion, but have a distinctive quality that makes them as beloved as a

---

Freezing

Cut into pieces, removing heavy stalks. Blanch in boiling water for 2 min. Refer to the FREEZING section.
2–3 pounds = 1 quart cooked

KOHLRABI STORAGE

Canning

Possible, but quality is poor.

Cold Storage

Remove large leaves, trim roots, and pack in damp material in root cellar, or pull with roots and "replant." Refer to the COLD STORAGE section.

Drying

Slice thinly or shred. Steam about 5 min. to cook through. Dry until hard. Refer to the DRYING section.

Freezing

Texture is damaged by ice crystals, but acceptable if precooked. Refer to the FREEZING section.

LEEK STORAGE

For CANNING, DRYING, and FREEZING refer to the ONIONS section, but

vegetable can be by those who know them well. Leeks are delicious enough when cooked plainly to be eaten every day of the week, and they are equally delicious in fancy dishes. Simple leek and potato soups have been satisfying daily fare in countless European homes for centuries, while Vichyssoise, a chilled leek soup so rich it has been called leek ice cream, is on the menu in the most elegant restaurants. There have been disputes for a century or two about the ingredients in the Scottish leek soup, Cock-a-leekie. While some may question the presence of prunes, most agree that the soup must be thick with leeks.

Growing the largest thick, white-stalked leeks is a gardening challenge, and in Wales there are leek growing contests. However, ordinary, even scrawny leeks keep well, have excellent flavor, and are easily grown in most gardens. Wild leeks are among the best tasting wild onions. Where plentiful they can be used in recipes instead of cultivated leeks.

HANDLING LEEKS

Leeks are planted in early spring for a fall and winter crop and are rarely harvested before the first frosts. Where winters are not too severe, leeks can be mulched and left in the garden to be pulled as needed. They also keep very well in a root cellar or any cool dark place if replanted in containers of sand or soil and kept slightly damp.

The lower white and light green part of the leek is the most tender, and is the part called for in recipes. The coarser, upper leaves are often cut off and discarded, but they are very flavorful, so save them for making soup stock. Or chop them small to add to soups and stews. If chopped and dried they can be used like dried onion.

After the outside leaves are pulled off and the top leaves and roots trimmed, carefully wash the leeks. Dirt becomes embedded in the folds of the leaves as they grow and will not easily rinse out. If the leeks are to be sliced, rinse them after slicing, with special attention to the section where the leaves start. If the leeks are to be used whole, make a slit, from just below the beginning of the leaves up to the top, so the leaves can be spread apart and rinsed.

Though leeks are almost always cooked, small amounts are good minced and added raw to salads.

COLD STORAGE (following) is the preferred method.

Cold Storage
Pull, and pack upright in damp sand or soil in root cellar, or in any cool, dark place, or mulch in garden through winter. Refer to the COLD STORAGE section.

LEEK IDEAS
Poor Man's Asparagus
As this name for leeks suggests, they can be steamed or stewed whole and seasoned in the same ways as asparagus.

Leek Salads
Steam leeks until just tender, let cool, and pour over them a dressing of oil and lemon juice or vinegar, or any favorite salad dressing. Crushed dill seeds make a lovely addition to the dressing. Marinate the leeks for a while or serve immediately if desired. Garnish with minced parsley or scallion, sliced or mashed hard-boiled eggs, or other salad ingredients. For a special treat, marinate mushrooms with the leeks for a few minutes.

Lettuce

Lettuce comes in several different types: head (or cabbage) lettuce, loose leaf lettuce, Bibb (or butterhead) which forms a soft loose head, cos (or romaine) which forms a loose, oblong head, and stem lettuce (or celtuce) with thick stems and narrow leaves. These all have noticeably different flavors and textures, but can be prepared in the same ways and are freely interchangeable in salads. Endive, escarole, and chicory are sometimes called lettuce, but they are a different plant. (Refer to the CHICORY section.)

To have a salad made with homegrown lettuce every day of the year would be ideal, but it is not easy. There is no practical way to store fresh lettuce except for short periods of refrigeration, so a constant supply depends on the cleverness of the gardener. The choice of varieties, timing of plantings, and the use of cooling shade in summer, and window sills, cold frames, and greenhouses in winter all help extend the lettuce season, but there may still be lettuceless times. Fortunately, there are alternatives other than buying tasteless lettuce from the store.

LETTUCE STORAGE
Cold Storage
Solid heads keep refrigerated about 1 month. Loose heads, leaves keep a few days to 2 weeks. See CLEANING AND CRISPING LETTUCE, below. Refer also to the SAUERKRAUT section.

LETTUCE IDEAS
Squeezed Lettuce Salad
When there is extra lettuce, shred a large amount, then squeeze it hard, a handful at a time. Let the water that comes out drain away. Mix with oil and vinegar or any other dressing. Much more lettuce than usual will be used, and the dressing will be absorbed more completely. Though everyone generally likes this salad, few can guess how it was made.

HANDLING LETTUCE

Pick lettuce when it is cool in the garden, and during hot sunny weather pick in the morning before the day's heat drains out its crispness. Properly handled, it will stay crisp for several days. Limp lettuce will sometimes revive if handled in the same way.

Cleaning and Crisping Lettuce

Wash lettuce soon after picking. If it is nearly clean, a quick rinsing in cold water is enough. If there is dirt between the leaves, separate them and put them in a big pan of cool water. Swish around gently and lift the lettuce out of the water, leaving the dirt behind. Repeat if necessary, using fresh water. If dirt still clings, rinse the leaves individually.

There are various ways to dry lettuce, from shaking the leaves, or patting them dry with a towel, to using a salad spinner that spins lettuce making the water fly off it. For handy home-style lettuce spinning, put the wet lettuce on a big, cloth dish towel. Gather the corners of the towel to make a "bag," take it outdoors, hold firmly, and swing the bag around several times in a full circle so that the water flies out. If the lettuce will be made into salad immediately, other leafy ingredients can be rinsed and swung in the towel with it.

To crisp limp lettuce, or to store it, leave the damp towel around it, and put the whole bundle in a big plastic bag in the refrigerator. The lettuce will be crisp after several hours, and should keep several days to a week wrapped in this way.

Though lettuce is most important as a raw vegetable, there are some very good ways to cook it. These are useful when it is most plentiful and threatening to go to seed in the garden. As well, firm varieties can be fermented for sauerkraut. (Refer to the SAUERKRAUT section.)

Melons 🌿

Down through the centuries there have been so many varieties and variations of varieties of melons that it would be impossible even to begin to evaluate them all. The melons best known in western countries are sweet fruits, delicious eaten fresh, but in China and other Asian countries, some melons are prepared as a vegetable, and a few varieties are grown for their seeds which are dried and eaten like nuts. Melons that are used as vegetables may be cut in pieces and stir-fried, or added to soups and stews. They taste something like cucumber or the white part of watermelon rind.

Sweet melons can be loosely divided into three groups: cantaloupes and muskmelons; honeydews, Persians, and casabas (sometimes called winter melons because they keep well); and watermelons. As watermelons have a different structure from other melons they are used somewhat differently. (Refer to the WATERMELONS section.)

HANDLING MELONS

Do not pick melons until they are completely ripe, as they do not gain sweetness after harvest. It is easy to tell when cantaloupes and muskmelons are ripe because they slip or separate from their stems by themselves. When a crack shows around the stem where it connects to the fruit the melon can be

---

MELON STORAGE

Canning

Not feasible unless pickled. Refer to *Spiced Pickled Fruit,* in the PICKLING section.

Cold Storage

Honeydews, Persians, casabas only. Storage life 1–2 months in root cellar.
Refer to the COLD STORAGE section.

Drying

Slice thinly. Dry to leathery. Refer to the DRYING section.

Freezing

Cut slices, cubes, or balls. Package plain, or in juice or syrup. Best eaten when partly thawed. Refer to the FREEZING section.

Melons

158

picked. Melons that do not separate can be judged for their ripeness by their color, their smell, and a slight softness when pressed at their stem end. Once picked, some melons will develop a richer flavor if kept for a day or two in a warm place, and afterwards will keep best in a cool, humid place. Cantaloupes and muskmelons should be eaten within a week or so. Others may keep for several weeks up to 2 months. However, melons are best as a fresh fruit, and something is lost when they are preserved for long storage, no matter which method is used. After freezing they will lose texture and are best eaten before they thaw completely. Dried melon has a sweet, odd flavor that only some people like. Melon juice and purée is best when mixed with lemon juice or another tart juice. (Refer to COMBINING SWEET AND TART FRUITS, in the FRUITS section.) For pickling, use those melons caught by the weather before they ripen completely. (Refer to the *Spiced Pickled Fruit* recipe, in the PICKLING section.)

Melon Seeds

Melon seeds are as nutritious and flavorful as pumpkin or sunflower seeds, but are too small to shell successfully. Some, which have very thin shells, can be dried or roasted, shells and all, and eaten as a snack. Otherwise, the seeds can be ground with water, then strained to make a "milk" to be used like coconut milk, or see the *Melon Seed Drink* recipe, below.

MELON RECIPES
Melon Seed Drink

(MAKES 4–5 GLASSES)

1 cup melon seeds, separated from pulp and fibers

2 tablespoons honey, or to taste

tiny sliver of rind from a lemon or lime

a few almonds, optional

Put all ingredients in a blender with a cup or so of water, and blend until smooth. Add 4 to 5 cups of water to the seed purée and let sit for half a day. Strain into a bowl through a damp cloth. Gather the edges of the cloth and twist and squeeze to get as much milk out of the seeds as possible. Chill, or serve over ice. This beverage (with or without a hint of almond) is a summertime favorite with young and old.

MELON IDEAS
Melon Appetizers

A section of melon with a sprinkle of lemon or lime juice makes a refreshing appetizer or first course. If a paper-thin slice of ham is laid on the melon it is deliciously elegant as well.

Melon Mixers

Though fresh, ripe melon is perfectly delicious unenhanced, it is fun to mix with other fruits and flavorings. Cherries, or chopped orange, grapefruit, or pineapple intermingle pleasantly. Add a sprinkle of minced mint leaf, nutmeg, powdered coriander seed, or grated fresh ginger for distinction. Some find that a dash of sweet wine or liqueur makes the mixture irresistible.

Mulberries

Mulberries are often ignored and left unused, yet they can be quite delicious. There are two kinds, red and white. Red mulberries, which are a dark, reddish purple or "mulberry" color when ripe, taste very good and can be eaten fresh like other soft berries or used in the same recipes as blackberries. White mulberries, which can be pale green to almost beige in color, are very sweet and can be eaten out of hand, though they tend to be dry. They are excellent dried and ground into a meal to use in baking. White mulberry meal is a common food in Afghanistan. Since many mulberry trees are wild there is considerable variation in the quality of the fruit. With luck and persistent tasting it is possible to find mulberry trees with exceptionally good fruit.

HANDLING MULBERRIES

To gather mulberries in quantity, it is usually easiest to spread an old sheet or large drop cloth under the tree, and shake the branches over it. If the tree is too big to shake, spread the cloth, weighted down with a few rocks, and leave it there to catch the berries as they fall by themselves. Then collect the berries once a day.

Red mulberries need no preparation to be eaten fresh, except a quick rinsing if dusty. Their small stems can be removed, but that is optional. Where people object to the axis or core that goes part way into each berry, try making them into juice. Red mulberry juice is delicious. Make from fresh berries by mashing and straining them, or by squeezing them in a cloth. (Refer to MAKING FRUIT JUICE AND SAUCE, in the FRUITS section.) A little lemon juice brings out the flavor, or try mixing it with the tart juices. (Refer to COMBINING SWEET AND TART FRUITS, in the FRUITS section.)

Do not wash white mulberries collected for drying unless really necessary. If they require washing, do it just before the drying starts, as they turn brown and spoil quickly once they become wet. The dried mulberries are easily ground to meal in a blender, grain mill, or other grinder. This meal is quite sweet with a delicate flavor, so can be added to most baked goods for sweetening. (Refer to USING DRIED FRUIT, in the DRYING section.)

MULBERRY STORAGE
Canning

Not practical except for red mulberry juice. Add 1–2 tablespoons lemon juice per quart. Refer to CANNING FRUIT JUICE AND SAUCE, in the FRUITS section.

Drying

Best for white mulberries. Dry until hard. Grind to meal. Refer to the DRYING section.

Freezing

Acceptable for red mulberries. Refer to the BLACKBERRIES section.

MULBERRY IDEAS
Mulberry-Ade

In the Middle East, red mulberry syrup is mixed into ice water to make a delicious, cool drink for hot weather. For a concentrated syrup, boil 1 part mulberry juice with 1 part honey, or 1½ parts sugar, adding lemon juice, if desired. One tablespoon of this will flavor a glassful of ice water. Or make mulberry-ade by simply mixing mulberry juice, lemon juice, water, and then sweetening to taste.

Mushrooms

To the scientist the mushroom is a fleshy fungus; to the epicure it is a gastronomic delight. To the country dweller it is a delicious food, expensive to buy but practical to grow and gather wild.

The mushroom most often home grown is white button, the variety usually sold fresh in stores. Some seed catalogs sell starter kits for these and other kinds of mushrooms, including royal tan, shiitake, and portabella.

Before edible wild mushrooms can be safely gathered it is essential to learn to identify the different kinds, but it is not necessary to become a mycological expert. A few delicious wild mushrooms are easy to identify, once their characteristics are learned. The more confusing and potentially dangerous ones can be avoided, even though some among them may be good to eat.

Truffles, which are subterranean fungi, are a relative of mushrooms, and are used in very small amounts for flavoring the same kinds of foods that go well with mushrooms. Most come from Europe and are available only at very high prices. The various dried mushrooms and wood fungus found in Chinese grocery stores and other specialty shops are interesting and much less expensive.

HANDLING MUSHROOMS

When gathering mushrooms, whether cultivated or wild, brush off loose soil and trim the stem end before putting them in a container. Soil clinging to one mushroom can stick here and there to others, making the whole batch hard to clean. If carefully gathered, wiping with a damp cloth may be all that is required. If they must be washed, do so quickly, in cool water, and pat dry with a towel. If allowed to soak, they become soggy and easily spoil. For large or mature mushrooms it is best to separate the caps and stems, as the stems tend to be tougher and slower cooking than the caps. Use them for adding flavor to sauces. Use the caps whole or sliced in dishes ranging from salads and appetizers to main courses.

MUSHROOM STORAGE
Canning
Pressure can only! Trim, wash, cut to uniform size. Blanch 4 min. in boiling water. Optional: To prevent darkening, add 1 tablespoon vinegar per quart blanching water, or add ⅛ teaspoon ascorbic acid to each pint jar, and ¹⁄₁₆ teaspoon to half pints. Pack in jars, add fresh boiling water, ½ in. headroom. Process 240°F, 11 pounds pressure. Both pints and half pints: 40 min. Refer to the CANNING section.

Drying
See DRYING MUSHROOMS, below.

Freezing
Trim, clean with damp cloth. May be quartered or sliced. Sauté, and pack in cooking juices, or steam blanch in single layer, 3–5 min. Quality retained 8–10 months. Refer to the FREEZING section.

1 pound fresh mushrooms = 4–5 cups sliced (1–1½ cups cooked); 1 pound fresh = about 3 ounces dried

MUSHROOM IDEAS
Mushroom Extract
Clean and chop several cups of mushrooms, including stems. Put them in

The different wild mushrooms vary greatly in taste and in the way they respond to cooking, and simple directions are impossible. Those who like to experiment should enjoy trying them in different ways.

Generally, drying is the best way to preserve mushrooms, and the flavor of some varieties is even enhanced by drying. When canned or frozen, they tend to lose flavor, and may lose texture as well.

Drying Mushrooms

There are two approaches to drying mushrooms. One is to dry them whole or in thick slices, for reconstituting as a featured ingredient in various dishes. The other is to chop them small before drying, or to grind them after drying, both for use as seasoning in sauces, soups, and other dishes. It is often most practical to dry the caps whole and chop the stems. Dry the stems of large mushrooms separately, in any case, since they dry more slowly than the caps.

If mushrooms are to be dried whole or in slices, trim them and wipe them clean with a damp cloth. It is best not to wash them. Sometimes soil that sticks when they are fresh will brush off after a day of drying. Wash off any remaining soil just before soaking the mushrooms to reconstitute them. They usually need about 30 minutes of soaking in warm water. Soil settled in the soaking water will be left behind when the clear part is poured off. Dried mushrooms and wood fungus from Chinese groceries usually need washing and trimming when they are soaked.

Mushrooms dried for seasoning may have to be washed, since they will be used without pre-soaking. If chopped small before drying, they will need only a few minutes of cooking. If ground in a mill or flaked in a blender they can be added just before a dish is served. (Refer to USING DRIED VEGETABLES FOR SOUP, in the DRYING section.)

Mushrooms will dry easily in any dry, airy place, whether in the sun or shade. Use drying trays or string them on a thread and hang them up to dry. Once they are hard or brittle store them in airtight containers.

a dry pan over low heat. Sprinkle with salt. Cover and cook 20 to 25 minutes. Drain, saving the liquid. Return mushrooms to the heat for a few more minutes, then drain again, saving liquid. Add water to the pan to cover the mushrooms, and simmer, uncovered, until the liquid is reduced to ¼ the original amount. Drain off liquid and mix with the other liquid. Discard the spent mushrooms. Simmer, uncovered, until the extract is quite strong and slightly thickened. Keeps a month or longer in the refrigerator. A teaspoon or less will season sauces, soups, and meat and poultry dishes.

Mushroom Catsup

To make this old-fashioned condiment, add a few whole peppercorns, allspice, and cloves, and perhaps a clove of garlic, to the mushroom liquid above, just before simmering it down to a concentrated extract. Strain and refrigerate. Use like mushroom extract, or instead of commercial sauces like Worcestershire.

Mustard
(Greens and Seeds)

The mustard plant got its name from a condiment made by mixing must, which is wine in the first stages of fermentation, with the powdered seeds of the plant. Most gardeners cultivate mustard for its greens, not its seeds, but both are valuable. The lightly hot taste of mustard greens distinguishes them from blander greens, making them a favorite with many. Mustard seeds make a good seasoning used whole or powdered, and home prepared mustard is excellent. The seeds are easy to collect from wild plants, so it may be more practical to gather them than to grow them. Wild mustard greens are good in early spring, but their season is short compared to cultivated greens.

Most varieties of mustard can be grown for both greens and seeds. Black mustard is an ancient variety still cultivated for both. It is also the most common wild variety. White mustard is often cultivated for its large white or yellow seeds but the greens are also good. Chinese or Indian mustard is mild flavored and is grown primarily for its greens. The greens and seeds of many mustard relatives can be used like mustard. Radish tops and turnip greens can be cooked like mustard greens, and their seeds, as well as Chinese cabbage seeds, can be used for seasoning. Arugula, or garden rocket, is a relative of mustard whose leaves are used as a fresh herb. Their strong and distinctive taste goes well with fresh tomatoes.

HANDLING MUSTARD

Mustard greens are cool-weather vegetables that grow very quickly. In the South they are a winter crop. Further north they are a fall crop or the first spring crop harvested from a spring planting. The early small leaves are very good in salads, but larger leaves are best cooked. If mustard plants are left to go to seed, the flower buds and flowers can be eaten, but these are usually saved to develop seeds. Gather seed pods before they are dry enough to split open and scatter seeds. Seed stalks can be picked when the lowest pods have begun to split, or pick pods individually. Lay stalks or pods on cloth or plastic to finish

---

MUSTARD (GREENS AND SEEDS) STORAGE

To preserve mustard greens refer to the SPINACH section.

Mature dry mustard seeds keep indefinitely in closed containers.

MUSTARD (GREENS AND SEEDS) IDEAS
Mustard Greens Patties

Chop cooked mustard greens to bite-size or smaller, and mix them with 1 or 2 beaten eggs, and a tablespoon or two each of flour and grated cheese. Shape into patties, then fry in oil or another fat until nicely browned on both sides.

Chinese Mustard Sauce

Put a spoonful of powdered, dry mustard in a small dish and stir in enough soy sauce to make the texture of thin cream. Mix an hour or two before meal time, and use as a dip for stir-fried or deep fried vegetables or meats. This sauce is very hot, so a little goes a long way. It can also be made with water or milk instead of soy sauce.

drying. They can then be crushed and winnowed to separate the seeds. (Refer to THRESHING AND WINNOWING, in the SEEDS section.)

Whole mustard seeds are good for seasoning pickles and meat marinades, and they can be sprouted. (Refer to the SPROUTS section.) Crushed or powdered, the seeds can be added to stews, sauces, and salad dressings.

Prepared Mustard from Seeds

Dry, powdered mustard is made by pulverizing mustard seeds. The powder can then be made into a creamy, prepared mustard.

The simplest preparations combine powdered mustard with vinegar or another liquid. Seasonings such as tarragon and turmeric may be added. Turmeric intensifies the yellow color. For less hot preparations, flour or another bland ingredient is added. The flour can be lightly browned to take away the raw taste. If vinegar is used the prepared mustard will keep indefinitely.

Other kinds of edible seeds with a hot, peppery flavor can also be made into a condiment like mustard. Dry nasturtium seeds and Chinese cabbage seeds have been used in this way.

MUSTARD RECIPES
Prepared Mustard

(MAKES ABOUT I CUP)

¾ cup (about) vinegar

OPTIONAL SEASONINGS:
(May use one alone, or any combination.)
slice of onion
sprig of tarragon, or ½ teaspoon dried
½ teaspoon celery or lovage seeds
1 clove garlic, crushed
4 tablespoons powdered mustard

1 tablespoon flour, lightly browned in a dry frying pan
½ teaspoon pepper
½ teaspoon turmeric
½ teaspoon salt, optional
1 tablespoon honey or sugar
1 tablespoon oil

Mix the vinegar with any optional seasonings used, and let sit overnight.

Crushed Mustard Seed Seasoning

Use crushed mustard seeds as a seasoning for salad dressings, cream sauces, and meat and vegetable dishes. Crush a few seeds as needed with a mortar and pestle, or with the back of a spoon against the side of a small bowl. Their flavor is fresher and less harsh than that of the commercial dry powdered mustard. Crushed seeds can be used instead of the commercial powder in many recipes.

Pot Likker

The liquid left from cooking mustard greens or turnip greens is called pot likker in the southern United States. One of the most flavorful and nutritious of vegetable cooking waters, it is a good "dunk" sauce for cornbread, and very good added to soups and stews.

"Must"-ard

Take out a little of the must when making wine and mix powdered mustard seeds into it to make a strong, flavorful condiment. Or use fermenting ap-

The next day combine the mustard powder, flour, pepper, turmeric, and salt, if desired, in a bowl. Heat the vinegar, seasonings, and honey or sugar to a boil, then strain out and discard seasonings. Pour boiling hot into the bowl, stirring while pouring. If too thick, heat and add a little more vinegar. Mix the oil into the prepared mustard and store in a jar in the refrigerator. This keeps indefinitely. A doubled recipe can be made. Flavor will vary with seed varieties. Most are excellent used like commercial prepared mustards.

Sunflower Mustard Butter

(MAKES ABOUT 1 CUP)

½ cup sunflower seeds
1 tablespoon mustard seeds

2 tablespoons oil
dash of salt, optional

Mix the sunflower and mustard seeds and cover them with water. Let them soak several hours or until swollen. Put them in a blender with their soaking water. Add oil, and salt, if desired, and blend until smooth and thick. If necessary, add a little more water to make the blender function. Very good with vegetables, or spread on crackers, or in sandwiches.

ple cider for the must. This idea goes back at least to Roman times. Use like prepared mustard with anything from fish to hot dogs.

NUTS STORAGE

Canning

Dry hot pack only! Spread nutmeats in a shallow layer, bake at 250°F for 30 min. or until hot, dry, but not brown. Pack hot, in pints or half pints only. Process 228°F, 5 pounds pressure, 10 min. or boiling water bath, 20 min. Keep water level below jar rims or jars may float. Refer to the CANNING section.

Cold Storage

See STORING NUTS, below.

Drying

See CURING NUTS, below.

Freezing

Leave in shells or shell, and freeze whole, chopped or ground. Package airtight. Quality retained 1–2 years. Refer to the FREEZING section. Also see

Nuts 🍃

Nuts are rich in flavor and rich in protein, fat, and B vitamins. They have been a highly valued food since the beginnings of the human race, and the gathering and storing of nuts for winter was essential for survival for many primitive people. In the modern world, nuts are valued more as a luxury than as a necessity, but they are still an excellent food to gather and store.

Just about everywhere in the United States and southern Canada there are kinds of nuts that can be cultivated or gathered from wild trees and shrubs. The uses of the different varieties are generally the same in spite of their assorted sizes, shapes, and flavors. Notable exceptions are chestnuts, which are starchy rather than oily, and peanuts, which are legumes rather than true nuts. (Refer to the CHESTNUTS and PEANUTS sections.)

SOME NORTH AMERICAN NUTS

Acorns

Oak trees of many species are common in eastern North America, and several species also grow in the west. The acorns from different species vary considerably in taste. Some are sweet enough to eat raw, but many kinds are too bitter to eat unless the tannin has been leached out of them. Tasting is the best way to tell whether acorns from a particular tree will need treatment.

Acorns are easier to peel if soaked overnight in water to make the shells split. The nutmeats can be roasted, then ground to make a dark meal or flour for baking. They can also be roasted and brewed for a beverage.

Almonds

Almond trees are cultivated in the warmer areas of the Pacific coast. Besides the familiar, sweet almonds there is a bitter variety used in small amounts for flavoring some almond pastes and ground mixtures. Soft, immature (green) almonds are good to eat, as well as the mature dry nuts. There is a botanical relationship between almonds and the stone fruits that can be tasted in the slightly bitter almond flavor of the kernels inside the pits of apricots, peaches, and plums. (Refer to the APRICOTS section.) Sometimes the kernels of those fruits are used to replace almonds in paste and other preparations.

Beech Nuts

Beech trees grow throughout the eastern United States and southern Canada, but they produce more and larger nuts in the northern part of their range. Beech nuts are thin shelled, small, and triangular in shape with a sweet, pleasant flavor.

Black Walnuts

Black walnut trees grow throughout the eastern United States, but they are becoming scarce because so many have been harvested for their valuable wood. The nuts fall from the trees with thick green hulls around them which later blacken. They must be crushed and removed before the hard shells are cracked and the nutmeats picked out. In spite of these difficulties, black walnuts are prized for their rich flavor. They are especially good in baking.

PICKLING WALNUTS OR BUTTERNUTS, below.

1 pound nuts in shells = about ½ pound shelled = 1½–2 cups nutmeats

NUTTY IDEAS
Roasted Nuts

Freshly roasted nuts make the ultimate snack food. For plain roasted nuts spread them on a baking sheet, and roast in a moderate, 350°F oven for about 10 minutes or until lightly browned. Stir once or twice, and watch closely to prevent burning. For salted nuts, mix a teaspoon of oil with each cup of nuts, and sprinkle with salt before roasting. For an almost smoky flavor, mix 1 teaspoon soy sauce and 1 teaspoon oil with each cup of nuts before roasting. A stove top version can be made by using any nuts in the BEER NUTS recipe, in the PEANUTS section.

Seasoned Nuts and Grains

Cook a grain such as rice, bulghur wheat, or barley, in soup stock instead of water. When done and the liquid is

Butternuts (White Walnuts)

Like black walnuts, these also grow wild in North America, with about the same range. Butternuts are difficult to shell, but their flavor is excellent. They can be used like regular walnuts or like black walnuts.

Cashews

Cashews can be cultivated only in the warmest regions of the United States. The trees are evergreen, related to poison ivy. The nuts must be roasted before they are shelled to dispel the irritating oil that surrounds them. Cashew butter is as flavorful and as versatile as peanut butter, though not as well-known.

Chinquapins

This name is applied to several different trees or shrubs that grow in various locations, primarily in the southern half of the United States. Their nuts are good-tasting but are used only locally. There is also a chinquapin oak whose acorns are quite bitter.

Hazelnuts or Filberts

Native American hazelnuts are smaller than European filberts, but they taste the same. Hazelnuts grow on shrubs rather than trees in scattered locations throughout the United States. Filberts can be cultivated in the same range as peaches, but they excel along the Pacific coast.

Hickory Nuts

Most species of hickory trees bear good-tasting nuts. There is, however, the Bitter Hickory tree, whose nuts are inedible. The nuts of the pignut hickory are reputed to be bitter, yet often they taste quite good. The best test is to taste the nuts of individual trees. Most hickories grow in the eastern United States and southeastern Canada.

Pecans

Pecans are the largest and meatiest of the hickory nuts. They are cultivated and also found growing wild in the southeastern United States.

---

absorbed, stir in chopped nuts, minced parsley, and other herbs and seasonings to taste. This makes a nutritious side dish or main course. It is also a delicious stuffing for vegetables such as green peppers or squash.

Nut Shakes

Pulverize 1 or 2 tablespoons of nuts in a blender, add about a cup of milk or water, an ice cube, and fresh or canned fruit and honey to taste. Blend until smooth. The nuts thicken and enrich this classic beverage.

Nut Soup

Pulverize ½ to 1 cup nuts in a blender, and add soup stock to make a purée. Include 1 or 2 cloves garlic, if desired. Mix in more soup stock as needed for a thin, creamy texture. Heat to a boil and season to taste. Freshly ground black pepper and a little milk or cream are very nice. Serve with a sprinkle of

Pine Nuts

Several species of nut pines produce nuts large enough to eat. The piñon pine is probably the best known. Usually the pine cones are gathered and then roasted to loosen the nuts, so that they fall out or are easily removed. As their flavor is unique, they are not usually interchangeable with other nuts in recipes. Pine nuts are often used as garnish or for flavoring in Middle Eastern and Mediterranean cooking.

Pistachios

In North America these nuts can be cultivated only in some interior California valleys. They are set apart by the unusual green color of their kernels, and their special, rich flavor. Their shells are sometimes dyed red for a decorative effect, but they seem to taste best in their natural beige shells.

Walnuts

English walnuts, the most familiar kind, are cultivated in the southern United States and along the Pacific coast. One variety, the Carpathian walnut, can stand colder temperatures, so family orchards farther north sometimes include them. Walnuts can be used in salads or in cooking when they first fall from the tree, but cured walnuts are most familiar, as curing is necessary for them to keep well (see below). Immature walnuts are very good pickled.

HANDLING NUTS

Nuts should be allowed to fall naturally from the tree when they become mature. They should not be picked, or hit to knock them loose, but branches can be shaken, if low enough to reach, so that mature nuts fall. Gather nuts from the ground soon after they fall so that squirrels, worms, and mold do not take too large a toll. People have been known to gather nuts before dawn to beat the squirrels to those that fell during the night.

Hulling Nuts

Many kinds of nuts grow surrounded by a thick hull or husk covering the nutshell. Usually these split open when mature, and the nuts fall out or easily separate. The hulls of black wal-

minced parsley, or a dash of paprika for color. Slivered nuts are also an attractive garnish.

Nut Meal Vegetable Topping

Mix 1 cup nut meal or finely chopped nuts with about 2 tablespoons melted butter. Sprinkle over vegetable casseroles, stuffed vegetables, and anywhere that a bread crumb topping might have been used.

Maple Nuts

Heat about a cup of maple syrup in a saucepan. When it boils, remove from heat and drop in some walnut halves, acorns, hazelnuts, or what have you. Dried fruits can also be included. Stir to coat all ingredients, then lift them out with a slotted spoon. Eat right away. Great as a sticky treat for unexpected company! Leftover syrup can be saved for cooking or another sticky treat.

nuts are an exception. They must be crushed or broken to free the nuts. Suggestions for doing this range from grinding each nut under the heel of one's boot to driving a car back and forth over them. If a wooden trough is made to fit the car's tire it will hold the nuts and they will not spin out from under the wheel.

Remove hulls from nuts when they are gathered or soon afterwards to prevent them from staining the nuts or giving them a bitter flavor. Walnut hulls are used for making a fabric dye, and they will also dye the hands of anyone who handles them. Such stains are almost impossible to wash off, so wear gloves when gathering and hulling.

After nuts are hulled put them in a container of water to separate any that are diseased or rotten. These will float and can be discarded. Drain the good nuts and immediately spread them out to dry.

Curing Nuts

Most freshly gathered nuts taste better and keep better if cured (dried in their shells) for several weeks to a month before being eaten or stored. For curing, spread them out in a dry, airy, shaded place. Old window screens make good curing trays. If the nuts are piled up more than two nuts deep, stir or rearrange them every few days to make sure they cure evenly. Screened porches or well-ventilated attics make good drying places. Of course, squirrels and other rodents must be kept out.

To check if the nuts have cured long enough, crack one and inspect the nutmeats. Any green or bitter taste should be gone, and the kernels should be brittle enough to snap when bitten or broken.

Storing Nuts

Cured nuts keep best in their shells unless they are to be canned or frozen. Some varieties, particularly walnuts, pecans, filberts, and hickory nuts, will keep as long as a year in a cool storage place. Containers should allow some ventilation for moisture to escape, otherwise mildew or mold may develop. Dry peat moss can be packed around nuts to absorb moisture.

Shelled nutmeats become rancid rather quickly when exposed to air and light. They will keep several months in the refrigerator, but for longer storage they should be canned or frozen.

Shelling Nuts

Some nuts have shells so thin they can easily be cracked with teeth or fingers and some are so tough they can resist a sharp blow with a hammer. Nuts are most easily cracked, and the nutmeats will come out in larger pieces, if the nuts are placed in the nutcracker the long way, or held upright and hit on their most pointed end. Once the shell is broken, a nut pick can be used to pry out hard to reach nutmeats, but it may be easier to crack the shell again. Place halves (or quarters, if need be) the long way in the nutcracker or hold them upright as when cracking whole nuts. Shrivelled and dark looking nutmeats are usually bitter and are best discarded.

CRACKING THE TOUGHEST NUTS

- Soften nut shells by pouring boiling water over them, then let them sit 15 to 20 minutes. Drain and shell.
- Freeze nuts to make the shells brittle. Remove only a few at a time from the freezer, and crack them before they start to thaw.
- Use a vise to crack the nuts. Position the nuts the long way and tighten the vise slowly so that it cracks without mashing them.
- Try roasting the nuts in the shell in a low oven for 20 to 30 minutes before cracking. This makes some nuts easier to crack.
- As a last resort smash nuts and shells together, then cook in plenty of water, until oil and nutmeats rise and shells sink. Skim off oil and nuts for use. The liquid can be strained through cloth to make nut milk. See NUT OIL, NUT MILK, and NUT FLOUR, below.

Blanching Nutmeats

Nutmeats are blanched by pouring boiling water over them, waiting 1 minute, then draining them. This loosens their thin, dark skins so they can be peeled or rubbed off. Nuts are blanched for their white appearance, but the procedure is not otherwise desirable, since the skins add flavor and nutritional value.

BASIC NUT PREPARATIONS

Nuts are so good plain that it is easy to eat a great many just as they come from the shell. However, there are several worthwhile nut preparations that offer variety, and can be the basis of some very delicious dishes.

Nut Butter

When nuts are ground in a way that crushes them the result is smooth nut butter. Only the oiliest nuts will turn to butter in a blender without added oil. (Add oil as for making peanut butter. Refer to the PEANUTS section.) A meat grinder can be used to make butter from most kinds of nuts without adding oil. It will take 2 or 3 grindings. To store, refrigerate in a closed container.

Use nut butters like peanut butter or regular butter. They are very delicious mixed with hot, cooked vegetables. A mixture of nut butter and maple syrup or honey is very good on bread.

Nut Meal

Nuts can be grated, flaked, or finely chopped to make meal. Most kinds can be flaked in a blender if they are done in small batches, a few tablespoons at a time. Some meat grinders have grating attachments that can be used to make nut meal, or the small hand-turned rotary graters for hard cheese can be used. Nuts can also be grated, one at a time, on a vegetable grater, or chopped finely with a knife, but these methods are very slow.

Use nut meal instead of some of the flour in baked goods. It is delicious in pancake batter and pie crusts. Nut meal is also good sprinkled over foods or used as a coating for sticky dried fruit, doughnuts, or any food that might otherwise be rolled in powdered sugar.

Nut Milk

A purée of nuts and water is a nut milk that can be used in many ways, often instead of regular milk. If a perfectly smooth nut milk is wanted, strain through cloth. To make nut milk in a blender, first pulverize the nuts, then add water, and blend until smooth. For a fairly thick milk, pulverize ½ cup nuts and add 1 cup of water. If the milk is strained, use the leftover nut pulp in baked goods, puddings, and vegetable loaves or patties.

Cooking Nuts for Oil, Milk, and Flour

Nuts were often made into oil, milk, and flour by the eastern American Indians. It is possible to make all three from the same batch of nuts.

Grind or chop the nuts, then add 4 or 5 times their volume of water. Cook until the nut oil rises, then pour through a sieve into a tall, wide-mouthed jar. This will make it easier to skim the nut oil off the top with a spoon. Some kinds of nuts may have very little oil. Use nut oils in salad dressings, or for seasoning cooked vegetables and other hot foods. Use the cooking liquid like milk in baked goods, desserts, and fruit-flavored beverages. To make nut flour, dry the sediment or bits of nut left after the milk is strained off. When completely dry, grind to a fine texture in a blender or a grain mill. Once their oil has been removed, the nuts will not clog a mill.

Pickling Walnuts or Butternuts

An old-fashioned, strong-flavored pickle can be made from walnuts or butternuts picked in early summer, when the nuts are almost full size and tender enough for a needle to go through them easily. The nuts are pickled hulls and all, and can be eaten about a month after they are finished though they are said to improve in flavor if kept 1 or 2 years. They are a unique treat and, like other pickles, good for snacking, or to accompany bland foods.

Okra

Okra evokes love often, dislike sometimes, but indifference? Never! This vegetable belongs to the mallow family which in general has the mucilaginous, sticky texture that cannot be ignored. (Another member is the marsh mallow, from which the original marshmallows were made.)

Okra is best known and best loved in the southeastern United States where it is highly productive. Southern varieties do not do well in the North because they require a long warm growing season, but now the development of some excellent short season varieties is extending its range and popularity. In the South another name for okra is gumbo. This can be confusing to the non-Southerner, since gumbos are also stews or soups thickened with okra, or filé (powdered, dried sassafras leaves).

HANDLING OKRA

Only okra pods picked when very young will be tender—pick them within a few days of the time the blossoms fall, as the pods quickly become woody if left on the plant. To keep the plants producing, pods must be picked every second or third day. As canned, dried, and frozen okra are all excellent, the choice of storage depends on individual preferences. It is handy, however, to have a supply of thinly sliced dried okra or dried, powdered okra that can be quickly added to stews and soups to thicken and flavor them.

Powdered okra can be added to foods at the last minute be-

OKRA STORAGE

Canning
Hot pack only! Trim stems, but leave caps, and blanch 1 min. in boiling water. Pack whole or slice, discarding cap. Add boiling water, ½ in. headroom. Process 240°F, 11 pounds pressure. Pints: 25 min. Quarts: 40 min. (Process mixtures with tomatoes or tomato juice as for okra alone. Refer to the CANNING section.)

Drying
For soup, slice thinly, and dry raw. For whole young pods, steam blanch to tender, about 10 min. (optional), trim off caps. Dry until hard or brittle. Refer to the DRYING section.

Freezing
Trim stems, but leave caps, and blanch in boiling water. Small pods: 3 min. Large pods: 4 min. Trim caps, package whole or sliced. Refer to the FREEZING section.

1½ pounds pods = about 1 quart stewed

fore serving, or put it on the table in a shaker for people to add as they wish. Filé, a similar thickener, is made of dried, powdered sassafras leaves, with powdered okra and spices sometimes included. A chewed sassafras leaf has the same mucilaginous quality as okra.

Fresh okra will take from 15 to 30 minutes to cook, depending on the size of the pods and the cooking method. If it is precooked in boiling water or steam, the pods should be left whole with the caps on. Cutting into the seed chamber before cooking will cause the loss of juice and flavor. When cooked, the caps can be trimmed off and the okra sliced, if desired.

A quite different way to use okra is to cook the seeds like peas. They have a distinctive, interesting flavor.

Okra Stuffed Tomatoes
(MAKES 6–8 SIDE SERVINGS)

6–8 tomatoes	½ cup onion, minced
4 tablespoons butter	1 clove garlic, minced
1 pound okra, sliced medium	1½ cups cooked rice
2 tablespoons parsley, minced	pepper, salt, optional

Hollow out the tomatoes, reserving the pulp. Melt the butter and sauté the okra, parsley, onion, and garlic in it. Stir often, until the onions and okra are soft, about 20 minutes. Then add the tomato pulp, rice, pepper, and salt, if desired, and cook another 5 minutes. Stuff the tomatoes with this mixture and place them close together in a buttered baking dish. Bake for 10 minutes in a 400°F oven. The tomato and okra flavors go very well together.

Onions 🌿

Everywhere in the world, humankind eats onions, and onions are called for in recipes more often than any other vegetable. They are eaten raw and cooked in every style, using every method ever devised. They are as delicious tossed into the coals of a campfire and roasted, as they are mingled with the rarest ingredients in the haughtiest cuisines. In addition, onions are credited with most of the same medicinal values as garlic, though in a milder way, and are eaten to maintain health and prevent disease. And last but not least, they are said to repel both insects and witches.

Onions come in many forms and varieties. Most familiar are the mature, papery-skinned bulbs. These range anywhere from marble sized to grapefruit sized, and they may be any color from white-beige yellow-brown to purplish-red. Their flavors and aromas may range from sweet and mild to harsh and tear jerking. Next most common are slender, young, green scallions. All young onions with green tops may be called scallions, no matter what they will be like at maturity. The bunching types of onions, and the multiplier (Egyptian) onions never produce large bulbs. These are valuable because they can over-winter in the garden and provide scallions in very early spring and late fall. Shallots are close relatives of onions, grown like garlic but eaten like onions. Their special flavor is prized by many cooks. (For other onion relatives refer to CHIVES, SCALLIONS, OTHER ONION GREENS, in the HERBS section, and to the LEEKS section.)

Many kinds of wild onions are worth gathering, and there is one species or another growing over most of North America. Some are so strong they can be used only for seasoning, but others can be used like cultivated onions.

HANDLING ONIONS

It would be ideal to always have a supply of homegrown onions in the store room, and a stand of small, green onions ready to pull in the garden, but in most places, this is difficult to achieve. It is not so difficult, however, to have homegrown onions of one kind or the other on hand throughout the year. Recipes can then be adjusted to suit the available onions, with no need to purchase any.

Green Onions (Scallions)

To be good these have to be fresh. If dried they are tasteless. They may retain their flavor when frozen, but their texture will be poor. The longer they can be maintained in the garden, the better.

The earliest green onions of the season are likely to come from overwintered multiplier or bunching onions. These can be pulled as scallions, or the greens can be cut off at ground level to use like chives, leaving the bulbs to produce more greens. Later in the season, scallions will come from the thinnings of onions grown from sets or seeds. In winter, it is possible to grow onion greens by planting sets in pots on the

---

ONION STORAGE

Canning

Resulting texture or color may be poor. Small (about 1 in. diameter) preferred. Trim, peel, push large needle or ice pick into root end to help hold shape. Boil 5 min. Pack hot in jars, add boiling cooking water, ½ in. headroom. Process 240°F, 11 pounds pressure. Pints: 25 min. Quarts: 30 min. Refer to the CANNING section.

Cold Storage

See CURING AND STORING MATURE ONIONS, below.

Drying

See DRYING ONIONS, below.

Freezing

Mature Onions Blanch 3–7 min. (Texture poor. Best used to flavor cooked

window sill. Sets collected from the tops of multiplier onions in the summer can be used.

When green onions are not available for the table, a slice of mature onion can be minced and used instead. Conversely, green onions, including their tops, can be chopped and used in cooking instead of mature onions. As they cook quickly, it is best to add them towards the end of the cooking time. They are excellent in soups and stews. If fried the cooking time should be very brief.

Curing and Storing Mature Onions

Onions are ready to harvest when the tops have stopped growing and have fallen over. After pulling or digging them, spread the onions out in a single layer in a dry airy place to cure for about a week. If the weather is dry they can be left outdoors on the ground, with their tops flopped over them to protect them from the sun. Otherwise they can be spread out in any sheltered, well-ventilated place. When cured the onion tops will be dry and shrunken at the neck of the bulb. Set aside any onions with thick necks to be used first, as they will not keep long. Cut the dry leaves off about an inch above the bulbs.

Store onions in net bags, or in well-ventilated boxes in a dry, cool place. A root cellar is too damp. They are better off in a dry place that is too warm than in a cool, damp place. An unheated attic or a spare room that stays above freezing is excellent. The length of time that cured onions will keep depends on their variety as well as storage conditions. Many varieties will keep 2 to 3 months. Only the long keeping, winter varieties can be stored until spring.

Check stored onions occasionally for softness, spoilage, or sprouting. The sprouts can be used like scallions. Dry any that show signs of sprouting or spoiling before they can be used.

Small onions with tough tops can be braided and hung like garlic (refer to the GARLIC section for directions), but they are not likely to keep as well as those cured and stored as above.

Drying Onions

Drying mature onions is easy, and they are convenient to use. For drying, simply slice them thinly and evenly and spread them on drying trays. Dry until hard or brittle. Onions do not

dishes.) Refer to the FREEZING section. Also see FREEZING HERBS, in the HERBS section.

1 pound onions = about 3½ cups, chopped

ONION IDEAS
Onions Stewed in Fruit Juice

To make a side dish that goes especially well with roast meats, put peeled onions, whole or quartered, in a saucepan; add a dab of butter or other fat; and pour in enough apple cider, orange juice, or another fruit juice to about half cover them. Simmer covered until the onions are tender, from 30 to 40 minutes. Season to taste with mint or thyme, and perhaps a little grated lemon peel.

For a sauce texture, chop the on-need blanching. So that all slices are uniform it is best to use a vegetable slicer. With varying thicknesses extra-thin slices may turn brown before thicker slices have dried completely. Onions may also turn brown if they are dried in heat over about 130°F. However, this coloring is not necessarily a bad thing. Brown onions can give color and flavor to some soups, gravies, and meat stews.

Dried onions can be added directly to liquid mixtures as long as they are allowed about 20 minutes of cooking time. For instant seasoning, they can be ground to meal or powder in a blender or other grinder, but they must be completely hard or brittle. Sometimes during storage, dried onions become limp or leathery, and though they will continue to keep, they must be heated briefly to make them brittle again before grinding.

Peeling and Preparing Onions

Though onions taste good roasted, steamed, or boiled in their skins and peeled when done, they must be peeled before being cooked in mixtures. Peeling a few onions for immediate use is easy, but when preparing many onions time can be saved if they are blanched in boiling water for about half a minute, then dunked in cold water to chill them. This will loosen the skins so that they slip off easily.

When cooking whole onions, cut a small X in their stem ends, or poke a hole in them with a large needle, or ice pick. This will cause the inside to cook almost at the same speed as the outside, making the splitting off of the outside layers or the pushing out of inner layers less likely.

To chop onions quickly, first cut them in half the long way, through the root and stem end, then lay the halves flat on the cutting board. Make several cuts the long way, leaving the root end intact to keep layers from sliding apart. Then, slice across the grain, starting at the stem end. To mince, make the long cuts closer together and slice more thinly.

The fumes that rise when peeling and slicing the stronger types of onions cause many harmless tears. The best preventive is probably a very sharp knife that will cut without crushing and releasing fumes, but relief can be found in other ways as well. If onions are cold, they will give off fewer fumes and cause fewer tears. When they are stored in a cold place, leave them there until just before preparing them. Other suggestions are keeping a piece of bread in one's mouth, using a fan to blow

ions, then stew them only 10 to 15 minutes. If thickening is needed, add fine, dry bread crumbs, a spoonful at a time, until it is thick enough. Try with hamburgers as a change from catsup.

Onions Roasted Over Coals

Put whole, unpeeled onions into the coals around the edge of a camp fire, or a fireplace fire, or put them on the rack of a charcoal broiler. Turn them often, roasting them slowly until they are charred on the outside and very soft and brown on the inside. Large onions may take an hour and a half. They are delicious by themselves, with no added seasonings. The American Indians often cooked wild onions in this way.

fumes away, and peeling them under the cold water faucet. Or the more drastic measures for horseradish in the HERB ROOTS section can be tried.

Onion Juice

Occasionally onion juice is wanted as a flavoring. A pulpy juice can be made by grating onions with a fine grater. Juice can also be pressed from a cut onion half using the reamer style of juicer. For just a little juice, scrape the cut side of an onion with a teaspoon, or press a small piece of onion in a garlic press.

As onion juice loses its flavor quickly, do not make it until ready to use it.

Cooking Onions

Onions cooked quickly at higher temperatures will have a sharper taste than those cooked more slowly. High heat also causes a strong onion odor that many people find objectionable. Onions are usually preferred cooked slowly over low to moderate heat. Prepared this way, they become soft, translucent, and almost sweet-tasting, without browning. They also taste delicious cooked very slowly until brown and reduced almost to a purée.

PARSLEY STORAGE
Drying
Lacks flavor as seasoning. Pleasant for mild tea. Refer to DRYING HERBS, in the HERBS section.

Freezing
Best in cooked foods. Refer to FREEZING HERBS, in the HERBS section.

Live Storage
Extend growing season in cold frames, greenhouses, window sill pots, etc. for constant fresh supply.

PARSLEY IDEAS
Parsley Bouquet
To keep a bunch of parsley fresh for several days after it is picked, put it in a glass of water as if it were a bouquet of flowers. For extra long keeping put it, glass and all, in the refrigerator.

Parsley Tea
Dry extra parsley leaves and stems for making herb tea. Though not parsley-ish, their flavor will be mild and pleasant, and will blend well with stronger flavors. Second year parsley plants that are tough and almost ready to go

---

Parsley

A good first step when preparing a meal is into the garden to gather a bunch of fresh parsley, as there is sure to be a need for it at some point. Parsley is the most useful fresh herb anyone can grow. It goes well with virtually every kind of main course, side dish, and salad—sometimes as an ingredient, sometimes as a garnish, and sometimes both. Besides color and flavor, it adds nutritional value, thanks to its rich vitamin and mineral content.

There are three types of parsley: curly leaf, plain leaf or Italian, and turnip-rooted or Hamburg. Curly-leafed parsley has a mild taste and looks pretty in salads and as a garnish. Plain-leafed parsley is more flavorful, and is the best kind to use in cooking. It is also chopped or minced for salads and for sprinkling on foods as a garnish. The large roots of turnip-rooted parsley are cooked and eaten like other root vegetables. (Refer to the CELE-RIAC section.) Its leaves are good used like plain-leafed parsley. (Sometimes fresh coriander leaves are called Chinese parsley, but they are an entirely different plant with a different stronger flavor.)

PARSLEY RECIPES

Spanish Parsley Sauce

(MAKES 1—1 ½ CUPS)

1 small clove garlic
1 small potato, boiled
medium bunch parsley
pepper, salt, optional

2 tablespoons oil (preferably olive)
1 tablespoon wine or
    cider vinegar

Combine all ingredients in a blender. Add a few tablespoons of water to make the blender work, and blend until smooth. This sauce can also be made with a mortar and pestle, first mashing the garlic, potato, and parsley, and then adding the other ingredients.

Parsnips

The parsnip is an old-fashioned vegetable that lost importance when modern storage methods were developed. Few now appreciate the value of a vegetable that can stay frozen in the ground all winter and still be sweet and ready to eat with the first spring thaws. Today's parsnip eaters can only appreciate parsnips for their fine sweet flavor when fried or mashed, for the delicious way they blend into beef stews and boiled vegetable dishes, and for the way they soak up meat juices when cooked in the roasting pan.

HANDLING PARSNIPS

Parsnips are not worth eating until after a few weeks of near freezing or below freezing fall weather. The cold turns the starch in the roots to sugar, giving them their typically sweet flavor. Store-bought parsnips often have a poor flavor com-

to seed are good dried for tea. Refer to the HERBS section.

PARSNIP STORAGE

Canning

Slice or dice, boil 5 min., pack hot. Cover with boiling cooking water, ½ in. headroom. Process 240°F, 11 pounds pressure. Pints: 30 min. Quarts: 35 min. Refer to the CANNING section.

Cold Storage

Pack in damp material. Will keep all winter in root cellar, or similar place. Refer to the COLD STORAGE section.

Drying

Slice, or shred raw. May steam whole until tender, then trim, slice. Dry to hard or brittle. Refer to the DRYING section.

Freezing

Slice across, or lengthwise. Blanch in boiling water 2–3 min. Refer to the FREEZING section.

Live Storage

(Easiest, most practical storage method.) Leave in ground, mulched. Dig up during fall, winter thaws, and early spring.

pared to homegrown ones, which suggests that some store parsnips may be harvested too early. When home grown it is not usually necessary to harvest parsnips in large numbers for storage, since they can be dug a few at a time as needed in the fall and spring. Some can be kept in a root cellar or another cool place for winter use.

Clean parsnips by washing and scrubbing with a vegetable brush. Avoid paring or scraping off skin since it contains nutrients. If parsnips are to be precooked, steam them whole, and trim off the top and root ends, and slice them only after they are cooked. Less flavor is lost in this way. Never boil parsnips in water that is later discarded, as some old recipes advise. The sugars that give parsnips their special flavor are dissolved and lost in the cooking water, along with water soluble vitamins and minerals.

Sometimes a fibrous or woody core develops in parsnips, and this must be removed, but gardeners seldom have this problem with homegrown roots. If necessary, the cores can be cut out of raw parsnips after they are cut in halves or quarters the long way. Whole parsnips can be steamed until tender, split open the long way, and the cores lifted out in one piece.

PEACH STORAGE

Note: Process nectarines like peaches, but do not peel.

Canning

Peel and halve or slice, removing pits (see below). Optional: Add one pit per jar for flavor.

Raw Pack

Add boiling syrup, juice, or water, ½ in. headroom. Process boiling water bath. Pints: 25 min. Quarts: 30 min.

Hot Pack

Simmer fruit 2–3 min. in boiling syrup, juice, or water. Pack, add boiling cooking liquid, ½ in. headroom. Process boiling water bath. Pints: 20 min. Quarts: 25 min. *Caution:* If fruit is overripe, add 2 teaspoons lemon juice per pint, 4 teaspoons per quart. Refer to the CANNING section. Also see

Peaches

Peaches are universally popular. Their sweet juiciness when fresh, and their excellence when canned, dried, and frozen, make them a "peach" of a fruit. They probably originated in China since they are mentioned about 2,000 years ago in Chinese writing, and from there they spread throughout the world. Peaches were one of the first fresh fruits brought to America by colonists, and they adapted so well that they now grow wild in some parts of the southern United States. They can be cultivated through most of the United States and parts of southern Canada.

Nectarines are, in these pages, included with peaches. Though sometimes described as crosses between plums and peaches, botanically they are the same as peaches. There is only the minor difference of the nectarine's smooth and the peach's fuzzy skin. They both come in yellow and white varieties, and can be either cling or freestone. Both yellow varieties are high in vitamin A, while the white varieties are low in it. Nectarines grow more successfully in western North America than in the East. Generally they are not as satisfactory as peaches when canned, dried, or frozen, but they are handled in the same ways, and can be used in the same recipes.

HANDLING PEACHES

Usually peaches are picked after they have started to ripen and before they become soft, but those with their own trees can wait until the peaches are fully ripe and eat or process them immediately after picking. Peaches picked when soft bruise easily and do not keep long. If picked green they never ripen properly. Pick them gently by tilting and twisting them off their stems. If grabbed at and yanked they are sure to be bruised.

Peeling Peaches

Peaches can be eaten fuzz, peel, and all, or the fuzz can be gently rubbed off with a towel, but many people like their peaches peeled. When the fruit is very ripe the peels pull off easily. If just underripe, blanch in boiling water for 30 to 60 seconds, then dip in cold water. The peels will slip off easily. Nectarines are almost never peeled since their skin is smooth.

Peach Skin Juice

When peeling large numbers of peaches for canning or freezing, collect the skins in a saucepan as they are removed. Cover them with water, heat, and simmer about 10 minutes. Strain through cloth. This juice can be used as the liquid for canning or freezing the peaches, but it is more fun to drink it as peachade. (This is not, of course, recommended if the peaches have been sprayed with insecticides.)

Pitting Peaches

The pits, or stones, easily come out of freestone peaches and nectarines when the fruit is cut in half. The flesh of clingstone fruits is firmly attached to the pits, as the name implies. There are special sharp-edged pitting spoons that can be pushed in, starting at the stem end of the fruit, and going to the bottom of the pit to free it. If a pitting spoon is not available, cut completely around the peach or nectarine along its crease, making

CANNING FRUIT JUICE AND SAUCE, in the FRUITS section.

Drying
Peeling optional. Halve, removing pits. Quarter, or slice for faster drying. Dry until tough and leathery. Or purée for leather. Refer to the DRYING section.

Freezing
Peel, and halve or slice, removing pits. Pack, cover with liquid (refer to LIQUIDS IN WHICH TO FREEZE FRUIT, in the FREEZING section), or mix with ¼ teaspoon ascorbic acid and ¼ cup sugar per quart, and package. Refer to the FREEZING section. Also see FREEZING FRUIT JUICE AND SAUCE, in the FRUITS section.

2–3 pounds = 1 quart prepared, canned, or frozen

1 bushel = 18–24 quarts canned, or frozen

sure to cut down to the pit all the way around. Then hold the fruit with both hands and twist the halves in opposite directions. If the pit still does not come loose, cut around it as closely as possible with a small sharp knife. Hold the fruit over a bowl while pitting, to catch the dripping juice.

There are red fibers in the cavities of some types of peaches that turn brown and unattractive when cooked. To avoid this, the fibers can be scraped out with a spoon when the peaches are pitted.

A few peach pits or the kernels inside the pits are often cooked with peaches because they add flavor. There are warnings not to eat the kernels because of the prussic acid (hydrogen cyanide) in them. However, the pits are used for flavoring without harmful effects. (Refer to USING APRICOT PITS, in the APRICOTS section.)

Peanuts

The peanut is well-named—"pea" because the peanut plant is a legume which grows like the pea, except that the pods form underground, and "nut" because the seeds in the pods are nut-like. The peanut's big advantage over true nuts is that a crop can be planted and harvested in the same season, while nut trees must grow for years before they come to bearing age.

Peanuts are native to tropical America, but they have become an important crop in such far flung places as India, China, and West Africa. Large quantities are also grown in the southeastern United States. Gardeners in moderate climates farther north can grow short-season varieties very successfully.

In the South peanuts are sometimes called goobers, and elsewhere in the world they are known variously as groundnuts, groundpeas, and earthnuts. The two best known varieties are the small round Spanish peanuts, and the larger oval-shaped Virginia peanuts. These are somewhat different in flavor, but are handled and used in the same ways. All peanuts are rich in oil and vitamins, and, in combination with cooked grains or whole grain bread, make a very high quality protein food.

HANDLING PEANUTS

Peanuts are harvested in the fall when the seeds are fully formed, and the veins inside the shells are darkening. The whole plant is dug or pulled with peanuts attached. Most peanuts are cured (dried) before use, but they can also be boiled and eaten fresh.

Curing Peanuts

Cure peanuts for about 2 months in a dry airy place that is not too warm. If too hot they dry too quickly and their flavor will be poor. They can be cured in an airy shed, or a well-ventilated attic. In cooler climates an attic is best. Dryness and good ventilation are important to prevent development of aflatoxin, a carcinogenic mold. Peanut plants can be stacked or hung, and the peanuts picked off after curing, or they can be picked off when they are harvested, and spread on screens or trays for curing.

Cured peanuts used without roasting are called raw peanuts. They are very good in many cooked dishes, but their roasted flavor is the most familiar.

Roasting Peanuts

Though usually roasted in their shells, peanuts taste just as good if roasted after shelling. However, they keep best in their shells. Spread peanuts in a single layer on baking sheets in a 300°F oven until they are just barely browned, from 20 to 30 minutes for peanuts in the shell and 10 to 15 minutes for raw shelled peanuts. Shake the sheets, or stir several times to brown them evenly. Taste to test for doneness. A light roasting saves nutrients, especially the B vitamins, and their flavor will be excellent.

Making Peanut Butter

Peanut butter is simply roasted, ground peanuts. Raw peanuts can also be ground for a butter, but the flavor will not be of a typical peanut butter. Though the thin skins covering each peanut are sometimes removed before grinding, this is unnecessary. Skins add flavor and nutrients, and are not noticeable after grinding. Adding salt is optional, with up to ½ teaspoon per cup as the usual amount.

dishes, and let everyone sprinkle them on for themselves. The peanuts add protein as well as a crunchy texture. They go especially well with chili beans and with curries. A dish of chopped raw scallions or onions is nice for sprinkling along with the peanuts.

Peanuts in Salads

Toss some roasted and chopped peanuts with lettuce or shredded cabbage salads. Finish with a tangy dressing of oil and lemon juice, with a few crushed mustard seeds, and a drop of honey.

Beer Nuts

Heat a cast iron or other heavy frying pan until quite hot, and fry 2 cups raw peanuts in about a teaspoon of oil for 5 to 10 minutes until golden brown. Meanwhile mix 2 tablespoons honey, 1 teaspoon soy sauce, and ¼ teaspoon cayenne pepper. Remove the pan from the stove, and immediately put in the honey mixture. Stir until peanuts are well-coated. They will stick together in a clump when hot, but will easily break apart after cooling. A very good snack with or without beer.

Peanuts can be ground to butter by putting them through a meat grinder several times. The first grinding will be difficult, but subsequent ones will be easy. Blenders and food processors will also grind peanut butter. If using a blender, add 1½ to 3 tablespoons of oil per cup. Begin by flaking the nuts in the blender. Then gradually add the oil, and continue blending until the texture is right. For chunky peanut butter, set aside some peanuts after the first grinding with a meat grinder, or some chopped in the blender, then mix into the smooth butter.

To store homemade peanut butter, always refrigerate, can, or freeze it. It will become rancid more easily than most commercial peanut butters, because the germ (heart) of the nut is not removed, and because it is not treated to retard rancidity. If freshly roasted peanuts are used, homemade peanut butter is far more delicious than any that can be purchased, including most health food store offerings.

Blanching and Peeling Peanuts

To change their appearance, shelled peanuts are sometimes blanched to loosen the thin, dark, inner skin covering each nut and then peeled. However, this is an unnecessary and undesirable procedure. The flavorful skins contain nutrients, and are too thin to be troublesome when eaten. They are blanched by dropping them in boiling water for 3 minutes. After draining and chilling the skins are easily rubbed off.

PEANUT RECIPES

Indonesian Peanut Sauce

(MAKES ABOUT 2 CUPS)

1 tablespoon oil	1 cup coconut milk, or water
1 medium onion, minced	1 teaspoon honey
1 clove garlic, minced	2 teaspoons soy sauce
1 slice ginger root, minced, optional	1 tablespoon lemon juice
	½ cup peanut butter

1 small hot pepper, minced, or ½–1 teaspoon hot pepper flakes or powder

Heat the oil in a saucepan and add the onion, garlic, ginger root, and hot pepper. Sauté over medium heat, stirring, until the onion is soft but not brown.

In a bowl, mix together the coconut milk or water, honey, soy sauce, lemon juice, and peanut butter. Stir into the onion mixture and simmer for 5 to 10 minutes. Watch closely and stir often, because it easily sticks and burns.

It is delicious used as a dip with raw vegetables, or mixed with hot cooked vegetables. Try it with green beans, cabbage, cauliflower, or carrots. Serve with rice.

Pears

Pears are good mixers. They like all kinds of spices and flavorings, and they fit into every kind of fruit situation, from beverages and compotes to baked desserts. They are also favorites for eating plain whether fresh, canned, or dried. In fact, in temperate climates, they rate just after apples as the second most popular fruit.

There are many pear varieties, and some that excel for a particular purpose, such as anjous for winter storage, or sekels for pickling and stewing. Most make good juice and sauce. Several varieties of pear trees are likely to be included in even a small home orchard.

HANDLING PEARS

Most kinds of pears have a better texture and keep better if picked when they show the very earliest signs of ripening—when their skins turn a lighter shade of green, and the stems separate easily from the fruiting spurs as the pears are lifted. If pears must be pulled from the tree, it is best to wait a little longer to harvest them. Pears left unpicked until fully ripe are more apt to turn brown in their center, or to form stony granules in their flesh, and they will not keep long in cold storage.

Peeling and Coring Pears

Most pear skins are thin and not troublesome to eat so peeling is not necessary. Even canned pears taste good with the peels on, but many do not like their appearance. Pears can be pared like apples, or blanched in boiling water from 1 to 3 minutes to loosen the skins, then peeled. Blanching time depends on the variety of pear. Though the skins do not slip off as easily as do blanched peach skins, it is faster than paring.

PEAR STORAGE

Canning

Peel (optional—see below), halve, and core. Optional: Add flavoring to each jar such as a sprig of mint, a slice of ginger root, a lemon slice, or a few whole cloves or coriander seeds.

Raw Pack

Halves, quarters, slices. Add boiling juice, syrup, or water, ½ in. headroom. Process boiling water bath. Pints: 25 min. Quarts: 30 min.

Hot Pack

Cook halves or quarters in boiling syrup, juice, or water for 2 min. Drain, pack, add boiling cooking liquid, ½ in. headroom. Process boiling water bath. Pints: 20 min. Quarts: 25 min. Refer to the CANNING section. Also see CANNING FRUIT JUICE AND SAUCE, in the FRUITS section. *Caution:* If fruit is overripe, add 2 teaspoons lemon juice per pint, 4 teaspoons per quart. Also see *Piquant Pear Relish,* below, and *Spiced Pickled Fruit,* in the PICKLING section.

Cold Storage

Winter varieties. Pick green and hard. Cure 1 week in airy place no warmer

Pear cores can be eaten since they are soft enough to be chewable, but most people do not enjoy them. Cores, and the fibrous veins that go from the stem to the core, are easily cut or scooped out after the pears are cut in half.

As pears darken quickly after they are peeled or halved, they can be sprinkled with lemon juice, or dipped in an ascorbic acid solution, made by dissolving 1 teaspoon crystalline ascorbic acid in 1 cup water. However, this can be omitted if the pears are prepared quickly, in small batches.

PEAR RECIPES

Piquant Pear Relish

(MAKES 4–5 PINTS)

3 quarts (about) hard green pears (windfalls are excellent)	4 tablespoons flour
	1 tablespoon cumin seeds
2 medium onions	1 tablespoon turmeric, optional (for color)
4–6 sweet red or green peppers	½ teaspoon salt, optional
1 fresh hot pepper, or dry flakes, or powder, to taste	3½ cups vinegar
	½ cup honey

4 tablespoons mustard seed or mustard powder (seeds are milder)

Grate the pears, onions, and sweet and hot peppers, or grind them with a meat grinder or food processor. (If using dry flakes or powder, add to the following mustard mixture.)

Mix the mustard, flour, cumin, turmeric, and salt, if desired, in a large pot. Moisten with enough of the vinegar to make a paste. Then add the rest of the vinegar and the honey, and heat, stirring often. Simmer about 5 minutes, until the mixture thickens. Add the pear mixture, and bring to a boil, stirring to prevent sticking. Pour into hot canning jars, leaving ½ inch headroom. Process in a boiling water bath, 10 minutes. (Refer to the CANNING section.)

This distinctive relish improves with several months of storage.

---

than 70°F. Store like apples. (Refer to the APPLES section.) Storage life 2–7 months depending on variety. Ripen for several days at room temperature before eating. Refer to the COLD STORAGE section.

Drying

Use ripe, but still firm pears. Halve, core, set on tray cut side up, or for fast drying, slice thinly, and core (optional). May separate outside skin-covered slices, which dry more slowly. Dry to leathery. Also purée for leather. Refer to the DRYING section.

Freezing

Use ripe, but firm pears. Halve or quarter, and core. Cook several at a time, 1–2 min. in liquid, lift out, cool, pack. Cover with cooled cooking liquid. (Pre-cooking improves texture.) Refer to the FREEZING section. Also see FREEZING FRUIT JUICE AND SAUCE, in the FRUITS section.

2–2½ pounds fresh = 1 quart canned or frozen; 1 bushel = 20–25 quarts canned or frozen

Peas

Fresh shelled green peas are a delicacy known only to those who have them growing in the garden. Eaten right out of the pod when picked, there is no tastier raw vegetable. Any sensible child soon finds his or her way to the pea patch to shell and eat some on the spot. Adults would be well-advised to do the same. After everyone has had a fresh snack, peas can be picked for cooking, freezing, or canning. Peas were among the first vegetables to be canned when the process was invented, and later among the first to be frozen. They are still among the best for either purpose.

Two other types of peas can be grown in the garden: edible podded peas, and mature dry peas. The edible, podded snow peas that come from China and other Asian countries are picked while the pods are flat, tender, and crisp. Snap or sugar snap peas are a new edible, podded variety that remain tender even after the peas are fully developed in the pods. Dry peas, to be shelled and used like dry beans, can be collected from any variety of pea by leaving the pods to dry on the vine, or a split pea variety can be grown.

Chick peas, cow peas, and black-eyed peas are all beans rather than peas. (Refer to the BEANS, DRY section.)

HANDLING PEAS

Green Peas

Pick green or garden peas, also called English peas, after the peas are swollen in the pods but before the pods lighten in color. If picking is delayed too long they will become hard and bitter. However, such peas can be left on the vine to mature and then harvested as dry peas.

Eat or process fresh peas as soon after picking as possible. If they must be kept for any length of time, refrigerate them. The sugar in the peas rapidly turns to starch after they are picked and they lose sweetness. Shelling is the only preparation peas need. Small batches are easily shelled by hand, but preparing large batches for freezing or canning becomes tedious. Pea shelling can be a family project with everyone helping, or a bean or pea sheller can be purchased. There are manual and

---

PEA STORAGE

Canning

Use only shelled green peas.

Hot Pack

Cover with boiling water, return to boil. Drain, fill jar loosely, pour over boiling cooking water, 1 in. headroom. Process 240°F, 11 pounds pressure. 40 min. both pints and quarts; extra large peas 50 min.

Raw Pack

Fill jars loosely, 1 in. headroom. Add boiling water, 1½ in. headroom (½ in. below level of peas). Process as for HOT PACK. Refer to the CANNING section.

Drying

Not suitable for green peas or edible podded peas. The sweet flavor is lost. See DRY PEAS, below.

Freezing

Shell green peas. Pull strings from edible podded peas. Blanch in boiling water, 1½ min. Refer to the FREEZING section.

electrical models that quickly shell both fresh beans and peas.

Freshly shelled peas need not be washed if hands and utensils are clean. The pod protects the peas so well that they are likely to be cleaner without washing.

Homegrown green peas are ideal for freezing. If picked at their prime and quickly processed and frozen, they will be far sweeter and more tender than commercially sold frozen peas. Canned peas are also good, but they cannot match the fresh flavor of frozen peas.

Green pea pods are lined with a membrane too stiff to eat, but the fleshy part of the pod has a good flavor. Take advantage of this by using pea pods when making soup stock and then straining them out. The pods can also be dried for later use.

---

1 pound in pods = about 1 cup shelled; 1 bushel in pods = 6–8 quarts, shelled and canned, or frozen

PEA IDEAS

Steamed Snap Pea Salad

String snap peas and steam them for about 2 minutes, just until they change color. Toss with oil and vinegar, or another favorite salad dressing while they are warm. Cool and add any preferred salad vegetables and seasonings. Chopped scallion, parsley, sweet pepper, and celery are very good. The steamed snap peas are also delicious added to potato or egg salads. They add color and flavor.

Peas with Herbs

Fresh herbs make perfect seasonings for hot peas. While the peas are cooking, mince some fresh basil, savory, mint, fennel, or parsley, and put it in the serving dish with a pat of butter or a spoon of oil. Put the hot peas in the dish, stir, and serve. Dried herbs can be used if fresh are not available.

Edible Podded Peas

Both snow peas and snap or sugar snap peas can be harvested over a longer season than green peas, providing they are consistently picked and not allowed to mature on the vine. Snow peas must be picked while the pods are still flat. They become too tough and stringy to enjoy when they fill out. Snap or sugar snap peas remain tender until the pods are swollen and the peas have reached full size. As much of their flavor is in the pods, they do not compare with the green peas when shelled.

Both types of edible podded peas are best fresh since freezing is the only practical way to store them, and then they lose the crispness that makes them so delightful to eat. Snap peas are really salad vegetables, and some should be picked every day or two for eating raw as a snack or adding to salads. Snow peas are known for their excellence when stir-fried, but they are also delicious raw. Steam both snap and snow peas for 2 or 3 minutes for eating as a hot vegetable, or add them to soup for the last minute or two of cooking. If cooked longer they will lose both texture and flavor.

There are strings along the seams of edible podded peas that are hardly noticeable if the peas are raw, but they can become bothersome after cooking. To remove the strings, break off the tip of the pod and pull. The strings will come off with the tip.

Edible podded peas are practical both as early pods to be picked for eating raw, and later (when many other garden vegetables are available) to mature for a crop of dry peas.

Dry Peas

Dry peas, also called soup peas, make good soup or stew no matter what their variety. Cooked larger dried peas are very much like beans. Split peas are a special variety listed in seed catalogs and intended only for dried use. Dry peas are picked, shelled, and stored like dry beans. (Refer to SHELLING AND STORING DRY BEANS, in the BEANS section.)

Pea flour can be made by grinding dry peas in a grain mill. It can be used for making quick pea soup or small amounts can be used for some baking. (The pea flavor is strong, and may not be appreciated in more delicate baked goods.) It is also possible to sprout dry peas and use them like bean sprouts, but they are not as easy to sprout as smaller sized seeds. (Refer to the SPROUTS section.)

Herbed Pea Pod Soup

(MAKES ABOUT 6 MEDIUM BOWLS)

pods from shelling 2 or more
    pounds of peas
4 tablespoons butter
2–3 scallions
2 tablespoons flour

½–1 cup peas, optional
sprig mint or savory,
    minced
⅓ cup milk or cream,
    optional
pepper, salt, optional

Put the pea pods in a pot and add about a quart of water. The water should cover only half the pods. Cover and cook about 30 to 40 minutes, until the pods are very soft. Stir several times. Put through a food mill or strainer to remove membranes and strings.

Melt the butter in the soup pot and sauté the scallion in it until limp. Stir in the flour until completely blended, then add the liquid from the pea pods, the peas, and the mint and savory. Heat and simmer, stirring often, until the soup is smooth and slightly thickened. Remove from heat, stir in the milk or cream, and season, if desired. Though this delicately flavored soup can be reheated, do not let it boil.

Pectin

Pectin is the substance in fruit that causes it to jell. For jelling to occur, cooking is necessary to extract or activate pectin. Other

Peas' Special Greenness

When cooked just enough to brighten them, both shelled and edible podded peas have an intense, fresh green color guaranteed to make any dish containing them look more appetizing. Add snow or snap peas to soups, especially clear ones, a minute or two before serving time. Mix fresh, cooked, shelled peas, or frozen peas, cooked just enough to thaw them, with hot cooked potatoes, macaroni, onions, or any root vegetable. Layer peas in casseroles, or add them to stews, or stuffings, or cooked grains. They will add flavor as bright as their color.

PECTIN STORAGE
Canning

Homemade (below): Pour boiling hot into hot jars. Seal as for OPEN KETTLE CANNING, in the CANNING section, or process in a boiling water bath, 10 min. Refer to the CANNING section generally.

requirements are the presence of acid, which most fruits contain naturally, and the addition of a true sugar or other concentrated sweetener. Apples and quinces are especially high in pectin, and a liquid pectin can be easily extracted from raw apples, apple peels and cores, or apple pomace by boiling them in water. (Pomace is the pulp left from making apple cider. Refer to the APPLES section.)

Homemade pectin is most often used to make jelly and other preserves from low-pectin fruits, but it is also valuable in other ways. Its smooth texture and flavor blends well with more intense fruit juices. It is the ideal liquid in which to freeze fresh fruit, helping to prevent darkening of the fruit and improving texture and flavor. When made from apple parts that would otherwise be wasted, pectin exemplifies the proverbial "something from nothing."

A special kind of pectin, low methoxyl, is extracted from citrus fruits by a process impossible to duplicate at home. It jells when certain calcium compounds are present. Since sugar is not necessary for jelling, it will be of interest to those who want to make sugarless or low-sugar preserves. Low-methoxyl pectin and directions for its use are available from some health food stores and mail-order catalogs. Directions for making preserves with homemade pectin, and a discussion of other jelling agents, are in the JAM AND JELLY section.

THE PECTIN CONTENT OF FRUITS

Fruits contain varying amounts of pectin, depending on their variety and ripeness. As fruit ripens its pectin content diminishes, so that overripe fruits have very little. Skins and cores contain more pectin than the pulp.

Pectin can be extracted from any high-pectin fruit by boiling it in water. Apples are the most popular because their flavor does not overwhelm, and because cores and peels, or pomace from making cider are often available in large amounts.

High-Pectin Fruits

Apples, sour, and crabapples	Lemons and the white part
Blackberries, sour	of citrus peel
Cranberries	Loganberries
Red currants	Plums, except prune plums
Gooseberries	Quinces
Eastern Concord grapes	

Freezing

Homemade (below): Cool, pour into containers, leave air space. Refer to the FREEZING section.

HOMEMADE PECTIN IDEAS

Pectin Pack for Freezing Fruit

Use pectin that has been boiled down to half its original volume as the covering liquid for fresh fruits to be frozen. It is especially good with fruits that darken easily, such as peaches, pears, apricots, sweet cherries, and figs. Refer to the FREEZING section.

Pectin with Fruit Juice

Dilute strong-flavored fruit juices and frozen juice concentrates with thin pectin instead of water for a smoother, sweeter drink.

Moderate-Pectin Fruits

(A few sour apples can be cooked with these to ensure jelling.)

Ripe apples · Grapefruit
Ripe blackberries · California grapes
Sour cherries · Oranges
Chokecherries

Low-Pectin Fruits

(An acidic juice, such as lemon, as well as pectin, may be needed to jell some of these.)

Apricots · Pears
Blueberries · Prune plums
Sweet cherries · Raspberries
Figs · Rhubarb
Western Concord grapes · Strawberries
Peaches · Overripe fruit

High-pectin fruits and juices may be mixed with low-pectin fruits and juices to obtain jelling combinations. Often the flavor is improved as well. (Refer to COMBINING SWEET AND TART FRUITS, in the FRUITS section.)

MAKING PECTIN

Pectin is usually made from fresh apples or apple leftovers, but dried apple can be used if it was dried raw without blanching. When whole apples, such as windfalls, are used, they should be sliced with peels and cores retained. Underripe quince or another high-pectin fruit can be used instead of apple, but the flavor may be strong.

To make pectin, put the apple pieces or pomace in a pot and cover with cold water. Bring to a boil and simmer for 20 to 30 minutes, or until the fruit is soft. Strain through cloth until it stops dripping. If the pectin is to be used for jelly, do not press or squeeze the cloth, as that causes cloudy jelly. Otherwise pressing saves time. Return the fruit pulp to the pot, add more water, and cook another 10 to 15 minutes. Strain through cloth again, and let it drain overnight, or press, if cloudiness does not matter. Combine the juice from both strainings.

The next step is to boil down the juice to make a concen-

Sour Fruit Cooked in Pectin

Use thin pectin as the liquid for cooking rhubarb and other very sour fruits. Pectin adds smoothness and sweetness so that less sweetening is needed. Tart fruits can also be canned in pectin.

Pectin Syrup

Boil down homemade pectin to a thin syrup. Add honey or sugar to taste, and cook to blend. Very little sweetening is needed. Such flavorings as a cinnamon stick, a slice of ginger root, or a sprig of mint can be included.

Hair Setting Liquid

Comb thinnish homemade pectin into hair, and set as usual.

trate. For most uses it should be reduced to half its original volume, when it will have a smooth and somewhat slick, or slippery, texture. It should jell low-pectin juices if mixed half and half. When boiled down to about ¹⁄₁₆ or ⅛ of its original volume, it becomes a ropy syrup that should jell in a ratio of ½ to ¾ cup pectin per 4 cups of fruit juice. For storage, can or freeze pectin at the preferred concentration.

It is possible to test fruit juices or mixtures of juice and homemade pectin for jelling, as below. Juice must be cooked before testing. If the test shows a lack of pectin, more can be added before the jelly is made.

Pectin Test with Alcohol

Measure 1 teaspoon of the fruit juice or juice and pectin mixture. Add 1 tablespoon of standard, 70% rubbing alcohol. If this forms into one clot, enough pectin is present for jelling. If several small dabs form, more pectin is needed. Do not taste this! The alcohol is poison.

Pectin Test with Magnesium Sulfate (Epsom salts)

Measure 2 tablespoons of the juice or juice and pectin mixture. Stir in 1 tablespoon magnesium sulfate, then stir in 2 teaspoons sugar. Set aside for 20 minutes. If the mixture jells, there is enough pectin for making jelly.

(Refer to the JAM AND JELLY section for other requirements and procedures.)

Peppers, Hot

There are people who love food seasoned with peppers until it is fiery hot, while others can tolerate only a hint of hotness. These are heartfelt differences, so neither type is likely to change preference. They must agree to disagree, and the family cook must pepper foods to suit family tastes. In any case, the required hot peppers—whether few and mild, or many and fiery—can be grown and processed at home. Fresh hot peppers can be used in many recipes, and they can also be dried and ground for pepper flakes or powder, pickled, or made into hot sauce. For those who prefer to grow their own seasonings, hot pepper flakes and powder can be used instead of imported black or white pepper. The flavor is not quite the same, but the results are good.

There are many varieties of hot peppers, with many levels of intensity.

Some that grow well in temperate climates are the relatively mild Hungarian Hot Wax, the red-hot Cayenne, which is thin-fleshed and easily dried, and the very hot, green Jalapeño. Jalapeños are thick-fleshed, with a hotness that does not manifest itself immediately after tasting. Their heat builds and spreads gradually, lasting a long time. The initial mildness may fool the unsuspecting into taking a large bite and suffering the fiery consequences.

Chili peppers are often thought to be a variety of hot pepper, which leads to some confusion. In Mexico, chile is the general name for peppers, while the different kinds are known by such names as chile pequin and chile poblano. Mexican recipes will specify whether a hot or a sweet pepper is required, and often call for a particular variety. If American recipes call for chili peppers, any hot pepper can be used, though specific varieties are intended in some regions. (To make chili powder, which is a blend of many ingredients, refer to the PEPPERS, SWEET section, following this section. For Chili Sauce, which is not generally very hot, refer to the *Tomato Catsup* recipe, in the TOMATOES section.)

HANDLING HOT PEPPERS

Hot peppers can be picked and used as soon as they reach a reasonable size, but they are hottest when fully mature. Red and yellow varieties are mature when they have lost all green coloring and become completely red or yellow. The hotness of homegrown peppers can be erratic. In the same garden, and even on the same plant, one pepper can be considerably hotter than another that looks the same. The hotness evens out once they are dried and ground, or pickled.

Thin-fleshed varieties of hot peppers are usually preserved by drying. Fleshy varieties can be dried, but they are also excellent pickled, or canned, or frozen as for sweet peppers.

Drying Hot Peppers

The thin-fleshed peppers, like cayenne or tabasco, are dried whole. They can be spread on trays, or threaded through their stems and hung for drying. The whole pepper plant can also be pulled and hung in a warm, dry place. When the peppers are completely dry and hard, they can be stored whole in airtight containers, or they can be flaked, or powdered. If stored

---

HOT PEPPER STORAGE
Canning
Process like sweet peppers, except may leave whole if small. Refer to the PEPPERS, SWEET section.

Drying
See DRYING HOT PEPPERS, below.

Freezing
(Drying is more practical for seasoning.) Leave whole, or cut to convenient size. Pack dry. Refer to the FREEZING section.

HOT PEPPER IDEAS
Hot Peppers and Cheese
Fresh or pickled hot peppers are delicious with most kinds of cheese. Put slivers of hot pepper in cheese sandwiches, or with cheese on crackers. Add minced hot peppers to cottage cheese and other fresh cheeses, or add them to cheese sauce. All of these are "pepper uppers."

Peppers in Sherry
Pack whole fresh cayenne, or other thin-fleshed hot peppers, in a jar, and cover with sherry. This preserves the peppers and flavors the sherry. Both can be added to sauces and stews, or try using the sherry when some is called for in stir-fried dishes.

whole, pieces can be broken off or crumbled as needed. The stems are discarded but the fiery seeds are usually retained.

Thick-fleshed peppers are usually sliced or chopped, and spread on trays for drying. They can be flaked or ground for seasoning.

Be sure that dried peppers are brittle before grinding. If still leathery, they will gum up the grinder or blender. For flakes, grind peppers coarsely in a grain mill, or whirl briefly in a blender. Grind finely or pulverize for powder. Seal in airtight containers. Powder will cake if exposed to air in a humid climate.

Hot pepper flakes and powder gradually lose flavor so replace the supply each year. For blends that sometimes include hot pepper, refer to the PEPPERS, SWEET section. (Also refer to the DRYING section.)

HOT PEPPER CAUTIONS

- To prevent burning skin when handling batches of fresh hot peppers, wear rubber gloves, or rub hands with oil. The gloves or oil may not be necessary when chopping just one hot pepper. Anyone who rubs his or her eyes, or puts in contact lenses after handling peppers is going to be very miserable for a while. Burning hands can be soothed by rubbing them with salt; eyes should be rinsed with a lot of cool water.
- When flaking or pulverizing dried hot peppers in a blender, keep the lid on until the dust has settled in the container. Otherwise, the dust is likely to cause an attack of sneezing and crying.
- Cook large batches of hot peppers in a well-ventilated room to avoid a build-up of irritating fumes.

Hot Pepper Pickle

Jalapeños, red cherry peppers, or other fleshy peppers	vinegar (refer to the PICKLING section)

OPTIONAL INGREDIENTS:

garlic cloves	onion slices, or tiny, whole onions
bay leaves	carrots, sliced thickly
whole cloves	salt

Put whole peppers with stems into hot, sterilized jars. If desired, a garlic clove, a bay leaf, and a few whole cloves can be put in each jar, and onion and carrot slices can be included among the peppers. Leave about 1 inch headroom. Heat a mixture of half vinegar, half water, and a little salt, if desired. Prepare 1 cup vinegar, 1 cup water, and ¼ teaspoon salt per quart jar. Pour the boiling hot vinegar mixture over the peppers, filling the jars almost to the rims. Seal immediately. Cool and store. (Refer to the CANNING section, and CANNING PICKLES in that section.)

Hot pickled peppers are excellent minced and added to cooked dishes, and mixtures of all kinds. Many enjoy them plain for snacking, or as an accompaniment with meals.

Peppers, Sweet

Thanks to Columbus, who ostensibly tasted a hot vegetable in the New World and called it pepper, there are two completely unrelated plants with the same common name. One is the tropical pepper tree, which is the source of both black and white peppercorns, and the other is the plant that produces the fleshy green, red, and yellow peppers grown in gardens almost everywhere. The fleshy peppers remain a confusing group even after they have been distinguished from black and white peppercorns.

There are at least a hundred varieties and, since they cross-pollinate readily, endless variations are possible. If sweet and hot peppers are grown in the same garden, cross-pollination is likely to cause sweet pepper seeds saved for planting to produce hot-tasting peppers, no matter how sweet they look.

Peppers can be green, red, yellow, purple, or brownish-black when mature, and they vary from large, globular, thick-fleshed types to small, narrow, thin-fleshed types. Green peppers usually refer to large, sweet peppers, while red peppers usually mean small, hot peppers. Yet there are many mild, sweet peppers that are red, and some of the hottest peppers imaginable are green. In countries like Mexico and Hungary, which use peppers extensively, the different varieties are used with great discrimination. Though there are said to be 61 named varieties in Mexico, according to one source, 9 varieties are as many as most cooks need. Elsewhere, 2 or 3 are usually enough: a large, sweet one for salads and vegetable dishes, a hot one for drying, pickling, and making spicy dishes, and perhaps a pimiento for preserving and for making paprika, or a medium-hot kind for peppery but not burning

---

SWEET PEPPER STORAGE

Canning

Hot pack only. Cut out stems, cores. Halved or sliced, optional. Cook 3 min. in boiling water. Optional: Dip in cold water and peel. Pack in hot jars, 1 in. headroom. Add 1 tablespoon vinegar to pints, 2 tablespoons to quarts. (*Note*: A standard vinegar is necessary for safety.) Add boiling cooking water, ½ in. headroom. Process 240°F, 11 pounds pressure. Pints: 35 min. Quarts: 45 min. Refer to the CANNING section. Also see PIMIENTOS, below.

Cold Storage

Ideal temperature 45–50°F with high humidity. Will keep 2–4 weeks in refrigerator vegetable bin.

Drying

Cut out stems, cores. Chop and dry raw for seasoning. Steam quarters, or large pieces 10–12 min. Dry until hard, or brittle, and reconstitute as vegetable. Refer to the DRYING section. Also see PAPRIKA, below.

hot fried peppers. As hot peppers are handled quite differently from sweet peppers, they are discussed separately. (Refer to the PEPPERS, HOT section.)

HANDLING SWEET PEPPERS

Sweet peppers can be harvested as soon as they become firm, glossy, and heavy, or they can be left on the plant until they turn red or yellow. Most green varieties eventually change color if left on the plant. Red, sweet peppers are especially high in vitamin C, while green peppers are lower in vitamin C, but higher in vitamin A. Both are exceptionally healthy.

Peppers should be cut rather than pulled, leaving part of the stem on the plant, otherwise whole branches may break off with the pepper. When frost threatens, pick all peppers, including the very small ones. Those that are almost mature will continue to ripen for a while after picking. Small, immature peppers can be cored, seeded, and chopped, then dried, or frozen. They are good as seasoning for tomato sauces, vegetable stews, and other dishes. The cores and seeds of sweet peppers should always be removed because they have a strong and sometimes hot flavor.

Peeling Peppers

Most peppers are eaten without peeling, which takes advantage of the skin's vitamin content, but peeled peppers are sometimes preferred. The peels will slip off easily if whole peppers are blanched in boiling water for 4 to 5 minutes, then dunked in cold water. They can also be roasted 5 minutes in a very hot oven and peeled when cool enough to handle. The most interesting method is to char the skins, then peel. This will add the special flavor associated with pimientos and green chiles (see below).

To char peppers, hold them on a fork or skewer over hot coals, turning constantly until mostly blackened. Or lay the peppers directly on the top of a hot wood stove, or on a baking sheet in a very hot oven. Turn as necessary to blister and lightly char all sides. Wrap them in a damp cloth to cool and then peel them, or put them in a pan of cool water and rub to remove the skins.

Pimientos

Pimiento pepper varieties are thick-fleshed, red, very sweet, and usually medium sized. They require a longer growing sea-

---

Freezing

Cut out stems, cores. Cut rings, strips, or dice. Pack dry. Optional: Blanch halves 3 min. to render limp for packing. Refer to the FREEZING section. Also see PIMIENTOS, below.

3 average peppers = about 1 pint canned or frozen; 1 pound peppers = about 3 cups, chopped

SWEET PEPPER IDEAS
Stuffed Pepper Salads

Hearty salads, such as tuna, chicken, potato, or egg salad are delicious in green pepper halves. Cut the peppers lengthwise, and remove stems and cores. Fill with the salad, and set on lettuce leaves.

For an eye-catching salad, cut the top and core out of a large green pepper, and pack cottage cheese into it. Chill for an hour or more in the refrigerator, then cut into slices ½ to 1 inch thick. This makes pepper rings filled with cottage cheese. Arrange the rings on lettuce, and garnish with minced scallion, parsley, or other fresh herbs, and a dusting of paprika. Add some

son than some other varieties, but can be garden grown in most moderate climates. Home preserving is an excellent alternative to the small, expensive jars of commercially prepared pimientos. In addition, any sweet pepper that becomes completely red when ripe can be preserved and used like pimientos. Green chiles are thick fleshed and can be mild, medium hot, or very hot.

Both pimientos and green chiles are prepared by roasting, peeling, and removing stems, cores, and seeds. The heat necessary for peeling them should make them limp enough for freezing, canning, or packing in oil. They have a wonderful, smoky flavor when charred and peeled as described above. The peeled and cored peppers can be left whole, cut into large pieces, or into strips. Freezing is the easiest preserving method, and it best retains color and flavor. Wrap small portions of prepared peppers in freezer wrap or foil and pack them in a freezer container. The wrapping makes it possible to separate portions as needed. If used in cooking, the peppers can be added frozen. For salads, salsas, or garnish, thaw for about half an hour.

To can, pack the prepared peppers in hot, half-pint or pint jars, leaving ½ inch headroom. Add 1½ teaspoons vinegar to half pints, and 1 tablespoon vinegar to pints. Do not add any other liquid. Process at 240°F, 11 pounds of pressure, for 20 minutes for half pints and pints. (Refer to the CANNING section.)

To preserve in oil (usual only for pimientos), first put the prepared peppers in a bowl and cover with vinegar. Cover and refrigerate for 2 days. Drain completely. (The vinegar will have a pleasing flavor and can be used for salads and cooking.) Pack the pimientos in jars and cover with oil. Olive oil is excellent, but any oil will do, except cold pressed oils that easily become rancid. Close the jars tightly and refrigerate or keep in a cool, dark place. These will keep all winter. They taste delicious, but the color is not as good as when frozen. The oil can also be used.

Paprika

There are at least six named blends or flavors of Hungarian paprika, ranging from mild and delicate to hot, so why not create a special, homestead blend. Any sweet pepper varieties that have ripened to a full, red color can be dried and ground for paprika. Pimiento varieties are excellent. Stems, cores, and seeds should be removed before drying, and the pepper pieces must

slices of tomato or sweet onion for color and flavor.

Corn Peppers

Cut peppers in half lengthwise, and remove stems and cores. Fill the halves with a mixture of cooked corn and grated cheese, then bake about 20 minutes in a moderate oven. Put 2 or 3 tablespoons of water in the pan around the peppers. 1 cup corn mixed with ½ cup cheese fills 2 to 3 large pepper halves. Minced onion and a dash of hot pepper can be added to the corn mixture if desired. If very soft peppers are preferred, steam the pepper halves about 5 minutes before filling them.

Stuffings for Sweet Peppers

Most mixtures made with beans, bread crumbs, meat, or vegetables are tasty in sweet peppers. Try the CELERY BREAD CRUMB STUFFING, in the CELERY section, and SEASONED NUTS AND GRAINS, in the NUTS section. If the stuffings do not require long cooking, the peppers can be prebe brittle, not leathery, when ground in a mill, or pulverized in a blender. Seal tightly in jars to prevent the paprika from caking during storage. For a hotter paprika, add ground, hot, red pepper to taste.

Chili Powder

As sold in stores, chili powder is a blend of powdered sweet and hot peppers, with the addition of other herbs and spices. These usually include cumin, oregano, coriander, cloves, and garlic powder. Other possibilities are allspice and turmeric. A basic formula is 3 tablespoons sweet paprika, ¼ teaspoon hot pepper, 1 teaspoon cumin, and 2 teaspoons other herbs and spices mixed. This can be premixed, or the various seasonings can be added to taste during cooking. In Mexico, premixed chili powder is not used.

---

cooked by steaming or roasting for 5–10 minutes, then baked without lids.

For small portions, cut peppers in half lengthwise and core them to make 2 shells.

PERSIMMON STORAGE

Canning

Purée, and add 2 tablespoons lemon juice per quart. Heat, pour in jars, ½ in. headroom. Process boiling water bath. 30 min. for both half-pints and pints. Refer to the CANNING section.

Drying

(Excellent, very sweet.) Halve or slice, remove seeds. Dry whole if small, or purée for leather. Refer to the DRYING section.

Freezing

Pack whole, or purée, with lemon juice to taste, or ⅛ teaspoon crystalline ascorbic acid per quart. Refer to the FREEZING section.

Persimmons

The persimmon deserves more attention than it usually receives. A soft, sweet fruit with a remarkable orange color, it is delicious fresh, and exceptionally good dried or frozen. There are two basic types: the native American, or wild, persimmon, and the cultivated Japanese or Chinese varieties. Both may be used in the same ways.

The American persimmon tree grows wild in moderate parts of the eastern and midwestern United States, where it is also cultivated. Its fruits are small, about an inch in diameter, but they can usually be gathered in large quantities. As the quality of the wild fruits varies, it is wise to taste samples from different trees to find the best. Sometimes trees bear unpollinated, almost seedless fruits. However, the flavor of seedy fruit is just as good. The Japanese and Chinese persimmon trees grown in the south of the United States produce tomato-shaped fruits.

Persimmons are an excellent source of vitamins C and A. They have been known to occasionally cause the buildup of a ball of indigestible fiber in the stomach, but this has only occurred with regular consumption of large amounts over a number of years, and should not discourage anyone from enjoying them in reasonable amounts.

HANDLING PERSIMMONS

Persimmons are ready to eat in the fall, as soon as they become soft. This may happen before or after frosts. Because they ripen slowly, and may stay on the tree into mid-winter, it is often mistakenly thought that frosts are necessary for ripening. Fully mature persimmons tend to become squashed when picked, or smashed if they fall to the ground, but they can be picked when just beginning to soften, and kept in a warm room to finish ripening. Wild persimmons can be gathered by spreading a large sheet under the tree and shaking the branches to make the almost-ripe fruit fall. Underripe persimmons are so mouth-puckering that it is hard to believe they will ever taste good.

Persimmons lend themselves naturally to freezing, as they do not lose texture or flavor, like many fruits. In fact, frozen persimmons picked from wild trees in mid-winter can be perfectly ripe and delicious when thawed. Dried persimmons are almost as sweet as figs or dates, and can be substituted for either in recipes.

It is not necessary to peel persimmons, since the skins are thin. However, if peeling is preferred, first rub the skins with the dull side of the knife to loosen them. Persimmons are excellent with yogurt, with acidic fruits like oranges and grapefruit, or simply sprinkled with lemon juice. Their amazing color and sweetness make them welcome in fruit mixtures. (Refer to the FRUITS section for combinations.)

Soft, fresh persimmons are easily puréed, and many recipes call for them in that form. Use a sieve or food mill, as blenders whip in too much air. (Refer to FRUIT SAUCE, in the FRUITS section.)

Pickling

Pickling is a method of flavoring and preserving foods in acidic solutions. The use of salt solutions for preserving foods is sometimes also known as pickling, but the foods so preserved are salted, or salt cured. They are not pickled according to most people's understanding of the word, and they are not called "pickles." There are two basic ways to pickle foods with

---

PERSIMMON IDEAS
Frozen Persimmon Desserts
Freeze whole, ripe persimmons until solid. Just before serving, grate them into individual dishes. Garnish with shredded coconut, chopped nuts, mint leaves, or a sprinkling of lemon juice and grated rind. Serve the persimmon while it is still icy.

PICKLING STORAGE
Canning
Refer to CANNING PICKLES, in the CANNING section.

Cold Storage
See STORING PICKLES, below.

IDEAS FOR USING THE LIQUID FROM VINEGARED PICKLES
(The pickle liquid can be strained through cloth to clarify it and make it more attractive.)

Pickling

❧

198

acidic solutions. The most common method requires the use of vinegar, which contains acetic acid. The other is by a process of natural fermentation that produces lactic acid. Sauerkraut (made from cabbage) is the best-known fermented pickle, but other vegetables can also be fermented. Many vegetables can be pickled in either way, and occasionally pickling is begun by fermentation, with vinegar added later as a preservative. Meats, fish, and fruits are virtually always pickled with vinegar. Meats and fish tend to spoil rather than ferment in a favorable way, and fruits can, of course, be fermented, but the result is an alcoholic beverage or vinegar, not a pickle.

THE NUTRITIONAL VALUE OF PICKLES

Pickled foods can be nutritious, but often they are not. Water soluble vitamins and minerals are leached out and discarded with the soaking water or pickling liquid. Excessive amounts of salt and sugar are used, and commercially pickled foods may contain questionable additives. Such defects are often dismissed as insignificant because pickles are seldom eaten in quantity. However, healthy pickles can be made at home and then enjoyed without reservations. Neither salt nor sugar is necessary to the process of making vinegar pickles, as the food is preserved by the vinegar. Salt can simply be omitted from many recipes, while the amount of sweetener in most sweet pickle recipes can be reduced. Very sweet pickles will taste cloying to anyone used to a more piquant flavor.

Some salt is necessary for making most fermented pickles, as it draws out moisture and sugars from vegetables, allowing fermentation to begin. However, the amount of salt ingested per serving is small. Sugar is not necessary in fermented pickles, and the lactic acid in them has been recommended for its healthiness.

Relish and Chutney

Most relishes are spicy blends of chopped or ground vegetables, pickled with vinegar. Chutneys are similar mixtures of fruit or vegetables spiced for an East Indian flavor. Relishes and chutneys can be exceptionally healthy pickled foods when made with fresh, unsoaked vegetables and fruits, and little or

---

*Eggs or Beets
Marinated in Pickle Liquid*

If the pickling liquid has a good flavor, pour it over shelled, hard-boiled eggs, or cooked, sliced beets. Unsweetened pickle liquid is ideal for beets. Marinate from several hours to several days in the refrigerator before serving.

Pickle Liquid Salad Dressings

If pickle liquid is strongly flavored, mix it with oil, or add to mayonnaise for salad dressings. These dressings go well with hearty salads, such as potato, egg, or chicken. Refer to QUICK POTATO SALAD, in the POTATOES section.

Spiced Fruit Pickle Beverages

Strain and dilute the liquid from spiced, pickled fruit to make a delicious hot or cold drink.

Pickle Liquid Sauce

If the flavor is pleasant, pickle liquid can be poured over rice, or other

no salt and sweetening. Since there is no liquid to discard, no nutrients are lost. Relish and chutney are exceptionally good substitutes for fatty sauces and gravies, or excessively salty or sweet condiments. In colonial times, large quantities of different relishes were put by every fall, to accompany meals all winter. It would be worthwhile to revive this practice.

MAKING FERMENTED PICKLES

Fermenting vegetables to make pickles can have its ups and downs, because it depends on the action of naturally present lactic acid–producing bacteria. Conditions must be arranged to suit the bacteria. Vegetables are usually sliced or shredded, and mixed with enough salt to draw out moisture and natural sugars. Approximately 3 tablespoons salt to 5 pounds vegetables are required. If the vegetables are too dry to produce their own moisture, or if making large pickles, use a solution of salt water, about 3 to 4 tablespoons of salt per quart of water. It is possible to use less salt, but the chances for spoilage or a mushy texture increase as the proportion of salt is decreased. On the other hand, if too much salt is added, the necessary bacteria may not grow.

The best temperature for fermentation is between 60 and 70°F. At higher temperatures the vegetables may become soft, or spoil. (Fermented pickles are seldom successful in hot summer weather unless there is a cool basement in which to keep them.) At temperatures below 60°F the fermentation process becomes very slow. Also essential is the use of pure salt, pure water, and high quality vegetables. See the requirements for vinegared pickles, below. There are helpful basic directions for making any fermented pickles in the SAUER-KRAUT section.

MAKING VINEGARED PICKLES

The basic requirements for successful pickling with vinegar are as follows.

Vegetables and Fruits

Use only fresh vegetables and fruits of high quality. If produce is bruised, overripe, or overgrown, the pickles are apt to be either mushy or woody. A spot of mold can affect the flavor of a whole batch of pickles, even after being cooked to kill bacteria.

cooked grains for a Middle Eastern touch.

Flavored Vinegar from Pickling

When full-strength vinegar has been used for pickling, it can be drained off and used like an herb vinegar. (Refer to the VINEGAR section.) It will have the flavor of the fruit or vegetable it covered.

Dried Vegetable Pickles

Reconstitute dried vegetables by soaking them in pickle liquid for a few hours, or overnight. If the vegetables were dried raw, they may taste best cooked in the liquid for a few minutes after soaking. Refrigerate them, and use within a few weeks. This is a surprisingly delicious way to use any dried vegetable that pickles well, such as beets, green beans, and some kinds of dried mushrooms.

Misshapen or blemished but fresh, firm vegetables can be trimmed and used for sliced or chunked pickles, or for relish.

Water

Water that contains such minerals as iron or sulphur can darken pickles, calcium can shrivel them, and other impurities can affect the flavor. Pure, soft water is best.

Salt

Ordinary table salt can darken pickles because it contains iodine and other additives. However, this problem is minimal when pickles are made with very little salt. Sea salt and kosher salt are excellent, as well as plain and pickling salt.

Vinegar

All modern vinegared pickle recipes are designed for vinegar with 4% to 5% acetic acid. Commercial vinegars are standardized at that level. Homemade vinegar is not generally recommended for pickling because its acid content is unknown, and its flavor is too distinctive. As well, it is likely to cause cloudy or dark pickles. For a few specific uses, refer to the VINEGAR section. Use white vinegar when a clear pickling liquid is desired. Cider or wine vinegar can be used whenever their flavor is compatible.

Sweeteners

Because it adds neither color nor flavor, white sugar is often used, but sweet pickles taste just as good made with mild honey. Dark honey or brown sugar will add more flavor. As honey should not be boiled for a long time, add it near the end of the pickle's cooking time. In many pickle recipes the sweetening can be reduced by half and still give a pleasant, sweet-sour flavor.

Herbs and Spices

The most common pickling herb for vegetables is dill. Heads of dill give the best flavor, but seeds can also be used. Other good seasonings are garlic, horseradish, hot pepper, bay leaf, tarragon, mustard seed, celery seed, coriander seed, whole cloves, whole allspice, cinnamon bark, and mace spears (pieces). Blends of various herbs and spices are used for some pickles. These can be bought already mixed, or added to taste. Powdered spices are seldom used because they cloud the pickling liquid and dull the flavor.

Risks with Additives for Crispness

Alum and calcium chloride are used to make pickles more crisp. However, even a speck too much of one of these can give food a bitter taste, and larger amounts of alum can cause stomach upsets, so they are best avoided. They are not necessary if the foods to be pickled are fresh and of high quality. The use of grape leaves is a traditional way to add crispness. A layer of grape leaves in the bottom of the pickling crock, and another on top of the pickles, or one or two grape leaves in each jar of pickles is all that is needed.

Utensils

Use only enamel, stainless steel, or other non-corrosive pots for cooking pickles or pickling mixtures. Aluminum reacts with the acid. Glass jars, stoneware, or pottery crocks are best for storing pickles. If plastic containers are used they will smell like pickles from then on.

STORING PICKLES

In the past, pickled foods were packed in crocks and stored in the cellar for the winter. Most pickles are now canned, with a boiling water bath, and stored like other canned foods. Canning is the best way to store pickles that require cooking to prepare, but some pickled foods, including most fermented pickles, have a better texture and flavor if kept raw. Some vegetables can be pickled by packing them raw in jars, pouring a boiling hot vinegar solution over them, and sealing without further processing. (Refer to CANNING PICKLES, in the CANNING section.)

Pickled eggs and meats, and some raw pickles and relishes must be made in small amounts and refrigerated for use within days, or at most a month or two. For keeping all winter, pickled foods must be quite acidic, carefully packed, and kept where the temperature stays between freezing and 40°F. Full strength vinegar will preserve pickles packed in crocks better than the half-vinegar, half-water blend used for many canned pickles. Plenty of liquid must be used, and the food must be kept well below its surface so it is never exposed to air. Crocks and other containers must be tightly covered to keep out dust and other contaminants, and to protect them from high humidity. It is also necessary to inspect them frequently to remove any mold that begins to grow on the surface. For fermented pickles refer to KEEPING SAUERKRAUT IN COLD STORAGE, in the SAUERKRAUT section.)

BASIC PICKLE RECIPES

Spiced Pickled Fruit

(MAKES 6–7 PINTS, CANNED)

8–12 pounds fruit, about 4 quarts prepared (Use any fruit. Firm or slightly underripe give the best texture.)

1 quart vinegar (can be homemade; refer to VINEGAR section)

1 cup (about) honey or 1½ cups sugar, or to taste

3 tablespoons mixed, whole pickling spices (or 1 tablespoon each cinnamon stick and cloves, and ½ tablespoon each allspice and mace spears)

Small fruits for pickling whole should be unblemished. Larger fruits can be trimmed and cut into chunks or slices.

To make the pickling liquid, put the vinegar, sweetening, spices, and about 1 quart water in a pot. If the fruit is very juicy, use less water. Tie the spices in a cloth bag to be removed just before the pickling liquid is poured in the canning jars, or add them loose. Heat the pickling liquid to a boil, and proceed as described below for the different fruits. For fruits not listed, especially slices or chunks, cook and can as follows.

Add a small portion of fruit to the boiling liquid. Cook just until the fruit is heated through, then dip it out with a sieve or slotted spoon, and put into hot canning jars. Add more fruit to the liquid and repeat. When all the fruit is in the jars, heat the liquid to a full boil and pour over the fruit, leaving ½ inch headroom. Process in a boiling water bath for 20 minutes, both pints and quarts. (Refer to the CANNING section.)

Small Whole Peaches, Sekel Pears, or other Small Pears

Among peaches, clingstones are best. Peel peaches. Blanching will make them easier to peel. Peel pears carefully, leaving stems on for handles, or omit peeling. A slice of ginger root can be included with the spices. Heat the liquid to a boil, and cook the peaches or pears a few at a time for 2 or 3 minutes, or until heated. Lift out fruit with a sieve or slotted spoon, and put it into a bowl or pot. Pour the boiling liquid over it, then let stand overnight. Pack fruit in hot canning jars. Bring the pickling liquid to a boil and pour over fruit in jars. Process as above.

Crabapples, Whole Plums

Leave stems on crabapples for handles. Pierce each crabapple or plum deeply with a needle to help prevent bursting. Heat the pickling liquid, then let it cool. Add the fruit and heat to a boil. Remove from heat and let sit overnight. Reheat the next day, and process as above.

Watermelon Rind, Melons, Cherries

Trim outer skin from watermelon rind or melon, and cut in slices or chunks. Leave cherries whole and unpitted, with stems on. Heat the pickling liquid to a boil, and pour over the fruit. Let sit overnight. Next day, drain off the liquid, heat it to a boil, and pour over the fruit. Repeat these steps the third day. On the fourth day, heat the fruit and liquid together and can as above. This procedure improves texture, preventing soft or mushy pickles.

Spiced Cucumber Pickles

Although not a fruit, cucumbers can be pickled like the watermelon rind, above. (Use standard 4% or 5% vinegar, rather than homemade.) Slice the cucumbers without peeling. Overly ripe cucumbers can be seeded, cut in chunks, and pickled in this way also.

Plums

Plums are grown in more places in the world than any other stone fruit, resulting in a wide and interesting array of plum recipes. There is someone, somewhere, who will know a good way to use every kind of plum, whatever its size, shape, color, or flavor. Strange as it seems, however, the most traditional of plum dishes, Christmas plum pudding, does not contain a single plum.

Several distinctly different kinds of stone fruits are called plums. European plum varieties are the best known and most widely cultivated. They include prune plums and all the common fresh and canned varieties. Japanese and Chinese varieties are gaining acceptance. They are very good fresh or canned, but less good dried. The various small, tart-tasting plum varieties are excellent for making juice or preserves, but not sweet enough to enjoy as fresh fruit. Most wild plums fall into this group, as do damson plums, which are most appreciated in Europe for making all kinds of preserves.

PLUM STORAGE
Canning
Leave whole, pierced with needle to prevent bursting, or halve and pit.

Hot Pack
Cook fruit 2 min. in boiling syrup, juice, or water. Let stand 20–30 min. Drain, pack, add boiling cooking liquid, ½ in. headroom. Process boiling water bath. Pints: 20 min. Quarts: 25 min.

Raw Pack
Add boiling syrup, juice, or water, ½ in. headroom. Process as for HOT PACK. Refer to the CANNING section. Also see CANNING FRUIT JUICE AND SAUCE, in the FRUITS section.

Drying
See PRUNES, below.

Freezing
Whole, or halved and pitted. Pack dry, or cover with liquid. Refer to the FREEZING section. Also see FREEZING FRUIT JUICE AND SAUCE, in the FRUITS section.

Plums

🌸

204

Pick plums for canning and freezing while they are still firm and a little tart, as these retain the best texture and flavor after processing. Fully ripe plums are quite soft and sweet, very good for eating fresh, making sauce, and drying.

Plums are easy to prepare. They never need peeling and can often be used unpitted. Flavor is lost if they are peeled. When cooking plums whole, pierce them with a needle to help prevent bursting. Though the skins will still crack, they will not curl off. Freestone varieties are easily separated from their pits after they are cut open. It is easier to cook clingstone varieties and pick out the pits afterwards, or the flesh can be sliced off fresh plums in several pieces. The pits will still have fruit on them and can be used for making juice. To do so, cover them with water, cook a few minutes, and strain off juice. Drink it as plumade, or use as the liquid for canned or frozen plums.

Prunes

The word "prune" usually refers to the dried fruit, but it can also mean a fresh plum intended for drying whole. Dried prunes were once a winter staple, used in all kinds of dishes, from main courses to desserts and snacks. Because of modern freezing and canning methods, prunes are no longer of vital importance, but they are still among the best-tasting and sweetest dried fruits.

Prune plums are not a specific plum variety, but any kind of plum with a sugar content high enough to allow drying without pitting. When sugar content is too low, whole plums are likely to ferment rather than dry. Such plums can be cut in half, pitted, and dried like a peach. They will taste good, but they will not be prunes. (Refer to the DRYING section.)

Most prune plums will hang on the tree and continue to sweeten even after they are completely ripe and soft. The best prunes come from plums left to drop from the tree by themselves. They must be gathered from the ground every day or two, or, for easy gathering, a sheet can be laid on the ground, and the tree shaken over it to make loose plums drop. The plums can be spread immediately on trays for drying in the sun or in a dryer, or they can be treated first to crack or check the skins so as to speed the drying process. Though lye treatments

---

2–2½ pounds = 1 quart canned or frozen; 1 bushel = 20–30 quarts, canned or frozen

PLUM AND PRUNE IDEAS
Plum and Wine Gelatin
Drain and reserve the juice from canned or stewed plums. Pit the plums, and put them in a mold or serving dish. Measure the juice, and mix in and soak 1 tablespoon powdered gelatin per cup. Heat to dissolve the gelatin. Add ½ cup wine for each cup of juice, sweeten, if necessary, and pour over the plums. Sweet wines are excellent in this. White wine is attractive with green or yellow plums, and red wine with red or purple plums. Chill to set the gelatin. Very pleasant as a side dish with a meal, as well as for dessert.

Plum Soup
Flavor puréed plums with lemon juice and grated rind. If too tart, add a little honey. Mix a tablespoon of tapioca or cornstarch into each quart of the purée. Heat gradually, stirring often,

have been used, there are more agreeable home methods. One is to simply nick each plum with a knife, so that the skin is broken. Another method is to soak the plums for 20 minutes in hot water to soften the skins. This will speed drying without breaking the skins. Plums can also be blanched briefly in boiling water to check their skins, but this may cause pieces of skin to curl off. Before blanching the whole batch, test a few plums to see how it works.

In a hot, dry climate prunes are dried for 4 to 5 days in the sun, and then moved to an airy, shaded place to finish drying. Each prune is turned over after 2 or 3 days in the sun. It takes from 12 to 24 hours to dry them in a mechanical dryer. The prunes will be leathery when finished. (Refer to the DRYING section.)

Old fashioned, home-dried prunes are quite different from most of those now sold in grocery stores. Commercial prunes are usually "moisturized," which means, among other things, less prunes per pound and less flavor per prune. Home-dried prunes are harder and drier, with a fuller flavor. Children enjoy chewing them for a snack but their jaws will get more exercise than usual. (Refer to MOISTURIZING DRIED FRUITS, in the DRYING section.) Very dry prunes will need soaking for several hours or overnight before they are cooked.

Potatoes

People can stay healthy on a diet of white or Irish potatoes and very little else, if they eat enough of them. Many of the poor of Europe have done so at different times in history. According to one estimate, it takes two pounds of potatoes to make a nutritious meal for one person. The Irish were eating an average of eight pounds per person, per day, before the disastrous famine of 1845 and 1846 when their potato crops were destroyed by a blight. Though the famine illustrated all too graphically the danger of depending entirely on one food crop, it also demonstrates the potato's exceptional food value. A whole people could never have come to depend on them so completely had they not been so nutritious.

until thickened. Serve hot, with a spoon of yogurt in each bowl, as a smooth, satisfying cold weather treat.

Prune Bits Instead of Raisins

Cut up prunes with scissors or a knife, and use like raisins in baked goods, salads, and snack mixtures.

POTATO STORAGE
Canning

(Small new potatoes best.) Rub or scrape off skins. Leave whole, or dice.

Hot Pack

Pour boiling water over, boil 10 min. Drain, pack in jars, add boiling cooking water, ½ in. headroom. Process 240°F, 11 pounds pressure. *Whole Potatoes* Pints: 30 min. Quarts: 40 min. *Diced Potatoes* (because of denser pack) Pints: 35 min. Quarts: 40 min. Refer to the CANNING section.

Cold Storage

See KEEPING POTATOES IN COLD STORAGE, below.

Besides starch, potatoes contain vitamins, minerals, and some high quality protein. There is not very much of any of these in one potato, but when many are eaten the cumulative amounts are significant. Their vitamin C and protein are especially important whenever potatoes are a major part of the diet. Contrary to some opinion, they are not a high calorie food, and eating a potato is about as fattening as eating an apple. Their bad reputation comes from the gravy, butter, and cream that so often accompany them.

Potatoes are a good crop for homestead gardeners. They are productive in a small space, require no special equipment for growing and harvesting, and are easily stored for winter. They are more productive per acre than grains, even when calculated by their dry weight. Mature potatoes will keep in any dark place for several months, and long-keeping varieties will last into spring in a root cellar.

Potatoes were first cultivated by the Incas in the Andes Mountains of Peru and Bolivia, and many unique potato varieties are still grown by Indians living there. The early Spanish explorers of South America took potatoes back to Europe where they spread rapidly, and early settlers brought them to North America. Most present day American and European varieties came from the same beginnings and are basically alike. A few seed companies do sell distinctive sets, like the yellow fingerling potatoes that make such good potato salads, and the blue-fleshed novelty varieties, but otherwise potatoes are white fleshed with similar flavors. The different varieties bred to suit particular climates and to resist diseases have not changed the basic character of the vegetable.

Sweet potatoes and yams are from an entirely different plant. (Refer to the SWEET POTATOES section.)

HANDLING POTATOES

Potatoes that are harvested early, soon after the plant's blossoms form, are called new potatoes. They are thin skinned, delicately flavored, and can be as small as one inch in diameter. As new potatoes do not keep well, they are usually gathered a batch at a time from around the potato plants, leaving the rest of the crop to continue growing. For long storage, they can be canned.

Drying
See DRYING POTATOES, below.

Freezing
(Quality poor if raw.) May bake, cool, and wrap; or french fry to light color, cool, and wrap; or cook in mixtures. Refer to the FREEZING section.
 1 pound raw = 2 cups mashed; 2½–3 pounds raw = 1 quart canned

POTATO IDEAS
Baked or Boiled Potatoes with Yogurt
Instead of bathing baked or boiled potatoes in butter, gravy, or other rich accompaniments, serve them with dishes of yogurt and minced onion or scallion. Each person can then mash a potato, and add yogurt and onion or scallion to taste. Minced parsley or some other herbs like fresh dill, tarragon, or fennel can also be included.

Oven Browned Potatoes
Scrub potatoes and cut them in uniform pieces. They can be large or small, diced, sliced, or cut in sticks.

Mature potatoes can be dug as soon as most of the plant tops have turned yellow. If the weather is cool and dry, they can be left in the ground until the first frosts. Potatoes keep so well in any cool, dark place that other methods for preserving them are unnecessary. Most varieties can be stored for two or three months, and long keeping varieties will last until late spring in a root cellar.

If they are cooked and dried, potato quality is good, while it is acceptable if they are cooked and frozen. Raw potatoes do not freeze well in home freezers because ice crystals form, rupturing the flesh and causing a watery texture when thawed. Commercially frozen potatoes are more successful because extreme low temperatures are used, bypassing the crystal stage.

Keeping Potatoes in Cold Storage

Before they are stored, potatoes need about 2 weeks of conditioning at 60 to 70°F. This allows skins to toughen and any scraped places to heal. Spread potatoes out in a spare room or shed—anywhere away from sun and wind. Set imperfect potatoes aside to use first. Conditioning is less important for potatoes left in the ground for a month or 6 weeks after their tops died back, but that is not possible in damp or warm weather.

When ready, pack the potatoes in boxes, bins, or other containers, allowing for some air circulation, and put them in the cold storage area. Ideal conditions are 40°F, with a humidity of 80–90%, as in a root cellar, but they will keep in outdoor pits, or cool, dark basements. Keep them in the dark to prevent them turning green, and protect them from freezing. A brown ring will show inside frozen potatoes when they are cut open, and they soon turn watery, blacken, and spoil. If the temperature stays between freezing and 35°F for very long, the starch in the potatoes begins to turn to sugar, and they become hard and difficult to cook. This can be corrected by holding the potatoes at room temperature for 1 or 2 weeks before cooking them. The sugar will then turn back into starch.

Break the sprouts off potatoes as soon as they appear. If they are left to grow the potatoes will soon wither, but if they are removed the potatoes will often be good to eat for several more months. It may be necessary to go through stored potatoes several times in late winter or spring to remove sprouts.

Rub or toss them with oil to coat all cut surfaces. Spread in a baking pan, and bake in a moderate oven until evenly browned. This may take 30 to 60 minutes, depending on the size of the pieces. Shake the pan, or stir the potatoes several times, for even browning. If desired, sprinkle with paprika when done. These are convenient to make when the oven is to be used for other baking for the same meal, and their browned flavor is pleasant and satisfying without butter or rich gravy.

Seasoning Potatoes for Mashing

Potatoes for mashing can be made more flavorful by adding seasonings to their cooking water. Cook any of the following with the potatoes: a small onion, a cut clove of garlic, a bay leaf, a sprig of celery leaves, or other herbs. Remove the seasonings before mashing the potatoes.

Leftover Potato Patties

Mix leftover mashed potatoes with egg and seasonings to taste. Shape into patties, and sauté until brown on

Always store potatoes and apples separately. If stored together the potatoes will make the apples musty. (Refer to the APPLES and COLD STORAGE sections.)

If there are more potatoes in cold storage than can be used, dry, or cook and freeze the extras.

Drying Potatoes

Potatoes must be cooked before they are dried, unless being dried for flour. Steam or boil them (unpeeled) until they are cooked through but not mushy. For slices, peel and cut them about ¼-inch thick. Spread on drying trays and dry until hard. To reconstitute, put the slices in a saucepan, pour boiling water over them, and simmer over low heat until they are expanded and heated through. Add extra water if necessary.

Riced dried potatoes are very useful. After the potatoes are cooked, spread them out in a pan or colander, in a cool, airy place for a day or two so that they will be light and fluffy when riced, rather than sticky. Peel the potatoes just before ricing. Push them through a ricer or food mill, and let them fall directly onto drying trays, lined if necessary. (Refer to DRYING FRUIT AND OTHER PURÉES, in the DRYING section.) Move the ricer or food mill around over the tray for a loose, even layer. Do not press or push the potato around after it is on the tray, as this will make it mat or stick together. Dry to a crumbly meal. To use for mashed potatoes, pour hot water or hot milk over the meal to cover, and let sit over very low heat until the liquid is absorbed. If too thick add a little more liquid. Potato meal is also good for making potato soup or for thickening soups and stews.

Raw potatoes can be sliced or grated, then dried, and ground for flour. They are likely to discolor while drying, even when treated with an ascorbic acid solution, and the flour will have a greyish appearance.

Making Potato Starch

Pure white potato starch can be extracted from raw potatoes and dried to use for thickening like cornstarch or arrowroot starch. Grate several pounds of potatoes as finely as possible.

---

both sides. Minced onion, leftover cooked, chopped vegetables or meat, or any kind of canned or cooked fish, or shellfish are very good in these patties. For a quick lunch or supper, serve potato patties with homemade relish or catsup.

Quick Potato Salad

Mix diced, leftover potatoes with liquid from dill pickles, or with a prepared Italian or French salad dressing, and add vegetables, herbs, and garnishes to taste.

Mashed Potato Crust

Oil a pie pan or shallow baking dish. Press mashed potato evenly against the bottom and sides. If the mashed potato is too stiff to be workable, mix a little milk into it. Bake in a hot, 375–425°F oven until the crust is browned, then fill it with creamed vegetables, creamed tuna, or other mixtures. Serve immediately, or sprinkle with bread crumbs and dots of butter and brown under the broiler.

Add about twice their volume of cold water and stir well. Pour through a fine sieve, or a cloth lined colander, using cloth that is not tightly woven. After the water sits for a few minutes, the starch will settle to the bottom, and the water can be poured off. To obtain as much starch as possible, stir fresh, cold water into the potato gratings, let sit, and drain several times more.

After collecting and draining all the starch, rinse it by adding more cold water, mixing, then letting it settle again. Pour off the clear water. The starch will remain as a damp, caked paste in the container. Spread it in a shallow pan, or on a lined drying tray, and dry it in a food dryer or in the sun. If the starch is lumpy after it is dry, sift it or roll over it with a rolling pin. It will keep indefinitely in a closed container. A pound of potatoes yields from ¼ to ½ cup of starch. The potato gratings can be cooked for soup or for feeding livestock.

Potato starch is popular in many northern European countries for thickening fruit purée, or for making puddings from juice.

Saving Potatoes' Nutrients

Peeling potatoes is the classic before-dinner chore. It is also the way to throw out the most nutritious part of the potato, since most of the vitamins and minerals are concentrated immediately under the skin. Peeling raw potatoes cuts most of these away, even when parings are thin. If peeling is delayed until after potatoes are cooked, the skins will slip off without taking any flesh, and most nutrients are saved. Another alternative is to eat the peel with the potatoes. If potatoes are scrubbed with a brush and well-rinsed, they can be sliced and fried, or cooked in most other ways, without peeling. As the skins do not have much flavor after they are cooked, it is largely the habit of seeing completely white potatoes that makes peeling seem necessary.

Damaged skin or green areas should be cut off. The green, caused by too much exposure to light, contains a toxic substance (solanine), and should not be eaten. Once green areas are cut away the rest of the potato can be eaten.

Another common practice that removes potato nutrients is soaking them, and then throwing out the soaking water, with its water soluble vitamins and minerals. Soaking to prevent discoloration is not necessary if potatoes are prepared just before they are cooked. To avoid losing nutrients in discarded potato cooking water, steam the potatoes, or boil them in a minimum of water, and then use the water as a cooking ingredient. It is excellent in bread dough, or sour dough, or added to soups and stews.

Quinces 🌿

The quince is an ancient fruit eaten in the Mediterranean area at least since the time of the early Greeks. It was brought to America by early settlers who valued it highly for making jelly and preserves. In the last half century it has, regrettably, lost much of its popularity. Many have never heard of it, and the fruit on many old quince bushes or trees goes unused because no one knows how to enjoy it. Most varieties are too hard and astringent to eat raw. They require long cooking to soften them and to bring out their delicate flavor and color. They are delightful fruits when well-prepared, and deserve to be rediscovered.

Quinces grow on small, bush-like trees. The fruit is greenish yellow to yellow, with the look of a lumpy apple or pear. When fully ripe, the flesh is cream to apricot colored. Quince trees grow like other fruit trees, but take less space. They are an attractive and practical addition to any garden.

HANDLING QUINCES

Quinces can be left on the tree until after the first fall frost, to be picked as needed. For long keeping in a root cellar or other cool place, harvest them a few weeks before frosts while they are still a little underripe. They are best used like tart cooking apples, and can be stewed, baked, and made into sauce or juice. The slight fuzz on their skins can be rubbed off with a cloth before they are cooked. Peeling is not necessary. If the quinces are very hard, and difficult to core, cook them first, and then core them. As quince skins and cores are flavorful, and rich in pectin, do not discard them but cook them in water and strain them for juice. This juice can be made into jelly, or mixed with bland, low-pectin fruits. (Refer to the PECTIN and the JAM AND JELLY sections.)

To precook hard quinces, cover them with boiling water and let stand a few minutes, then boil or steam until soft, when they can be cored and sliced. Always save the cooking water to use with the fruit, or for juice. Quinces hold their shape even after they are tender. Traditionally, they were tested for doneness by poking with a straw to see if it would penetrate completely. Some varieties turn a pretty, rosy red color when completely done, which usually takes from 40 minutes to an hour.

QUINCE STORAGE

Canning

Cook whole in water to soften, about 20 min. Slice or chunk, removing cores. Pack, cover with boiling syrup made from cooking water, ½ in. headroom. Process boiling water bath. Pints and quarts: 60 min. Refer to the CANNING section. Also see CANNING FRUIT JUICE AND SAUCE, in the FRUITS section.

Cold Storage

Pick before fully ripe. Store like apples. Will keep 2–3 months. Refer to KEEPING APPLES IN COLD STORAGE, in the APPLES section.

Drying

Handling easier if cooked whole until soft. Slice, core, dry to hard. Thick cooked sauce makes good leather. Refer to the DRYING section.

Freezing

Must be precooked. Refer to FREEZING FRUIT JUICE AND SAUCE, in the FRUITS section.

QUINCE RECIPES
Quince Compote

(MAKES ABOUT 6 DESSERT SERVINGS)

2 pounds (about) quinces
¼ cup honey, or to taste

lemon juice and grated rind to taste, optional

Rub fuzz off the quinces, cover with boiling water, and simmer about 30 minutes, until softened. Drain, saving the cooking water. Peel, remove cores, and slice. Simmer the slices in the cooking water for about 30 minutes more. If there is too much juice, boil it uncovered until reduced. Add honey and lemon, and bring to a boil to blend flavors. Chill before serving.

Radishes

Round, red, raw radishes are a familiar and delightfully crisp nibble, and a salad favorite, but they are an embellishment rather than a food staple. It is the large winter radishes commonly grown in East Asian countries, and in some places in Europe, that are a basic vegetable crop. They are similar to turnips, and used in many Chinese and Japanese dishes. They are practical to grow because they can be started late in summer as a second planting, after the harvest of some other crop, and because they can be stored through the winter. There are many shapes and colors of winter radishes, but all of them are large in size. Roots weighing one or two pounds are common, and 50 pound roots are quite possible. Daikon, a Japanese, long, white winter radish, is perhaps the best known. Most seed catalogs carry a few winter radish varieties, as well as many spring varieties.

Radishes are not very high in nutrients, but as there is an old belief that they are good for digestion, they may have hidden virtues. Radish leaves are also good to eat, and are more nutritious than the roots. They make a good cooked vegetable, like their close relatives, turnip tops and mustard greens. Radish seed pods, picked while young and tender, make a surprisingly

---

QUINCE IDEAS
Baked Quince

Rub the fuzz off the quince with a cloth, and cut out the core as for baked apples. Precooking makes coring easier. Put a spoon of honey and a dab of butter in each quince, and set them close together in a baking dish. Sprinkle with ginger, or pepper, or other spices if desired. Add water to the baking dish halfway up the quince and bake in a hot, 375–400°F oven for about an hour if raw, 30 minutes if precooked.

Quinces in Apple Recipes

Quinces are often a delicious replacement for apples in cooked recipes. A longer cooking time will be necessary, unless the quinces are precooked. Quince sauce is a very good substitute for applesauce. Refer to the recipes in the APPLES section.

RADISH STORAGE
Canning

Pickled only! For winter radishes, refer to CANNING SAUERKRAUT, in the SAUERKRAUT section.

good, if peppery, vegetable for eating raw, and for cooking or pickling. The pods which form on radish plants after they flower look like small, pointy-ended green beans. If left to mature and dry, their seeds can be collected for sprouting, or for a seasoning like mustard seeds. (Refer to THRESHING AND WINNOWING in the SEEDS section, and to the SPROUTS and MUSTARD (GREENS AND SEEDS) sections.)

HANDLING RADISHES

The fastest growing radishes taste best. Pull spring radishes as soon as they reach a reasonable size. Those that stay in the ground too long will become hot, and may turn woody. Some can be left growing to produce pods or seeds for gathering during the summer. Winter radishes can withstand light frosts, but should be pulled before hard freezes.

The only preparation small radishes need is washing and trimming. If the tops are attractive, leave them on as a handle, and include the radishes with other vegetables for dipping. Do not soak radishes in cold water, because they will lose flavor. Keep them crisp by putting them in a closed container in the refrigerator. Large radishes are usually sliced or shredded.

Small, young radish leaves are good raw in salads. Chop finely and they will lose their scratchy quality. Large or mature tops are best cooked.

Using Very Hot Radishes

To tone down the taste of radishes that are too hot or peppery, marinate them for a few minutes in vinegar, soy sauce, or any salad dressing. Fermenting them like pickles will also tame them. (Refer to the SAUERKRAUT section.) A way to take advantage of their hotness is to dry and grind them, or grate them finely before drying, for a peppery seasoning to sprinkle on salads, soups, and other dishes.

Radishes that become tough or woody as well as hot are difficult to use except for making soup stock.

Marinated Salad Radishes

To prepare extra hot radishes for use in salads, slice and marinate them in vinegar for 2 to 3 hours, using about ½ cup vinegar for 2 cups radishes. The drained slices will pep up green salads,

---

Cold Storage

Winter varieties Harvest after frost. Do not wash or trim roots. Cut tops to about ½ in. Will keep 2–4 months in root cellar. Refer to the COLD STORAGE section. Also see KEEPING SAUERKRAUT IN COLD STORAGE, in the SAUERKRAUT section.

Drying

Shred, or slice thinly. Dry to hard. May grind to use as seasoning. Refer to the DRYING section.

Freezing

(Not practical, except if for cooking.) Dice winter radish. Blanch 1 min. in boiling water. Refer to the FREEZING section.

potato, egg, and tuna salads, and even some fruit salads. Use leftover vinegar in salad dressings, or for the next batch of radishes.

Raspberries

Nothing tastes better on a summer day than a bowl of freshly picked raspberries, but the raspberry aroma, flavor, and color are just as welcome in winter. Sparkling raspberry juice, and rich, red raspberry sauce are winter luxuries known only to those who freeze and can their own.

Red raspberries are the most familiar, but there are black, purple, white, and yellow varieties. All berries that separate from their cores when picked, leaving their centers hollow are raspberries. Some wild, black raspberries are called "black caps," because picking them is like taking tiny caps off very tiny heads. In some places, wild raspberries, especially the red varieties, are so abundant and easy to pick that there is no need to cultivate them. All raspberries are hardy and well-suited to northern climates.

HANDLING RASPBERRIES

Raspberries are ripe and ready to pick when they come off their cores with a gentle touch. If pressing and pulling is necessary, they are not ready. As ripe raspberries are soft, pick them into shallow containers to keep them from packing down and crushing each other. (Immediately use any crushed raspberries for sauce or juice.) While picking, remove and discard any moldy berries on the plants, because the mold can quickly spread to other berries, spoiling them for later picking. This is worthwhile even for wild berries, if one intends to return to pick the same spot again.

Washing is not necessary for raspberries growing in a clean, dust free place. If they must be washed, do not do so until just before using them, as the water and handling make them spoil quickly. Wash them gently, by putting them in a large pan of cool water, swishing them around by hand, then lifting them out into a colander to drain.

RASPBERRY STORAGE
Canning
Berries become very soft, juice is excellent. Pour about ½ cup boiling water, juice, or syrup in jars, fill with berries, shake to pack, add more boiling liquid, ½ in. headroom. Process boiling water bath. Pints: 10 min. Quarts: 15 min. Refer to the CANNING section. Also see CANNING FRUIT JUICE AND SAUCE, in the FRUITS section.

Drying
Refer to DRYING SOFT BERRIES, in the DRYING section. Leaves for herb tea: Refer to DRYING HERBS, in the HERBS section.

Freezing
Pack dry, unsweetened, or spread in shallow layer; sprinkle with about ¼ cup sugar or honey per quart, pack gently. Or pack and cover with liquid. Refer to LIQUIDS IN WHICH TO FREEZE FRUIT, in the FREEZING section.

5–8 cups fresh = 1 quart canned, or frozen

Some kinds of wild raspberries are very seedy but still make good juice or sauce. (Refer to SEEDINESS IN BLACKBERRIES, in the BLACKBERRIES section.)

RASPBERRY RECIPES

Raspberry Shrub

This old-fashioned beverage retains the heady aroma of raspberries on a hot summer day better than any other raspberry preparation.

raspberries, freshly picked (washed, if necessary)	vinegar (preferably home-made, or raw cider vinegar)

Pack the raspberries into a jar and add vinegar to fill it. Run a knife around the sides of the jar to release air bubbles. The vinegar must fill all spaces between berries. Close or cover the jar, and keep it in a dark place at room temperature for a month. Then strain through cloth and pour the raspberry vinegar into sterile bottles for storage. Store in a cool, dark place.

To make a refreshing glass of raspberry shrub, put several spoonfuls of the raspberry vinegar in a glass, and add cold water. Sweeten, if desired.

Blackberry or Strawberry Shrub

Use either of these instead of raspberries.

Rhubarb

Rhubarb—the fruit that is not a fruit—is actually the stalk of a plant related to buckwheat. It grows best in the North where winters are cold. Among its many advantages are its permanence in the garden (once established it is always there), and its earliness. It can be harvested long before any true fruits mature. An old name for rhubarb is pieplant, which describes one popular use, but there are many other ways to prepare it.

Rhubarb's one disadvantage is the large amount of sweetening commonly added to counter its tartness, but even this tart-

---

RASPBERRY IDEAS

Raspberry-Orange

This flavor combination is always a winner. Fresh raspberry and diced orange fruit cup, chilled and sprinkled with coconut or chopped nuts, is superb. Half raspberry and half orange juice is delightful to drink and makes an outstanding gelatin, to say nothing of its sherbet and ice cream possibilities. When the raspberry supply is limited, there is no better way to extend it.

Raspberry Orange Sauce

Cook raspberries with very thin slices of orange with the rind, and sweeten with a little honey or maple syrup. For a stronger orange flavor add extra orange juice, especially concentrated frozen juice. Simmer over moderate heat for 10 to 15 minutes, stirring often as it heats up to prevent sticking. This sauce is very nice with meats, or enjoy it with breakfast or for dessert. To can, pour hot in jars and process for 10 minutes in a boiling water bath. Refer to the CANNING section.

Raspberry Juice Blends

Raspberry juice blends deliciously with apple, currant, peach, and other fruit juices, as well as orange juice. As good for gelatin, sherbets, and jelly-making as it is for beverages.

ness can be turned to advantage. Rhubarb or its juice can be used like lemon to enliven the flavor of bland, sweet fruits, or used like tomato to perk up meat stews or soups. Rhubarb, onion, and beef flavors, for instance, go surprisingly well together. Why not grow a rhubarb plant near the kitchen door, beside the patch of herbs, to inspire such uses?

Only the stalks of rhubarb plants are edible. The leaves contain enough oxalic acid to be poisonous and sometimes fatal. Do not confuse rhubarb leaves with rhubarb chard, which is a red-stalked variety of Swiss chard, and quite safe to eat.

HANDLING RHUBARB

Rhubarb stalks should be pulled rather than cut, as cutting leaves the stalk's base in the ground to rot. Grasp the stalks near the base and pull with a slight twisting motion. Cut the leaves off outdoors. A brisk whack with a knife works best, and the leaves can go directly onto the compost pile. The bottom of the stalks can also be trimmed outdoors. Rinsing and slicing is the only other preparation necessary before cooking. Do not peel rhubarb stalks. Many old cookbooks advise it, but as the newer varieties are less stringy, as well as redder and sweeter, this advice no longer applies.

Rhubarb is most tender and sweet in spring and early summer, so these are the best times to can or freeze it. As rhubarb contains a lot of water, add only a tiny bit in the bottom of the pot when stewing it, to keep it from sticking as it begins to cook. Rhubarb can also be baked in a covered dish in the oven without adding water. Or it can be mixed with a little honey or sugar after it is sliced, and left sitting until enough juice has collected for cooking it.

Reducing the Sweetening

Rhubarb recipes usually call for ½ cup or more of sugar per quart of chopped fruit. Reduce this amount to 3 to 4 tablespoons honey or ⅓ cup sugar for a flavor that is still pleasantly sweet and sour. The reddest, sweetest varieties can be tried with even less sweetening. Add a dab of butter to mask some of the acidity.

RHUBARB STORAGE
Canning
Cut ½–1 in. slices, mix in 3–4 tablespoons honey, or ⅓ cup sugar per quart. Let stand 3–4 hours to draw out juice. Bring slowly to boil, then boil ½ min. Ladle into jars, ½ in. headroom. Process boiling water bath. Pints and quarts: 10 min. Refer to the CANNING section. Also see CANNING FRUIT JUICE AND SAUCE, in the FRUITS section.

Cold Storage
Refer to COLD WATER CANNING, in the COLD STORAGE section.

Drying
Slice or chop, dry to hard. Good in *Herb Teas* (refer to the HERBS section). Or grind for FRUIT MEAL or purée for FRUIT LEATHER. Refer to the DRYING section.

Freezing
Slice. Optional: Blanch 1 min. in boiling water to set color and flavor. Pack dry or cover with liquid. Refer to LIQUIDS IN WHICH TO FREEZE FRUIT, in the FREEZING section, and to the FREEZING section generally.

An excellent way to reduce the amount of sweetening is to cook it with sweet fruits. Use dried fruits like raisins, figs or dates. A mixture with berries is often very good. Such juice combinations as rhubarb and bland wild berry juice, rhubarb-sweet cherry juice, or rhubarb-pear juice, can all be extraordinarily delicious. (Refer to COMBINING SWEET AND TART FRUITS, in the FRUITS section.)

Winter Forcing

Dig roots in late fall, replant in containers. Leave outside until frozen solid. (Freezing is required for new growth to begin.) Bring into cellar, or other cool, humid place. Harvest new stalks as they grow.

2 pounds fresh = about 1 quart canned or frozen

ROSE STORAGE
Canning

Rosehip juice or purée. *Caution:* Add 2 tablespoons lemon juice to each pint to increase acidity. Refer to CANNING FRUIT JUICE AND SAUCE, in the FRUITS section. Also see *Rose Petal Syrup*, below.

Drying

Rosehips Spread out, dry until brittle or hard. Optional: Blanch briefly or nick with knife to crack skins and speed drying. Crush or grind if for teas. *Rose Petals* Trim off base of petals (see below). Dry until papery. Use for tea or flavoring. Refer to the DRYING section.

Freezing

Rosehips May trim blossom and stem ends. Package dry. *Rose Water* (see below) Freeze as ice cubes. Refer to the FREEZING section.

Roses

A rose is more than a pretty flower. It is the blossom of the rosehip—a highly respected fruit, and its petals can be an exotic flavoring in food. Particularly useful are wild roses and some old or standard rose varieties. Most modern hybrids have too little fragrance to be used for flavoring, and they produce no fruits. Those who wish to eat their roses as well as look at them must find some wild ones, or else plant varieties known to produce rosehips or a strong scent. *Rosa rugosa* is a variety often advertised for its hips. Damask roses are famous for their scent, but are rarely found in nurseries or garden catalogs. They are used to make rose attar, a perfume or fragrant oil. The rose geranium is known for its scent, but it is not botanically related to roses.

Since the discovery of rosehips' high vitamin C content, they have often been regarded as vitamin supplements to take dutifully rather than fruits to be enjoyed. Yet rosehips were enjoyed long before anyone ever heard of vitamins. In Scandinavian countries they have always been a favorite fruit. The American Indians always appreciated them, as did the early American colonists, and they can be just as enjoyable today. Well-prepared rosehips are both a taste treat and a nutritional bonus.

Besides the petals and hips, the rose plant has other edible parts. Its first spring leaves, and the blossoms can be added to salads. The leaves, both fresh and dried, can be made into herb teas, and the roots can be slivered and dried for rose root tea. The flavor of all of these will be mild and pleasant without any distinctive rose taste.

HANDLING ROSES

Gather only those rose petals and hips that have not been sprayed with insecticides. Wild roses growing along roadways, and ornamental roses are often heavily sprayed.

Gathering and Preparing Rose Petals

Gather the petals from strongly scented roses on a dry morning, before the heat of the day has dissipated their fragrance. Choose blossoms in full bloom. The white or yellow area at the bottom of each petal must be trimmed off, as it is bitter tasting. This is easy to do while picking the petals. Pick a "pinch" of petals at a time, snip off the bottoms with scissors, and put them in a container. Or hold the petals with the fingers of one hand and twist off the bottoms with the other. (There is no need to trim petals for sachets.)

If the petals come from a clean location and are picked neatly, washing will not be necessary. If they must be washed, put them in a colander and lower them into a pan of cool water. Swish them gently, lift them out, and let them drain. They are then ready for drying or using in one of the recipes below, or for making into rose water.

Making Rose Water

Rose water is an intensely rose flavored liquid used like vanilla to flavor desserts, beverages, and other foods. True rose water is distilled from rose petals, but flavorful imitations can be made by simmering trimmed, crushed rose petals in a small amount of water, then straining through cloth to remove the spent petals. The temperature must stay below a boil or the flavor will be dissipated. Another possibility is to put 2 parts rose petals with 1 part hot water in a blender, liquify, and strain through cloth.

A sort of kitchen drip still for rose petals can be made as shown in the diagram. It takes about a pound of trimmed rose petals to make a cup of rose water. Place a rack in the bottom of a large pot and bring a quart of water to a boil in it. Then add the rose petals. Put in the bowl with the ice cube, being sure it is centered on the rack. Place the lid on upside down and put ice cubes in it. Keep the heat fairly high. The rose flavored steam will hit the cold lid, condense, run down to the center of

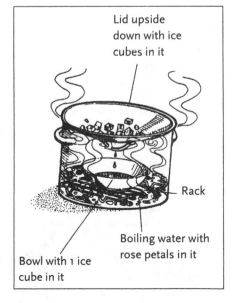

Lid upside down with ice cubes in it

Rack

Boiling water with rose petals in it

Bowl with 1 ice cube in it

the concave lid, and drip into the bowl. The ice cube in the bowl keeps the collected rose water from re-evaporating. Stop when there is about a cup of rose water, because after that the flavor becomes too weak.

Rose water kept in a tightly closed bottle in the refrigerator will last for months. It can also be frozen in small cubes of 2 or 3 tablespoons each, adding a cube to flavor a food. Rose water is widely used in Middle Eastern recipes.

Gathering and Preparing Rosehips

One or two rosehips can be nibbled fresh, but as they are too dry and seedy to enjoy raw in large quantities they are best cooked in some way or dried for making tea. Rosehips have their best flavor and highest vitamin C content in the fall when they are fully colored and fully ripe. They are usually picked after the first frost. If they shrivel on the plant before they are picked, the fibers around the seeds become scratchy. This will not affect teas or juices, but for purées they should be picked earlier.

Rosehips picked in a clean place can be dried or made into juice without washing or other preparation. Loose bits of the blossom end and stems are harmless. If the hips must be washed, put them in plenty of cool water, and rub them between the hands to remove bits of blossom and stem. Float off as much debris as possible, then lift the hips out of the water, leaving heavier dirt behind.

To make juice or purée, cover the hips with water and cook them until soft. Strain through cloth or a fine sieve for juice. Purée them by pushing them through a sieve or other device to remove seeds. (Refer to MAKING FRUIT JUICE AND SAUCE, in the FRUITS section.) Rosehip juice and purée are good in combinations with tart fruits.

Rosehips vary in size from smaller than a pea to almost as large as a plum, and it is best to dry tiny hips for tea or to use them for juice, so as to avoid tedious trimming. Large fleshy hips can be stewed or made into preserves. For these, trim the blossom and stem ends, then slit them open on one side to scrape out the seeds.

ROSE IDEAS

Rosehip Applesauce

Cook apples for making sauce in rosehip juice, or cook rosehips and apples together and purée them using a sieve or other straining device to remove the seeds.

Raisin Stuffed Rosehips

Use large, fleshy rosehips. Trim the blossom and stem end and slit the hips open on one side to scrape out the seedy centers. Put in several raisins. Eat as a fresh snack, or cook gently in a little water to make stewed fruit. For preserves, cook the stuffed hips in a syrup. Refer to the JAM AND JELLY section.

Rose Custard

Make a plain custard, and flavor it with 2–3 teaspoons rose water, or add a handful of fresh or dried, trimmed rose petals.

Rose Vinegar or Brandy

Fill a bottle with fresh, trimmed rose petals. Add vinegar or brandy to cover, close the bottle, and steep. After a month, strain off the vinegar or brandy and rebottle.

Rose Petal Syrup

(MAKES ABOUT 1 PINT)

1 cup rhubarb juice or
   ½ cup lemon juice
1 cup honey or 1½ cups sugar

1 cup rose petals, trimmed
   (see above)

Put the rhubarb juice and 1 cup water, or the lemon juice and 1½ cups water, in a saucepan with the sweetening. Heat to a boil, then simmer, uncovered, for 10 minutes. Add the rose petals and simmer without boiling for another 10 minutes. Strain to remove the rose petals, if desired, or they can be left in the syrup.

To can, pour hot into jars, and seal as in open kettle canning, or process in a boiling water bath for 5 minutes. (Refer to the CANNING section.)

Rose Beverages

For a roseade, put several spoons of rose petal syrup in a glass, add ice water, and stir. For a rose milk drink, add cold milk to the syrup. These can also be made with hot water or hot milk.

Rutabagas

Rutabagas are a vegetable of the north. They grow best and are most appreciated in the Scandinavian countries, Russia, Scotland, Canada, and other northern locations. They do not grow well in warm climates, even as a winter vegetable.

Rutabagas are sometimes confused with ordinary, summer turnips, but the confusion is in the name and not in the taste. Rutabagas are also known as Swedish turnips, Swedes, Canadian turnips, and winter or yellow turnips. In Canada they are often just called turnips. Though both rutabagas and turnips are members of the cabbage family, they are different species. Rutabagas have edible cabbage-like leaves and look like cabbage plants until their roots start to swell, while turnip leaves look and taste like mustard greens. Rutabagas have a sweeter taste and denser

---

RUTABAGA STORAGE

Canning

Not recommended. (They discolor and develop a strong taste.)

Cold Storage

(Excellent, the preferred storage method.) Trim tops to 1 in. Lay in bins in root cellar, or pack in damp sand or other damp material in any cool place. Will keep all winter. Refer to the COLD STORAGE section.

Drying

Slice thinly, or grate. Steam to precook (optional). Dry until hard. Refer to the DRYING section.

Freezing

Cut in cubes, blanch 2 min. in boiling water, or cook, and mash. Refer to the FREEZING section.

RUTABAGA IDEAS

Rutabaga in Salads

Raw rutabaga is an excellent salad ingredient when thinly sliced or grated.

Salsify

220

A mixture of grated rutabaga, grated apple, and alfalfa sprouts makes a delicious winter salad. Raw rutabaga slices are also good to eat like carrot sticks, and go well with vegetable dips. In winter a rutabaga in the refrigerator is a boon for salad makers to add here and there, as needed.

Sautéed Rutabaga Slices

Cut ½-inch thick slices of rutabaga and steam them for 3–4 minutes. Then sauté them in butter or another fat. They will be very good sautéed in the fat of the meat with which they are served.

Neep Purry

This is Scottish style mashed rutabaga. Cut the rutabaga in pieces, then cook and mash it like potatoes. Season with butter, pepper, powdered ginger, and salt, if desired. Make plenty, as everyone will want a second helping.

SALSIFY STORAGE
Canning

Steam, or boil whole roots about 15 min., then peel. Pack whole or slice,

texture than turnips. They are very good eaten raw and are, in fact, as versatile as carrots. They can very often be substituted for carrots, turnips, and other root vegetables in recipes.

HANDLING RUTABAGAS

Do not harvest rutabagas until after fall frosts, as before frost they have a hot, strong flavor. When harvested for storage in a root cellar or similar place, trim the tops but leave the roots as they are, and do not wash them. There will be no need for the paraffin or wax coating that is sometimes used commercially if the rutabagas are stored in a humid place or are packed in a damp material.

Before use, scrub rutabagas with a vegetable brush to clean them. Peeling is unnecessary, unless the skin is blemished or has been waxed. Often rutabagas are too big to eat at one time, but cut sections keep very well covered in the refrigerator.

RUTABAGA RECIPES
Finnish Rutabaga Pudding
(MAKES ABOUT 6 SIDE SERVINGS)

¼ cup fine bread crumbs
¼ cup milk
2 eggs
4 cups mashed rutabaga
⅛ teaspoon nutmeg

pepper, salt, optional
2 teaspoons molasses
   or honey
1 tablespoon (about) butter

Soak the bread crumbs in the milk for a few minutes. Then beat in the eggs with a fork. Add the rutabaga, pepper, salt, if desired, and molasses or honey. Mix well and pour into a buttered baking dish. Dot with butter, then bake uncovered for an hour in a moderate, 350°F oven. The pudding will set and should be lightly browned. Serve as a side dish instead of potatoes, or as a light supper, or lunch.

Salsify (Oyster Plant)

Salsify is primarily a root vegetable, though its leaves and flower stalks are also good to eat. The roots have a distinctive, oyster-like flavor which accounts for its other names, oyster plant and vegetable oyster. A century ago salsify was well-known and quite popular in North America. It has lost importance probably because it is not a good market crop, since the roots shrivel after a few days in the open air. It is ideal, however, for gardeners who want to extend their gardening season. Salsify is dug late in fall and early in spring when there is little else to harvest, and the roots will keep well if protected.

There are several varieties of salsify. In the past, the white rooted kinds were most common in North America, but many seed catalogs now carry Scorzonera (black salsify). From Northern Europe, it has black-skinned roots and is more flavorful than the white varieties. Wild salsify, also called goatsbeard, is as good to eat as the cultivated plant. It is most common in areas with somewhat dry climates. All of the salsifies can be prepared in the same ways.

HANDLING SALSIFY

Salsify roots have a richer, more oystery taste after heavy frosts. Their best season is probably early spring, before they sprout. Use the roots soon after they are dug, or pack them in damp sand, peat moss, or another damp material to keep them from shrivelling.

Young salsify leaves are very good in salads, and, if cut before the buds begin to open, the flower stalks are good prepared like asparagus. As the plant is a biennial, the flower stalks do not appear until the second year. Since the roots are harvested the first year, the stalks are seldom cultivated, but they can be gathered from wild plants. Salsify has a milky sap that can be allowed to congeal for chewing like chewing gum.

Clean salsify roots by scrubbing with a brush instead of peeling them, unless the skins are very rough. They discolor quickly after they are scraped or pared. Though directions often say to put them in water with a little vinegar in it after cleaning them, this can be avoided if they are prepared quickly and cooking is begun immediately. Salsify roots are rich in minerals, and soaking removes some of them as well as some of the flavor of the vegetable. Another way to handle them is to steam them whole, peeling and slicing them after they are done.

Salsify

221

add boiling water, 1 in. headroom. Process 240°F, 11 pounds pressure. Pints: 30 min. Quarts: 35 min. Refer to the CANNING section.

Cold Storage

Dig late, after frosts. Pack roots in damp sand, soil, or peat moss. Will keep all winter in root cellar or similar place. Refer to the COLD STORAGE section.

Drying

Steam to precook, peel, slice, dry until hard. (They discolor badly if dried raw.) Refer to the DRYING section.

Freezing

Peel, slice, put immediately into boiling water, blanch 2–3 min. Refer to the FREEZING section.

Live Storage

(Most practical method.) Leave in ground, mulched. Dig during late fall, winter thaws, or early spring.

SALSIFY RECIPES
Mock Oyster Chowder

(MAKES 6—8 MEDIUM BOWLS)

2—3 pounds salsify roots
2 cups (about) milk
2 tablespoons butter
cayenne or black pepper, to taste

1 teaspoon celery seeds, dried
celery leaves, or 1 tablespoon
fresh celery leaves, minced
salt, optional

Wash, trim, and scrape the roots. At the same time, bring several cups of water to a boil. Slice the salsify into a pot, then quickly cover it with boiling water. Simmer until tender, 15 to 20 minutes. Stir in enough milk to make a chowder texture, and add butter, celery seeds or leaves, pepper, and salt, if desired. Reheat slowly, without boiling. Flavor will be best if the chowder is kept covered over very low heat from 30 to 60 minutes before it is served.

Sauerkraut 🌿

Cabbage is known as the sauerkraut vegetable, but sauerkraut made from other vegetables is equally delicious. All result from a natural fermentation process in which the vegetable's sugars are changed to lactic acid through the action of naturally occurring bacteria. The shredding or slicing, and the addition of salt draws out vegetable juices which the bacteria then act upon. Fermented pickles are made in a similar way. (Refer to MAKING FERMENTED PICKLES, in the PICKLING section.)

There is lactic acid in sour or fermented milk products, as well as in sauerkraut and fermented pickles. Foods containing it are exceedingly healthy, especially when eaten uncooked. Fresh, homemade sauerkraut can be as beneficial as yogurt, and should receive more praise than it normally does. It should be noted, however, that made in the standard way, it contains considerable salt, and salt from other sources should be avoided when eating it. (Low- and no-salt versions are possible [see below], but many find their texture, if not their flavor, unacceptable.) Sauerkraut juice is delicious in juice

---

SALSIFY IDEAS
Mashed Salsify

Steam whole salsify roots until tender, about 20 minutes. Mash them through a sieve or food mill to remove any coarse fibers. Serve as a mashed vegetable side dish, or make them into patties. For mock oyster patties, mix with an egg, pepper, and a little melted butter. Shape into patties, dust with flour, and brown in butter or oil on both sides.

SAUERKRAUT STORAGE
Canning

Excellent for cabbage sauerkraut or firm textured krauts. See CANNING SAUERKRAUT and SAUERKRAUT MADE IN CANNING JARS, below.

mixtures, and is as beneficial as the sauerkraut itself. Both are known for improving digestion.

MAKING SAUERKRAUT

To make sauerkraut, use cabbage, savoy cabbage, Chinese cabbage, collard greens, kale, firm lettuce, white or winter radish, or rutabaga or turnip. Weigh the vegetables after they are ready for use, and measure 3 tablespoons plain, pickling, or sea salt for each 5 pounds of vegetables. (2½ % salt measured by weight. For a low-salt version, see LOW-SALT SAUERKRAUT, below.)

Prepare leafy vegetables by cutting out the cores or heavy stalks and slicing them thinly into shreds. Root vegetables must be very thinly sliced. If large, cut the roots into fourths or eighths before slicing. A vegetable slicer or cabbage cutter helps to quickly make even slices or shreds.

Have ready a crock, large jar, or other non-porous container which is large enough to leave room above the vegetable for the brine to rise. Mix together the vegetable and salt, put it in the container, and tamp it down. If making a large amount, mix 5 pounds of the vegetable with 3 tablespoons of salt in the container, then tamp it down to make the first layer. Mix the required amount of salt with the rest of the vegetable and also tamp it down in layers. Letting the vegetable and salt mixture sit a few minutes before tamping will make it easier to handle. Firm vegetables, like cabbage, must be tamped hard enough to start juices flowing. More delicate vegetables, like Chinese cabbage or lettuce, must be tamped only gently. Use a wooden mallet or a jar bottom for tamping. A sturdy mallet can be made with a piece of wood the size of a baseball bat with the tip cut off to make a flat surface.

When all of the vegetable and salt have been tamped into the container, cover with a clean cloth tucked in around the edges. (Dip the cloth in boiling water to clean it.) Set a plate or wooden follower on the cloth. The follower should fit the container without much room to spare. Put a weight such as a large jar of water or a clean rock on the follower.

After 24 hours enough juice or brine will come out of the vegetable to completely cover it. If there is not enough brine, add cold water to cover.

Keep the sauerkraut container where the temperature will go no higher than 72°F. It is likely to turn soft and may spoil rather than ferment, if temperatures are too high. If the tem-

Cold Storage

Excellent. See KEEPING SAUERKRAUT IN COLD STORAGE, below.
Vegetables Suitable for Sauerkraut: All cabbages, including savoy. (Red cabbage fades; is least attractive.) Chinese cabbage, collard greens, kale, lettuce (firm), radish (white or winter), rutabaga, turnip (when fermented called "Sauer Rüben").

5 pounds vegetables = about 2½ quarts sauerkraut

SAUERKRAUT IDEAS
Sauerkraut Sandwiches

Drain sauerkraut well. Fresh sauerkraut is outstanding, but canned is also good. For a simply delicious sandwich, spread rye bread with butter or mayonnaise, add sauerkraut,

perature is near 70°F, fermentation will take from about 10 days to 2 weeks. If it is below 60°F, fermentation may take as long as 4 to 6 weeks. Some prefer the flavor of slowly fermented sauerkraut, but it tastes very good either way.

Check the fermenting sauerkraut every day or two. Skim off any scum that forms, and replace the cloth with a clean one. Clean or scald the follower and weight before replacing them. Some directions advise changing the cloth every day, but unless problems develop, it is not necessary. While it ferments, bubbles will show in the sauerkraut, and the level of the brine may rise. If the container is filled too full it may overflow. There will also be a strong sauerkraut aroma, which some people enjoy, while others do not.

Partly fermented sauerkraut is quite delicious. Some can be removed to eat when the cloth is changed, making sure the surface is leveled to allow the brine to completely cover it. When all fermentation activity ends, or when the sauerkraut tastes pleasantly tart, it can be prepared for cold storage or canned.

Low-Salt Sauerkraut

Proceed as above, using 1½ to 2 teaspoons salt per 5 pounds of prepared vegetables. The finished texture tends to be overly soft, but the flavor will be pleasantly tart. To store, refrigerate it for a month or so, or can it like regular sauerkraut (see CANNING SAUERKRAUT, below). It is not recommended for keeping long term in cold storage.

Cabbage can also be fermented without the use of salt, but most find both flavor and texture poor and failures frequent.

Seasoned Sauerkraut

Many kinds of flavorings, such as herb seeds and herbs, are good in sauerkraut. They can be mixed in with the salt or sprinkled between the layers as they are tamped down. Caraway, dill, or celery seeds each add an excellent flavor. Other good seasonings are bay leaf, peppercorns, tarragon sprigs, garlic, onion rings, and shreds of horseradish root. For interest and an agreeable flavor, a layer of grape leaves can also be included.

Cabbage and Apple or Quince Sauerkraut

Thinly slice 1 or 2 tart apples or quince for every 5 pounds of cabbage and mix them in. If making a large quantity of sauerkraut a few whole apples can be distributed through it. The apples are deliciously flavored as well as the sauerkraut.

---

and that is it! Sauerkraut is excellent in sandwiches with roast beef and other leftover cooked meats.

Sauerkraut in Mixed Salads

Small quantities of drained, fresh sauerkraut add a very nice flavor to tossed green salads and vegetable salads, especially to bean salads. Reduce the amount of vinegar or lemon juice in the dressing and omit salt when adding sauerkraut.

Sauerkraut-Tomato Juice and Other Mixtures

Half sauerkraut juice with half tomato juice makes a very good beverage. Sauerkraut juice combines very well with many vegetable juice mixtures.

Keeping Sauerkraut in Cold Storage

Some people believe that fresh, uncooked sauerkraut is more nutritious than cooked sauerkraut because of its beneficial bacteria and enzymes, and so prefer to keep it in cold storage. When cold storage is not possible, canning retains an excellent flavor and the sauerkraut is still nutritious. To prepare for storage, take the cloth off the sauerkraut. Clean or scald the follower and return it to hold the sauerkraut under the brine. A weight will no longer be needed. Close the container tightly. Cover with aluminum foil if there is no lid. Store in a cool place between freezing and 45°F, check frequently, and remove any surface film or mold.

Canning Sauerkraut

For canning, sauerkraut made from firm vegetables is best. (Lettuce or Chinese cabbage sauerkraut will become soft.) Heat the sauerkraut and its juice in a pot until almost boiling. Pack it into hot jars leaving ½ inch headroom. The sauerkraut can be drained and packed, and the juice brought to a boil and added, or tongs or a slotted spoon can be used to lift the sauerkraut out of the pot and directly into the jars, and then the juice added to fill them. If there is not enough juice add a little boiling water. Process in a boiling water bath. Pints: 11 minutes. Quarts: 16 minutes. (Refer to the CANNING section.)

Sauerkraut Made in Canning Jars

Mix shredded cabbage with salt as described above, and let sit for a few minutes until wilted, for easier packing. Press firmly into clean canning jars, leaving 1 inch headroom. Make a weak brine of 1 teaspoon salt to 1 quart water, and add to fill jars to ½ inch headroom. Close with canning lids and rings, but do not tighten. Set jars in a pan to catch any overflow and leave to ferment as above. Check often to make sure cabbage is covered with brine, and add more, if necessary. Fermentation may take from 2 to 4 weeks. When it stops and the cabbage looks, smells, and tastes like sauerkraut, remove jar lids and rings and boil them in water for 5 minutes to soften the sealing compound. Clean jar rims, seal jars, and process as described above. Since the jars are cold, put them in hot rather than boiling water and time from when the water starts boiling.

HINTS FOR SUCCESSFUL SAUERKRAUT

- Use only fresh, firm vegetables. Using old, wilted, or woody vegetables results in poor texture or flavor.

• Use pure water. Water containing chlorine, calcium salts, or other salts or minerals may interfere with the fermentation process.
• Make sure the salt/vegetable ratio is right and that they are well-mixed. If the sauerkraut becomes too soft there may not be enough salt. Softness can also be caused by high temperatures, air pockets, and uneven salt distribution. Too much salt, or its uneven distribution, can cause unwelcome yeasts to grow which will turn the sauerkraut pink and inedible.
• Make sure the vegetable stays covered with brine. If not properly covered or weighted down, it can turn pink, turn dark, or even rot on the surface, and must then be discarded.

USING HOMEMADE SAUERKRAUT

The tartness of sauerkraut will vary considerably with different batches and with fermentation time. Partly fermented sauerkraut is mild, and very good as a fresh condiment with meals, or as a snack. Mild sauerkraut will not need rinsing, and its juice can be used in recipes. If sauerkraut is very tart it may be necessary to drain it, rinse it in cold water, then drain again. If possible use the juice.

As often as possible eat sauerkraut fresh rather than cooked.

Seaweed

Seaweed is amazingly flavorful, as well as nutritionally valuable. Important vitamins, minerals, and protein in seaweed have brought it to the attention of the health conscious, but in North America it has often been swallowed in pill form or choked down in powdered form, when it could so easily be enjoyed as a tasty vegetable. In Hawaii, limu (seaweed) is a favorite food, and the Japanese and many other Asian peoples know how to appreciate seaweed as a food. Anyone who has had the good fortune to eat some of the Japanese snacks and vegetable dishes using it will know why, as they are delicious. Scotland is another country with a long seaweed-eating tradition, complete with tasty traditional recipes. During colonial times New Englanders and other East Coast North Americans made use of seaweed, but

---

SEAWEED STORAGE
Drying

Trim. If rinsing is necessary, use sea water. Spread on trays or racks, or hang on indoor or outdoor clotheslines. Dries in warm, airy, shaded place, in 1–2 days. Seal in containers. Keeps 1 year or more. Refer to the DRYING section.

Freezing

Trim, rinse, break or cut to convenient size. If tender, blanch by pouring boiling water over and steeping ½ min. If tough, blanch several min. in boiling water. Refer to the FREEZING section.

SEAWEED IDEAS
Seaweed Salads

Very tender seaweeds are good chopped raw and added to salads. Tougher varieties can be cooked, then chopped for salads. A mixture of lettuce, chopped radishes, scallion, oranges, and seaweed, with a little orange juice poured over for a dressing makes a good salad. Another good mixture is cucumber, cooked flaked fish or shellfish, and chopped seaweed.

then it gradually lost its importance. The current revival of interest in seaweed foods is sure to last once people discover what an excellent vegetable it is.

In primitive times all coastal people gathered and ate seaweed, and some inland people made journeys to the coast to gather a year's supply. Gathering one's own is still the best way to obtain a supply of seaweed. It is sold in some health food and Asian food stores but the price may be prohibitively high. Since there is abundant free, edible seaweed growing along both North American coasts, inlanders might take a hint from their ancestors, and make seaweed foraging a part of a seaside vacation. It could easily become the most memorable part of the trip!

COMMON EDIBLE SEAWEEDS

(For the identification and use of less common, regional varieties, see the reference sources at the end of this section.)

Dulse

This reddish seaweed is common along the New England coast and around the Maritime provinces of Canada. Though most often dried and chewed as a snack, it is also good in cooked dishes. When fresh its flavor is not as good as it is after drying.

Irish Moss or Carrageen

This is an exceedingly useful seaweed. Many additives for emulsifying, thickening, and stabilizing processed foods are derived from it. It can be gathered and used fresh or dried to make aspics and desserts. Though it is often left outdoors to bleach in sun and rain before use, this removes its flavor as well as its color. In most dishes, the sea tang of unbleached Irish moss is quite pleasant. Though Irish moss can be cooked and served as a vegetable, usually the stock or liquid extracted from it by boiling in water and straining is preferred. This liquid will set like gelatine when cooked, though with a less rubbery texture. Irish moss is very much like agar agar, which comes from a similar kind of seaweed.

Laver

Many kinds of laver are eaten around the world. Nori, a Japanese variety, is cultivated in bays and inlets, and made into thin

DULSE

IRISH MOSS

LAVER

KELP

sheets that can be used for food wrappings or toasted for a snack. Laver is generally tender enough to be nibbled raw, and is one of the best seaweeds to cook as a vegetable. Dried fronds of laver can be stuffed like cabbage leaves. They may need a brief blanching in boiling water to make them pliable. The "sloke" used to make the *Sloke Jelly,* below, is a kind of laver.

Kelp

There are many edible kinds of kelp. The Japanese call them "kombu." They generally take longer to cook than other seaweeds. Dried and powdered kelp makes a good seasoning, or the base for a seaweed soup. When dried and shredded it also makes a good vegetable dish.

HANDLING SEAWEED

Some seaweeds can be gathered when they wash ashore, but others must be cut or pulled from underwater. Cutting is best as it leaves the roots to continue growing, especially where large quantities are harvested.

Seaweed is generally dried to preserve it, though it can also be frozen. If it is dried, it will usually need soaking for a few minutes to an hour before it is cooked. Most seaweeds can be substituted for each other in recipes, if soaking and cooking times are adjusted. Seaweeds of all kinds, as well as Irish moss, become gelatinous when cooked, making them good for thickening and flavoring soups and stews. The seaweed flavor goes well with onions, and is usually improved by the addition of lemon or orange juice, or another tart flavor.

SEAWEED RECIPES

The following instructions from *The Scot's Kitchen* for preparing sloke, a kind of laver, can also be used for other seaweeds.

Sloke Jelly

"The weed is brought home from the rocky pools and carefully washed to remove all sand and dirt. It is then steeped for a few hours in cold water, sometimes with a little salt, sometimes with a little bicarbonate of soda, which is said to remove bitterness. [Drain and rinse after steeping.]

Put the prepared sloke into a thick-bottomed pot with wa-

Seaweed Soup

Seaweed broth makes a good soup all by itself, as well as being a base for heartier soups. For the broth, soak dried seaweed, cut it in pieces, and simmer until the water is thickened slightly and the seaweed is tender. Onion adds a nice flavor simmered with the seaweed. Straining is optional. Powdered seaweed can also be used in this way. Good seasonings for the broth are pepper, and lemon juice or vinegar. For a creamed version, make a strong seaweed broth and add milk, or milk with a little cream, to thin it. A Korean version calls for seaweed broth with shredded beef, garlic, scallions, and soy sauce. A hearty vegetable soup can be made by adding chopped vegetables and cooked rice and beans.

Toasted Seaweed Garnish

Dried dulse or sheets of nori can be toasted by putting them briefly on the top of a hot wood-burning stove or close under the oven broiler. They are done when they change color. Crumble them on salads, cooked vegetables, potatoes, eggs, and over cooked rice. Immediately after toasting, these seaweeds also are a delicious snack.

ter to cover and boil gently to a jelly, stirring constantly with a wooden spoon. When thoroughly cooked, it becomes a dark green. Let it cool, then store in earthenware jars. It will keep good for two or three weeks. [In the refrigerator or another cool place.]"

The jelly was often spread on bread. The Caithness fishermen used to take a supply of it with them when they went to sea, and ate it with oatcakes.

Sloke Sauce

"Prepare the sloke as for jelly, and add pepper and lemon juice to taste. The juice of a bitter orange goes excellently with sloke, as with carrageen. Serve very hot. It is especially good with roast mutton."

EDIBLE SEAWEED REFERENCES

Guberlet, Muriel Lewin, *Seaweeds at Ebb-Tide,* University of Washington Press, 1971. (For identifying Pacific Coast seaweeds.)

Hilson, C. J., *Seaweeds,* Pennsylvania State University Press, 1977. (For identifying Atlantic Coast seaweeds.)

Seeds

There are edible seeds so unique in character that they cannot be classed with grains or nuts or other groups of seeds. These special seeds are all high in food value as well as pleasing in taste. They merit attention in the kitchen and, when possible, space in the garden. Some notable seeds are described below.

Alfalfa Seeds

Alfalfa is a good food for people as well as for livestock. Its tender shoots and leafy tips can be added to salads or cooked with mixed greens, and the leaves can be dried for making herb tea, but the seeds are the most valuable part. They are easily sprouted at home for a vegetable that rivals lettuce in its versatility. For many people alfalfa sprouts serve as a basic winter salad and sandwich green. They can be sprouted regularly and a fresh, crisp, raw homegrown vegetable will always be on hand. (Refer to the SPROUTS section.)

Alfalfa seeds can be harvested on a small scale from wild plants, or from cultivated alfalfa that is allowed to mature. They are also economical to buy, considering the quantity of sprouts they produce. Only 1 to 2 pounds of seeds will keep the average

> ### SEED STORAGE
> *Note:* If mature and dry, most seeds can be stored a year or more in any dry place.

family well-supplied with sprouts for a whole winter. Be sure to buy only seeds intended for sprouting, as those for planting may have been treated with chemicals.

Amaranth Seeds

Amaranth, also known as pigweed or redroot when it grows wild, is a native American food plant, once cultivated for its seeds by the Indians in many parts of North, Central, and South America. Cooked amaranth leaves are popular in southern Asia, Africa, and the West Indies, while in North America there is increasing interest in both its seed and its greens. Some seed catalogs offer two varieties, one primarily for greens and the other for seeds.

Growing and harvesting amaranth seeds on a small scale is easier than raising most grains, and the seeds are immediately likeable in cooked cereals. They are also good ground into flour, for breads and other baked goods. Use ¼ to ⅓ part amaranth flour in yeast breads, fruit breads, pancakes, and muffins. For a nutty flavor, roast the seeds, or pop them in a dry frying pan. They can also be sprouted.

Wild amaranth is widespread all over North America. Its young greens can be eaten, and later the seeds can be gathered and used like the cultivated varieties.

Chia Seeds

Chia grows wild in the Southwest, in the dry parts of California, and in Mexico, where the Indians collect them in large quantities. They are often roasted or parched and ground into meal to mix with wheat flour or cornmeal, for mush or bread. When crushed or soaked in water, the seeds become mucilaginous. In Mexico a smooth, slightly thickened drink is made by soaking them in water, and then flavoring it like lemonade and chilling it. Chia seeds can also be sprouted. (Refer to the SPROUTS section.)

Flax Seeds

Flax is a plant with many uses. The fibers are made into linen and the pressed seeds yield linseed oil. The seeds can also be added to cereal, or sprouted. (Refer to the SPROUTS section.) Like chia, flax seeds become mucilaginous when soaked in water. To make a healthy drink from them, put some in boiling water and leave for about 3 hours. Drink hot or cold. Soaked flax seeds are a very good natural laxative.

Poppy Seeds

Seed varieties of poppies will grow in most gardens, but because they are similar to, and sometimes the same as, opium varieties, their cultivation is illegal in North America. However, the seed never contains opium, which occurs only in the immature fruits.

Poppy seeds are good sprinkled on bread and other baked goods, and mixed into dough or batter. Crushing them before cooking brings out the poppy seed flavor. A very special and delicious filling for cookies and pastries can be made from them. (See the *Poppy Seed Filling* recipe, below.)

Pumpkin Seeds

Refer to the SQUASH, WINTER AND PUMPKIN section.

Sesame Seeds

Sesame needs a long, warm growing season, but otherwise it is easy to grow. The seed pods are harvested in the fall, before they become dry enough to shatter, and are then spread out on trays or screens to finish drying. The seeds still have thin hulls after they are separated from the pods, but as they taste good with hulls left on, there is no need to try to hull them. They are sold both unhulled and hulled. Unhulled seeds are especially flavorful if toasted in a dry frying pan for a few minutes. Ground sesame seeds make a smooth butter known as Tahini, that can be used like peanut butter or other nut butters. It is common in Middle Eastern cooking. (Refer to the PEANUTS and NUTS sections.)

Sunflower Seeds

Refer to the SUNFLOWERS section.

HANDLING SEEDS

Harvesting

When small plots of seed plants are grown in the garden they can be harvested like herb seeds. (Refer to HARVESTING, in the HERB SEEDS section.) With larger plantings the seed stalks or heads are usually cut or reaped like grain. Some kinds of seeds fall out of their pods by themselves as soon as they are thoroughly dry. Others must be crushed or threshed to release the seeds.

Threshing and Winnowing

Seed heads must be completely dry before they are threshed. Some kinds can be left to dry on the plant in the field or garden. Others must be cut slightly green, before the seeds fall out, then dried on trays in the sun, or in another dry airy place.

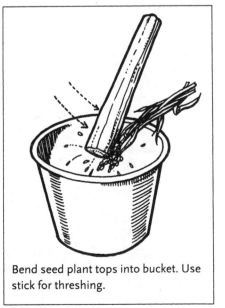

Bend seed plant tops into bucket. Use stick for threshing.

There are quite a few different ways to thresh seed heads, and different methods can be tried to find out what works best for a particular plant. Sometimes the seed stalks can be laid on a firm surface and hit with a heavy stick or flail, as in threshing grain. Or a bunch of seed stalks can be hit against the inside of a bucket or other container, causing the seeds to fall into the container. It may be possible to bend the tops of the seed plants over the edge of a bucket without cutting them and then hitting them with a stick to knock off the seeds. Seed pods which are separated from the stalks can be crushed to release the seeds by rolling over them with a rolling pin or by tamping them in a bucket using a mallet or heavy stick. Be careful not to hit so hard that seeds are damaged.

After they are loosened from the pods the seeds will usually still be mixed with bits of chaff, and stems. Winnowing is a way of blowing off this light debris. Do this outdoors on a breezy day, or set up a fan to provide the breeze. Pour the seeds slowly from one container to another, and the heavier seeds will fall straight down into the container, while the lighter debris is blown away. The containers must be wide topped and deep enough to catch bouncing seeds. After pouring the seeds back and forth 5 or 6 times the light debris should be gone. It is best to begin pouring cautiously to be sure the breeze is not strong enough to blow away seeds as well as chaff. Traditionally seeds have also been tossed in the air and caught instead of being poured.

If any heavier debris still remains, shake the seeds through a screen or sieve with mesh of just the right size to let the seeds through and catch any sticks, or lumps of dirt. If the seeds are then still not clean, just before using them, cover them with water, so that they sink, while the debris floats and can be poured off.

SEED RECIPES
Poppy Seed Filling

(MAKES ABOUT 2 CUPS)

1 cup poppy seeds
1 cup milk
2 tablespoons butter
2 tablespoons molasses
    or honey

¼–½ cup raisins or pitted,
    chopped prunes
½ teaspoon lemon rind,
grated, optional
¼ cup almonds, grated
    or ground, optional

Grind the poppy seeds, or bruise them by whirling them in a blender. Put them in a saucepan with the rest of the ingredi-

Winnowing seeds.

ents, and cook, stirring often, until the mixture blends and thickens. Very good used as a pastry filling.

Hamantaschen, or Three Cornered Hats

Roll out small balls of bread dough to make 4- to 5-inch diameter circles. Put a spoon of poppy seed filling on each circle, then fold up the sides to make 3 corners. Pinch the seams well to keep the filling from running out. Set on oiled baking sheets and brush with warm honey if desired. Let rise about 20 minutes, then bake in a moderate, 350°F oven until lightly browned. These are traditional for the Jewish holiday of Purim. An enticing pastry, and less rich than most.

Hummus (Chick Pea Tahini Dip), Middle Eastern Style

(MAKES ABOUT 1 QUART)

1 cup sesame Tahini (sesame butter)
½ cup cold water
juice of 3 lemons
1 clove garlic, crushed
½ teaspoon salt, optional

2 cups cooked chick peas (or garbanzo beans)
1 tablespoon olive oil
parsley, minced (for garnish)
paprika (for garnish)

If oil has separated from the Tahini, stir it in until smooth. Then stir in the water, which thickens it dramatically. Then stir in the lemon juice, which will thin the mixture to a butter texture again. Mix in the garlic, and salt, if desired. Mash the chick peas through a sieve or food mill, and mix them in, stirring until smooth. Spread in an attractive shallow dish, such as a pie pan. Dribble oil over the surface. Arrange the parsley around the edge in a ring, and in any interesting pattern over the middle, like decorating a cake. Sprinkle lightly with paprika.

Serve as a dip with raw vegetables, or with flatbread. Tear the bread, rather than cutting it, as the ragged edges seem to taste best.

Soybeans

Soybeans are well-known for their high protein content. Their composition also differs from all other beans in its higher fat and lower carbohydrate content. Though dry soybeans can be cooked like other dry beans, their flavor and texture are quite different, and the usual bean seasonings do not suit them. In

Soybeans

⚘

234

North America the tendency has been to prepare them like other dry beans, and then to reject them because they are not as good as expected. In Asian countries, where soybeans have been an important food for many, many centuries, special preparations are made from them, totally unlike western bean dishes. A few of these, like soy sauce and tofu (soybean curd), are gaining acceptance everywhere, and the soybean may eventually be appreciated in all of its ramifications in the West as it is in the Far East.

Soybeans are easily grown as a garden crop in most climates. They can be harvested as fresh, shelled, green soybeans, or as mature, dry soybeans, and used in all kinds of savory ways.

Soybeans are also known as soya beans, and the products made from them are named accordingly.

SOYBEAN PREPARATIONS

Miso

Miso is the Japanese name for a flavorful, fermented soybean paste. It is usually made from a mixture of soybeans, grain, and salt. There are also Chinese versions. Miso is often used as a base for soups, and as a seasoning for meat, fish, and vegetables. It is possible, but difficult, to make miso at home. (See REFERENCES at the end of this section.)

Soybean Sprouts

Soybeans germinate easily, but conditions must be just right to grow large, tender sprouts from them. (Refer to the SPROUTS section.)

Soy Flour

The flour made by grinding dry soybeans is useful for making soy milk, and as a nutritious addition to baked goods, and pasta. Because of their oil content it is not always possible to grind them in a home grain mill. However, a mill that cannot grind them alone will grind them if they are mixed with two or three times their quantity of wheat or another grain.

The flour ground at home will be whole or full fat soy flour. Health food stores often sell low fat soy flour or other soy powders intended for special purposes, such as making low fat soy milk. It is not possible to make these at home.

SOYBEAN STORAGE

Canning

Fresh, green Shell (see below). Cover with boiling water, boil 1 min. Drain, pack in jars, add boiling cooking water, 1 in. headroom. Process 240°F, 11 pounds pressure. Pints: 55 min. Quarts: 65 min. Refer to the CANNING section.

Drying

Fresh, green Steam in pods 10 min. Shell (see below). Dry until hard or brittle. Refer to the DRYING section. For mature soybeans, refer to HANDLING DRIED BEANS, in the BEANS, DRY section.

Freezing

Fresh, green Blanch in boiling water 5 min. Shell (see below), or freeze in

Soy Grits

Coarsely ground soybeans can be used in baked goods, breakfast cereals, and meat or vegetable dishes to add a chewy or nutty texture. Few enjoy their flavor alone, but they blend well in mixtures. Often soy grits are added precooked, but this is not necessary in moist mixtures to be cooked 30 minutes or longer.

Soy Milk

Soy milk can be made from soy flour or from whole, dry soybeans. Making milk from dry soybeans is the first step when making tofu. To make milk from soy flour, mix the flour with enough warm water to make a paste, then stir in more water, and cook over low heat for about 15 minutes, stirring very often. A good mix is 1 cup soy flour to 6 cups water, but this can be varied to taste. Strain the milk through cloth for complete smoothness.

Soy milk can be substituted for dairy milk in many recipes and milk mixtures. Instant soy milk powders are available in some stores. Though soy milk is not a tasty beverage by itself, it is excellent in mixtures. Yogurt can be made from soy milk in the same way as from dairy milk, using the same starter.

Soy Nuts

Whole dry soybeans can be soaked, cooked, and then roasted to eat as a crunchy, nut-like snack.

Soy Oil

The oil pressed from soybeans is among the best vegetable oils for use in cooking and for salads. Unfortunately it is not possible to press the beans at home.

Soy Protein

This is a commercial concentrate made from soybeans, often used as an extender for sausage and other ground meat preparations such as hamburger patties and meat loaf. It cannot be duplicated at home, and the additives in it make its use questionable in any case. Cooked, ground soybeans can be made at home and used as meat extenders in most of the same ways.

pod for snack (see below). Package dry. Refer to the FREEZING section.

⅛ cup dry soybeans = about 1 cup flour

SOYBEAN IDEAS
Brown Soybeans

Add several tablespoons soy sauce to dry beans' soaking water. Soak overnight. Next day cook the beans in the soaking water. When they are tender, remove the lid and cook until the water is absorbed, and all of the soy sauce flavor and color is in the soybeans. Serve cold as a snack, add to salads, or use instead of plain soybeans for patties or other dishes.

Green Soybean Snack

Cook green soybeans in the pod in plenty of well salted boiling water for

Soy Sauce

Natural soy sauce, without chemicals, is pressed from a fermented mixture of soybean, wheat, and salt. It might possibly be made at home, but could take as long as 2 years—an impractical endeavor for most people.

When buying soy sauce look at the ingredients on the label. If made with chemicals the label will list acid hydrolyzed vegetable protein, sweeteners, and caramel coloring. Naturally fermented soy sauce contains only soybeans, wheat or another grain, and salt. Tamari is one natural soy sauce sold in many health food stores. Low-salt, naturally fermented soy sauce is also available in some places.

Tempeh

Tempeh is an Indonesian food made from soybeans. The soybeans are cooked, and then inoculated with a starter of special mold spores. They are then held at a temperature of 90°F for several days while mycelium grow from the spores, binding the beans together into a sort of cake. This can be cooked and eaten in a variety of ways. Most people like the flavor the first time they try it. Tempeh is easily made at home, if an incubator can be arranged to hold the temperature at 90°F. Mold starters are available from several mail order sources.

Tofu

Tofu is the Japanese name for soybean curd. It is also made in China and other far eastern countries.

MAKING TOFU

The preliminary step for making tofu is to make soy milk. The best tofu comes from milk made from whole, dry soybeans, but it is also possible to use milk made from soy flour. (Refer to SOY MILK, in the SOYBEANS section.) Only one other ingredient besides soy milk is required—a solidifier to separate the tofu curds from the whey. Nigari, a by-product of the extraction of salt from sea water, is the preferred solidifier. (Bittern is its English but little-used name.) Other solidifiers are fresh sea water, lemon or lime juice, vinegar calcium sulfate,

---

Tofu Box

Follower to fit into box. Handles for easy removal.

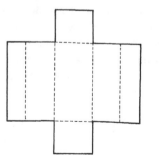

Box: Good dimensions are 8" × 4" × 3". Can be changed for larger or smaller amounts. Bottom board: A little larger than the box, with legs to raise it for drainage. Drainage holes are about 3/8" diameter.

Cloth liner: Cut to fit neatly into tofu box when the sides are folded up on the dotted lines. The flaps must be long enough to fold over the top of the tofu.

or magnesium sulfate (Epsom salts). Nigari is available in many health food stores and by mail order from some natural foods catalogs.

Most kitchens have the necessary utensils for making tofu, except for a mold or box in which to drain and press it. A colander or a cheese mold can be substituted, but anyone who makes tofu regularly will appreciate having tofu molds. They can be homemade from untreated wood, such as maple. (Avoid pine, as it could give an unwanted flavor.) The cloth liner should be cotton with a somewhat coarse weave, to allow easy draining.

MAKING SOY MILK FROM DRY SOYBEANS

(The quantities of ingredients may be doubled or halved, as desired.) Soak 2 cups of dry soybeans in 2 quarts of water for about 10 hours. Increase soaking time if the temperature is much below 70°F, or decrease it if the temperature is much above 70°F. After soaking, drain the soybeans, rinse them, then drain again. If it is not possible to make the soy milk immediately, the drained soybeans can be refrigerated for about a day.

The next step is puréeing or grinding the soaked beans. If using a blender, add 6 cups of water to the soybeans and purée them in small batches that the blender can handle. Meanwhile start heating 2½ quarts of water in a large pot. If using a meat grinder, grind the soybeans twice using the finest blade, and heat 4 quarts of water.

Add the ground or puréed soybeans to the heated water. The blender or grinder parts can be rinsed with a little water and that too can be added. Heat to a boil, stirring often, and watch carefully, as it will foam up suddenly as it begins to boil.

Line a colander with a sturdy piece of cotton cloth and set it over a large container. When the soybean mixture boils, pour it into the cloth to strain off the milk. Pull the sides of the cloth together to form a bag and squeeze to remove as much milk as possible. Use a large spoon, potato masher, or other tool for pressing, since the bag will be too hot for the hands. The grainy material left in the cloth is known as okara. Put it into a container with a quart of warm water. Stir it, then pour it back into the cloth-lined colander to strain off more milk. As this is less hot, it can be squeezed by hand to remove as much milk as possible. Combine the milk from the two squeezings. There will be 3 to 4 quarts.

about 10 to 15 minutes, until the pods start to open slightly. Drain and eat hot or cooled. Everyone shells their own soybeans by putting the pods in their mouths and sucking out the beans. This Japanese snack is for both young and old. The salt can be omitted.

Green soybeans frozen in the pod can be dropped in boiling water while still frozen for a quick snack.

Green Soybean Succotash

Green shelled soybeans are very good cooked with corn, instead of ordinary fresh shelled beans, to make succotash. (Refer to *Succotash*, in the BEANS, FRESH section.) In the winter use dried or frozen green soybeans and sweet corn to make the dish.

MAKING TOFU FROM SOY MILK

Put soy milk in a large pot, and heat to simmering. Simmer from 5 to 7 minutes, stirring often and watching closely, as it will easily stick and burn. If using a thin-bottomed pot or an electric burner with "hot spots," use an insulating ring under the pot to prevent scorching. Remove from heat after it has simmered, and have ready one of the following solidifiers:

2 ½ teaspoons dry nigari dissolved in 2 cups water, or

2 cups fresh sea water, or

5 tablespoons lemon or lime juice, with water to make 2 cups, or

4 tablespoons vinegar with water to make 2 cups, or

2 ½ teaspoons magnesium sulfate (Epsom salts) or calcium sulfate dissolved in 2 cups water

Begin to stir the very hot soy milk and slowly pour in ⅔ cup of the solidifier. Stir 5 or 6 times, and hold the spoon still until the liquid stops moving. Remove the spoon and dribble another ⅔ cup of the solidifier into the soy milk without stirring. Cover the pot and wait 3 minutes. Then dribble the rest of the solidifier over the soy milk and stir just the top half-inch for about 10 minutes. Cover the pot again and wait 3 to 6 minutes. If clouds of white curds have not separated from the whey, stir the surface and they should appear. If the whey is milky looking, wait another minute, then stir again. If the whey still looks milky it will be necessary to mix another ⅔ cup of the solidifier and stir it in. When using magnesium sulfate for the solidifier, it takes longer and may be more difficult to make the curds separate. Sometimes with nigari the curds will separate before the full amount of solidifier has been added. If the whey is clear the remainder need not be used.

Line a tofu box or other mold with cotton cloth. Dip out a little of the whey from around the tofu curds, and pour it over the cloth to dampen it. Then use a ladle or cup to dip up the curds and whey mixture and pour it gently into the mold. If the mold fills up, wait a minute or two for it to drain, then add more curds and whey.

When all of the curds are in the box and most of the whey has drained off, fold the cloth over the curds and set the follower in place. Set a 1–1 ½ pound weight, like a small jar of water, on the follower, and leave for about 15 minutes.

Slide the tofu, still wrapped in cloth, into a large container of cold water. Let cool for a couple of minutes, then gently unwrap the tofu while it is under water. If it is rectangular, cut it in half to make 2 square cakes while still immersed. Leave in the water a few more minutes to chill thoroughly. It will become firmer as it cools. Use the tofu right after taking it out of the cold water, or store it in the refrigerator for as long as a week. If stored, keep it in a container covered with cold water, and change the water every second day.

HANDLING SOYBEANS

While seed catalogs sell separate strains of soybeans for shelling green and for maturing to dry beans, in a small garden it works quite well to plant only one variety and harvest some green, leaving the rest to mature.

Harvesting and Shelling Green Soybeans

Pick soybean pods after the beans have formed in them, and before they begin to lose their green color. As it is very difficult to shell raw green soybeans, blanch them in boiling water or steam them for about 5 minutes. This will make the pods open easily for shelling. Squeeze them over a dish and the beans will pop out into it, or shell them directly into freezer containers. Green soybeans cooked in the pod are a common snack in Japan.

Harvesting and Using Mature Soybeans

Gather mature soybeans after the pods have turned yellow, but before they have dried enough to shatter and scatter the beans. If the pods are not completely dry, spread them out to dry in an airy place. Shell and store like regular dry beans. (Refer to the BEANS, DRY section.)

To be digestible, soybeans must be well-cooked before they are eaten. Dry soybeans can be ground into flour or grits and then cooked in various ways, or whole beans can be soaked in water and cooked. This is the first step for many different dishes. Soaking and cooking times will vary according to the strain and age of beans, but overnight soaking and several hours of cooking are usually necessary. Some sources suggest cooking them from 7 to 8 hours to make them as soft as possible. They can be pressure cooked, adding a teaspoon of oil for each cup of beans to prevent them from clogging the steam escape valve, but they are as good or better when slow cooked. If the soaking water from soybeans is discarded and they are cooked in fresh water, they are less apt to cause gas when eaten.

SOYBEAN RECIPES
Soybean Patties

(MAKES ABOUT 6 DINNER SERVINGS)

3 cups cooked soybeans, drained,
　and mashed or ground

2 eggs
3–4 tablespoons oil or butter

VARIATION 1:

1 cup cooked rice
1 cup bread crumbs
1 clove garlic, minced
2 tablespoons parsley, minced

1 teaspoon dill leaves or other
　herbs, minced
2 tablespoons soy sauce
dash pepper

VARIATION 2:

2 cups mashed potatoes
1 small onion, minced
pepper, salt, optional

1 cup raw vegetables, grated,
　minced, or ground (try carrot,
　green pepper, or celery)

Combine the soybeans, eggs, and the ingredients for the chosen variation. Shape into patties. Sauté them in the oil or butter, turning to brown on both sides, or set them on a greased baking sheet with a dot of butter on each, and bake in a moderate, 350°F oven for about 20 minutes.

　Patties made with rice and bread crumbs are very good served with a cream or cheese sauce, and those made with potato are good with tomato sauce. Either one is delicious served with homemade relish instead of a sauce.

Spinach

Spinach is the prototype of potherbs—the greens to which all other greens are compared. When Popeye, the cartoon sailorman, began swallowing it by the canful to give himself amazing strength, he made spinach interesting to modern children, but it was respected and cultivated for many centuries before that. It dates back to 8th century China, to Persia even earlier, and only became known in Europe in the 12th century.

　Most gardeners raise spinach, or similar greens, of which there are many. Lamb's quarters, which grow wild in many gardens, taste so much like spinach that they almost make its cultivation unnecessary.

HANDLING SPINACH

Spinach can be harvested by cutting the whole plant, but often in home gardens only the outside leaves are gathered, leaving the plant to produce more leaves. If soil is caught in the creases the spinach leaves will need thorough washing. It is best to wash spinach just before use, so that water does not stand on the leaves, making it spoil more quickly. If it must be washed ahead of time, dry it immediately as lettuce is dried.

Rinse spinach leaves individually under running water or put a bunch in a large pan of water, swish it around vigorously, and lift it out. It may take several changes of water to clean it completely. Never leave spinach soaking in water, allowing water soluble vitamins and minerals to be lost.

Cooking Spinach

Spinach must be cooked quickly to retain its many vitamins and minerals. Steaming is not an efficient method, because the leaves mat down and the steam fails to penetrate. The best simple, quick way to cook it is with only the water that clings to the leaves after they are washed. Put the damp spinach in a pot, cover, and set it over moderately high heat. After 2 or 3 minutes, when the bottom leaves have wilted, and steam is coming up around the edges, turn over the whole mass of spinach using forks or a small spatula. Cover, and continue cooking another 2 or 3 minutes, until the spinach is limp and soft, but still bright green. Serve hot with seasonings, or use in recipes calling for precooked spinach. If there is a bit of cooking water left in the pot, use it with the spinach or in any vegetable mixture, or drink it to give strength to the cook.

Oxalic Acid in Spinach

When cooked spinach has a harsh taste with a teeth-on-edge quality, it is because it contains a lot of oxalic acid. This taste does not occur in raw spinach, and its intensity can vary considerably in different batches. The presence of oxalic acid is unfortunate, as it ties up the calcium in the spinach, so that it cannot be used. (The many other vitamins and minerals in spinach are not affected.)

SPINACH STORAGE
Canning

Trim stems, midribs. Cook until wilted in minimal water (see below). Pack hot, add boiling water, 1 in. headroom. Process 240°F, 11 pounds pressure. Pints: 1 hr. 10 min. Quarts: 1 hr. 30 min. Refer to the CANNING section.

Drying

Trim coarse stems, midribs. Optional: Steam blanch 4–6 min. to wilt. Spread on trays with minimal overlap. Dry until crumbly. Refer to the DRYING section.

Freezing

(Best storage method.) Trim, blanch 2 min. in boiling water. Chill, package. Refer to the FREEZING section.

2–3 pounds fresh = 1 quart canned or frozen

SPINACH IDEAS
Cold Spinach and Yogurt

Chop leftover cooked spinach and mix it with yogurt. Season with crushed garlic and pepper to taste. Serve as a cooling side dish with curries, chili beans, or other hot spicy dishes.

There are several ways to neutralize this unpleasant taste. Cooking it with high-protein foods like milk, eggs, or cheese works well. A sprinkling of lemon juice also works, because of the lemon's high calcium content.

Sprouts 🌿

Sprouting seeds is a phenomenally easy way to grow fresh vegetables in winter. This method of cultivation requires no soil, no sun, no growing lights, no greenhouse, not even a south-facing window sill. All that is necessary are seeds, a jar or other container that can be drained, and a room temperature place to keep them. Some seeds, particularly bean seeds, need an even temperature round the clock to sprout well, but others, like alfalfa seeds, sprout perfectly well in a room that is warm in the daytime and cool at night.

The sprouting of seeds is not a new idea. For centuries mung beans and soybeans have been sprouted in China, and lentils have been sprouted in India. Sprouting oats for winter feed for chickens is an old farm practice, and sprouting is the first step for making barley malt. Alfalfa sprouts are, however, a more recent innovation, and they make fresh, homegrown winter salads possible for everyone at negligible expense. Only one or two pounds of alfalfa seeds will keep an average family in salads throughout an entire winter.

Along with their other virtues, sprouted seeds are very nutritious. Dormant seeds already have a high food value, and when sprouted their value increases, particularly in their vitamin content.

HANDLING SPROUTS

Sprouts from plain, untreated seeds of the majority of food plants can be eaten, but there are exceptions. Do not eat sprouted potato, tomato, sorghum, Sudan grass, castorbean, apple, or stone fruit seeds, because they can be toxic. Also do not sprout seeds purchased for planting in the garden, as they may have been chemically treated in some way that does not show either on the seed or on the label. The best sources of sprouting seeds are health food stores and seed catalogs selling

---

SPROUTS STORAGE

Note: Long storage is counter to the purpose of sprouting. For a constant, fresh supply, start sprouts weekly.

Canning

No tested methods for home canning available.

Drying

Spread on trays. Dry until hard or papery. (Texture varies with type of sprout.) May grind to powder for soups. Refer to the DRYING section.

Freezing

Steam blanch 3 min. Chill. Package. (Will be limp when thawed.) Refer to the FREEZING section.

seeds intended specifically for sprouting, and of course, seeds collected from one's own garden. For harvesting seeds refer to the SEEDS section.

SPROUTING ARRANGEMENTS

Most seeds sprout best in darkness, to mimic natural growing conditions. Their container must allow good water drainage, and while they grow they must be kept damp by frequent watering or rinsing. They are ready to eat in 3 days to a week. An uncommon approach to sprouting is the planting of seeds in a thin layer of soil to be tended like seedlings for the garden. This is possible only for the larger seeds—beans, grain, or sunflower seeds. Such sprouts are often difficult to use because of the tangle of roots and dirt. Sometimes the shoots are cut for use and the root section discarded. Many styles of sprouters are available from catalogs that sell seeds for sprouting.

Sprouting Jars

Any wide mouthed glass jar of quart size or larger can be used for sprouting. A cover is needed that will let in air and retain the seeds when the jar is tipped and drained. A piece of a nylon stocking, nylon netting, or plastic screening can be used. If using a canning jar, the covering can be held in place with a canning lid ring. Otherwise use a rubber band. Another possibility is to punch many small holes in a regular lid. The seeds are soaked in the jar, drained, rinsed, and drained again, and then put in a dark or shaded place, preferably near the sink so it's easy to remember to water them. To keep the seeds moist, the jar is filled with water and drained several times a day. Between rinsings, the jar should be propped on its side so that moisture can drain out. If the seeds sit in water they will rot.

Opaque Sprouting Containers

Boxes made of plain, untreated wood, with small holes drilled in the bottom make good sprouting containers. With a lid to keep them dark inside, they can be kept in plain view for convenience in watering. Wooden boxes should be soaked in water for a few minutes, before the seeds go in. The moisture held by the wood will help keep the seeds evenly damp. Scald the sprouters with boiling water or leave in the sun for a while between uses to clean them.

A set of wooden sprouting boxes that stack one above the other can be made. Each box should be 3 inches deep to give the sprouts growing space. The whole stack can be watered at once by filling the top box, then letting the water trickle down through the other boxes. A different kind of sprout can be grown in each box.

Sprouting Trays

A baking pan or plastic container of shoebox size can be made into a sprouter by punching or drilling holes in the bottom and propping it over a drainage pan. For the first day or two of sprouting, a damp paper towel can be kept on the bottom of the container to hold moisture. However, if left too long, the paper may promote spoilage, especially in damp climates. Cover with cloth or a piece of wood. If transparent, keep the tray in a dark place. Pour water over the sprouts as needed to keep them damp, and empty the drainage tray every day. In this kind of sprouter the seeds are undisturbed as they grow. They will look like a dense miniature forest by the time they are ready for use.

BASIC STEPS OF SEED SPROUTING

- Measure an amount of seeds that will not crowd the sprouting container. For an average sized sprouter, such as a quart jar, use 2 tablespoons of tiny seeds like alfalfa or radish, ¼ cup of medium seeds, like grains or small beans, or ½ cup large seeds like sunflower or large beans.
- Cover the seeds with plenty of lukewarm water and soak about 8 hours, or overnight. Drain the seeds, rinse them in lukewarm water, and drain again. (Use the soaking water for watering house plants, as it contains beneficial nutrients.) Spread the seeds out in their sprouter, then keep them in the dark at room temperature, ideally 70°F, but many kinds of seeds will sprout even when nighttime temperatures are considerably lower. Excessively warm temperatures, however, encourage mold or other spoilage.
- Rinse or water the seeds 3 or 4 times a day. Water more frequently when the seeds are just beginning to germinate, especially where humidity is low. Use room temperature water, as icy water will discourage growth. Make sure the sprouter's drainage is good.
- When the sprouts are big enough to use, some kinds are improved if uncovered or put in the light for a day to make their leaves turn green.
- Wash the sprouts in a large pan of cool water to remove loose seed coverings. The coverings will float and can be poured off. Seed coverings that stick will not impair the taste of the sprouts. Lift the sprouts out of

the wash water, leaving unsprouted seeds behind. Drain well and store in a closed container in the refrigerator. They will keep about a week.

SEEDS FOR SPROUTING

The seeds described below can all be home grown and harvested.

Sprouting Alfalfa, Red Clover, and Fenugreek

The seeds of these three legumes are easily sprouted, taking 4 to 7 days. Cool night temperatures slow their growth, but do not affect their taste. They are ready to eat when tiny leaves appear. Their flavor and vitamin content are improved if they are kept in the light for a day to turn the leaves green. Red clover sprouts are smaller than alfalfa, and fenugreek sprouts are larger. All are delicious raw in salads and sandwiches.

Sprouting Radish, Mustard, and Cress

The sprouts of radish, mustard, and cress are all peppery in flavor, and are liked more as garnishes or flavorings than as main salad ingredients. As these seeds sprout in about the same time as alfalfa, a few can be mixed in with alfalfa seeds to be sprouted together for a slightly peppery salad mixture.

Sprouting Chia and Flax

These seeds become sticky or gelatinous when soaked. To keep them from sticking together in a clump, start them soaking by sprinkling them over water in a dish. Many prefer the taste of chia sprouts when very small, about ¼ inch. Grow flax sprouts until leaves appear. They can be left in the light to turn the leaves green.

Sprouting Mung Beans and Lentils

The familiar sprouts found in Chinese cooking are mung bean sprouts. Mung beans and lentils are easy to sprout if there is a place to keep them that stays near 70°F. If it is too cool, they will grow slowly and have a woody, uncooked, bean taste. When they grow as they should, the sprouts burst out of their seed coverings, and these are easily floated off when washing the sprouts. These sprouts are tender and taste very good raw. They will be 1 or 2 inches long and have two tiny leaves in 4 to 5 days. They taste especially good if kept in the light for a day to turn the leaves green. Once they turn green, mung bean sprouts do not look like typical Chinese bean sprouts, but they will be excellent used in the same ways.

Sprouting Soybeans

Soybeans germinate easily if the seeds are less than a year old, but it is difficult to grow them to full-sized, tender sprouts, like those sold in Chinese grocery stores. Black soybeans are best for sprouting. To prevent mold, commercially sprouted soybeans are often watered with a very mild solution of chlorinated lime. For the best chances of success without using chemicals, keep the soybeans at an even 70°F and keep them evenly moist. Large batches of sprouts will generate their own heat after 2 or 3 days, and must be cooled down with ice water to prevent rot. They take 6 to 8 days to grow and become 2 to 3 inches long. A brief blanching before they are eaten will improve their flavor.

Sprouting Dry Beans

All bean seeds make better sprouts if kept near 70°F while sprouting. After they have soaked, discard any seeds that float, as they will not sprout. Small-sized beans make sprouts that can be used like mung bean sprouts. They usually are ready in 3 to 5 days, when they are about an inch long. Use large-sized bean sprouts when the sprout is only as long as the seed it grows from, as the sprouts begin to taste bitter if grown longer. Large sprouted beans must be cooked before they are eaten. They are very good added to soups, stews, and vegetable dishes.

Sprouting Grains

All grains can be sprouted, except sorghum, whose sprouts are toxic. Grains with tight hulls, like barley, must be sprouted unhulled. There are two basic approaches to sprouting grains. One is to sprout them like other seeds in a sprouter, until the shoots are only as long as the original seed. These can be used in baking for their pleasant, chewy taste. They can also be dried and ground. The other way is to cover the grain seeds with a thin layer of soil, and grow them in a sunny window for their grassy green tops. Cut the tops when they are 2 or 3 inches high, then mince them for salads. Chew them for their sweet flavor, but the "cud" must be spat out.

It will take 2 to 5 days for grains to sprout until the shoot reaches the length of the seed. Grains generally sprout very well regardless of differences in day and night temperatures.

Sprouting Sunflower Seeds

Use only unhulled seeds. If grown in a sprouter, use the sprouts as soon as the shells have split open, when they can be easily removed. Perhaps the best way to enjoy sprouted sunflowers is to grow them in about ½ inch of soil in a sunny window, and cut the shoots when they are 2 or 3 inches tall, with two green leaves. The shoots are sometimes called sunflower lettuce and are very good in salads.

SPROUTS RECIPES

Essene Bread

(MAKES 6 THICK OR 12 THIN PATTIES)

The Essenes were an ancient Jewish sect whose asceticism precluded all but the purest and simplest foods, as exemplified by this bread.

2 cups whole grain, for sprouting (rye, wheat, triticale or a mixture of these is excellent)

¼ teaspoon caraway or other herb seeds, optional (refer to the HERB SEEDS section)

¼ cup dried fruit, soaked, drained and chopped if necessary, optional

oil for baking sheets, or several tablespoons sesame seeds

Sprout the grain until the shoots are about the same length as the kernels. If noticeably damp, let the sprouted grain sit exposed to the air for a few hours, until no wetness shows. Grind to a dough in a meat grinder or food processor. If using caraway or other herb seeds, grind them along with the grain. Dried fruit can also be ground in, or it can be chopped small and worked into the dough after grinding. Knead the dough to distribute herb seeds or fruit evenly throughout.

Shape the dough into 6 large, inch-thick patties or make twice as many thin patties. Lightly oil baking sheets, or sprinkle them with sesame seeds, and set the patties on them. Let dry in the sun, in a food dryer, or in another warm, airy place, such as near a stove, until the tops of the patties are dry to the touch. This usually takes about 1 hour. Then turn them over and bake them in a very low, 250°F oven for about an hour. Thin patties will take less time than thick ones. The bread will rise slightly and darken in color. (It is also possible to put the dough in small, oiled baking dishes or loaf pans and bake it for several hours in a very low, 250°F oven, but the texture will tend to be more pudding-like than bread-like.)

This bread has a somewhat sweet flavor and a moist, dense texture. It tastes very good by itself, or with butter or other toppings. Keep it a week to 10 days in the refrigerator, or freeze it for long storage.

Squash, Summer

Summer squash is any squash eaten young, while the skin is tender and the seeds undeveloped. Zucchini is the all-round favorite, but yellow straightneck and crookneck, and patty pan or scallop squash are also popular. Winter squash varieties make good summer squash if picked when very small. All varieties can be prepared in the same ways, though there will be differences in flavor and texture.

A well-known characteristic of most summer squash is their tendency towards bursts of rampant productivity. When weather and growing conditions are right, a great many squash can appear in a very short time. Though an overwhelming supply has been known to dampen enthusiasm for eating them, it need not do so. Summer squash are an excellent summertime staple, and there are so many good ways to prepare them that they can be eaten every day of their growing season, yet still be missed when the season ends. There are also good ways to put them by for winter, though they will not retain the delicate crispness of raw squash, or the firm bite of freshly cooked squash.

Marrow or vegetable marrow is a large, oval summer squash, best known in England, though a few North American seed catalogs do include it. The cymling or simlin, sometimes mentioned in old cookbooks, is patty pan squash. Courgettes, the French name for small summer squash, is also seen in some English language cookbooks.

HANDLING SQUASH

Summer squash can be harvested at any size, from fingerling with blossom attached to quite large, as long as the skin is still tender. Even the occasional overgrown squash hidden under its leaves can be used, though it will lack the good flavor and texture of the small ones.

Nothing is easier to prepare than summer squash. All they need is a rinse to take off dust or dirt. (Peeling would remove so much flavor and color that little of value would remain.) Only an overly mature squash will need seeding.

Squash Blossoms

The blossoms of both summer and winter squash are very good to eat. They can be gathered from different varieties, and used

---

SUMMER SQUASH STORAGE

Canning

Slice ½ in. thick. Cut slices in uniform pieces. Cover with boiling water, return to boil. Drain, pack. Cover with boiling cooking water, ½ in. headroom. Process 240°F, 11 pounds pressure. Pints: 30 min. Quarts: 40 min. *Zucchini and Tomato* Boil chopped tomatoes until juicy. Add onion, basil, other herbs, to taste. Add zucchini, sliced or diced. Boil 5 min. Pack in jars, ½ in. headroom. Process as above. Refer to the CANNING section. Also see ZUCCHINI DILL PICKLES, below.

Drying

Slice thinly, or grate. Dry until papery. *Crisp Chips* Slice ¼ in. or thinner. Optional: Season with garlic juice, cayenne pepper, salt. Dry in electric or other steadily heated dryer until crisp. Good with dips. Refer to the DRYING section.

Freezing

(Texture soft when thawed.) Slice or cube. Blanch 1–3 min. Blanch about

together in one dish. However, note the difference between male and female blossoms. Usually, only the male blossoms are gathered since they do not affect yield. (A few are left for pollination.) When a female blossom is picked, the result is one less squash. These are meatier than the male blossoms and quite delicious fried in batter, so try them if they can be spared. See the recipe below for a way to prepare blossoms.

SUMMER SQUASH RECIPES

Patty-cake Squash

(MAKES ABOUT 6 SIDE SERVINGS)

4 cups summer squash, grated
1 small onion, grated
2 eggs, lightly beaten
¼ cup flour
pepper, to taste
¼ teaspoon salt, optional

2 tablespoons (about) fine dry bread crumbs
2–3 tablespoons butter or oil, for frying
yogurt, to taste

Put the grated squash and onion in a strainer and press out extra liquid. Then mix with eggs, flour, pepper, and salt, if desired. Add bread crumbs as needed for a medium thick batter. Heat butter or oil in a frying pan, then put in large spoonfuls of the squash mixture. Flatten with a spoon to make pancake thickness. Brown lightly on both sides, and serve the patty-cakes with yogurt. They are good for breakfast, lunch, or dinner.

Squash Blossom Corn Cakes

(MAKES ABOUT 2 DOZEN SMALL CAKES,
OR 1 DOZEN MUFFINS)

1 cup whole cornmeal
2 tablespoons honey or sugar
salt, optional
1 cup boiling water
½ cup butter, or oil
¾ cup milk

2 eggs
1 cup squash blossoms, coarsely chopped
1 cup flour
1 ½ teaspoons baking powder

Put the cornmeal, honey or sugar, and salt in a heat-proof bowl and stir in the boiling water. Add the butter or oil and stir until melted or mixed. Then mix in the milk, eggs, and squash blos-

5 min. Or grate. Pack without blanching. *In Tomato* Cook slices or chunks of squash in boiling stewed tomatoes, or juice, for 5 min. Chill. Pack in containers. Refer to the FREEZING section.

2–2½ pounds fresh = 1 quart canned, or frozen
1 pound = about 4 cups grated

SUMMER SQUASH IDEAS

Steamed Fingerling Squash

Pick very small (2- to 5-inch) summer squash when they are plentiful. (If blossoms are still attached, separate them and fry them in batter.) Steam the squash about 5 minutes, long enough to brighten their color but not long enough to soften them. These are exquisite eaten plain without any seasonings, or cooled and seasoned with olive oil, a sprinkling of minced fresh herbs, such as scallions and basil, pepper, and salt, if desired.

Yellow Squash and Onions

Slice the yellow squash, and then slice about half as much onion. Simmer these 10–15 minutes in just enough

soms. Mix or sift together the flour and baking powder, and add to the batter. Drop by spoonfuls on a hot, greased griddle and bake, turning to brown both sides, or bake in muffin tins in the oven for about 20 minutes. Either way these are delicious. Have them for breakfast or any other meal.

Dandelion Blossom or Elderflower Corn Cakes

Instead of squash blossoms use either dandelion blossoms or elderflowers. For the dandelion blossoms, take off the green part at the base of the blossoms, letting the petals fall free. The elderflowers must be stripped from their stems.

Zucchini Dill Pickles
(MAKES 6 PINTS, CANNED)

6 heads of dill	6 grape leaves, optional
6 cloves garlic	4 cups vinegar
5 pounds (about) zucchini, in chunks or slices	salt, optional
	5 cups water

Put 1 dill head and 1 whole clove of garlic in each of 6 hot pint canning jars. Fill with zucchini, leaving ½ inch headroom. If desired, put a grape leaf on top for flavor, and to help keep pickles crisp.

Heat the vinegar, water, and salt, if desired, to a full boil, then pour into jars to just cover ingredients. Run a thin knife around the inside of the jars to remove air bubbles, and, if necessary, add more vinegar solution. Adjust lids and process in a boiling water bath canner for 10 minutes. Wait 6 weeks before using the pickles. They are as good as, or better than, most canned dill cucumber pickles.

water to keep them from sticking, until both are tender. Stir once or twice. Season with pepper and butter, and serve hot.

Stir-fried Summer Squash

Slice the squash thinly, ⅛ inch if possible. In a wok or heavy frying pan, heat 1 or 2 tablespoons lard or oil, then stir-fry minced garlic and ginger root (optional) in it briefly. Over high heat add and stir-fry the squash about 2 minutes. Add a little soy sauce or water and a dash of pepper. Cover and cook over moderate heat about 5 minutes.

Grated Summer Squash

Because grated squash is mild in flavor it can be added to a variety of foods to extend them and add moisture. It is good added to most kinds of salad, and can be mixed with ground meat and other ingredients to make meatballs, patties, or meat loaf. It is also very good added to such baked goods as muffins, pancakes, and fruit or nut breads.

Zucchini Tomato Bake

This is an excellent way to use canned, or frozen and partly thawed zucchini and tomato mixtures. Spread the zuc-

Squash, Winter and Pumpkin

Winter squash and pumpkins are somewhat different botanically, but they are quite alike as foods. Some, wanting the best of both, choose to eat winter squash and call it pumpkin. The flesh of pumpkins is apt to be more watery and stringy than that of winter squash, but the name pumpkin or "punkin" has a friendlier, more toothsome sound. The best pumpkin pies are made of winter squash. The range in size, shape, and skin color of the different kinds of squash is remarkable, yet the flesh inside all of them is pumpkin colored. Its yellow to orange color indicates high vitamin A content. Japanese varieties of winter squash are becoming well-known and popular. They have dense, dry, flavorful flesh that is excellent in pumpkin recipes. As their skin is quite thin, it can be eaten with the flesh, but this thinness means they may spoil sooner when stored. Squash and pumpkins are widely valued as winter food because they are so easily grown in quantity for long storage.

HANDLING WINTER SQUASH

Winter squash and pumpkins are harvested in fall, around the time of the first frosts. Hard shelled varieties are not damaged by light frosts, but thinner skinned varieties must be protected or brought in before the first frost. Winter squash and pumpkins keep so well in a cool, dry storage place that no other storage methods are necessary for fall and winter use. Any extra squash in storage can be canned or frozen during late fall or winter, when there is spare time. They also dry well, but their quality will be best if they are dried as soon as they are harvested.

Immature winter squash and pumpkin can be prepared like summer squash, and their blossoms used together with summer squash blossoms. (Refer to the recipes in the SQUASH, SUMMER section.)

Curing and Storing Winter Squash and Pumpkins

For long storage use only completely mature winter squash and pumpkins that were harvested with their stems on, and that are free of bruises and scrapes. Set aside any with broken stems or other damage for early use. (Butternuts are an exception in that they will keep without stems.)

After harvesting, cure winter squash and pumpkins from 10 days to 2 weeks to toughen their skins. They can be left outdoors in dry sunny weather, but must be covered at night to protect them from frosts. Or they can be cured indoors, at room temperature. If thick skinned varieties are washed in a solution of about a tablespoon of chlorine bleach to a gallon of

chini and tomatoes in an oiled, shallow baking dish or deep pie dish. Sprinkle with parsley, oregano, or other herbs, and pepper. Then pour 1 or 2 lightly beaten eggs over. Sprinkle generously with bread crumbs, and top with grated cheese or dots of butter. Bake in a moderate, 350°F oven until set, 30 minutes, or a little longer, if the vegetables are icy from the freezer.

WINTER SQUASH AND PUMPKIN STORAGE

Canning

Peel, cut in 1-in. cubes. Bring to boil in water to cover. Drain, pack, add boiling cooking water, ½ in. headroom. Process 240°F, 11 pounds pressure. Pints: 55 min. Quarts: 1 hr. 30 min. *Purée* (see below) Heat to simmer, stirring. Fill jars, ½ in. headroom. Process 240°F, 11 pounds pressure. Pints: 65 min. Quarts: 80 min. Refer to the CANNING section.

Cold Storage

See CURING AND STORING WINTER SQUASH AND PUMPKINS, above.

Drying

(Solid fleshed varieties best.) Peel, slice, or grate. Optional: Steam

water, their skins will be disinfected, discouraging mold or rot. Dry them immediately after doing this, as lingering dampness can also cause spoilage.

A dry, airy storage place with a temperature between 45 and 60°F will be needed. (Root cellars are too damp.) Use an attic, spare room, or a cool bedroom. Storage at temperatures above 60°F will make squash and pumpkins stringy. Spread out the squash in the storage place so they do not touch each other. Check them occasionally for mold, and wipe them with vegetable oil if any is found, to remove it and seal that spot.

Most winter squash and pumpkins will keep from 3 to 4 months in a good storage place. A few, like Hubbard squash, will keep for 6 months.

Pumpkin Seeds

The seeds of all pumpkins and mature squash have a nice, nut-like flavor, but their shells can be a problem. There is, however, a naked seeded pumpkin called "Lady Godiva" that is grown for its seeds alone. Its flesh is too watery and stringy to enjoy. Ordinary squash and pumpkin seeds can be eaten in spite of their shells. Roast them like nuts (see the NUTS section), and eat them shell and all. They can be boiled about 15 minutes to soften shells before roasting. Some people become adept at shelling the seeds with their teeth, eating the nutty part and spitting out the shell. Other possibilities are to grind seeds and shells to use in baking, or to experiment with shelling them like sunflower seeds. (Refer to the SUNFLOWERS section.) As the seeds of different kinds of squash and pumpkin vary in size and toughness of shell, a system that works poorly for one may do very well for another.

For an easy way to separate seeds from the fibers and pulp around them, scrape out the centers of the squash, put them in a bucket or pan, cover them with warm water, and let them sit at room temperature for several days. As they begin to ferment, the pulpy parts will rise and float and the seeds will sink. Pour off the pulp and drain and dry the seeds. Spread them out in a warm, airy place so that they dry quickly, or use a food dryer.

Use naked pumpkin seeds or shelled seeds in the same ways as sunflower seeds or nuts. They are delicious in muffins, cookies, and breads.

blanch, 6 min. Spread on trays, or slice thick rings and hang. Dry until leathery or brittle. Dry purée as for fruit leather. Refer to the DRYING section.

Freezing

Purée (see below) Fill containers, leaving airspace. Refer to the FREEZING section.

about 3 pounds whole raw = 1 quart canned or frozen

WINTER SQUASH AND PUMPKIN IDEAS
Seasonings for Baked Chunks

Cut serving sized chunks of winter squash or pumpkin and set them in a baking pan. Sprinkle with pepper, and dot with butter, or cover with a slice of bacon. Or, dribble with honey, molasses, or maple syrup, and dot with butter. Or, spread with a mixture of orange juice concentrate, a little honey, and dots of butter or bacon slices, if desired. Put a few tablespoons of water in the pan around the squash or pumpkin and bake until tender, usually 40 minutes to an hour.

Winter Squash and Pumpkin Purée

Before it is puréed, squash or pumpkin must be cooked by baking, steaming, or stewing. To bake, cut the squash or pumpkins in half, scoop out the seedy centers, and set the halves, cut side down, on an oiled baking sheet. Bake in a moderate, 350°F oven until soft. The time will vary with the thickness of the flesh, taking from 30 to 60 minutes. Test with a fork for doneness. When cool enough to handle, scrape out the flesh, discarding the peel. To steam or stew, cut the squash or pumpkin in pieces and slice off the peel. Steam on a rack, or stew in a minimum of water until soft. If watery after stewing, continue to cook uncovered to evaporate moisture. The cooked flesh can be mashed like potatoes, but the texture will not be smooth. For smoothness, put it through a sieve or food mill.

Spaghetti Squash

This unusual squash makes a virtue of stringiness, as its long, spaghetti-like strands are its claim to fame. Boil or steam it whole, or cut the long way, and steam half, saving the other half for another meal. When soft, scrape the flesh out of the skin. It will come out in long strands that can be seasoned and served immediately while they are hot. They can be served with spaghetti sauce, but in spite of the name, they may be better liked with vegetable seasonings.

WINTER SQUASH AND PUMPKIN RECIPES

Out-of-This-World Pumpkin Pie

(MAKES ONE 9- TO 10-INCH PIE)

2 cups puréed winter squash
½ cup honey or ¾ cup brown sugar
2 tablespoons molasses
1 teaspoon cinnamon
1 teaspoon ginger
½ teaspoon cloves
½ teaspoon nutmeg
1 egg white, lightly beaten
1 nut topping recipe, below

¼ cup whiskey, rum, or brandy
1¼ cups light cream, or evaporated milk
3 eggs and 1 yolk, lightly beaten
single 9- to 10-inch pie shell

Sautéed Winter Squash or Pumpkin

Slice peeled squash or pumpkin thinly, and sauté slowly in butter or another fat. Sliced onion, minced garlic, or other sliced vegetables can be sautéed with it. Season with pepper, and such minced herbs as parsley and mint. If a sauce is wanted, add apple cider or a little light cream for the last few minutes of cooking.

Herb Tossed Spaghetti Squash

While the spaghetti squash is cooking (see above), mix minced fresh chervil or parsley, or dried herbs, such as thyme, mint, or celery leaves, with melted butter, oil, or with bacon fat and crisp, crumbled bacon. Toss the mixture with hot strands of spaghetti squash and serve immediately. If oil was used the leftovers will be good later as a salad or cold vegetable dish. As a variation, chopped onion, celery, carrot shreds, and other vegetables can be sautéed in the fat and tossed with the spaghetti squash and herbs.

Mix the puréed squash, honey or sugar, molasses, spices, whiskey or other liquor, and the 3 eggs and yolk. Beat until smooth. Brush the bottom and sides of the pie shell with the egg white. Pour in the pie filling. Put in a hot, 450°F oven and bake 10 minutes. Then reduce heat to 325°F, and bake from 30 to 40 minutes more, until the pie has set. Make a small slit with a knife to test for firmness.

Let the pie cool completely, then add the following topping.

NUT TOPPING:

⅔ cup brown or grated maple sugar	½ cup pecans, walnuts, hickory nuts, or butternuts, chopped
3 tablespoons butter, melted	nut halves, optional
1 tablespoon heavy cream	(for garnish)

Mix all topping ingredients, except nut halves. Spread the mixture on the cold pie. Arrange the nut halves on top. Put under a broiler, about 3 inches from the heat. Broil until the topping is bubbly and lightly browned, about 2 or 3 minutes. Watch closely because it will easily burn. (If the phone rings do not answer it!) Serve in small slices—it is very rich.

Sweet Potato Pie

Use mashed sweet potato instead of winter squash. Because sweet potato is sweeter than squash, reduce sweetening to ⅓ cup honey or ½ cup brown sugar. Spices are optional.

Steam Cooking

Steaming is highly recommended as a nutritious way to cook foods, especially vegetables, but it is not always as highly esteemed for its flavorful results. The difficulty lies not with the method itself, but with its implementation. If steamed foods seem dull, flavorless, or unimaginative, then the potential of steam cooking has not been realized.

In some parts of the world, ovens are not common and steam cooking replaces baking as a basic way to prepare food. Steamed breads and puddings replace baked bread, and meat, poultry, and fish are steamed rather than roasted. The moist,

Squash Cornmeal Mush

In a heavy saucepan or double boiler, mix about 2 cups thin puréed winter squash or pumpkin, ½ cup cornmeal, and 1 tablespoon butter. Cook together slowly, stirring often, until very thick. It will take from 30 to 40 minutes. Stir in about ½ cup diced mild cheese. Serve hot, like mashed potatoes, or cool in a mold, slice, and sauté the slices.

Winter Squash for Summer

When winter squash forms too late in the season to have a chance to mature, pick them tiny, 2 to 3 inches, and steam them whole. Season to taste. A dish of tiny, recognizable squash shapes, such as acorn or butternut, has a whimsical look as well as a fine flavor.

STEAM COOKING IDEAS
Bedfordshire Clanger

This idea originated among English working women long before such short cuts as frozen dinners were possible. The clanger would be put on to steam in the morning and served as both main course and dessert at dinner.

tender goodness of foods perfectly cooked with steam need only be tried to be enjoyed.

Steaming Under Pressure

Though pressure cookers use steam for cooking, they function at such high temperatures that the gentleness of regular steam cooking is lost. These high temperatures are essential for canning low-acid foods, but otherwise, the main advantage of pressure cooking is speed. The flavor and texture of meats and most other foods are better with the use of conventional methods. Since most vegetables cook quickly, there is a tendency to overcook them in a pressure cooker, and in any case, little time is saved. A pressure cooker does make a good utensil for steaming vegetables when used with the vent open.

This section will deal with steam cooking without pressure. (However, when pressure is used it is important to carefully follow the manufacturer's instructions, especially those concerning safety.)

There are several different ways to use steam for cooking. Foods can be set on a rack directly over boiling water, or placed in a dish or mold, and set on a stand in a pot with boiling water. Old-time bag puddings are made by tying the pudding mixture in a cloth and either placing it in, or suspending it over, boiling water. Another way to use steam (which is not always known as steaming) is to cook foods, especially vegetables, with only a little water in a pot with a tight lid. The water turns to steam when heated, and the steam cooks the food.

STEAM COOKING VEGETABLES

Vegetables retain more of their vitamins and minerals when steamed than when they are boiled, as boiling water leaches out most water soluble nutrients. Although the water in a steamer may collect some food value and flavor from the vegetables, it is not as valuable to save for soup and other cooking as the water from boiled vegetables. Both flavor and food value of most green and root vegetables are better when they are steamed rather than boiled—with a few exceptions. Such leafy greens as spinach mat down in a steamer and do not cook efficiently. (Refer to COOKING SPINACH, in the SPINACH sec-

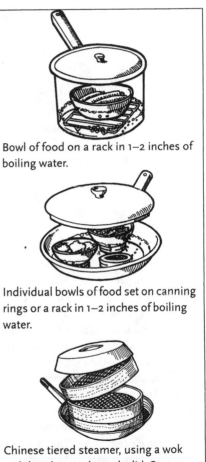

Bowl of food on a rack in 1–2 inches of boiling water.

Individual bowls of food set on canning rings or a rack in 1–2 inches of boiling water.

Chinese tiered steamer, using a wok with bamboo racks and a lid. Steams several foods at once to make a meal, with the food requiring the longest, hottest cooking on the bottom tier.

tion.) Green vegetables requiring a quick, high cooking heat may cook too slowly if the steamer is not hot enough, or if it is too, crowded. Green beans, for instance, taste better cooked quickly in plenty of boiling water than they do cooked in most steamers. If steamed, they should be cooked in small batches over plenty of boiling water for quick, hot steam, in a steaming pot with a tight lid.

STEAM COOKING FOODS IN OPEN DISHES

For this Chinese steam cooking method, put fish, meat, vegetables, or mixtures of these in uncovered dishes, and set them on a rack in boiling water. The moisture that collects in them will make a flavorful sauce for the food, which is served in its steaming dish. It is best to use heat resistant dishes, but ordinary serving dishes will suffice if they are protected from sudden temperature changes. Warm them before putting them in the steamer, or put them in before the water in the steamer starts boiling. Start timing when the water can be heard boiling or when steam comes out around the lid. Never open the steaming pot during the cooking time. Tongs can be used to lift the dishes out of the steamer.

STEAM COOKING CAUTIONS

- Pots used for steaming must have close fitting lids to hold in the steam. Do not lift the lid unnecessarily during the steaming because heat will be lost.
- Do not mistake a cloud of water vapor for steam. Vapor often rises from hot, but not boiling, water. Foods will not cook properly if the water is not heard or seen boiling. Start counting time only when the water is visibly boiling.
- When steam cooking foods for long periods of time, occasionally check the level of the water and add more boiling water as needed. Never add cold water because it will interrupt the cooking.
- Keep face and hands away from the steam that pours out when opening a steamer, and tilt the lid to direct the steam away from people. The steam will dissipate in a minute or so, when the food can be removed from the steamer. Tongs are handy for lifting out racks or containers of food.

Pastry or biscuit dough (using minced suet instead of lard or other shortening) is rolled out in a big rectangle. A strip of dough is cut from the long side and laid down the center, dividing the dough the long way. One half is spread with ground beef, minced onion, and seasonings. The other half is spread with jam or other preserves. The dough is dampened around the edges and rolled up, keeping the divider in place. The whole thing is then tied in a well-floured pudding cloth and steamed in a pot of boiling water for several hours.

Stir-Frying 🌿

Stir-frying is the Chinese way to quickly cook all kinds of vegetables, meats, poultry, and fish. The foods are cut small (preparation takes considerably longer than cooking), then stirred over high heat in a minimum of fat or oil. The average cooking time for stir-fried dishes is only 5 minutes. Because of this quick cooking, foods retain fresh flavor, texture, color, and a high nutritional value.

Although stir-frying is a Chinese cooking method, vegetables stir-fried with plain seasonings go very well as side dishes with western style meals. There are in fact some western recipes, particularly from the Mediterranean area, that use the same principle as stir-frying. Thinly sliced meats or vegetables are sautéed quickly in very hot olive oil, seasoned, and served immediately.

Stir-frying is a valuable cooking technique for everyday use. It is a way to give familiar, sometimes boring, vegetables a new look and a new flavor. It is a way to stretch small amounts of meat with large amounts of vegetables to make nourishing family meals. It is also a very good way to ensure satisfied after-dinner smiles all around the table.

All ingredients for stir-frying must be prepared and set out ready to use before cooking begins. Stir-frying is too quick to allow time for chopping last-minute ingredients or hunting for last minute seasonings. One Chinese cookbook calls the procedure "blitz cooking." Usually, all ingredients for a particular stir-fried dish are cut in the same approximate size and shape. If the meat is in small, thin slices, the vegetables are also thinly sliced. If the meat is shredded, then so are the vegetables. Chinese stir-frying is done in a wok, but a large frying pan that holds heat well can be used instead.

Stir-frying with a Wok

The wok is a unique Chinese cooking pan. Ideal for stir-frying, it can also be used for steaming and deep fat frying. Woks are shaped as if cut from a sphere. Their shallow, curved shape has many advantages. Less oil or fat is needed in stir-frying or deep frying than in western utensils. The curved sides of the wok transfer heat along with the bottom, creating a large, hot surface area that cooks the foods faster. Foods are easily stirred and turned in the curved shape. Woks also fit nicely into the openings of old-fashioned wood or coal burning cookstoves when a stove lid is removed. For use with gas or electric stoves, woks come with a metal ring to support them over the burner. Gas works better than electricity when cooking with a wok, because gas heat adjusts more quickly.

The best woks are made from thin tempered iron. They must be seasoned and cared for like cast iron cookware. Avoid stainless steel and aluminum woks because they do not heat as hot or as evenly. There are woks with one long handle which are easier to move around when hot than those with a small handle on each side. A large-sized wok is most practical, since it can be used to cook both small and large amounts. Woks are sold in many stores carrying kitchen utensils. Lids and spatulas with a curved edge to fit the wok often go with them. Though a spatula is nice to have, it is not essential, and any large lid will work as well as a wok lid.

Preparing Vegetables for Stir-frying

Most vegetables are very good stir-fried. Stir-fry slow cooking vegetables over high heat for a minute or two, then add a few tablespoons of liquid, cover, and cook them for 3 to 5 minutes more. There are many different ways to cut vegetables depending on their size, shape, and texture, but thin slices are the most common. A vegetable slicer can make slicing easier. When one part of a vegetable cooks more slowly than another, separate the parts. For instance, the stalks of Chinese cabbage are sliced separately to be cooked longer than the green, leafy parts.

It is best not to prepare vegetables too far ahead of time, because exposure to air after slicing causes loss of nutrients. If early preparation is necessary refrigerate them in the meantime.

Fats and Oils for Stir-frying

Lard or a good quality cooking oil is preferred for stir-frying. Peanut oil is often used.

Seasonings for Stir-fried Dishes

Stir-fried dishes do not require particular or special seasonings. If served as part of a western style meal, pepper, herbs, and salt, if desired, do very well. The basic Chinese seasoning for stir-frying is soy sauce, but garlic, fresh ginger root, and dry sherry (as a substitute for Chinese rice wine) are all common. (Dry powdered ginger is not a good substitute for fresh ginger root, as the taste is quite different.)

Chinese recipes often call for both soy sauce and salt, but the salt should be omitted, because soy sauce is salty enough. Chinese stir-fried dishes are highly seasoned because they are eaten in relatively small amounts with a lot of (unsalted) rice. However, as westerners tend to eat more of the stir-fried dish and less rice, less seasoning will be needed in the stir-fry.

Liquids and Thickeners for Stir-frying

Several tablespoons to ½ cup of liquid will be required for many stir-fried dishes. Though plain water can be used, soup stock or the soaking water from dried vegetables will add a better flavor. Soup stock (usually chicken stock) can be frozen in small containers or as ice cubes for use in stir-frying. Thaw and warm them before use, as cold liquids will slow down the cooking too much.

Cornstarch or another starch is often used to thicken the sauce around stir-fried foods. This thickening is optional, depending on personal preference, and on the wetness and type of ingredients in a particular dish. Arrowroot starch is preferred by some over cornstarch, as they consider it healthier. Homemade potato starch (see the POTATOES section) also works very well. Always mix the starch with water or another liquid before adding it. It can be mixed with soy sauce and other ingredients, or with water or stock and added last, just before the dish is served. But all the liquids and thickenings for a particular dish should be measured, mixed if necessary, and set out with other ingredients before cooking begins.

BASIC STIR-FRYING STEPS

- Assemble and prepare all ingredients. If many different ones are included, arrange them in the order in which they will be added. Have in mind the procedures to be used. Long pauses to find ingredients or figure out the next step will lead to over-cooked foods. With practice the preparation will become second nature.
- Heat the wok or frying pan, add fat or oil, then heat it almost to smoking before adding anything else. If the pan is not hot enough foods may stick. Perfection depends on high heat.
- Add an ingredient and stir or toss it constantly, so that the heat sears the pieces on all sides, especially the cut edges. This step seals in juice and flavor. Minced garlic and ginger root can be added first and stirred for a second or two, followed by a meat or vegetable.
- If an ingredient is to be stir-fried briefly and taken out of the wok or frying pan while another is added, have a dish ready to hold it. The serving dish can be used for this.
- When adding liquids, pour them in around the sides of the pan or clear a place in the center to pour them. They will heat faster if they contact the pan before the food. If the pan is to be covered, do it quickly after the liquid is added so that it does not steam away. Reduce the heat to medium while the pan is covered.

- Ideally, each ingredient in a stir-fry is cooked for the exact time it needs. The pace can be hectic when a real effort is made to do this, especially when learning. Eventually, though, a free-wheeling style develops that makes stir-frying fun and an invigorating way to cook. Fortunately, stir-fried foods almost always taste good, whether this ideal is met or not.
- To enjoy it at its best, everyone should be ready to eat as soon as the stir-fry is done. (A Chinese proverb says it is better for the diners to wait for the dish, than for the dish to wait for the diners.)

Strawberries

The heady fragrance of a patch of ripe strawberries on a hot summer afternoon is unforgettable. It lingers with every strawberry put by for winter, whether domestic or wild. The large, sweet strawberries cultivated in the garden are superb, and the tiny, intense strawberries gathered from their wild hiding places are superlative. Always for strawberries the larger question is not how to use them, but how to get enough of them.

HANDLING STRAWBERRIES

Strawberries must be completely ripe when picked. Gather them on a dry day, and handle them gently, without squeezing or pinching. If carefully picked from a clean patch they can be used without washing. If they must be rinsed, do it just before they are hulled and used. Do not allow them to be hit with the full force of the water from the kitchen faucet, but dunk them in a pan of water, or pour water gently over them.

As strawberries keep best with hulls on, use them within a day if they are hulled as they are picked. Wild strawberries are easiest to hull as they are picked, and it is tedious in the extreme to go through the tiny berries later, hulling each one. If berries must be rinsed after hulling, do it quickly. Wild strawberries can be eaten without hulling, but they will have a scratchy texture. There is no need to hull strawberries when making juice or purée, as the hulls can be strained out.

STRAWBERRY STORAGE

Canning

Berries tend to fade, lose flavor. Juice is excellent. Hull, spread in pans, drizzle with ¼ cup honey or ½ cup sugar per quart. Let stand until juice collects, 2–4 hrs. Heat slowly without boiling. Pack hot in jars, ½ in. headroom. Process boiling water bath. Pints: 10 min. Quarts: 15 min. Refer to the CANNING section. Also see CANNING FRUIT JUICE AND SAUCE, in the FRUITS section.

Drying

Not recommended for whole berries. Most of the flavor lost. Refer to FRUIT LEATHER, in the DRYING section. *Leaves* Dry *completely*, as wilted leaves may be toxic. Refer to DRYING HERBS and *Herb Teas*, in the HERBS section.

STRAWBERRY RECIPES

Strawberry Butter

(MAKES ABOUT 1 CUP)

½ cup strawberries, trimmed, fresh or frozen

½ cup butter

2 tablespoons honey, optional (omit if berries are pre-sweetened)

Put ingredients in a blender and blend until smooth, which will take several minutes. The delicate pink color and fresh flavor make this a very special spread for waffles, pancakes, or toast, or try a dollop on warm baked or steamed desserts.

Sunflowers

Sunflowers are native to North and South America and have always been appreciated by American Indians. The seeds are valued for their versatile nut-like meats and for the high quality oil that can be pressed from them. But though they are the most important part of the plant, all parts can be used: the sprouts or seedlings in salads, the buds as a cooked vegetable, the roasted shells steeped for a beverage, the leaves for livestock feed, the petals for dye, and the fibers in the stalks for making cords and ropes like those from hemp.

Sunflowers grow well in gardens everywhere. They are cultivated like corn, but they can be grown successfully farther north. They make a practical crop once the problem of shelling the seeds has been solved. They are also the only cool climate crop suitable for pressing on a small scale to make vegetable oil.

HANDLING SUNFLOWERS

It is best to harvest sunflower seed heads after the seeds are fully formed but before they are mature and completely dry. Too many things are likely to happen to seeds left on the plant. Birds may take an unfair share, or worms may get into them, or they may fall to the ground and be lost. As there is a lot of mois-

Freezing

Better color and flavor if presweetened. Hull, slicing optional, mix in about ¼ cup honey or maple syrup per quart. *Unsweetened* Pack, cover with solution of 1 teaspoon crystalline ascorbic acid in 1 quart water. Refer to the FREEZING section.

6–8 cups unhulled = 1 quart canned or frozen

SUNFLOWER STORAGE

Note: With shells, store in a cool, dry place, protected from insects. Should keep for a year or more.

Cold Storage

Shelled seeds Keep in closed container in refrigerator, or other cool place. Quality retained for months. *Home pressed oil* Keeps 2–3 months refrigerated.

ture in the seed heads when they are harvested early, they must be hung or spread out in a dry place. Do not stack or leave them in a damp place, or they will mold. If there are signs of worms, remove the seeds from the heads as soon as they are harvested, and dry them immediately in a food dryer or oven at its lowest setting, 150–200°F. If worm free, the seeds can be removed at any time after the heads are dry.

For a few sunflower heads, the seeds can be rubbed off by hand. Wear gloves to protect fingers, or use a stiff brush or similar tool. When there are many, rub the heads on ½-inch mesh hardware cloth laid over a box or wheelbarrow. Some use a wire brush attached to an electric motor to remove seeds. Bits of debris can be winnowed out (refer to the SEEDS section), or they can be removed later, with the shells.

SHELLING SUNFLOWER SEEDS

For snacking, sunflower seeds can be shelled one by one. Some people are good at holding them on end between their teeth, cracking them, and spitting out the shells. For shelling larger quantities some ingenuity is required. (Hopefully someone will eventually market a handy shelling device for small scale use.) One way is to sort them according to size and then put them through a grain mill or grinder adjusted to crack the shells without crushing the meats. The seeds can be sorted for size by shaking them on ¼-inch mesh hardware cloth so that small seeds fall through. These seeds can be further sorted by putting two layers of ¼-inch mesh hardware cloth together, but slightly offset to make smaller holes. To crack the shells a grain mill must be adjusted so that the space between the plates is just slightly smaller than the size of the seeds. Some mills adjust more easily than others so it is necessary to experiment. For some sizes of seeds, a meat chopper with the coarsest chopping plate might work. This system will only work if the sunflower seeds are thoroughly dry, so that the shells crack easily.

Once the shells are cracked they can be removed by winnowing, or by floating them off with water. Shelled sunflower seeds do not winnow as easily as most grains and seeds, because the seeds and shells are too close in weight; if the breeze is not just right the seeds will blow away with the shells. To float off

---

Freezing
Shelled seeds Quality retained 1 year or longer.

SUNFLOWER SEED IDEAS
Sunflower Seeds Instead of Nuts
Use sunflower seeds in recipes instead of nuts. Since the seeds are small they can replace coarsely chopped nuts without any chopping. As sunflower seeds go further than most kinds of nuts less will be needed. When recipes call for ½ cup nuts, use 4 to 6 tablespoons sunflower seeds. For a nuttier taste, roast sunflower seeds for about 15 minutes in a moderate, 350°F oven, or shake them for 5 to 10 minutes in a hot, dry frying pan until lightly browned.

Snack Mixes
Mix sunflower seeds with raisins and other dried fruits, nuts, and coconut for snacking. When sunflower seeds

the shells, put seeds and shells in a large container and fill with water. Stir to loosen any seeds stuck to shells and then let sit about 5 minutes until the seeds settle. Pour off the shells and drain the seeds. If necessary, repeat the procedure. Then spread out the seeds to dry completely before storing them.

PRESSING SUNFLOWER SEEDS FOR OIL

Oil seed sunflowers yield considerably more oil than the eating varieties, but both can be pressed. Oil varieties can be ground, shells and all, in a meat grinder or other grinder, and then pressed. Eating varieties must be shelled first and then ground. Though a fruit or lard press will remove some oil, a heavier press is necessary to obtain oil in practical quantities and to avoid waste. If a small press is used, try cooking the leftover material to recover more oil and perhaps milk and flour as well. (Refer to COOKING NUTS FOR OIL, MILK, AND FLOUR, in the NUTS section.) Perhaps it will eventually be possible to buy the necessary equipment for small scale pressing.

Home pressed oil must be refrigerated for storage.

SUNFLOWER SEED RECIPES
Sunflower Seed Cakes

(MAKES 18–24 SMALL CAKES)

3 cups shelled sunflower seeds
2 teaspoons honey or maple syrup
2–4 tablespoons oil, for frying

6 tablespoons (about) flour or fine cornmeal

Put the seeds in a heavy saucepan with 3 cups of water, then simmer, covered, over low heat for 1 hour. If water remains, cook further, uncovered, to evaporate it. Grind the seeds, or press them through a food mill. Mix in the honey or maple syrup, and work in flour or cornmeal, a spoon at a time, for a stiff dough. Shape into thin, about 3-inch diameter cakes, and brown in oil on both sides. Very good with plain apple or apricot sauce for breakfast. Or sweeten the sauce, add powdered coriander seed or other spices, and have them for dessert.

Sunflower Seed Crackers

Add 1 tablespoon of oil to the dough, along with the honey or syrup. Roll out thinly on a floured board, and cut into square or

and peanuts are combined, the protein value is especially high.

Sunflower Seed Meal

Grind sunflower seeds to a meal with a blender or food chopper. (They are too oily for a grain mill.) Use in place of about ¼ of the flour in baked goods, or add to vegetable loaves, patties, and stews. The meal enriches baked goods, and thickens stews without overwhelming other ingredients' flavors.

Sunflower Peanut Butter

When making peanut butter, use 1 part sunflower seeds (roasted, if desired) to 3 parts peanuts. (Refer to ROASTING PEANUTS and MAKING PEANUT BUTTER, in the PEANUTS section.) The blend makes a pleasant change from plain peanut butter, and the protein value is increased.

rectangular crackers. Bake 10 to 15 minutes on an oiled baking sheet, in a hot, 375°F oven until lightly browned. If the crackers are not crisp, dry them in a very low oven or food dryer.

REFERENCES FOR SUNFLOWERS
Organic Gardening Magazine, April 1979.

Sweet Potatoes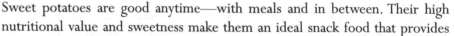

Sweet potatoes are good anytime—with meals and in between. Their high nutritional value and sweetness make them an ideal snack food that provides staying power. Sweet potatoes, native to Central and South America, once were the basic life-sustaining food for groups of American Indians. However, their worth is lost when they are candied in sugary syrups. It is hard to understand the compulsion to add quantities of sugar to a food that is naturally very sweet, especially when there are numerous and delicious ways to fix it.

Sweet potatoes grow as perennials in tropical climates, but they are easily cultivated as annuals in temperate regions with fairly long growing seasons. Sweet potato flesh ranges from creamy white and orange to a purplish color. Moist, orange fleshed sweet potatoes are often known as yams. True yams, however, are an entirely different tropical plant requiring a full 12 month growing season, and are seldom seen outside the tropics. Sweet potatoes are not related to white potatoes.

HANDLING SWEET POTATOES

Sweet potatoes can be dug at any time after they are big enough to eat, but their main harvest is in the fall. In the South they are dug when the leaves turn yellow, while further north they are dug at about the time of the first frost. They will deteriorate if left in the ground after it turns cold. Sweet potatoes must be dug carefully, because the skins are tender and likely to rot if damaged. Before they are stored, sweet potatoes must be cured to toughen the skins and heal slight scrapes.

SWEET POTATO STORAGE
Canning

Steam, or boil to half-cooked, about 20 min. Dunk in cold water, peel. If large, cut uniform pieces.

Dry Pack

While hot, press close together in jars without mashing, 1 in. headroom. Add nothing. Process 240°F, 11 pounds pressure. Pints: 1 hr. 5 min. Quarts: 1 hr. 35 min.

Wet Pack

Fill jars without pressing, add boiling water, 1 in. headroom. Process 240°F, 11 pounds pressure. Pints: 55 min. Quarts: 1 hr. 35 min. Refer to the CANNING section.

Cold Storage

See CURING AND STORING SWEET POTATOES, below.

Drying

Steam until cooked, 30–40 min. Peel, slice or shred, and dry until leathery or

Curing and Storing Sweet Potatoes

Sweet potatoes are cured by holding them between 80 and 85°F, and between 85 and 90% humidity, for 4 to 7 days. If cured longer than 7 days they will start to shrivel. Any warm place can be used for curing if they are loosely covered with plastic or another material to maintain humidity. After curing, store them where the temperature is between 55 and 60°F, with high humidity. If the temperature is too low the sweet potatoes will blacken and rot. A basement or spare room may be a good storage place. The sweet potatoes can be loosely covered to increase humidity, but they need circulating air and should not be sealed in.

Sweet potatoes will become sweeter during storage as their starch gradually turns to sugar. If well-cured and carefully stored, they may keep as long as 6 months, though 3 to 4 months is more common.

Preparing Sweet Potatoes

Raw sweet potatoes should never be peeled, as too many nutrients will be lost. The skins are thin and good to eat, so peeling is unnecessary. However, if desired, the peels can easily be removed after the sweet potatoes are cooked.

For slightly firm sweet potatoes, steam or bake them from 30 to 45 minutes, depending on size. With longer cooking they will become very soft and easy to mash.

Sweet potato tops can be cooked like spinach and eaten as greens.

SWEET POTATO RECIPES
Sweet Potatoes, Japanese Style

(MAKES 6–8 SNACK OR SMALL SIDE SERVINGS)

3–4 medium sweet potatoes, in
   1-inch chunks
1 cup (about) soup stock or water

1 tablespoon honey
2 teaspoons soy sauce
2 tablespoons sherry or
   white wine

Cook the sweet potato chunks in the soup stock or water until they are barely tender, about 10 minutes. Add honey, soy sauce, and sherry or white wine. Simmer, uncovered, until the liquid

brittle. Or slice raw, dry until hard, and grind to flour. Refer to the DRYING section.

Freezing
Cure (see above). Steam, boil, or bake until tender. Let cool at room temperature. Wrap individually, or peel. Slice as desired, and pack. Or mash (optional), add 1 tablespoon lemon or orange juice per pint to prevent darkening. Refer to the FREEZING section.

2–3 pounds fresh = 1 quart cooked

SWEET POTATO IDEAS
Sweet Potatoes Ahead

As there are so many ways to use cooked sweet potatoes, cook some extra when baking or steaming them for a meal. The extras can then be sliced or mashed for everything from salads to desserts. Use mashed sweet potato in recipes for puréed pumpkin, and use sliced, cooked sweet potatoes for frying or scalloping like white potatoes.

is reduced to a syrup and the sweet potatoes are soft, another 15 to 20 minutes. Taste and adjust seasonings, if necessary. An excellent snack and pick-me-up eaten warm or cold. Or serve them for dinner with rice and other Japanese or Chinese dishes.

Winter Squash, Japanese Style

Use a Japanese squash variety instead of sweet potatoes. This squash is thin skinned, and can be cut into cubes without peeling. The skins add a pleasant flavor to the dish.

Swiss Chard

SWISS CHARD STORAGE

Note: Often grown for a continual supply of fresh greens, rather than stored.

To store, handle like spinach. Refer to the SPINACH section.

SWISS CHARD IDEAS
Stir-fried Swiss Chard

Separate the stalks and thick midribs from the leafy greens, and cut them diagonally into about 1-inch pieces. Cut the greens into larger, irregular pieces. Heat oil or fat, then stir-fry the stalks for about 1 minute. Add several tablespoons of water or soup stock, cover, and let cook over medium heat about 5 minutes. Increase heat to high, uncover, and add the greens. Stir-fry about 2 minutes. Minced garlic and fresh ginger root can be included, if desired.

Swiss chard is good stir-fried in mixtures if the stalks and green parts are added separately. Meat goes especially well with it. Refer to the STIR-FRYING section.

Swiss chard is a gardener's delight. It is one of the few leafy greens that grows well over a long season, through both hot and cold weather. It seldom goes to seed, and no matter how often it is cut, it will soon grow a new set of leaves. One small planting of Swiss chard is enough to keep a family in greens for the entire gardening season. The catch may be that the cook is not as delighted with this constant supply as the gardener. When Swiss chard is merely cooked like any other green, the other greens are often preferred. The best recourse, then, is finding ways to make Swiss chard taste as good or better than other greens.

As Swiss chard has more body and does not cook down as much as most greens, it will hold its own better in mixed dishes. It is excellent combined with beans, grains, or meats. The thick stalks have a celery-like texture and are good prepared separately, while the leafy parts are very good in salads and other mixtures.

Swiss chard, also known simply as chard, is closely related to the beet, and rhubarb chard, a red-stalked variety, looks very beet-like. Cooked beet greens and Swiss chard cooked without its stalks are virtually indistinguishable, and are interchangeable in recipes.

HANDLING SWISS CHARD

Cut the outer leaves of growing Swiss chard without damaging the small inner leaves. Leaves can be harvested about once a week from an established plant, and it is best to harvest often to prevent the leaves from becoming coarse and overgrown. Chard's thick stalks and midribs take a little longer to cook than the green parts. When steaming or stewing, slice the stalks and put them in the bottom of the pot with green parts on top to give the stalks a little extra cooking time.

Tomatoes

Tomatoes are ideal for a first taste of food self-sufficiency. Most beginning gardeners are immediately successful growing them, and many home canners learn this skill by canning them. When fresh-from-the-garden tomatoes are eaten all summer and fall, and homegrown tomatoes are canned for the rest of the year, the bad old days of eating the expensive, lackluster store offerings quickly fade to nothing but an uneasy memory.

Botanically, the tomato is a fruit, but in practice it is a unique, much favored vegetable. Many gardeners grow several varieties at once for different purposes, including, perhaps, an early variety to extend the season, a large, sweet one for slicing, and a meaty Italian variety for sauce. Gardeners will enjoy especially good tomatoes if they raise their own seedlings, because then they can select the most flavorful varieties, rather than those bred to withstand mechanical harvesting and commercial storage conditions.

HANDLING TOMATOES

Tomatoes reach their peak in flavor and nutritional value when fully ripe, full colored, and still somewhat firm. If left until overripe, they become soft, and lose both flavor and acidity. Those that are picked green and ripened indoors never attain the flavor of vine-ripened fruits, but they are acceptable after frosts, when vine ripening is impossible.

TOMATO STORAGE
Canning
(See THE ACIDITY OF TOMATOES FOR CANNING, below.) Leave whole if small or medium. Halve if large.

Hot Pack only
To blanch, use about 4 cups boiling tomato juice, add 4–6 large halves, or more medium, or small tomatoes, return to boil, lift out with a slotted spoon or sieve. Optional: Slip off skins. Pack in jars. Blanch more tomatoes in same juice until jars filled. Add boiling cooking juice, ½ in. headroom. Process boiling water bath. Pints: 35 min. Quarts: 45 min. Refer to the CANNING section. Also see CANNING TOMATO SAUCE, PURÉE, OR JUICE, CANNING TOMATO PASTE, and TOMATO RECIPES FOR CANNING, below.

Cold Storage
If firm ripe, will keep refrigerated about 2 weeks. Refer to RIPENING GREEN TOMATOES, in the TOMATOES, GREEN section.

Though canning is the most popular way to preserve tomatoes, drying is almost as practical. The quality of cooked frozen tomatoes is equal to that of canned tomatoes, but the thawing time makes them less convenient. Raw, frozen tomatoes turn mushy when thawed, but some like them for color in salads. They taste best partly thawed.

PEELING TOMATOES

Peeling tomatoes is never a necessity, though it is sometimes preferred. Tomatoes eaten fresh are seldom peeled since skins are tender and flavorful. They are often peeled before canning to avoid curls of skin that separate during processing. An alternative to peeling before canning is to pick out bothersome curls of skin when the canned tomatoes are opened. There are differences of opinion about the flavor the peels contribute. If cooked with peels, tomatoes have a stronger, richer flavor. If cooked without, their flavor is sweeter and milder. Peeling is unnecessary when making sauce or juice, since peels are either strained out or puréed with the rest of the tomato, but some prefer the sweeter flavor of sauce made without peels.

Tomatoes are quick and easy to peel after they are scalded with boiling water. This loosens the skin enough to slip off almost in one piece. Dunk the tomatoes in boiling water 30 seconds, lift them out, and let them cool. Or dip them in cold water to cool more quickly. Dunk only a few at a time in a large pot of boiling water, so that the boiling hardly stops. Another method is to put the tomatoes in a container, pour boiling water over them, wait about a minute, and then drain them, before peeling.

DRYING TOMATOES

Both fresh tomatoes and tomato paste dry very well. Their flavor is excellent and they are convenient to use. (See DRYING TOMATO PASTE, below.)

Small-sized, fresh, ripe tomatoes are best for drying. Large tomatoes must be sliced, causing loss of juice. Long or pear-shaped tomatoes can be halved the long way and set on drying trays cut side up, which saves the juice. Peeling is not necessary. Small cherry tomatoes can be dried whole. Check their skins like those of firm berries (refer to the DRYING section) to make them dry faster, or they can be peeled completely, which is almost as easy. It takes several days to sun dry tomatoes, and

---

Drying
See DRYING TOMATOES, below.

Freezing
(Not as practical as canning or drying.) Pour cooled, stewed sauce, juice, or uncooked purée in containers.
Fresh, ripe (Will be soft to mushy when thawed.) Put wedges or slices on trays, freeze solid, then package.
Paste Pack in ice cube trays for convenient quantities. Unmold when solid and package. Refer to the FREEZING section.

1½ cups chopped fresh = 1 cup stewed or canned; 1 bushel fresh = 15–20 quarts canned

TOMATO IDEAS
Salad Stuffed Tomatoes
Cut off the tops of large, firm, ripe tomatoes, and scoop out the centers with a spoon. Stuff the shells with a hearty salad mixture such as tuna,

about 24 hours to dry them in an electric dryer. Opinions differ, but many believe that sun drying gives tomatoes a sweeter, more intense flavor.

Use dried tomatoes as a snack, like any dried fruit, or add them to soups, stews, and other cooked dishes. They can be soaked, and added with the soaking water, or they can be added to liquid mixtures without soaking if allowed to cook 30 minutes or longer.

THE ACIDITY OF TOMATOES FOR CANNING

Tomatoes can vary considerably in acidity, depending on their variety and their growing conditions or location. In some circumstances, modern varieties may be borderline for canning safely by the boiling water bath method. (Refer to REQUIREMENTS FOR CANNING HIGH- AND LOW-ACID FOODS, in the CANNING section.)

PRECAUTIONS FOR SAFE BOILING WATER BATH CANNING

- Avoid canning very low acid varieties, soft, overripe tomatoes with wrinkled skins, or those from dead vines. Tomatoes lose acidity as they ripen. Add lemon juice, or pure crystalline citric acid. The usual amounts per quart are 2 tablespoons lemon juice or ½ teaspoon citric acid. (Sour salt is another name for citric acid.)
- Can tomatoes by a hot pack method such as the one described in STORAGE at the beginning of this section, or make sauce or juice (see below). Cooking before canning concentrates flavor and acidity, and ensures a better pack. Add tomato juice if more liquid is needed. (Salt may be omitted, as it has no effect on the safety of the tomatoes.)
- Mixtures of tomatoes and other vegetables such as zucchini or okra must always be pressure processed for the time required by the other vegetable. (Exceptions are tested recipes for such mixtures as catsup which include vinegar, increasing acidity to a safe level. It is safe to include one basil leaf, one clove of garlic, or a small piece of hot pepper in the jar of canned tomatoes or tomato sauce, but larger quantities must not be added unless part of a tested recipe.)

egg, potato, or macaroni. These are delicious and attractive set on a bed of greens.

Broiled or Fried Tomato Slices
Cut tomatoes into ½- to ¾-inch slices, and sauté them in oil or butter. When done they are good seasoned with pepper, minced parsley, a sprinkle of lemon juice, and salt, if desired. Before frying, the slices can also be dipped in cornmeal, fine, dry bread crumbs, or flour.

Broiled Tomatoes with Cheese and Broccoli
Put thick slices of tomato on a baking sheet, and top with slices of cheese or a layer of grated cheese. Broil until the cheese is melted. Or broil this combination on toast. For a fancy broiled tomato treat, mix chopped, cooked broccoli, minced scallion or onion, and grated cheese, and spread

MAKING TOMATO SAUCE, PURÉE, OR JUICE

There are several different styles of tomato sauce and purée, and several different methods for making them. The choice will vary with personal preferences and intended uses. It may be practical to can more than one style for a greater variety of uses.

Crushed Tomato Sauce

Chop fresh, unpeeled tomatoes, or peel them first, and put them in the pot. Crush with a potato masher or any other tool to make plenty of juice. Heat to a boil, stirring often, then simmer, uncovered, until they are cooked through and thickened to taste. This may take from 15 minutes to an hour, or more.

Smooth Tomato Sauce or Purée

Italian or paste varieties of tomatoes make the thickest, most flavorful smooth sauce. The tomatoes can be cooked first and then put through a puréeing device, or they can be puréed while raw and then cooked. If the flavor of the peels is not especially wanted, it is easiest to purée them raw, as described below.

For the quickest way to prepare tomatoes for cooking before puréeing, wash and trim them as necessary, and then squeeze them by hand to break the skins to release their juice. Hold the tomatoes, one in each hand, over the cooking pot, squeeze, and drop them in. Children with clean hands are sure to enjoy helping with this chore. If squeezing is not appealing, the tomatoes can be quartered and dropped in the pot. Heat to a boil, stirring often, and cook uncovered, until the tomatoes are completely soft and juicy. Then put them through a sieve or strainer. A food mill works very well. For a thick sauce, cook the tomatoes down either before or after they are puréed, or strain off the thin juice to use in another way. However, the tomato flavor will be strongest if the sauce is thickened by cooking to evaporate extra moisture.

To make purée from raw tomatoes, a squeezing strainer will be the fastest way to remove peels and seeds before cooking. To avoid waste, put the peels and seeds through the strainer a second time to remove more of the pulp. Even so, there is likely to be a smaller yield of sauce with this method as compared to cooking

on the tomato slices before broiling. Other cheese-vegetable mixtures can also be tried.

Fresh Tomato Sauce

Mince fresh, very ripe tomatoes with seasoning vegetables and herbs, such as sweet peppers, scallions or onion, parsley, and basil. The texture when chopped by hand in a wooden bowl is excellent, but a blender can also be used. Serve with meat, fish, cooked vegetables, or pasta. Chill to serve with cold meats and salads.

For a Mexican style sauce mince the tomatoes with hot peppers, onion, and fresh coriander leaves. This goes with tacos, tostadas, egg dishes, and many meat, poultry, and fish dishes.

Whipped Tomato Cream

Fold smooth, thick tomato sauce into an equal amount of stiffly whipped

the tomatoes before puréeing. However, those who prefer a sweet, mild tomato sauce will find a squeezing strainer well worth the investment. Avoid buying one that is made of aluminum. The raw purée must be heated to a boil before it is canned. It is usually simmered uncovered to thicken it before canning.

Tomato Juice

Tomato juice can be made in any of the ways smooth sauce or purée are made, except that it is not cooked down to thicken it. It is actually not necessary to make canned tomato juice as a separate project, since the canned sauce or purée can be diluted when it is opened to make juice.

Canning Tomato Sauce, Purée, or Juice

(These should be plain full strength tomato without dilution of any sort.) Heat the sauce, purée, or juice to a full boil, stir to be sure it is evenly thick, and pour in hot canning jars leaving ½ inch headroom. Process juice and thin sauce or purée in a boiling water bath, both pints and quarts—15 minutes. Process thick sauce or purée in half-pint or pint jars only—30 minutes. (Refer to the CANNING section.)

MAKING TOMATO PASTE

The first step for making tomato paste is to make a smooth sauce or purée by one of the above methods. This is then thickened, either by cooking uncovered to evaporate more moisture, or by draining through a cloth to remove juice. If it is to be cooked, keep the tomato sauce or purée over low heat and stir it often to prevent sticking and burning. An insulating ring under the pot is a help. Cook the paste until it is as thick as mashed potatoes. It should have an intensely concentrated tomato flavor.

Either raw tomato purée or cooked sauce can be thickened by putting it in a cloth bag and hanging it to drain, or by draining it in a cloth-lined colander. Use the drained juice when canning whole tomatoes or add it to vegetable juice mixtures or cooked dishes. Tomato paste made in this way will be sweet and mild compared to the paste concentrated by cooking. If the paste is from raw tomatoes the flavor can be preserved by freezing it. Freeze it in ice cube trays, and then store the cubes in a freezer container, where they will be available in small quantities, as needed.

cream. Season with pepper and lemon juice. Use as salad dressing or as a dip for raw vegetables. It also adds a special touch to vegetable aspics, and cooked vegetable salads.

Home Canned Tomato Sauce Instead of Paste or Juice

It is not really necessary to can tomato purée in three thicknesses—thin for juice, medium for sauce, and thick for paste. Instead, dilute a medium sauce with water, vegetable juice, vegetable cooking water, or another liquid, such as the SAUERKRAUT-TOMATO JUICE, in the SAUERKRAUT section to make juice. A rich tomato sauce can replace tomato paste in most recipes, by adding twice or three times as much sauce as the called-for paste, and reducing the other liquids in the recipe proportionally.

Canning Tomato Paste

If the tomato paste was concentrated by cooking, spoon it hot into hot half-pint jars as soon as it is thick enough. If the paste was made by draining, heat it slowly, stirring often to keep it from sticking, then fill the jars, leaving ½ inch headroom. Process in a boiling water bath, in half-pint jars for 45 minutes. (Refer to the CANNING section.)

Drying Tomato Paste

Dry tomato paste like fruit leather. (Refer to DRYING FRUIT AND OTHER PURÉES, in the DRYING section.) Seasoning vegetables such as onion, garlic, celery, parsley, and other herbs can be cooked and puréed with the tomatoes to make the paste, but plain tomato paste will be more versatile. Tear or cut off pieces of tomato leather to add to soups, stews, or sauces, or roll the leather and slice small cross sections before storing it. The flavor is strong, so add sparingly. To reconstitute the leather as a paste, pour boiling water over it and let it sit about 30 minutes, until it softens.

TOMATO RECIPES FOR CANNING

This catsup is much more nutritious than its commercial counterparts, since it contains considerably less sugar and salt. In fact, it is excellent without any salt at all.

Thirteen Seasonings Tomato Catsup

(MAKES ABOUT 3 PINTS)

4 quarts tomatoes, chopped or squeezed
4 onions, chopped
1 sweet red pepper, chopped, optional
1 clove garlic, minced, optional
1 ½ teaspoons each whole cloves, allspice, and mace
1 small cinnamon stick
1 ½ teaspoons celery seed (or cook 1 stalk chopped celery with vegetables)
1 ½ teaspoons peppercorns
1–2 bay leaves
1 teaspoon mustard seed or ¼ teaspoon dry mustard
1 tablespoon paprika, optional
½ teaspoon cayenne pepper, optional
¼–½ cup honey or sugar
1 teaspoon salt, optional
1 cup (about) vinegar

Cook together the tomatoes, onion, sweet pepper, and garlic, uncovered, until they are all soft, from 30 to 40 minutes. Put through the finest screen of a food mill or another strainer for a smooth purée. (If using a blender the flavor will not be as good, because of the pulverized peels and seeds.) Return the purée to the cooking pot. Tie the whole spices, seeds, and bay leaves in a cloth bag and add them to the pot. (Powdered spices will darken the catsup's color.) Add dry mustard, paprika, and cayenne pepper, if desired. Stir in honey or sugar, and salt, if desired. Simmer, uncovered, over low heat until boiled down and thickened, stirring often to prevent sticking and burning. This may take 2 or more hours. Next, remove the spice bag and add the vinegar. Stir, taste, and adjust sweetener, vinegar, and any other seasonings. It should taste more piquant and less sweet than commercial catsups. (The flavor improves with age.)

Bring the catsup to a full boil, stir for even thickness, and pour in hot canning jars, ½ inch headroom. Process in a boiling water bath, for 10 minutes for both pints and quarts. (Refer to the CANNING section.)

Tomato Apple Catsup

Use 2 quarts apples and 2 quarts tomatoes instead of all tomatoes. The apples must be chopped, but peeling and coring are optional, if puréed through a sieve. Excellent, especially when the tomato supply is limited. The apple does not change the flavor drastically, but does add a pleasant fruitiness.

Chili Sauce

Chili sauce is made like catsup with a rougher texture, and a spicier, more intensely sweet and sour flavor. Chop the tomatoes small. They can be peeled to avoid curls of skin. Grind the onions and other vegetables. Sweet peppers can be increased to 2 or 3. Cook to a sauce without puréeing. Ginger and nutmeg can be used instead of cinnamon and mace. Increase hot red pepper to 1 tablespoon, or to taste, and, if desired, increase amounts of sweetener and vinegar.

Herbed Tomato Juice Cocktail

(MAKES ABOUT 3 QUARTS)

10 pounds firm, ripe tomatoes,
   chopped
8 whole cloves
2 bay leaves
½ teaspoon peppercorns or
   ground pepper
1 teaspoon dill seed, or 1 head
   dill

several sprigs parsley
sprig basil
sprig fresh marjoram or oregano,
   or 1 teaspoon dried
bunch chives, several scallions,
   or 1 small onion, chopped
1 tablespoon honey, or sugar
1 cup vinegar

Combine all ingredients, then cook, covered, 45 minutes, until the vegetables are soft. Purée through the fine screen of a food mill or another strainer. Taste and adjust seasonings, if desired.

Heat to a boil, stir for even thickness, and pour in hot canning jars, ½ inch headroom. Process in a boiling water bath for 10 minutes for both pints and quarts. (Refer to the CANNING section.)

Hot Tomato Bouillon

Heat tomato juice cocktail and pour it into bowls. Put a dab of butter in each bowl, and if desired, sprinkle with minced parsley. This makes a nice first course in cold weather.

Tomatoes, Green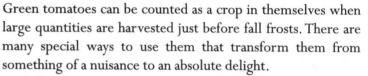

Green tomatoes can be counted as a crop in themselves when large quantities are harvested just before fall frosts. There are many special ways to use them that transform them from something of a nuisance to an absolute delight.

Not all green tomatoes taste alike. Full-sized, green tomatoes of the sweeter varieties are very good fried, stuffed, and added to mixed dishes. The less mature, more acidic green tomatoes taste too harsh to enjoy by themselves. They are best made into relishes, condiments, and other spicy mixtures. Green tomatoes ripened indoors attain full color and a reasonably good taste, but they can never match vine ripened quality.

Mexican green tomatoes, or tomatillos, are a different plant from regular tomatoes. They are grown in the southwestern United States and are used often in Mexican cooking. Seeds are available from some catalogs, and some specialty stores sell them canned.

HANDLING GREEN TOMATOES

After they have been picked green tomatoes should be sorted. Those beginning to change color can be set aside to ripen. The perfect, full-sized green fruits can be stored in a cool place, either to be used later in green tomato recipes or for slow ripen-

---

GREEN TOMATO STORAGE

Canning

See GREEN TOMATO RECIPES FOR CANNING, below.

Cold Storage

Keep in cool place 1–2 months. Also see RIPENING GREEN TOMATOES, below.

Drying

Possible, but harsh flavor allows few uses.

Freezing

Best for cooked mixtures. Refer to the FREEZING section.

GREEN TOMATO IDEAS
Green Tomatoes for Tartness

Add a chopped green tomato to stews, casseroles, and soups where a

ing. Small, misshapen, or very immature green tomatoes can be used in one of the canning recipes below.

RIPENING GREEN TOMATOES

Green tomatoes will usually ripen if they are picked after their skins have become glossy. Remove stems, then wash and dry them, if necessary. Tomatoes ripen fastest if kept at room temperature. Though they often are put on a window sill, they can sit anywhere. Spread them out in a single layer so that ripe ones show up readily and check them every day or two. Some people find that keeping them in brown paper bags speeds ripening.

To delay ripening so that some fresh tomatoes will be available over a longer period of time, store the green tomatoes in a cool place, ideally 55–58°F. If kept below 50°F for more than a few days, they may never ripen properly. Each tomato can be wrapped in newspaper, or packed in dry leaves, hay, or straw, but they keep about as well uncovered, and are much easier to check for signs of ripening or spoilage. Arrange them no deeper than two layers. Check once a week, and move those beginning to turn red to room temperature to finish ripening. Green tomatoes will keep from 4 to 8 weeks.

An easy way to store green tomatoes growing on small plants is to pull the whole plant, and hang it upside down in a cool place, such as a basement. Then pick the tomatoes as they ripen. Another way to extend the fresh tomato season is to devise protection for the tomato plants in the garden, using hay, straw, plastic, or another material. This allows the tomatoes to continue to ripen after early frosts.

GREEN TOMATO RECIPES FOR CANNING

Green Tomato Hot Sauce

(MAKES 8–9 HALF PINTS)

3 quarts green tomatoes, chopped small, or ground

1 quart ripe tomatoes, chopped small, or ground

1 onion, chopped, or ground

1–2 cloves garlic, pressed, optional

1 cup fresh, hot peppers, minced or ground, or ¼ cup hot pepper flakes

1 cup vinegar

1 teaspoon salt, optional

touch of tartness would be welcome. Green tomatoes go especially well in curries.

Green Tomato in Baked Goods

Use chopped green tomatoes in muffins, fruit breads, and other baking instead of berries or other fruits. Grated lemon or orange peel and spices such as cinnamon, ginger, and powdered coriander seeds complement the green tomato flavor.

Cornmeal Coated Green Tomato Slices

Select large, green tomatoes of a sweet variety, and slice them about ½ inch thick. Season the cornmeal with pepper, and salt, if desired, and dip the slices in it, coating them completely. Sauté in oil or fat until nicely browned on both sides. As an extra touch, put a crushed clove of garlic in

Combine all ingredients, and cook uncovered, stirring often, for about 20 minutes, or until thickened. Ladle into hot canning jars, ½ inch headroom, and process in a boiling water bath, for 10 minutes for both half pints and pints. (Refer to the CANNING section.) Serve with tacos and other Mexican foods, or as a hot, piquant sauce with other dishes.

Dilly Green Tomatoes

(MAKES 5 QUARTS)

5 cloves garlic
5 3- to 4-inch pieces celery stalk
5 small hot peppers, or pepper
   flakes, to taste
5 heads dill

5 quarts small, perfect green tomatoes
   (cherry tomatoes are excellent)
1 quart vinegar
2 quarts water
1 teaspoon salt, optional

Boil jars and lids in water to cover for 5 minutes.

Put garlic, celery, hot pepper, and dill in each jar. Fill with green tomatoes, leaving ½ inch headroom. Combine the vinegar, water, and salt, if desired, in a saucepan, heat, and boil 5 minutes. Pour boiling hot over the tomatoes, filling the jars almost to the brim. Seal immediately. (Because of the green tomato's high acidity, the ratio of vinegar to water is lower than usual for this pickling method, and the pickles keep exceptionally well. Refer to CANNING PICKLES, in the CANNING section.) Wait at least a month before opening. They will be a favorite with those who like their pickles strong.

Green Tomato Mincemeat

(MAKES ABOUT 6 PINTS)

4 quarts green tomatoes,
   chopped small
2 quarts cored apples,
   chopped small
1 pound raisins (about 3 cups)
   or other dried fruit
¼ cup lemon, orange, or other
   citrus peel, grated or minced

1 tablespoon cinnamon
¼ teaspoon allspice
¼ teaspoon cloves
1 cup molasses
1 cup vinegar, or ¾ cup
   vinegar and ¼ cup lemon
   juice

Combine all ingredients in a big pot, then cook, covered, about 1 hour. If the mixture is too thin, remove the lid for the last few

---

the oil or fat and stir it around once or twice, before adding the tomato slices.

Green Tomato Parmigiana

Sauté green tomato slices, as above, or dip them first in beaten egg, and then in cornmeal or flour. Set the sautéed slices next to each other in a shallow baking dish, or on a baking sheet. Spoon a well-seasoned tomato sauce over them, put a slice of mozzarella cheese on each, then sprinkle with Parmesan cheese. Bake 20 minutes at about 375°F, until hot and bubbly.

TURNIP STORAGE
Canning

Not recommended for roots. (Tend to discolor and become strongly flavored, except if fermented.) Refer to CANNING SAUERKRAUT, in the SAUERKRAUT section. *Greens* Can like spinach. Refer to the SPINACH section.

minutes of cooking. Ladle hot into hot jars, leaving ½ inch headroom, and process in a boiling water bath for 10 minutes, for both pints and quarts. (Refer to the CANNING section.)

Use this mincemeat like applesauce in dessert recipes or like regular mincemeat.

Turnips

Turnips are by reputation plain, unexciting, everyday fare, but their reputation does not do them justice. Turnips have been cultivated for centuries, during which time they have been food for livestock, for peasants, and the *pièce de résistance* on the tables of kings. They have often been boiled, but they have also been souffléed, gratinéed, stuffed with fruit, simmered in wine, and carved into elaborate shapes to grace fancy dishes. Today's turnip eaters are lucky, for this is a vegetable that is easy to grow and very productive, and it comes with a legacy of interesting recipes handed down through centuries of worldwide turnip eating.

Turnip greens are as good to eat as the roots, and some varieties are grown just for their greens. They taste like mustard greens and can be prepared in the same ways. (Refer to the MUSTARD GREENS AND SEEDS section.) To differentiate between turnips and rutabagas refer to the RUTABAGAS section.

HANDLING TURNIPS

Spring-planted turnips are best picked small, before the weather gets too hot, when they are crisp and mild enough to eat raw. The greens are also best when young. Turnips planted to mature in the fall can be left in the ground until after light frosts. If they are to be stored in a root cellar or outdoor pit, cut off the tops about an inch above the turnip. Do not wash them or trim the roots. Any turnips left in the root cellar in early spring can be re-planted for a very early crop of greens. Cut the greens before seed stalks develop. The tops that grow while the turnips are in storage are also good to eat.

Before cooking, trim and wash turnips, using a vegetable brush when necessary. They do not need peeling.

Cold Storage

Roots Plant to mature in fall. Pack in damp sand or other damp material. Keep 2–4 months in root cellar or similar conditions. Turnip odor affects fruit and penetrates living areas—outdoor storage preferred. Refer to the COLD STORAGE section. Also see KEEPING SAUERKRAUT IN COLD STORAGE, in the SAUERKRAUT section.

Drying

Roots Slice thinly, or shred. Optional: Steam to cook through. Dry to brittle or leathery. *Greens* Optional: Steam blanch 4–6 min. to wilt. Spread on trays with minimal overlap. Dry until crumbly. Refer to the DRYING section.

Freezing

Roots Dice or slice. Blanch in boiling water: 2 min. Steam: 2½ min. Or cook and mash. *Greens* Blanch in boiling water: 2 min. Refer to the FREEZING section.

Vegetables 🌿

The word vegetable is sometimes used to describe a person who leads "a monotonous, passive, or merely physical existence." Unfortunately, many vegetables intended for the table deserve the same description, though they should be one of the brightest, most enticing parts of a meal. It seems that monotonous vegetables are a North American tradition. Early American cookbooks, which are valuable sources of information on other subjects, usually recommend preparing fresh vegetables in ways that destroy flavor, texture, and nutritive value. Modern America carries on this tradition in another way. Agricultural and marketing techniques dictate the development of vegetable varieties suitable for machine cultivation and harvesting, for long distance shipping, and for long "shelf time" in grocery stores. Attributes such as tenderness, crispness, juiciness, and a sweet, delicate flavor have become either irrelevant or a hindrance. Because of this sad state of affairs, many people have never tasted really delicious vegetables, and cannot be blamed for not knowing the difference.

Anyone who doubts a difference in quality has only to taste an average store carrot, tomato, or cabbage, and then taste the same vegetable of a strain selected for its flavor, grown by organic methods, and picked fresh from the garden at its prime.

HOW TO GET FULL FLAVOR AND NUTRITIONAL VALUE FROM GARDEN VEGETABLES

- Depend, as much as possible, on vegetables that are fresh and in season. Plan the garden for an extended season, including early spring and late fall vegetables.
- Pick vegetables just before they are to be eaten. An empty refrigerator vegetable compartment, and a quick trip to the garden just before mealtime is a winning combination. If delay is unavoidable, refrigerate or keep vegetables in another cool, dark place in the interim.
- Do as little peeling, paring, and trimming as possible. Remove only tough parts, blemishes, or damaged areas. Many vitamins and minerals are in or just under the vegetable's skin. The skin also contributes valuable flavor.

VEGETABLE STORAGE
Canning
Refer to the CANNING section.

Cold Storage
Refer to the COLD STORAGE section.

Drying
Refer to the DRYING section.

Freezing
Refer to the FREEZING section.

VEGETABLE IDEAS
Uncommon Raw Vegetables and Dips
Most vegetables that are good raw taste good with dips. Some of the less common ones are kohlrabi sticks, cabbage leaves or other stiff leaved greens, asparagus spears, very thin beet slices, sugar snap peas, and snap beans of different colors. Some dips to try are the *Spanish Parsley Sauce,* in the PARSLEY section, the *Indonesian Peanut Sauce,* in the PEANUTS section, and the *Whipped Tomato Cream,* in the TOMATOES section.

- Never soak vegetables to clean them or to prevent discoloring. Wash in cool water, scrub with a brush if necessary, and rinse quickly. Use the vegetables immediately after rinsing to avoid discoloration, or sprinkle them with lemon juice, vinegar, or an ascorbic acid solution. Soaking removes water soluble vitamins, minerals, and natural sugars and flavors as well.
- Except for some kinds of blanching, do not cook vegetables in a large amount of water that is to be discarded. (Refer to BLANCHING VEGETABLES, in the FREEZING section.) Steaming, stir-frying, and simmering in a minimum of water are good cooking methods. (Refer to the STEAM COOKING and STIR-FRYING sections.) Use leftover cooking water in soups, or for the liquid in recipes.
- Avoid overcooking. Most vegetables taste best while still brightly colored and somewhat crisp or firm.

VEGETABLE JUICE

Raw vegetable juice is a popular health drink. It can be made with most kinds of vegetables, but a modern juice extractor will be needed for hard or tough vegetables. Carrot juice is best known, and some people drink a small glass every day. (Larger amounts have been known to turn a person's skin yellow.) An electric centrifugal juice extractor is expensive and only practical for making small quantities of fresh juice to drink immediately. It will make juice from raw apples, and grapes, but the amounts produced at one time are too small to be worth canning or freezing. There are less costly manually operated juice extractors, but they are still a fairly expensive tool if not used regularly. Moist, raw vegetables, like cucumbers, can be made into juice in the same ways as soft fruits. (Refer to FRESH FRUIT JUICE, in the FRUITS section.)

Another way to make juice using raw, firm vegetables is to chop them, and then to put them in a blender or food processor with water, vegetable cooking water, or another liquid, and purée them. Healthy mixtures sometimes called "green drinks" are made in this way, using green vegetables, herbs, and seasonings. One advantage of juice mixtures made from the whole vegetable is the inclusion of the fiber, which is known to be important for a healthy diet. For ideas for vegetable juice mixtures see CARROT DRINKS, in the CARROTS section.

The most common cold cooked vegetable juices are tomato and tomato vegetable blends (refer to TOMATO JUICE, in the TOMATOES section), but any thin puréed vegetable, flavored perhaps with lemon juice, can be chilled for a beverage. Hot cooked vegetable juice mixtures are most highly appreciated, but go by a different name—soup!

MAKING VEGETABLE SOUP

The quality of the vegetables used for making soups is very important. Poorly grown, or old, limp vegetables do not have enough flavor to give a good taste to their cooking water. However, clean vegetable trimmings and imperfectly shaped vegetables should certainly go in the soup pot, as long as they are fresh and homegrown for full flavor. European recipes calling for a carrot, a stalk of celery, and a sprig of parsley to flavor a whole big pot of soup, must be an enigma to anyone depending on American supermarket vegetables. Perhaps three or four times that quantity of depleted store vegetables will be needed to match their strength of flavor, and it will still not be as good. There is no way to replace missing natural sugars, aromatic oils, minerals, and vitamins. Regrettably the standard way to pep up the flavor is to add excess salt, MSG (monosodium glutamate), sugar, and artificial flavorings.

(Refer to individual vegetable sections for recipes.)

Vinegar

Vinegar can be as simple or as complicated as anyone wants to make it. Chemically it is nothing more than a dilute solution of acetic acid. White distilled vinegar, which is made from pure alcohol, is vinegar in its plainest form. Other common vinegars are cider vinegar made from apples, and wine vinegar from grape wine. Their distinctive flavors come from the fruit. Malt vinegar is made from malted barley. Many other kinds of fruits, grains, and even some starchy vegetables have been made into vinegar. In fact, any food that can be fermented to make alcohol can also be fermented to make vinegar. Homemade vinegar usually comes from fruit, because it is less complicated than making vinegar from grains or vegetables.

Since ancient times vinegar has been appreciated for its ability to preserve or pickle other foods, and raw vinegar has always been credited with medicinal value. It is certain also that

---

VINEGAR STORAGE

Note: If pasteurized, vinegar keeps indefinitely almost anywhere. See STORING HOMEMADE VINEGAR, below.

VINEGAR IDEAS

Vinegar as a Condiment

A small bottle of vinegar on the table is as good with many foods as catsup or mustard. It can also replace the salt shaker, and add flavor to vegetables, cooked grains, potatoes (especially French fried), and salads. Try it instead of lemon juice on fish or meat. Homemade vinegar, herb vinegar, and wine vinegar will contribute an extra special flavor.

raw, homemade apple cider vinegar tastes better than any standardized, pasteurized, store vinegar.

The usual home method for making vinegar is simply to set out a sweet, fruity liquid and wait for it to "turn." If the liquid is raw apple cider, containing no preservatives, success is almost guaranteed. Success with other fruit juices and liquids is less certain, but an understanding of the process will help to improve the odds.

MAKING VINEGAR FROM FRUIT

The fermentation of a sweet liquid into vinegar occurs in two stages. First the sugar is converted to alcohol by yeasts, and then the alcohol is converted to acetic acid by bacteria. When conditions are right, naturally occurring yeasts and bacteria do these jobs, but poor conditions can allow unfavorable organisms to interfere with the desired fermentation. The vinegar maker must see that conditions are right for the growth of the desirable yeasts and bacteria. Starters of yeast or acetic acid–producing bacteria can be added to assist the process.

The Alcoholic Fermentation

A sweet, fruity liquid set in a warm place should begin to ferment on its own. Look for a bubbling and foaming, with accompanying alcoholic smells and tastes. Fermentation will start within a day or two and continue for a week or more. Once enough alcohol has been produced, the change to acetic acid begins.

The liquid to be fermented may be fresh raw fruit juice, or juicy mashed fruits, or fruit trimmings and culls, with water added. If the fruit is not very sweet, add sugar, molasses, or another sweetener to give it a sweet, but not overly sweet, taste. Honey can also be used, but it must be pasteurized, because raw honey often contains unfavorable wild yeasts. To get fermentation off to a good start, a little baking yeast or wine yeast can be added. About ½ teaspoon dry yeast with 1 gallon of liquid is enough. To ferment cooked juice or fruit, a yeast starter will always be necessary, after which the process becomes the same as for making wine.

The ideal temperature for fermentation is between 80 and

Herb Vinegar Dressings and Marinades

Instead of plain vinegar, use herb vinegar in salad dressings and marinades for meats and vegetables. The herb flavors give extra zest wherever the vinegar is used.

Unplanned Fruit Vinegar

In hot weather, soft fruits like blackberries sometimes begin to ferment on their own, if they are left unrefrigerated after picking. If this should happen, take advantage of the situation by putting the fruit in a wide mouthed container, and let it turn to vinegar like the VINEGAR FROM MASHED FRUIT discussed below. With such a good start it is quite likely to succeed.

85°F, but it can also occur successfully at somewhat lower temperatures, or in a place where temperatures fluctuate. A warm room temperature is usually satisfactory. Temperatures rising too much above 90°F may kill yeasts and bacteria and stop fermentation.

Cover the vinegar container loosely, so that air can get in, and leave room for the liquid to rise while it ferments. If using mashed fruits or fruit trimmings, stir them once a day for the first few days. After fermentation is well started, strain out the solid material, and return the liquid to the container.

The Acetification

Acetic acid–producing bacteria are everywhere in the environment and will turn up when conditions are right—when enough alcohol has formed in a fermenting liquid for them to have something to work on. As they need air, use a wide mouthed container covered with a cloth to keep out dust and insects. They can work in a cool place, but their action will be slower, and it will take longer for the vinegar to form. The process may take from one month to several months, depending on circumstances.

As they work, the bacteria form a gelatinous surface layer on the vinegar which is called the "mother of vinegar." Push the "mother" aside to check on the progress of the vinegar, but do not stir it in. When acetification is complete, the mother of vinegar will sink to the bottom of the container. The vinegar may then be strained through cloth to remove the mother and any sediment that is present, and sealed in bottles. Any vinegar that already tastes good before the mother sinks is usable, but a new mother may form in it even after it has been strained and bottled.

The mother from one batch of vinegar can be added as a starter to a new batch that has just finished alcoholic fermentation, but a little raw vinegar makes a better starter, since the acid in it will give some protection against any unfavorable organisms that might interfere with the desired process. Never use pasteurized vinegar as a starter, since there are no live bacteria in it.

Mother of vinegar is quite harmless and can be eaten.

Cider Vinegar

Raw freshly pressed apple juice without preservatives will easily turn to a pleasant vinegar without special attention. Anyone who has tried to keep hard cider hard will know how easily this can happen. It is well worth letting a gallon or so of apple cider turn to vinegar every year, in order to enjoy the good flavor of the raw vinegar for salad dressings and as a condiment.

Though many directions advise leaving cider in a cool place to ferment, fermentation will be faster and the vinegar will also be excellent if it is kept in a warm place.

Wine Vinegar

Wine with an alcoholic content of 10% or more will not turn to vinegar and must first be diluted. (Too much alcohol will inactivate the acetic acid–producing bacteria.) As alcohol content increases up to 10%, however, the strength of the resulting vinegar also increases. Many homemade wines will turn to vinegar if left where air can reach them. However, commercial wines almost always contain additives that prevent them from turning. The quality of wine vinegar tends to vary considerably, but a good-flavored homemade wine is likely to make good vinegar.

The French and Italian wine vinegars with their superb flavors are homemade as an ongoing process in those countries, helped by the fact that untreated wine is routinely available. A permanent keg or jug is used, called a "vinaigrier" in France. It has a spigot at the bottom for drawing off vinegar, a place at the top for adding wine, and an opening for aeration. Vinegar-making begins with wine and a starter of wine vinegar. Once vinegar has formed, some is taken out regularly from the bottom of the keg, and more wine is regularly added to the top.

Sometimes sweet, fresh grape juice from ripe grapes will turn to vinegar as easily as apple cider, while at other times, the wrong kinds of organisms take over and results are poor. To guarantee success use pasteurized grape juice and proceed as for making wine.

Vinegar from Mashed Fruit, Fruit Trimmings, and Culls

Clean, fresh leftovers of many fruits, including apples, grapes, pears, peaches, plums, apricots, pineapples, and berries can be used for making vinegar. Or use the trimmings left from canning. Put the peels, cores, whole mashed or chopped fruit, juice, or a mixture of these into a container. The scraps must be fresh without traces of mold or other spoilage. Add water to cover all, unless there is plenty of natural juice. Usually sugar or another sweetener must be added, and a sprinkle of dry yeast is a good idea. If, after a day or so, fermentation has not begun, add a little more sweetening or yeast. (If worst should come to worst, and the mixture spoils rather than ferments, very little is lost, since the trimmings would have gone into the compost pile anyway.)

Stir the fruit mixture every day for the first few days. After 4 or 5 days, when it is fermenting freely, strain it to remove solids. They can be pressed or squeezed to obtain as much juice as possible. Then return the juice to the vinegar container to continue its fermentation.

STORING HOMEMADE VINEGAR

Homemade raw vinegar is less stable than pasteurized store vinegar, because a slight amount of bacterial activity may continue in it. Thin strands of mother of vinegar may form, or sediment may continue to settle. These in no way affect its quality. In fact, the flavor is likely to develop and improve during storage. If desired, strain the vinegar when it is to be used.

To minimize activity in the vinegar while it is stored, keep it in bottles filled as full as possible, leaving very little air space. A cool, dark storage place is best. After several months the vinegar can be strained through cloth, or carefully poured or siphoned out of the bottles, leaving sediment behind, and then re-bottled.

Raw vinegar can be heated to about 160°F to pasteurize and stabilize it, in the same way that milk is pasteurized, but its special flavor and possible health benefits will be lost.

THE ACIDITY OF HOMEMADE VINEGAR

Commercial vinegar is standardized at 4 to 5% acidity. Homemade vinegar may be either milder or stronger. This presents no problem for ordinary uses, because it can be added to taste. If it seems very strong or harsh it can be diluted with a little water before use. The uncertain acidity can be a problem, however, when making many kinds of pickles. Do not use homemade vinegar for pickling and canning vegetables or other low-acid foods, unless its acidity has been tested and found to be 4% or more (see below).

Some Pickling Uses for Homemade Vinegar

Besides the uncertainty of its acidity, homemade vinegar may present problems because of its tendency to cloud or discolor pickles, and because its flavor may not go well with some pickle flavors. There are, however, some kinds of pickles in which it will always taste good, such as pickled fruits. As long as the fruit is acidic enough for safe boiling water bath canning, there is no danger from lower than standard acidity vinegar. The flavor of homemade vinegar goes well with most fruits, and the color of the fruit is usually dark enough not to be affected by the color of the vinegar. Use homemade vinegar in *Spiced Pickled Fruit* (refer to the PICKLING section), and in fruit chutneys. Homemade vinegar can also be used to taste, for a quick pickled flavor, in pickled foods not intended for canning, such as meats marinated in vinegar.

Testing the Acidity of Homemade Vinegar

One way to test the acidity of vinegar is to use an acid testing kit for wine, sold in winemakers' supply stores and winemaking mail order catalogs. If the kit is not new it should be tested on standard vinegar to check for accuracy. The vinegar can be diluted with a measured amount of water before testing so as to use up the test kit less quickly. (Those who are familiar with titration can, perhaps, devise a test of this kind for themselves.)

VINEGAR RECIPES

Herb Vinegar

(MAKES 1–2 QUARTS)

1 handful fresh herbs, crushed, or 3 tablespoons (about) dried herbs (Basil and tarragon best fresh. Others fresh or dried. Try elderflowers or celery leaves.)

1–2 quarts vinegar (homemade cider vinegar or any mild-flavored vinegar)

Put the herbs in jars or another container, then warm the vinegar, pour it over them, and cover. Warm vinegar will more readily absorb the herb flavor. To retain the character of raw vinegar, warm it only slightly. Steep for about 3 weeks before using. The vinegar can be strained and rebottled, or attractive sprays of herbs can be left in the jar. Store in a cool dark place.

When an herb flavor is wanted right away, the herbs and vinegar can be heated just to a boil in a covered enamel or stainless steel pot, and left to cool. This vinegar can be used after several hours, but its flavor tends to be harsher than slowly steeped raw vinegar.

For ways to use herb vinegars, see VINEGAR IDEAS, above. To use vinegar as a way to preserve herbs, refer to the HERBS section.

Garlic Herb Vinegar

Partly crush one or more cloves of unpeeled garlic. Steep the garlic in the vinegar for 24 hours, then remove it. The garlic can be added with the herbs and fished out the next day, or it can be put in and removed before adding the herbs. Basil and garlic are a very good combination. Garlic can also be used alone.

Hay-time Molasses Switchel

(A REFRESHING BEVERAGE)

(MAKES 6—12 CUPS)

1 cup cider vinegar (preferably homemade or raw)

½ cup (about) molasses

½ cup (about) honey or brown sugar

1 teaspoon powdered ginger or
1 tablespoon grated ginger root

Mix ingredients with 1 to 2 quarts cold water. Taste and adjust flavors, as desired. This refreshing old-time drink was used for relieving thirst and giving energy to people cutting hay on a hot day.

WATERCRESS STORAGE

Live Storage

Keeps several weeks, or longer, with stems in water in a loose bouquet. (Often begins to grow.) Set in cool place inside, outside, or covered in the refrigerator. Change water every few days.

WATERCRESS IDEAS

Watercress Sandwiches

Plain watercress is good in bread and butter sandwiches, or try mincing it and mixing it with other ingredients for a special sandwich spread. It is sometimes mixed into cream cheese or softened butter, or included in hard-boiled egg mixtures to add a brisk, peppery flavor.

Watercress in Salad Dressings

Minced watercress adds a nice peppery flavor and green color to mayonnaise, oil and vinegar dressings, or yogurt dressings. For a smooth texture, make oil and vinegar watercress dressings in the blender.

Watercress

Watercress, with its delightfully peppery taste and crisp texture, is renowned as an herb, a salad green, and a green vegetable. There are several kinds of land cress with a similarly peppery taste, but their texture is more like other greens of the mustard family, to which cresses belong. (Refer to the MUSTARD (GREENS AND SEEDS) section.)

Wild watercress is widely distributed. It likes cool, shallow, slowly running water in a limestone region. It can often be started in springs and brooks where it does not already grow, or it can be grown as a garden crop if fresh, cold water can be provided daily.

HANDLING WATERCRESS

As watercress readily picks up pollutants, it must come from clean water, especially if it is to be eaten raw. Treatments with water purifying tablets have been suggested, but as a survival technique rather than a way to have a delicious salad.

Watercress is at its best during cool weather. Cut or pinch it off at water level to gather it, or trim off the bottoms later, when using it. The green stems as well as the leaves are good to eat, but the underwater stems and roots are tough. Watercress seeds are good sprouted. (Refer to the SPROUTS section.)

WATERCRESS RECIPES

Watercress Soup

(MAKES 10—12 MEDIUM BOWLS)

2—3 handfuls (about 1 pound)
   watercress
2 tablespoons butter
1 onion, chopped small
1 clove garlic, minced

2 medium potatoes, diced
1 ½ quarts chicken stock or
   other stock
pepper, salt, optional
1 ½ cups milk, buttermilk, or yogurt

Pick off a cup or so of watercress leaves and set them aside.
Heat the butter in a soup pot, then sauté the onion and garlic in
it over low heat until limp. Add the potatoes, and cook another
5 minutes or so, stirring. Add the stock and season with pepper
and salt, if desired, unless the stock is already seasoned. Bring
to a boil, then add the watercress, except for the reserved
leaves. Simmer, covered, until the potatoes are very soft, from
20 to 30 minutes. Then purée the soup in a blender or with a
food mill. Return it to the stove, add the milk, buttermilk, or
yogurt, and reheat without boiling. Add the reserved watercress leaves, and serve. Delicately flavored, and very attrac-
tively colored as well.

Watermelons

Watermelons have been in existence for so long that there is a
word for them in Sanskrit, and there are pictures of them in
early Egyptian works of art. They are well-named, since they are
as thirst quenching as a cool drink of water and as sweet to eat as
the very nicest of melons. Above all else, watermelons are a fruit
for eating fresh. Recipes for their use do not make sense unless
watermelons are so plentiful that they cannot all be eaten fresh.

HANDLING WATERMELONS

There are a great many ways to judge the ripeness of watermelons, but none seem to be foolproof. The novice can try several

Watercress Instead of Parsley
Sprigs of watercress can replace parsley as a garnish with many foods, including meats, molded salads, and
potato dishes. Watercress also does
well in most cooked recipes calling for
parsley, and since it is available early
in spring, before parsley can be grown,
it is very handy to use then.

WATERMELON STORAGE
Canning
Juice See WATERMELON SYRUP, be-
low. *Rind* Refer to SPICED PICKLED
FRUIT, in the PICKLING section.

Drying
Possible, if peeled, sliced, and seeded,
but less useful than other dried fruits.

Freezing
Cut 1 in. cubes or balls, seeds removed. Serve only partly thawed to
avoid mushiness. Refer to the FREEZ-
ING section.

WATERMELON IDEAS
Watermelon Wedges with Meals
Trim off rind, then cut watermelon
into small, easy to handle wedges, and

Watermelons

methods and pick the melon when all methods seem to indicate ripeness. With practice a sort of sixth sense develops, and then, regardless of which test is used, the chosen watermelon will be ripe. There is one catch, however: watermelons must ripen in hot weather. Those caught by cool weather will never become as sweet and juicy as they should.

TESTS FOR WATERMELON RIPENESS

- Knock on the melon with the knuckles. A hollow sound means it is ripe.
- Check the tendril nearest the melon. In most varieties it will die when the melon is ripe.
- Look at the underside of the melon. The light patch there will usually turn yellow and become slightly rough when ripe.
- Scratch the melon's skin with a fingernail. It becomes less tough and can be easily scraped when the melon is ripe.
- Cut a wedge-shaped plug out of the watermelon, and look or taste for ripeness. Replace the plug if underripe. (This has the obvious disadvantage of marring the fruit and making an entrance for ants.)

Watermelon will keep up to a week in the refrigerator after it is cut open if the exposed side is protected. The rinds and seeds are both edible, but it is difficult to find ways to use them. The white part of the rind can be made into pickles or preserves, but because considerable sweetening is required, only small amounts should be eaten. As a last resort, give them to chickens and other birds, who like the leftover rinds and seeds.

Watermelon Molasses or Syrup

To make an excellent natural sweetener from extra watermelons, cut off the rinds and white part, and make juice from the red flesh by crushing and pressing it, or by cooking and straining it. (Refer to MAKING FRUIT JUICE, in the FRUITS section.) Then boil the juice in an open kettle until it is concentrated to a syrup. It will look like molasses, and have a sweet, somewhat strong flavor. Towards the end of the boiling, watch closely and stir it often to prevent burning. Use instead of molasses or other kinds of syrup. To can, pour it boiling hot in hot jars and seal immediately. (Refer to OPEN KETTLE CANNING, in the CANNING section.)

---

put a plate of them on the table with a meal. They look nice on a bed of greens, and can take the place of a salad or a vegetable. A sprinkle of lemon or lime juice can be added for a sharper taste.

Watermelon Conserve

Dice or chop the white part of watermelon rind, or use parts with just a tinge of pink. Mix with chopped apple, thinly sliced, or chopped lemon or orange, with peel, and honey or sugar, for sweetening. Raisins and nuts can be included. To make the conserve, refer to *Fruit and Nut Conserves*, in the JAM AND JELLY section.

Watermelon Lotion

Collect the "water" when slicing a watermelon and use it as a face lotion. This is an old-time way to soothe the skin. It was also said to remove freckles, if applied often enough.

Watermelon Seeds

The meats inside watermelon seeds are as good to eat as the insides of pumpkin or squash seeds, but they are so difficult to shell that this is usually impractical. Reportedly, there are less hard, dried watermelon seeds of some Chinese varieties that can be eaten, shells and all. If using hard seeds, it is best to cook them in water for a short while to soften them before drying or roasting them. (Refer to PUMPKIN SEEDS, in the SQUASH, WINTER section.)

Some American Indian tribes used watermelon seeds to make a medicinal tea because it was thought to relieve high blood pressure and to expel worms.

WATERMELON RECIPES

Watermelon Cooler

(MAKES ABOUT 4–6 GLASSES)

3 pounds (about) watermelon, peeled, cut in chunks, seeded	1 tablespoon (about) honey
3–4 tablespoons yogurt	mint leaves, optional

Put the watermelon, yogurt, and honey in a blender and blend until smooth. The amounts of yogurt and honey can be adjusted to taste. Pour over ice cubes in a glass, and, if desired, add a mint leaf or sprig of mint. Pale pink and very refreshing.

Watermelon Popsicles

Freeze this mixture in popsicle molds. These popsicles can also be made from watermelon purée without the yogurt or honey.

Index of Recipes & Food Ideas

Apple Butter, 4
Apple Cider Butter, 6
Apple Desserts with Herb Seeds, 3
Apple Muffins, Pancakes, Baked
    Goodies, 2
Apple Slump, 3
Apple Tea and Apple Beer, 4
Apricot Chutney, 8
Apricot Nectar Milkshake, 7
Apricot Nectar Treats, 7
Apricot Nut Sauce, 8
Asparagus Instead of Bamboo
    Shoots,
    Stir-fried, 12
Asparagus Salads, 11
Asparagus Steamed with New
    Potatoes, 12

Baked Applesauce, 4
Baked Apricots, 7
Baked Asparagus, 12
Baked Beets, 20
Baked Cabbage, 30
Baked Corn-off-the-Cob, 77
Baked or Boiled Potatoes with
    Yogurt, 296
Baked Quince, 211
Baked Sprouts, 27
Barbecued Bean Bundles, 19
Basic Beans, 16
Bean Patties and Loaves, 15
Bean Porridge, 15
Beans with Noodles or Grains, 14
Bedfordshire Clanger, 254
Beer Nuts, 181
Beet and Horseradish Relish, 21
Blackberry Apple Combinations, 23
Blackberry or Strawberry Shrub,
    214
Black-eyed Peas, 14–15
Black-eyed Peas or Cowpeas,
    13
Blenderized Comfrey, 66
Blueberries with Breakfast Cereal,
    24
Blueberry Marmalade, 24
Boiled Chestnut Snacks, 54
Bouquet Garni, an Herb Bouquet,
    133
Brandied Grapes, 129
Broccoli in Salads, 25

Broccoli with Herbs, Roman Style,
    2
Broiled or Fried Tomato Slices, 269
Broiled Tomatoes with Cheese and
    Broccoli, 269
Brown Soybeans, 235
Bulghur Wheat, 165

Cabbage and Fish Salad, 29
Cabbage Instead of Lettuce, 29
Canned Corn Relish, Shaker Style,
    76
Canned Corn Relish, Yankee Style,
    78
Carrot Drinks, 45
Carrots, Celeriac, Chicory roots,
    Horseradish, Jerusalem
    Artichoke, Parsnips, Salsify, 62
Cauliflower Fried in Batter, 48
Cauliflower Greens, 47
Cauliflower Salads, 47
Celeriac in Soup Stock, 49
Celery and Carrots in Cider, 50
Celery Bread Crumb Stuffing, 50
Chestnuts and Corn, 55
Chestnut Stuffing, 54
Chinese Cabbage in Soup, 59
Chinese Mustard Sauce, 162
Chives, Scallions, Other Onion
    Greens, 134
Cider Butter Leather, 7
Cold Spinach and Yogurt, 241
Congee, 67
Cooked Cucumbers, 81
Cooking Beans Ahead, 13
Coriander, 144
Coriander (Chinese Parsley,
    Cilantro), 136
Cornmeal Coated Green Tomato
    Slices, 275
Cornmeal Layers for Casseroles, 69
Cornmeal to Replace Potatoes, 68
Corn Omelets, 76
Corn Peppers, 195
Corn with Nuts or Seeds, 70
Cranberries in Baking, 79
Cranberry Gravy, 79
Creamed Artichoke, Wild Thistle,
    or Cardoon Stalks, 10
Creamed Cabbage, 30
Creamed Chestnuts, 54

Creamed Collards, 64
Crispy Fried Kale, 153
Crushed Tomato Sauce, 270
Cucumber Pickles, 81
Cucumbers and Herbs, 80
Cucumber Soup, 81
Currant Juice, 83
Currants in Fruit Mixtures, 83

Dandelion and other Greens, 85
Dandelion and Pasta, 85
Dandelion Beet Salad, 85
Dandelion Blossom Punch, 86
Dilly Green Tomatoes, 276
Dried Blueberries in Meat Stews,
    24
Dried, Chopped Vegetable Soup
    Combinations, 97
Dried Elderberry Chutney, 102
Dried Figs in Fruit Juice, 104
Dried Vegetable Pickles, 199
Drying Chestnuts, 53

Eggplant Cakes, 100
Eggplant Dip, 101
Elderflower Face Cream, 102
Essene Bread, 247
Extra Special Cranberry Sauce, 79

Fats and Oils for Stir-frying, 258
Fennel, 136
Fenugreek, 145
Fines Herbes or Herb Seasoning for
    the Table, 134
Finnish Rutabaga Pudding, 220
Flavored Vinegar from Pickling, 199
Flax Seeds, 230
Fresh Beans with Nuts, 18
Fresh Currants in Baked Goods, 83
Fresh Elderberry Chutney, 102
Fresh Herbs with Meals, 131
Fried Artichokes, 10
Fried Cornmeal Slices, 69
Frosted Grape Clusters, 129
Frozen Horseradish Cream, 142
Frozen Persimmon Desserts, 197
Fruit Chutney, 9
Fruit Jelly with Honey, 149
Fruit Tempura, 120

Garlic Herb Vinegar, 285
Garlic Purée, 123
Gooseberry Chutney, 125

Index

292

Grapes in Salads, 128
Grated Jerusalem Artichoke in
    Soup or Salad, 152
Grated Summer Squash, 250
Green and Wax Beans in Salads, 18
Green Drink, 140
Green Soybean Snack, 245
Green Soybean Succotash, 237
Green Tomato Hot Sauce, 275
Green Tomato in Baked Goods, 275
Green Tomato Mincemeat, 276
Green Tomato Parmigiana, 276

Hair Setting Liquid, 189
Hamantaschen, or Three Cornered
    Hats, 233
Hasty Pudding, 70
Hay-time Molasses Switchel, 286
Herbed Scrambled Eggs, 132
Herbed Tomato Juice Cocktail, 273
Herb Teas, 139
Herb Tossed Spaghetti Squash, 253
Herb Vinegar, 285
Herb Vinegar Dressing and
    Marinades, 281
Hominy and Beans Stew, 70
Hominy Grits, 70
Horseradish, 142
Hot Beans with Raw Vegetables, 14
Hot Pepper Pickle, 192
Hot Peppers and Cheese, 191
Hot Tomato Bouillon, 274
Hummus (Chick Pea Tahini Dip),
    Middle Eastern Style, 233

Iced Herb Tea, 140
Indonesian Peanut Sauce, 182

Jelly Melt Cereal, 147
Jerusalem Artichoke Pickles, 152
Jerusalem Artichoke Salad, 152
Jim's Mother's Chestnut Butter, 55

Korean Chestnut Balls, 56

Last Minute Jam, 147
Leek Salads, 155
Leftover Cauliflower, Baked, 47
Leftover Potato Patties, 207

Maple Fruit Preserves, 150
Maple Nuts, 167
Marinated Salad Radishes, 212
Mashed Carrots, 46
Mashed Eggplant, 100
Mashed Potato Crust, 208
Mashed Salsify, 222

Melon Appetizers, 158
Melon Mixers, 158
Melon Seed Drink, 158
Mix 'n Match Greens or Fruits, 289
Mock Oyster Chowder, 222
Mulberry-Ade, 159
Mulled Fruit Juice, 113
Mushroom Catsup, 161
Mushroom Extract, 160
Mustard, 162
"Must"-ard, 163
Mustard Greens Patties, 162

Nasturtium, 137
Neep Purry, 220
North Woods Doughboys, 73
Nut Butter, 169
Nut Meal Vegetable Topping, 167
Nut Milk, 170
Nut Shakes, 166
Nut Soup, 166

Okra Stuffed Tomatoes, 172
Old-Time Hot Borscht, 21
Onions Roasted Over Coals, 175
Onions Stewed in Fruit Juice, 174
Out-of-this-World Pumpkin Pie,
    253
Oven Browned Potatoes, 206

Parsley Bouquet, 176
Parsley Tea, 176
Patty-cake Squash, 248
Peach Skin Juice, 179
Peanut Accompaniment, 180
Peanuts in Salads, 181
Peas' Special Greenness, 187
Peas with Herbs, 186
Pectin Syrup, 189
Pectin with Fruit Juice, 188
Peppers in Sherry, 191
Pickled Artichoke Hearts, Middle
    Eastern Style, 10
Pickled Cauliflower Stalks, 47
Pickled Grapes, 127
Pickled Kohlrabi Sticks, 48
Pickle Liquid Salad Dressings, 198
Pickle Liquid Sauce, 198
Pickling Walnuts or Butternuts, 171
Piquant Pear Relish, 184
Plum and Wine Gelatin, 204
Plum Soup, 204
Polenta, 68
Polish Style Beets for Roast Meats,
    22

Poor Man's Asparagus, 155
Poppy Seed Filling, 232
Pot Likker, 163
Prepared Mustard, 163
Prepared Mustard from Seeds, 163
Preserving Grape Leaves in Salt,
    130
Preserving Herbs in Vinegar or Oil,
    133
Prune Bits Instead of Raisins, 205

Quick Canned Grape Juice, 129
Quick Potato Salad, 208
Quince Compote, 211

Raisin Stuffed Rosehips, 218
Raspberry Juice Blends, 214
Raspberry Marmalade, 25
Raspberry Orange Sauce, 214
Raspberry Shrub, 214
Raw Beets in Salads, 21
Raw Cranberry Relish, 79
Relish and Chutney, 198
Rhubarb Chutney, 125
Roasted Nuts, 165
Roasting Peanuts, 181
Root Vegetables, (see individual
    vegetables) 61, 96, 108
Rose Beverages, 219
Rose Custard, 218
Rosehip Applesauce, 218
Rose Petal Syrup, 219
Rose Vinegar or Brandy, 218
Rutabaga in Salads, 219–220

Salad Stuffed Tomatoes, 268
Sautéed Apricots, 8
Sautéed Kohlrabi, 154
Sautéed Rutabaga Slices, 220
Sautéed Winter Squash or
    Pumpkin, 253
Savory, 138
Scarlet or White Runner Beans,
    14
Seasoned Nuts and Grains, 165
Seasoning Potatoes for Mashing,
    207
Seasonings for Baked Chunks, 252
Seasonings for Stir-fried Dishes,
    258
Seaweed Salads, 226
Seaweed Soup, 228
Seediness in Blackberries, 23
Sloke Jelly, 228
Sloke Sauce, 229

Small Eggplant, Roasted Whole, 100

Small Whole Peaches, Sekel Pears, or other Small Pears, 202

Smooth Tomato Sauce or Purée, 270

Snack Mixes, 262

Snap Beans as Dried Beans, 18

Sour Fruit Cooked in Pectin, 189

Soybean Patties, 240

Soybean Sprouts, 234

Spaghetti Squash, 252

Spanish Parsley Sauce, 177

Spiced Fruit Pickle Beverages, 198

Spiced Pickled Cabbage for Canning, 30

Spiced Pickled Fruit, 202

Spicy Stir-fried Dandelion Greens, 86

Squash Blossoms, 248

Squash Cornmeal Mush, 254

Squeezed Lettuce Salad, 156

Steamed Fingerling Squash, 249

Steamed Snap Pea Salad, 186

Stewed Garlic Seed Stalks, 123

Stir-fried Cabbage, 29

Stir-fried Summer Squash, 250

Stir-fried Swiss Chard, 266

Strawberry Butter, 261

Stuffings for Sweet Peppers, 195

Succotash, 19

Sunflower Mustard Butter, 164

Sunflower Peanut Butter, 263

Sunflower Seed Cakes, 263

Sunflower Seed Crackers, 263

Sunflower Seed Meal, 263

Sunflower Seeds Instead of Nuts, 262

Super Sweet Corn in Desserts, 77

Sweet Potatoes Ahead, 265

Sweet Potatoes, Japanese Style, 265

Sweet Potato Pie, 254

Tempeh, 236

Thirteen Seasonings Tomato Catsup, 272

Toasted Seaweed Garnish, 228

Tofu, 236

Tomato Juice, 271

Tomato Succotash, 19

Tomato Apple Catsup, 273

Tortilla Chips, 73

Tortilla Dough, 72

Uncommon Raw Vegetables and Dips, 278

Uncooked Jam and Jelly, 149

Vegetable Tempura, 120

Vinegar as a Condiment, 280

Vinegared Cucumbers, 81

Walnuts, 165, 166, 167,

Watercress in Salad Dressings, 286

Watercress Instead of Parsley, 287

Watercress Sandwiches, 286

Watercress Soup, 287

Watermelon Conserve, 288

Watermelon Cooler, 289

Watermelon Lotion, 288

Watermelon Popsicles, 289

Watermelon Seeds, 289

Watermelon Wedges with Meals, 287

Winter Squash and Pumpkin Purée, 253

Winter Squash for Summer, 254

Winter Squash, Japanese Style, 266

Yellow Squash and Onions, 249

Zucchini Dill Pickles, 250

Zucchini Tomato Bake, 250

Index

293

Subject Index

Acidity of food when canning, 7, 31, 42, 101, 119, 216, 269
Acorns, 165, 166, 167
Agar agar, 227
Alfalfa leaves, 139
  seeds, 229, 242, 245
  sprouting, 220, 242, 244
Almonds, 8, 51, 58, 165, 232
Altitude, high, canning at, 33–34, 37, 38
Aluminum pots, 71, 201
Amaranth seeds, 230
Anise seeds, 136, 143, 144
APPLES, 1–7
  baked, 1
  butter, 4
  ciders, 4–5
  cores and peels, 6
  crabapples, 2
  syrup, 5
APRICOTS, 7–9
  pits, 8
ARTICHOKES, 9–10
Arugula, 162
Ascorbic acid, 43, 111, 184
Ashes, hardwood, for hominy, 70, 71, 74
ASPARAGUS, 11–12
Aubergine. *See* EGGPLANT
Avocado, 112–13

Basil, 14, 18, 46, 81, 109, 132, 133, 134, 186
Bay leaves, 134
Bayberry, 134–35
BEANS, DRY, 12–16; BEANS, FRESH, 17–19
  fresh shelled, 18–19
  green, 17–18
  sprouts, 246
  varieties, 13–14
  See also PEANUTS; SOYBEANS
Beech nuts, 165
BEETS, 19–22
Belgian endive, 56, 58
Berries, wild. *See* BLACKBERRIES; BLUEBERRIES; CURRANTS; ELDERBERRIES; GOOSEBERRIES; MULBERRIES; RASPBERRIES; STRAWBERRIES
Bicarbonate of soda, 228

BLACKBERRIES, 22–23
  seediness, 23
Black caps, 213
Black-eyed peas, 13, 14–15, 19, 185
Black walnuts, 165, 167
Blanching vegetables, 108
BLUEBERRIES, 23–25
Boiling water bath canning, 36–37
Borage, 135
Borscht, 21
Botulism, preventing in canning, 32–33
BOYSENBERRIES, 22
Broad beans, 13
BROCCOLI, 25–26
  de-bugging, 26
BRUSSELS SPROUTS, 26–27
Bulghur wheat,
Burdock roots, 141
Butternuts (white walnuts), 166
  pickling, 171

CABBAGE, 27–30
  preventing digestive upsets, 29–30
  winter, 28–29
Camomile, 135
CANNING, 31–44
  boiling water bath, 36–37
  and botulism poisoning, 32–33
  cautions, 41, 44
  cold water, 63
  containers, 34–36
  fruits, 42–43, 119
  high altitude, 33–34, 37, 38
  high- and low-acid foods, 31
  liquids for, 42
  open kettle, 38
  pickles, 43
  pressure, 38–39
  steps for, 39–41
  vegetables, 43–44, 225
Cantaloupe. *See* MELONS
Caponata, 99
Caraway seeds, 143, 144
Cardoon, 9
Carrageen, 227
CARROTS, 45
  drinks, 45
Cashews, 166

Catsup, mushroom, 161
  tomato, 272–73
CAULIFLOWER, 46–47
Cayenne, 191
CELERIAC, 48–49
  leaves, 135
  seeds, 144
CELERY, 49–50
  leaves, 135
  root. *See* CELERIAC
  seeds, 143
Chard. *See* SWISS CHARD
CHERRIES, 50–52, 203
  pitting, 51
Chervil, 135
CHESTNUTS, 52–56
  flour, 54
  peeling, 53
  purée, 55
  roast, 54
Chia seeds, 230
  sprouting, 245
Chick peas, 13
CHICORY, 56–58
  bitterness in, 58
  roots, roasting, 56
  winter forcing, 56
Chili, peppers, 191, 195, 196
  powder, 192, 196
  sauce, 273
CHINESE CABBAGE, 58–89
Chinquapins, 166
Chives, 135–36
Chutney, 198–99
Cider,
  apple, 4–5
  syrup, 5
Citron, 113
  pickled, 113
Citrus fruits, 113
  candied peel, 113
  dried peel, 113–14
COLD STORAGE, 59–64
  apples, 2–3
  cabbage, 28–29
  in crocks, 64
  factors affecting, 60–61
  fruits, 62–63
  root cellar for, 60
  vegetables, 61–63

Cold water canning, 63
COLLARDS, 64—65
COMFREY, 65—66
Conserves, 148—49, 150
Coriander leaves, 136; seeds, 144—45
CORN, DRY, 66—74; CORN, SWEET, 74—78
  cobs, 76—77
  cream style, 75
  flour, 69
  hominy, 70—72
  husks, 70
  meal, 68
  mush, 67
  nutritional value of, 67—68
  parched, 69
  popcorn, 69—70
  shelling, 68
  starch, 69
  tortillas, 72—73
  whole kernel, 74
Cowpeas, 13
Crabapples, 2
CRANBERRIES, 78—79
  cold water canning, 63
Crocks, cold storage in, 64
CUCUMBERS, 80—82; pickles, 81, 203
CURRANTS, 82—84

Damson plums, 203
DANDELIONS, 84—86
  blossoms, 85
  greens, 85
  roots, 86
Dehydration. *See* DRYING FOODS
Dill leaves, 136
  seeds, 143, 145
Dryers, electric, 91; solar, 90
DRYING FOODS, 87—99
  figs, 103
  fruit leather, 7, 92—93
  fruits, 2, 92—95
  indoor, 90
  outdoor, 89
  potatoes, 208
  prunes, 204—5
  raisins, 129
  soup vegetables, 97—98
  steps, 91
  storage, 98
  tomatoes, 268—69

  trays, 89
  vegetables, 95—97
Dulse, 227

EGGPLANT, 99—101
  bitterness, 100—101
ELDERBERRIES, 101—2
Elderflowers. *See* ELDERBERRIES
Elephant garlic, 121
Endive, 56
Escarole, 56

Fennel, 136, 143
Fenugreek, 145; sprouts, 245
FIGS, 103—4
Filberts, 166
Flax seeds, sprouting, 245
FREEZING FOODS, 104—12
  cautions, 111—12
  to concentrate juice, 107—8
  fruit juice, 110
  fruits, 2, 110, 119
  vegetables, 108—10
French beans, 14
FRUITS, 113—21
  canning, 42—43, 119
  combining sweet and tart, 116
  drying, 2, 7—8, 92—95
  freezing, 2, 110
  insecticides in, 115
  juice, 116—19
  leather, 7, 92—93
  sauce, 116—19
  semi-tropical, 112

Garbanzo beans, 13
Garden rocket, 162
GARLIC, 121—24
  braiding, 121
  press, 122
Gobo, 141
Goobers, 180
GOOSEBERRIES, 124—25
  cold water canning, 63
Grapefruit, 113
GRAPES, 126—30
  juice, 127—29
  leaves, 130
  raisins from, 129
  seedy, 127
Green beans. *See* BEANS, FRESH
Green tomatoes. *See* TOMATOES, GREEN
Greens, canning, 44
  drying, 97

  freezing, 107
  See also COLLARDS; COMFREY; DANDELIONS; KALE; LETTUCE; MUSTARD; SPINACH; etc
Grits, hominy, 70, 72
Hazelnuts, 166
HERB ROOTS, 140—42
HERB SEEDS, 143—45
HERBS, 131—40
  bouquet, 133
  drying, 132
  freezing, 133
  garden, 134—38
  tea, 139—40
  vinegar, 285
Hickory nuts, 166
Hominy, 70
Honeydews. *See* MELONS
Horseradish, 142
Huckleberries, 24; *See also* BLUEBERRIES

Irish moss, 227

Jalapeños. *See* PEPPERS, HOT
JAM (AND JELLY), 146—50
  uncooked, 149
Jelled liquids. *See* JAM AND JELLY; PECTIN
JELLY (JAM AND), 146—50
JERUSALEM ARTICHOKES, 150—52
  cold storage, 151
Juice, apple, 4
  fruit, 117—19
  grape, 127—29
  vegetable, 279
Juniper berries, 143, 145

KALE, 153
Kelp, 228
Ketchup. *See* Catsup
Kidney beans, 14
Kiwi, 114
Knob celery. *See* CELERIAC
KOHLRABI, 48, 153—54

Laver, 227—28
LEEKS, 154—55
  Chinese, 121
Lemons, 113
  cold water canning, 63
Lentils, 14
  sprouts, 245

Index

296

LETTUCE, 156–57
  crisping, 157
Lima beans, 14
Limes, 113
  cold water canning,
Lingonberries, 22
Loganberries, 22
Lovage leaves, 135
  seeds, 144

Marjoram, 137
Marmalade, 148–49
Masa, 73
MELONS, 157–58, 203
  seeds, 158
Mint, 137
Miso, 234
Moussaka, 99
MULBERRIES, 159
Mung beans, 14
MUSHROOMS, 160–61
  wild, 161
Muskmelons, See MELONS
MUSTARD (GREENS AND SEEDS),
  162–64
  greens, 162
  prepared, 163
  seeds, 143, 163
  sprouts, 245

Nasturtiums, 137
Nectarines, See PEACHES
NUTS, 164–71
  butter, 169–70
  cracking, 169
  North American, 165–67
  pickling, 171

Oils, nut, 170
  sunflower seed, 263
OKRA, 171–72
Olives, 114–15
ONIONS, 172–76
  drying, 174–75
  for food coloring,
  fumes from, 175–76
  juice, 176
  varieties, 173
Open kettle canning, 38
Oranges, 113
Oregano, 137
Oyster plant. See SALSIFY

Paprika, 195–96
PARSLEY, 176–77

PARSNIPS, 177–78
PEACHES, 178–80
PEANUTS, 180–83
  butter, 181–82
  roasting, 181
PEARS, 183–84
PEAS, 185–87
  flour, 187
  varieties, 185
Pecans, 166
PECTIN, 5, 8, 187–90
  content in fruit, 188–89
  low methoxyl, 188
  making, 189–90
  testing for, 190
PEPPERS, HOT, 190–93; PEPPERS,
  SWEET, 193–96
  chili, 191, 195, 196
  paprika, 195–96
  pimiento, 194–95
PERSIMMONS, 196–97
Pickles, canning, 43
PICKLING, 197–203
  additives, 200, 201
  fermented, 199
  nutritional value, 198
  relish, 198–99
  safety, 201
  utensils, 201
  vinegar and, 198, 199–200
Pimientos, 194–95
Pine nuts, 167
Pistachios, 167
PLUMS, 203–4
  damson, 203
  prune, 203
  pudding, 203
  wild, 63
Polenta, 68
Pomegranates, 115
Popcorn, 69–70
Poppy seeds, 230–31
POTATOES, 205–9
  drying, 208
  nutrients, 205, 209
  starch, making, 208–9
  sweet. See SWEET POTATOES
Preserves, 148–49, 150
Pressure canning, 38–39
  cooking, 255
Prune plums, 203
Prunes, 204–5

PUMPKINS, 250–54
  seeds, 252
QUINCES, 210–11

RADISHES, 211–13
  hot, 212
  sprouts, 245
Raisins, 129
RASPBERRIES, 25, 213–14
Ratatouille, 99
RHUBARB, 214–16
  chard, 215
  cold water canning, 63
Rocket, garden, 162
Rosemary, 138
Roses, 216–19
  hips, 216, 218
  water, 217
Runner beans, 14
RUTABAGAS, 219–20

Sage, 138
SALSIFY, 220–22
SAUERKRAUT, 222–26
  vegetables for, 223
Savory, 138
Scallions, 135, 173
Scarlet beans, 14
SEAWEED, 226–29
  varieties, 227–28
SEEDS, 229–33
  alfalfa, 229–30
  amaranth, 230
  as cereals, 230
  beans, 246
  chia, 230
  flax, 230
  grains, 246
  harvesting, 231–32
  poppy, 230–31
  sesame, 231
  sunflower, 262–63
  See also HERB SEEDS; SPROUTS;
    SQUASH, WINTER
Sesame seeds, 231
Shallots, 231
Solar dryers, 90
SOYBEANS, 233–40
  milk, 238, 237
  preparations, 239
  sauce, 236
  tofu, 236–37, 238–39
  See also SPROUTS

Soy sauce. *See* SOYBEANS
Spaghetti squash, 253
Spices. *See* HERB SEEDS
SPINACH, 240–42; oxalic acid in,
     241
SPROUTS, 242–47
     containers for, 242, 243–44
     making, 244–45
     seeds for, 245–46
     trays for, 244
SQUASH, SUMMER, 248–50;
     SQUASH, WINTER, 250–54
     blossoms, 248–49
     pumpkin, 250, 251, 253
     seeds, 252
Starch, corn, 69; potato, 208–9
STEAM COOKING, 254–56
     arrangements, 255
     pressure, 255
     safety, 256
STIR-FRYING, 257–60
     steps, 259–60
     wok, 257–58

STRAWBERRIES, 260–61
String beans. *See* BEANS, FRESH
Succotash, 19
SUNFLOWERS, 261–63
     oil, 263
     shelling seeds, 262–63
     sprouts, 246–47
SWEET POTATOES, 264–66
SWISS CHARD, 215, 266–67
Syrup, cider, 5

Tamari. *See* Soy sauce
Tarragon, 138
Tempeh, 236
Tempura, 120
Thistles, 9
Thyme, 138
TOMATOES, 267–74; TOMATOES,
     GREEN, 274–76
     acidity, 269
     juice, 271
     paste, 271–72
     sauce, 270
Turnip rooted celery. *See* CELERIAC

TURNIPS, 277

VEGETABLES, 278–80
     blanching, 108
     canning, 43–44, 225
     cold storage of, 61–63
     drying, 95–97
     freezing, 108–10
     juice, 279–80
     nutritional value of, 278
     soup, 280
VINEGAR, 280–86
     acidity, 282, 284, 285
     varieties, 282–84

Walnuts, 167
WATERCRESS, 286–87
WATERMELONS, 203, 287–89
     seeds, 289
     syrup, 288
Witloof chicory, 58
Woks, 257–58

Yams, *See* SWEET POTATOES

Zucchini. *See* SQUASH, SUMMER

Index

297

Index

298

recipes, ooo
WATERMELONS, ooo
recipes, ooo
seeds, ooo
syrup, ooo
Water quality, ooo
WILD FOODS, ooo
plants, ooo
recipes, ooo
Witloof chicory, ooo
Woks, ooo
Yams, *see* SWEET POTATOES
Zucchini, *see* SQUASH, SUMMER